# Occupancy Cost Planning and Benchmarking

## A Survey for Public Real Estate Management

von

Dr.-Ing. Elisabeth Beusker

Oldenbourg Verlag München

Bibliografische Information der Deutschen Nationalbibliothek

Die Deutsche Nationalbibliothek verzeichnet diese Publikation in der Deutschen
Nationalbibliografie; detaillierte bibliografische Daten sind im Internet über
http://dnb.d-nb.de abrufbar.

Dissertation, Universität Stuttgart (D 93), 2012

© 2013  Oldenbourg Wissenschaftsverlag GmbH
Rosenheimer Straße 145, D-81671 München
Telefon: (089) 45051-0
www.oldenbourg-verlag.de

Lektorat: Dr. Stefan Giesen
Herstellung: Constanze Müller
Einbandgestaltung: hauser lacour
Gesamtherstellung: Books on Demand GmbH, Norderstedt

Dieses Papier ist alterungsbeständig nach DIN/ISO 9706.

ISBN    978-3-486-72656-5
eISBN   978-3-486-72977-1

# Acknowledgement

I developed this dissertation during my work as research assistant at the Institute for Construction Economics, University of Stuttgart, my appointment at the Building Management Department of the state capital Stuttgart and my stay as Visiting Scholar at the Graduate School of Design, Harvard University. The present thesis was supported by the Postgraduate Research Grants Program of Baden-Württemberg (LGF) and the German Academic Exchange Service (DAAD) for which I am extremely grateful and explicitly thank at this point.

I wish to express my sincere gratitude to Prof. Dr. Christian Stoy of the University of Stuttgart and Prof. Dr. Spiro N. Pollalis of the Harvard University for their continuous support and excellent supervision of my research. Special thanks are also due to the state capital Stuttgart, especially to Ms. Heike Brettschneider, the Director of the Building Management Department for public schools and sports facilities, as well as to my colleagues at the related departments, not only for their confidence and encouragement, but also for our great collaboration. I am very grateful for the offered opportunities of exchange and discussion which provided focus and direction to my research and made this empirical survey possible in the first place.

Moreover, I greatly thank my colleagues of the entire bauoek-team. Their valuable co-operation and support made it all to a memorable time and experience. Last but not least I want to express my sincere appreciation to my parents and brothers, my friend and to all my close friends for their generous and unwavering assistance during my PhD.

My heartfelt thanks to all those mentioned above!
Elisabeth Beusker

# Contents

# List of contents

## List of Abbreviations

| | |
|---|---|
| BCIS | Building Cost Information Service |
| BHO | Federal Budgetary Regulation (German: Bundeshaushaltsverordnung) |
| BKI | Baukosteninformationszentrum Deutscher Architektenkammern |
| BMI | Building Maintenance Information |
| CEEC | European Committee of Construction Economists |
| cf. | Compare (Latin: confer) |
| CL | Confidence limit |
| DAC-BW | Department of Asset and Construction of Baden-Württemberg |
| df | Degree of freedom |
| DIN | German Institute for Standardization (German: Deutsches Institut für Normung) |
| e.g. | For example (Latin: exempli gratia) |
| et al. | And others (Latin: et alli, et aliea) |
| etc. | And so on (Latin: et cetera) |
| et seq. | The following (Latin: et sequens) |
| et seqq. | The followings (Latin: et sequentes) |
| Fig. | Figure |
| GEFMA | German Facility Management Association |
| GemHVO | Municipal Budgetary Regulation (German: Gemeindehaushaltsverordnung) |
| GROFA | Gross floor area |
| GrStG | German property tax act (German: Grundsteuergesetz) |
| gym | Gymnasium (gym, sports hall) |
| H-GROFA | Heatable gross floor area |
| LH | State capital (German: Landeshauptstadt) |
| LP | working stage (German: Leistungsphase) |
| i.e. | That is (Latin: id est) |
| IFMA | International Facility Management Association |
| IT | Information Technology |
| MAPE | Mean absolute percentage error |
| MOMD | Management, operation, maintenance and development |
| N | Sample size |
| NEFA | Net floor area |
| No. | Number |
| OLS | Ordinary least squares |

| p.a. | Per year (Latin: per annum) |
| para. | Paragraph |
| $R^2$ adj. | Adjusted coefficient of determination |
| RICS | Royal Institution of Chartered Surveyors |
| UFA | Usable floor area |
| UFA 1 | Usable floor area for living and recreation |
| UFA 2 | Usable floor area for office work |
| UFA 3 | Usable floor area required for production, manual and machine work, experiments |
| UFA 4 | Usable floor area required for storage, distribution and sale |
| UFA 5 | Usable floor area required for education, teaching and culture |
| UFA 6 | Usable floor area required for healing and care |
| UFA 7 | Other usable floor areas |
| SEE | Standard error of estimate |
| SIA | Swiss Society of Engineers and Architects |
| Sign. | Significance |
| SLA | Service level agreement |
| St. Error | Standard error |
| T-value | Tolerance |
| Tab. | Table |
| Transf. | Transformation |
| VAT | Value added tax |
| VDI | Association of German Engineers (German: Verband Deutscher Ingenieure) |
| VIF | Variance inflation factor |
| VwV | Administrative regulation (German: Verwaltungsvorschrift) |
| vs. | Versus |
| yd. | Yard |

## List of Figures

## List of Tables

# Abstract

The tight budgets of federation, states and municipalities compel the responsible authorities to comprehensively control all cost-influencing factors that could negatively impact the long-term value of their investments. The operating and repair costs of public buildings have historically represented a large proportion of the overall municipal expenditure. They there-fore constitute decisive quantities for cost control which are fundamental for the realization of an enormous cost saving potential. To ensure an economically sustainable planning, provision and operation of real estate, as demanded on the institutional side, it is essential that cost-benefit analyses are developed for various planning alternatives and employed at the earliest possible stage in the planning process of new buildings, renovations or modernization measures. Occupancy cost planning and benchmarking moreover gain in importance during the operation of real estate in order to constantly monitor the regular expenditure associated with a preferred alternative, by either eliminating the crucial para-meters, or by their improved and prudent management. Although the economic relevance of iteratively planning, monitoring and controlling occupancy costs can be in principle described for optimizing real estate expenditure, leveraging that information into real estate manage-ment practice and establishing an agreed upon standard for effectively managing property costs have been proved to be rather challenging in recent years. The reason for this is that reliable predictions of occupancy costs, and especially the identification and quantification of the determinants influencing on individual cost types, represent considerable challenges for both the occupancy cost planning and benchmarking of real estate.

The present research study is dedicated to this issue and examines the relevant causal interrelations that exist between occupancy costs and their underlying factors. The ultimate objective is to determine the causes of significant differences which occur in the outlay for operating and repair measures of around 130 public schools located in Germany. Based on a definition of the significant control parameters, the study proceeds to present numerous distributions of cost indicators for evaluated building reference areas and factor levels examined. In addition, the practical application fields of the research findings are demon-strated in detail by means of various examples for early planning stages and benchmarking purposes.

The empirical study takes a wide range of not only theoretically, but also practically relevant factors into account which became evident as crucial factors in discussions, and were detailed over the course of this study in collaboration with the state capital Stuttgart and further experts. The investigation of the cost influential factors is carried out for the annual outlay of aggregate operating and repair costs and, more differentiated, for individual consumption and cost types at lower structural cost levels according to DIN 18960:2008-2. The research method applied comprises descriptive and inferential statistics and, in particular, multivariate analyses for the purpose of a uniform data evaluation. Revealed interrelations are validated in a multi-stage process that allows both a test statistical and practical assessment of introduced statistical models.

As a result, the empirical analysis reveals that the operating costs are to a great extent usage-dependent, and that the evaluation applied here for heterogeneous school profiles, including secondary utilizations such as gymnasiums and indoor swimming pools for teaching purposes, for example, is of decisive importance and enables a comprehensive investigation of the schools' annual outlay. Those differences in utilization constitute a substantial cause of cost variation, a fact which is frequently not taken into consideration in discussion and the publication of cost indicators for cost planning or benchmarking purposes. In general, the existence of a swimming pool on site is of particular relevance and substantiates a significant variation in the annual outlay incurred for aggregate and individual operating costs, such as for the outlay for utilities, the cleaning and care of buildings or for the operation, inspection and maintenance, for instance, that is around 1.3 to 1.5 times higher in comparison with the average cost values for schools without additional swimming facilities. A more differentiated examination carried out for individual operating costs allows further and more detailed assumptions for cost estimates and comparisons to be made. Measured differences between the annual outlay for water, heating and electricity supply, for example, that in total constitute a relevant part of around 37% of the overall operating costs, can particularly be explained with regard to the heatable gross floor area, the swimming pool utilization area and different conditions of the heat supply systems.

The repair costs are examined separately from the outlay for the operation, inspection and maintenance. The comprehensive survey of various condition categories, i.e. the condition of the building constructions, technical installations, grounds and outdoor facilities as well as of the fittings, furnishings and equipment, enables the monetary consequences to be assessed in relation to specific conditions of individual structural components. The respective cost values that are presented for different types of repair measures therefore establish a valid basis for cost estimates and comparisons of the public schools concerned. The distributions of repair cost indicator depicted in this study can be easily included in the practical planning and benchmarking approach, and are preferable to those costs predictions that are based on different age categories.

## Zusammenfassung

Die finanzschwachen Haushalte von Bund, Ländern und Gemeinden zwingen die Verantwortlichen zu einer umfassenden Steuerung aller kostenbeeinflussenden Faktoren, die sich negativ auf den Gesamtbetrag ihrer Investitionen auswirken. Dabei entsprechen die Betriebs- und Instandsetzungskosten öffentlicher Gebäude einem Großteil der kommunalen Aufwendungen und stellen somit bedeutende Kostenblöcke zur Verwirklichung von Einsparpotenzialen dar. Um die von institutioneller Seite geforderte Wirtschaftlichkeit in der Bauwerksplanung und -bewirtschaftung zu erzielen, ist es zunächst erforderlich, Kosten-Nutzen-Analysen für verschiedene Handlungsalternativen zu entwickeln und diese zu einem möglichst frühen Planungszeitpunkt (bspw. bei einer Neubau-, Umbau- oder Modernisierungsmaßnahme) in den Entscheidungsprozess einzubringen. Mit Fortschreiten des Bauwerkslebenszyklus kommen der Nutzungskostenplanung und dem -benchmarking darüber hinaus entscheidende Bedeutung für die fortwährende Überwachung und Steuerung des immobilienbezogenen Aufwands zu. Für das kommunale Immobilienmanagement stellen hierbei verlässliche Nutzungskostenprognosen und -bewertungen noch immer eine beachtliche Herausforderung in der Praxis dar.

An dieser Stelle setzt die vorliegende Arbeit an, indem sie die relevanten Ursache-Wirkungszusammenhänge zwischen den Nutzungskosten und ihren zugrundeliegenden Einflussgrößen am Beispiel von rund 130 öffentlichen Schulanlagen in Deutschland untersucht. Die Arbeit benennt und quantifiziert die maßgeblichen Ursachen für auftretende Unterschiede in den Betriebs- und Instandsetzungskosten und stellt darauf aufbauend differenzierte Nutzungskostenkennwerte für evaluierte Bezugsflächen und kostenrelevante Parameter zur Verfügung. Zahlreiche Anwendungsbeispiele veranschaulichen darüber hinaus die Implementierung der Forschungsergebnisse für vielfältige Zielsetzungen im Kontext der Nutzungskostenplanung und des -benchmarkings.

Die empirische Arbeit berücksichtigt eine Vielzahl von theoretisch und praktisch bedeutsamen Einflussfaktoren. Zu nennen sind hier insbesondere Angaben zu den Schulgebäuden und ihren Nutzungsprofilen, welche in der fachlichen Diskussion hervortreten und zu Beginn der Untersuchung u.a. in Zusammenarbeit mit der Landeshauptstadt Stuttgart als erfolgskritische Parameter für die betrachtete Stichprobe konkretisiert wurden. Die erhobenen Kostendaten der Untersuchung umfassen sowohl die jährlichen Beträge aggregierter Kosten als auch einzelne Kostenarten und deren zugrundeliegenden Verbräuche auf tieferen Gliederungsebenen nach DIN 18960:2008-2. Methodisch zieht die Arbeit deskriptive- und schließende Statistik, und hier insbesondere multivariate Analysemethoden, zur Datenauswertung heran. Sodann werden aufgedeckte Zusammenhänge in einem mehrstufigen Bewertungsverfahren validiert, das sowohl eine teststatistische als auch eine praktische Evaluierung der relevanten Einflussfaktoren erlaubt.

Im Ergebnis erweisen sich die Betriebskosten als vornehmlich nutzungsabhängig. Dabei ermöglicht die vorgenommene Auswertung heterogener Nutzungsprofile von Schulen eine umfassende Beurteilung des jährlichen Kostenaufwands. Insbesondere gewinnt die Betrachtung zusätzlicher Nebennutzungen wie Sporthallen und Schwimmbäder an Bedeutung. Demgegenüber wird ihr signifikanter Kosteneinfluss in der Erörterung und Publikation von adäquaten Kostenkennwerten vielfach nicht hinreichend berücksichtigt. Die Arbeit belegt sowohl für die Summe der jährlichen Betriebskosten als auch für einzelne Kostenarten der Versorgung, Reinigung und Pflege von Gebäuden sowie der Bedienung, Inspektion und Wartung einen durchschnittlich 1,3 bis 1,5-fach höheren Kostenaufwand für Schulen mit Schwimmbädern, als solche ohne diese Sporteinrichtung. Eine differenzierte Betrachtung der Betriebskosten auf tieferen Gliederungsebenen nach DIN 18960:2008-2 erlaubt es zudem, genauere Annahmen für Kostenschätzungen und -vergleiche zu formulieren. Beispielsweise können Kostenunterschiede in der Versorgung der betrachteten Schulen mit Wasser, Heizung und Strom (rund 37% der Betriebskosten) insbesondere anhand der beheizten Brutto-Grundfläche, der Schwimmbadfläche und dem Zustand der Wärmeversorgungsanlagen erklärt werden.

Die Instandsetzungskosten werden gesondert vom Betrag der jährlichen Bedienungs-, Inspektions- und Wartungskosten analysiert. Auf der Basis einer umfassenden Erhebung verschiedener Zustandskategorien von Bauteilen (wie bspw. der Baukonstruktionen, Technischen Anlagen, Außenanlagen oder der Ausstattung) erlaubt es die vorliegende Arbeit, die monetären Auswirkungen in Abhängigkeit von einem konkreten Zustand zu bewerten. Zusätzlich werden spezifische Kostenkennwerte für unterschiedliche Instandsetzungsmaßnahmen vorgestellt. Mit dieser Datengrundlage zeigt die vorgenommene Untersuchung valide und einfach umzusetzende Kostenprognosen und -vergleiche für die praktische Instandsetzungsplanung von öffentlichen Gebäuden auf, welche einer altersspezifischen Schätzung vorzuziehen sind.

# 1    Introduction

## 1.1    Background

Nowadays, municipalities are in a difficult situation to fulfil their sovereign duties despite limited budgetary conditions and sinking tax revenues (cf. Destatis, 2011a; Ernst & Young, 2010). Considerable cost savings must be undertaken in all social areas to act against increasing debt and improve the financial situation of municipalities. According to Cock and French (2001, p.4): 'Property costs are one of the largest sources of overhead cost for most corporate organisations, typically second only to staff costs.' A major possibility for municipal cost savings is therefore to reduce such costs for both internally and publically used buildings. A fundamental distinction of these costs into capital and occupancy costs is made for the evaluation of real estate expenditure, whereby, after a few years, the accumulated amount of the operating and repair costs basically increase above the capital cost outlay for planning and construction (cf. SIA 112/1:2004, p.46)[1]. Various cost analyses underline the fact that occupancy costs represent a significant proportion of the total real estate expenditure and that they determine therefore an enormous cost saving potential for public authorities. Among others, BCIS (2009), for example analyzed the amount of the total occupancy costs for two elementary schools in Great Britain, both of which with around 420 pupils, over a life span of 20 years and showed that, on average, the occupancy costs (exclusive costs for staffing) exceeded the initial capital cost after 12 years of operation. Although the economic relevance of iteratively planning, monitoring and controlling occupancy costs can be in principle described for optimizing total real estate expenditure, leveraging that information into real estate management practice and establishing an agreed upon standard for effectively managing property costs has been proved to be rather challenging in recent years.

According to SIA 112/1:2004, an economically sustainable planning strives for the lowest possible outlay for operation and repair while the value of a building is maintained. The implementation of this objective is hardly possible in practice, however, because of the limited financial means available. Municipalities therefore are concerned and regard budgetary restrictions as a negative impact on the performance of existing buildings and the long-term value of their real estate investments. Taking the state capital Stuttgart as example, a considerable repair deficit for municipal schools can be identified, which actual predictions rate as being an amount of around 350 million euros[2] (cf. LH Stuttgart, 2009). An economical provision of municipal real estate while simultaneously maintaining their substances represents therefore often a great challenge for the municipal real estate management and necessitates innovative solutions.

---

1  SIA: Schweizerischer Ingenieur- und Architektenverein (in German), Swiss Society of Engineers and Architects (in English).

[2]  The costs comprise the outlay for structural measures for the building constructions and technical installations. Neither repair costs for the grounds and outdoor facilities, fittings, furnishings and equipment, nor expenses for the Federal and State Government's capital investment program are included.

The federal and state governments (see §24 point 1-2, BHO, 2010-12)[3] have long been working on the standardization of the occupancy costs planning process (as defined by DIN 18960:2008-2, for example)[4] and its supplementation with the conventional approach of planning investment costs (according to DIN 276-1:2008-12, for example). The overall target of such efforts is to make the required outlay for occupancy costs transparent for all decision-making committees and to visualize the long-term economic success of an investment. The Municipal Budgetary Regulation[5] of the federal state of Baden-Württemberg (§12 point 1-2 GemHVO, 2009-11), for example, states that economic comparisons of various scenarios have to be carried out under inclusion of follow-up costs (point 1) and that payments for building projects may only be permitted when cost estimates on the annual budget burdening (after completion of a measure) are previously available (point 2).

In contrast to this, cost planning is to a great extent still exclusively limited in practice to the real estate investment costs, and it is therefore that the principles of a long-term and economically sustainable planning of the entire expenditure are often disregarded and not feasible in practice yet (cf. Kalusche, 2002, p.297). The efforts to establish occupancy cost planning at the point in time of the investment decision, i.e for new buildings, renovations or modernization measures according to DIN 276-1:2008-12, for example, and to promote overall economic comparisons and sustainability certifications can therefore mostly not be realized as required. According to BMVBS (2011), the reason for this lack of implementation is that reliable predictions of occupancy cost costs, and especially the identification and quantification of the determinants influencing on individual cost types, represent considerable challenges in occupancy cost planning. This points on the one hand to a lack of adequate and standardized calculation methods that can be translated into practice and enables to draw up reliable cost predictions as well as comparison of planning alternatives. On the other hand, cost comparisons and predictions in early project stages require valid cost indicators, which take various basic conditions in terms of crucial parameters into account. The present research is addressed to these issues. A detailed survey is made of schools complexes that often represent a major part of the total municipal building stock. In the example of Stuttgart, which has approximately 600,000 inhabitants, this is clearly illustrated by the structure of building asset, in which schools make up 54% of the total municipal building stock (cf. LH Stuttgart, 2007).

## 1.2    Objective of the investigation

Carrying on from the matter presented above on the establishment of strategic occupancy cost planning and benchmarking as an inherent part of public real estate management, this empirical study seeks to determine the crucial parameters for efficient occupancy cost predictions and comparisons for new and existing buildings, in order to accurately forecast, benchmark and evaluate the annual outlay for occupancy expenditure. The study is part of

---

[3]   BHO: Bundeshaushaltsordnung (in German), Federal Budgetary Regulation (in English).

[4]   DIN: Deutsches Institut für Normung (in German), German Institute for Standardization (in English).

[5]   GemHVO: Gemeindehaushaltsverordnung (in German), Municipal Budgetary Regulation (in English).

an actual attempt to enable occupancy cost planning and benchmarking to be implemented in the planning practice of structural engineering and to substantiate the approach for various basic conditions. The ultimate objective of this empirical study is to develop and introduce prediction models differentiated for both the operating and the repair costs of schools in Germany, to enable significant pre-calculations of future expenditure and, based on this, to provide valid occupancy cost indicators for the practice of cost planning and benchmarking. This also includes the determination of the appropriate building floor areas for the definition of reliable reference values as an essential basis for valid cost predictions and comparisons. For this purpose, the present study examines the annual amount of aggregate costs as well as various cost contributions and consumptions as defined on lower structural cost level according to DIN 18960:2008-2 (cost groups 300 and 400) by means of descriptive and inferential statistics. The underlying data base of this investigation comprises a uniform survey of property and usage-related descriptions of around 130 public school complexes in Germany, comprising around 300 school buildings and 140 sports facilities. The practical application fields of the research findings are additionally demonstrated for both the occupancy cost planning and benchmarking approach with regard to a concrete school building.

## 1.3    State of the art

Economic planning has a long tradition and is as old as the building and construction process itself. There is widespread consensus that the professionalization of the building or real estate management can be traced back to the 1980s, when the economic importance of operating and managing real estate was recognized as being essential for various industrial sectors in order to enable a successful running of the business (cf. Lucertini et al., 1995). Gibson (1994, p.9) identifies two substantial reasons for the remarkable development of the real estate management between the mid to late 80s: 'Two of the major criticisms were the lack of a strategic approach to property management and the limited recognition of the value of these assets by property users and operational decision makers.'

The origins and initial developments of the cost planning and benchmarking approach can also be dated to this period. According to Ashworth (2004, p.32 et seqq.), the first cost planning studies were introduced at that time with a view of optimizing design-related expenditure by either defining an overall cost budget or comparing the outlay of different building designs. Those first implications of building or construction economics focused on budget forecasts for the overall construction costs (including the building pricing and the architects' fee) and were in particular characterized by single-price estimates. Since then, the subject-matter of cost planning has been extended with regard to the scope of cost data that is examined in a cost determination. The development from a solely consideration of the initial building construction costs to a more comprehensive analysis of both the investment and occupancy costs can particularly ascribed to the evolution of the facilities management discipline. With the focus on effectively managing real estate during the operation stage, facilities management has become established as a management discipline in recent years, commonly defined as 'an integrated approach to operating, maintaining, improving and adapting the buildings and infrastructure of an organization in order to create an environment that strongly supports the primary objectives of that organization' (cf. Barrett & Baldry, 2003 cited in Facilities Society, 2011; Then, 1999 cited in Pathirage, et al., 2008). In addition, it can be stated that the prediction method applied to provide accurate forecasts has been further developed to more sophisticated techniques of multi-price cost estimates.

The rapid development of the benchmarking approach falls into the same period. The competitive study performed by the US American Xerox Corporation to reduce manufacturing costs for the production of copying machines is generally regarded as a groundbreaking milestone that marks the starting-point for the subsequent evolution and institutionalization of this approach. In 1979, the company adopted externally set benchmark targets for its business plan in order to compete and stay ahead on the global market (cf. Camp, 1992; McDougall & Hinks, 2000). Nowadays, numerous definitions of benchmarking exist parallel to each other which differ in particular in the scope of considered benchmarking tasks (see definitions by Williams, 1996 vs. Camp, 1992 or Shetty, 1993 for example). Furthermore, a specific aspect of the general approach is often highlighted and thus generalized by definition, such as an inherent competitive character with external companies i.e. best-practice leaders, for instance (see APQC, 2010; Shetty, 1993 or Lucertini et al., 1995). In contrast to this, the present study refers to a more general definition of benchmarking as provided by Williams (1996) and Walker (1992) for example. Williams (1996, p.31) defines benchmarking as the process of comparing a product, service or process (i.e. any activity or object) with the characteristics of another per group sample, with a view to the identification of 'best practice' and targeting oneself to emulate it. In addition, Walker (1992, p.9) determines benchmarking in general as a management technique and continuous approach of 'comparing yourself with, and learning from, others who have achieved high standards of excellence'.

According to these definitions, it can be summarized that each benchmarking study comprises the establishment and assessment of actual measures that are presently carried out in various business fields with regard to adequate reference data in order to reveal required changes that are essential to achieve improved performance. The benchmarking approach in general is seen as an inherent part of every quality management process according to EN ISO 9004:2000-12 that serves to evaluate the strengths and weaknesses of a business performance by means of comparison (cf. Shetty, 1993; Kouzmin et al., 1999). The basic idea behind benchmarking real estate is to obtain the best performance in the provision and operation of facilities with respect to certain quality standards and basic conditions. The performance of an operated property is compared with excellent figures of other facilities that are highly comparable with the actual property. A benchmark is determined as an outstanding measure of a comparative performance specified by a reference property or sample in order to indicate the possible level of optimization (cf. Watson, 2007, p.4). Among others, Loosemore & Hsin (2001) point out that the identification of this reference point that serves as a standard against which an actual performance under review may be judged, is the essence of every benchmarking approach. From the statistical point of view, the definition provided by OECD (2002) can also be stated as follows: 'Benchmarking refers to the case where there are two sources of data for the same target variable, with different frequencies, and is concerned with correcting inconsistencies between the different estimates, e.g. quarterly and annual estimates of value-added from different sources.'

In general, a solid data analysis and provision of reference values is necessary to achieve an adequate level of comparability and therefore enable a reasonable interpretation of observed cost indicators. In recent years, a process of continual specialization were carried out for both approaches, particularly with regard to certain fields of duties, such as technical, infrastructural and commercial management services according to DIN 31051:2003-6, specific building types of usage (such as offices, schools, healthcare, industry, etc.) and cost types, such as individual utility costs or aggregate expenditure, for instance. This development was accompanied by the effort to provide refined cost indicators with supplemental descriptions to support meaningful predictions and evaluations of occupancy costs to be made. According to GEFMA 300:1996-6, those supplemental characteristics that are required to specify valid cost indicators basically comprise descriptions regarding the building design and year, the type and intensity of utilization, specifications on the standard of technical installations as well as details on specified service level agreements (SLAs). Occupancy cost indicators as published by Jones Lang LaSalle (JLL, 2011), for instance, represent such a source for office buildings in the German-speaking region, which takes different building sizes, layouts, locations and standards of technical installation into account. At an international level, the data bases provided by the International Facilities Management Association (IFMA) in the USA, the Royal Institution of Chartered Surveyors (RICS) or by the Cranfield benchmarking consortium in the UK, for example, are often regarded as meaningful sources for the purpose of cost identification and comparison (see McDougall & Hinks, 2000 or Ashworth, 2004). Since 2010, BKI[6] publishes occupancy cost indicators in the form of object documentations for different utilization types (such as offices or buildings for culture, education and teaching) which serve for various occupancy cost planning and benchmarking purposes (see Stoy & Beusker, 2010 for instance). There has been further investigations being conducted in the international research environment on the determination of consumption and cost influential factors with the view of providing adequate classifications of indicators. A selection of the relevant research studies and standards which determine those for different utilization types and cost groups in the context of occupancy cost planning and benchmarking is shown in Tab. 1. The present investigation carried out for the operating and repair costs of schools refers to this theoretical basis in particular and takes all of the named factors in Section 2.2.2 into account for the specification of the relevant determinants for this empirical study. The literature review reveals that, in general, minor importance is given to the definition of adequate reference quantities for the normalization of consumption and cost data and that, in addition, office and residential buildings often represent the research subject of investigation. The present investigation takes the listed reference quantities into account and proceeds to determine the relevant building quantities for the practice of occupancy cost planning and benchmarking. The individual objectives and characteristics of both approaches are described in the following section in more detail.

---

[6]  BKI: Baukosteninformationszentrum Deutscher Architektenkammern (in German).

Tab. 1:    Overview of the relevant studies and standards

| Studies and Standards | Type of utilization and data base | Consumption and Costs | Determination of reference quantities | Determination of further influential factors |
|---|---|---|---|---|
| **Ages (2005)** Germany | Different utilization types and samples | Utility consumptions (Water, Heating, Electricity) | Heatable gross floor area | Utilization<br>Secondary utilization (sports facilities, etc.)<br>Building size<br>Type of energy source |
| **Bahr (2008)** Germany | 6 office buildings, 11 schools | Repair costs | - | Building size, design, layout<br>Building age<br>Standard of technical installations<br>Utilization<br>Maintenance strategy<br>Location, political environment |
| **Balaras et al. (2007)** Greece | Residential buildings (different samples) | Heating energy consumption | - | Thermal insulation of external walls and roofs<br>Facade (glazing, shading)<br>Standard of technical installations<br>Condition of technical installations<br>Maintenance strategy |
| **BMI (2000)** Great Britain | 2 office buildings | Object management costs<br>Operating costs<br>Repair costs | - | Building size<br>Design, Building specifications<br>Type of energy source |
| **BMI (2003)** Great Britain | Different utilization types and samples | Object management costs<br>Utilities<br>Cleaning and care of buildings | - | Building size, shape, layout<br>Building design, specifications<br>Intensity of use<br>Location |
| **BMVBS (2011)** Germany | - | Operating and repair costs (as part of life-cycle costs) | - | Type and standard of utilization<br>Service level agreements (SLAs)<br>Functional characteristics<br>Technical characteristics<br>Location, external climate |
| **DAC-BW (2005)** Germany | Different utilization types and samples | Operating consumptions and costs | - | Utilization<br>Building characteristics<br>Type of energy source<br>Service-level agreements (SLAs)<br>Characteristics of the plot<br>Location, topography |
| **DAC-BW (2006)** Germany | Different utilization types and samples | Energy consumptions and costs | - | Utilization<br>Building design, layout<br>Standard of technical installations<br>Type of energy source |
| **DETR (1997)** USA | Education facilities | Energy consumptions and costs | - | Utilization<br>Building design, layout<br>Building fabric<br>Standard of technical installations<br>Location, orientation |
| **DETR (1998)** USA | Schools | Energy consumptions and costs | - | Utilization (occupancy level)<br>Secondary utilization (sports facilities, etc.)<br>Building design and size |

*(continued)*

| Studies and Standards | Type of utilization and data base | Consumption and Costs | Determination of reference quantities | Determination of further influential factors |
|---|---|---|---|---|
| **DETR (1998)**<br>USA | | | | Standard of technical installations<br>Building age<br>Type of energy source<br>Location (external climate) |
| **DGNB (2008)**<br>Germany | Office buildings | Operating and repair costs<br>(as part of life-cycle costs) | - | Type of utilization<br>Service level agreements (SLAs)<br>Building quantities<br>(window surfaces)<br>Standard of building constructions<br>Standard of technical installations<br>Type of energy source |
| **DIN 18960:2008-2**<br>Germany | - | Occupancy costs | - | User behaviour<br>Functional characteristics<br>Technical characteristics<br>Organizational<br>characteristics (SLAs)<br>External influences<br>(location, environment) |
| **GEFMA 300:1996-6**<br>Germany | - | Occupancy costs | Building floor areas<br>(e.g. GROFA, NEFA)<br><br>Building volumes<br>Number of user | Utilization (type and intensity)<br>Building design<br>Building age<br>Standard of technical installations<br>Service level agreements (SLAs) |
| **GSD (2003)**<br>USA | 10,544 residential buildings | Administrative costs<br>Operating costs<br>Repair costs | - | Property size<br>Property age<br>Type of utilization<br>Design quality<br>Ownership type<br>Location |
| **IP Bau (1995)**<br>Germany | Residential and commercial buildings | Operating and repair costs | - | Type, standard and intensity<br>of utilization<br>Standard of building constructions<br>Condition of building constructions<br>Standard of technical installations<br>Condition of technical installations<br>Building design and size |
| **JLL (2011)**<br>Germany | 500 office buildings | Operating and repair costs | - | Building size, layout<br>Building design<br>Standard of technical installations<br>Location |
| **Kalusche (2008)**<br>Germany | - | Occupancy costs | - | Type of utilization, user behaviour<br>Functional characteristics<br>Technical characteristics<br>(Age, Type of constructions)<br>Organizational<br>characteristics (SLAs)<br>External influences (social, legal,<br>fiscal, climatic environment) |
| **KGSt (2009)**<br>Germany | - | Occupancy costs | Building floor areas<br>(e.g. GROFA)<br><br>Number of user | Type of utilization<br>Additional sports facilities<br>Organizational structure of<br>the building management |

*(continued)*

| Studies and Standards | Type of utilization and data base | Consumption and Costs | Determination of reference quantities | Determination of further influential factors |
|---|---|---|---|---|
| **McDougall & Hinks (2000)** Great Britain | - | Occupancy costs | - | Type of utilization<br>Environment conditions, market<br>Organization culture, social environment<br>External political conditions |
| **Riegel (2004)** Germany | Office buildings | Occupancy costs | - | Type and intensity of utilization<br>Building layout, specifications<br>Technical characteristics<br>Service level agreements (SLAs) |
| **SIA 380/1:2009** Switzerland | - | Heating consumption | Energy reference area according to SIA 416/1:2007 | Type and intensity of utilization<br>Building design (construction, windows)<br>Building size, layout<br>Standard of technical installations<br>Type of energy source<br>Location (climate, topography) |
| **SIA 380/4:1995** Switzerland | Different utilization types | Electricity consumption | Energy reference area according to SIA 416/1:2007 | Type and intensity of utilization<br>Building design, layout<br>Standard of technical installations<br>Location, orientation |
| **Stoy (2005)** Switzerland | 116 office buildings | Capital costs<br>Object management costs<br>Operating costs<br>Total maintenance costs | - | Strategy (e.g. maintenance strategy)<br>Building characteristics (e.g. standard, condition)<br>Utilization |
| **VDI 3807-1:2007-3** Germany | - | Utility consumption (water, heating, electricity) | Heatable gross floor area (H-GROFA) | Type of utilization<br>User behaviour<br>Standard of technical installations<br>Thermal insulation |
| **VDI 3807-3:2000-7** Germany | Different utilization types and samples | Water consumption | - | Type of utilization<br>Secondary utilization (sports facilities, etc.)<br>Building age<br>Technical state of sanitary equipment<br>Extend of watering grassed areas |
| **Zhang et al. (2011)** Great Britain | office buildings | Electricity consumption | - | Standard of technical installations (electric equipment and appliances)<br>User behaviour<br>Secondary utilizations (kitchens, etc.)<br>Temporal usage intensity |

## 1.4    Occupancy cost planning and benchmarking

The overview given on the beginnings of both the occupancy cost planning and benchmarking process and their recent developments at an international level forms the basis of a more detailed description of the individual objectives and endeavors of each of the approaches as carried out at different life-cycle stages. Both occupancy cost planning and benchmarking represent iterative processes of continuous identification, comparison and evaluation of the costs of actually incurred outlays.[7] They serve as a fundamental basis for cost control and the definition of optimization measures when required (see Lucertini et al., 1995). Each approach is based on a standardized calculation method which in particular requires valid cost indicators of a reference source and differentiated information for their respective purposes of cost prediction and assessment respectively. Descriptions are given in the following of the decisive requirements for the practical application of each of these procedures, together with the data base specifications required for individual working steps.

### Occupancy cost planning

As defined by DIN 18960:2008-2, occupancy cost planning comprises the entirety of all measures taken to determine, monitor and control occupancy cost during real estate planning and operation (cf. Tab. 2). The determination of occupancy expenditure (such as € or $ p.a.) generally serves as a basis for cost monitoring and control processes, whereby cost monitoring hereby comprises cost comparison and assessment with respect to pre-determined reference values. Any optimization measures that such monitoring reveals as being necessary are carried out within cost control. The overall process of cost determination is subdivided into five successive working steps or calculation methods which differ with regard to their purpose, the time period in which a cost determination is carried out and the detailing level of available information, such as property and usage-related specifications in the form of drawings or calculations. These different types of cost determination build up stepwise to the final statement. Tab. 2 shows the time periods in which they are applied in the course of the life-cycle of a building, i.e. different planning and operation stages. The first four types of cost identification (i.e. first projection, preliminary, approximate and final estimate) are dedicated to forecasting future occupancy expenditure of real estate, regardless of whether a cost prediction is carried out for a new building, renovation or modernization measure which is being considered according to DIN 276-1:2008-12, for example. Correspondingly to the progress in planning and the increase in detail, i.e. to the requirements planning and on to working stage (LP) 9 according to HOAI:2009-4, the various occupancy cost determinations are gradually substantiated and so allow more and more concrete cost predications to be carried out. These estimates clearly differ from the final occupancy cost statement that is performed at a certain time of building operation, such as after an accounting period of one year for example in that it comprises a survey of actual incurred occupancy costs (cf. DIN 18960:2008-2).

---

[7]   Iteration, gradual approximation (Latin: iterare).

The first projection of total occupancy costs should best be already part of the requirements planning as defined by DIN 18205:1996-4, for instance. Such an initial cost estimate not only serves for considerations on the profitability and financing of the investment for the proprietor at an early stage, but also provides an appropriate basis for cost planners to continued development of more detailed cost predictions and finer comparisons. In this way, reference can be made to initial budgets throughout each of the different planning stages. In addition, the subsequent cost determinations cannot only be evaluated from updated states of planning, but also with regard to an initial cost target and underlying reference value.

Tab. 2:     Constituent elements of occupancy cost planning

| Occupancy cost planning | | |
|---|---|---|
| Constituent element | Type | Time period |
| Cost determination | First projection | Requirements planning |
| | Preliminary estimate | Building planning (Preliminary design stage) |
| | Approximate estimate | Building planning (Final design stage) |
| | Final estimate | Start of operation |
| | Final statement | Building operation |
| Cost monitoring | | Building planning and operation |
| Cost control | | Building planning and operation |

Note: Occupancy cost planning according to DIN 18960:2008-2

Based on the first occupancy cost projection, the subsequent cost estimates are performed in compliance with the progress in the planning of the building construction costs according to DIN 276-1:2006-11. The standard and detailing level of each occupancy cost approximation is defined according to the classification structure of DIN 18960:2008-2. Each preliminary estimate is therefore dedicated to indicate the overall costs in the cost groups at least to the first structural cost level. Based on this, an approximate estimate specifies the expected outlay at least to the second cost level. Finally, both the final occupancy cost estimate and statement substantiate the occupancy outlay at least with respect to the third structural level of the cost breakdown. These requirements on cost determination described by the German standard are fulfilled in planning practice by the application of different calculation bases that are aligned to one of the structural cost level named above. The general procedure for predicting occupancy costs is to multiply a representative cost indicator (e.g. €/m² reference area or unit) or each cost group under consideration by the reference area or unit that is appropriate for it. The overall occupancy outlay can be accordingly roughly approximated by means of a single-factor estimation that uses just one cost indicator for aggregate costs and one building quantity such as the total size of a building measured in m² gross floor area. In contrast to this, the other types of cost determination that are conducted at lower structural cost level (i.e. preliminary, approximate and final estimate as well as the final statement) apply more specific cost indicators as well as reference areas or units respectively specified for individual cost groups. In general, it can be stated, that the predictions that result from such multi-factor estimates are more precise and reliable, but however they also necessitate more extensive efforts in the compilation of the required data.

The fundamental requirements of any cost determination can be described on the basis of the overview of the different constituent elements of occupancy cost planning and the individual procedures of cost identification. Transparency in both cost determination and monitoring at each stage of progress requires the inclusion of the following four items in each type of cost determination:

- Completeness and consistency in cost identification
- Designation of the time period under consideration and the preparation date
- Determination of the observation level
- Specification of the underlying calculation basis

According to DIN 18960:2008-2, completeness in cost identification means that each cost group considered in a specific cost determination shall include the entire occupancy expenditure as defined on a lower structural cost level. This requirement of a uniformly determined cost basis is particularly relevant when comparison is made between different cost determinations of one or different properties. Cost consistency means that a cost determination shall always specify whether, and in which manner, allowance has been made for value added tax (VAT). Furthermore the time period under consideration (such as one year, quarter or month, for example) as well as the preparation date of the cost deter-mination shall be stated for the costs identified. This reference to the underlying period of time is particularly necessary for further time-series observations of possible fluctuations that may occur, such as in the wage levels of facilities services or in weather conditions for instance. In addition, life-cycle costing and other dynamic investment calculations take differences of payments (or cash flow in general) incurred over time into account, so that the time period of cost contemplation is particularly essential for the calculation of the net present value. The disclosure of the completion date is also important to readily comprehend to which calculation basis and stage of progress a specific cost determination refers.

Besides these cost data specifications, every occupancy cost determination shall include information on the level of observation and the underlying calculation basis. Various observation levels can be specified and taken as a basis for the identification of real estate expenditure. These could be, for example, the consideration of an entire portfolio, property, building or, even more specifically, of an individual building section. According to the German standard, the smallest unit that can be determined in terms of functional or organizational items should be taken as the basis for the calculation. This recommendation is particularly dedicated to the elimination of specific boundary conditions that arise from heterogeneous functions on site of a property, for example, and would lead to generalized and therefore unspecified cost predictions. Although it is in practice not always possible to determine occupancy costs for the smallest unit that can be identified for a property under consideration, it is important to state the underlying level of observation to which a cost determination is addressed. It may also be found necessary to add further specifications on the scope of further property functions that are implemented, such as specific sports facilities or types of school educational programs for instance.

The latter aspect leads to the fourth fundamental item, the specification of the underlying calculation basis for each type of cost determination. In general, all information that is used for the prediction or compilation of occupancy expenditure and which could be of particular interest for subsequent cost monitoring procedures should also be included in the cost determination document. The scope of information required for each type of occupancy cost determination comprises cost data, real estate quantities and descriptions. As outlined above, the form in which the cost data is required depends mainly on the type of cost determination that is to be performed and therefore on the calculation method which is to be used. Whereas the first four of the five types of occupancy cost determination (i.e. first projection up to final estimate) employ cost indicators such as €/m² reference area p.a. or $/yd. reference area p.a. of comparable buildings or portfolios for the prediction of the total outlay (e.g. € or $ p.a.) for the real estate under consideration, the final occupancy cost statement employs the accounted cost postings as they are available for the actual property and is therefore directly dependent on the total expenditure.

Real estate quantities in general comprise building floor areas (such as the net floor area as defined by DIN 277-1:2005-2), surfaces of constructional components, such as the external cladding area according to DIN 277-3:2005-4, or individual functional units or technical components, such as the number of pupils, school classes or lifts for instance. These quantities are generally essential for the definition of representative cost indicators and the prediction of the total outlay for a property concerned, and moreover for cost classification and selection purposes in advance. The latter named aspect, i.e. a distinguishing feature for cost classification, is demonstrated by way of the following example. If an empirical study reveals that the variation in operating costs is particularly dependent on the total size of a property as measured in m² net floor area for instance, this building floor area represents a relevant factor for the estimation of the operating costs of the property concerned, and therefore represents a significant criterion for the definition of an appropriate cost indicator. In general, the cost data required for this calculation example can be provided by a single property that is highly comparable in the total size of the net floor area, or in an even more sophisticated way, by means of an empirical distribution that includes a classification of cost indicators for this building floor area, such as a classification of operating cost indicators for property sizes below and above 6,000 m² net floor area for instance by descriptive statistics. The specifications on the net floor area so become relevant for efficient estimates on operating costs and are therefore valuable to be provided for both the planned real estate and the reference property or portfolio.

In addition, a reliable determination of occupancy expenditure comprises further charac-teristics of real estate, such as details on the building type or usage for example, that are compiled in a uniform manner for the property under consideration (i.e. a planned or actual facility) as well as for the identified reference source. In the case of the final occupancy cost statement, details of property quantities and descriptions only have a marginal relevance for the calculation process and therefore for the determination of total occupancy expenditure.

These specifications gain particularly in importance for subsequent cost comparison and evaluation studies carried out during cost monitoring which in turn justify their designation in previous considerations. As opposed to this, these additional information in the form of qualitative and quantitative descriptions of the considered property and its reference source are substantial for the identification of appropriate cost indicators and therefore for the prediction of total occupancy expenditure. The difficulties existing in the definition of the relevant factors (as building quantities and characteristics) are well-known in practice and represent a major challenge for the estimation of occupancy expenditure in particular. This empirical study is addressed to this issue by evaluating the decisive parameters for the prediction of total operating and repair costs for the building type school. Based on that, specific occupancy costs indicators that are derived from the statistical analysis for various cost groups, factor levels and building quantities are provided (see Sections 3 to 5). In addition, examples of the practical application of the research findings for different types of cost prediction are given in Section 7.1 for a concrete school building.

**Benchmarking**

Based on a description of occupancy cost planning and its requirements for valid cost predictions, the following section gives an overview of the benchmarking approach and its limitations that exist in current real estate management practice. The general approach can be basically structured and thus operationalized into five consecutive working stages:

• Definition of the performance to be benchmarked and its influential factors

• Survey of the actual performance (status quo)

• Survey of the reference performance

• Comparison of both surveys and causal research

• Inference for achievement of the desired state of performance

According to the field of interest where optimization is desired, the decisive parameters that determine the actual level of performance are identified at the beginning of each benchmarking study. Watson (2001, p.50) points out that this initial stage is also often accompanied by defining the achievable level of performance by means of a vision. Subsequently, the performance measures and their underlying determinants of both the actual performance under review (i.e. a product, service or process) and the specified source of reference data are uniformly compiled for the purpose of comparison. As an example, actual costs and the initial budget figures are ascertained together with cost-relevant parameters. These two surveys then form the fundamental basis for each bench-marking study. Measured deviations between the observed value and the benchmark (i.e. the comparative performance measure) are assessed and the causes for the attainment of an actual level of performance are determined. Finally, this causal research is followed by the definition of those interventions that are essential to reach the desired state of performance and which should therefore be implemented. If the intended level of improvement is achieved, a new status quo will be defined that once it will contain other weaknesses in the future it will again be a new subject for a benchmarking study (cf. Watson 2001, p.52 et. seq.).

Based on this overview of the general benchmarking process, the targets and challenges for the application of this concept in real estate management are differentiated in more detail. The overall objective of benchmarking real estate is to obtain an adequate notion of the actual performance as a basis for decision making and the implementation of optimization measures if required. To this end, observed indicators of operated properties are being reviewed with outstanding reference values of other comparable buildings or portfolios.

In general, facilities benchmarking pursues three levels of improvement, i.e. the optimization of the physical, functional and financial performances with regard to different control parameters (cf. Loosemore and Hsin, 2000; Williams, 1996). Benchmarking the physical performance of a building or portfolio comprises, for example, an assessment of the fabric sustainability in terms of energy efficiency or structural durability. The relevant parameters for this benchmarking survey are kWh/m² GROFA p.a. or m² stone flooring/ m² GROFA among others. In contrast, the functional performance of a property concerns the economy of spatial characteristics with regard to determined quality standards or requirements in terms of the image and communication, flexibility or health, for example. These can be measured in m² UFA 5 per m² GROFA or school class, or in the average storey height, for example. Both, physical and functional characteristics influence the financial performance of real estate through the fabric standard and level of occupied space. The annual outlay for utility supply or for repair measures in €/m² GROFA can be taken, for instance, as being relevant key performance indicators for measuring the cost effectiveness of an operated property. The level of examination is basically determined by the objective of the client and therefore the scope of the data taken into account, such as the level of detail of con- sidered cost groups (i.e. individual or aggregate outlay) or of supplementary descriptions (i.e. building reference areas and influential factors). In contrast to this, the prediction of occupancy expenditure mainly depends on the planning stage of construction and thus on the information available at a certain period of time.

With regard to the reference source which is identified for a specific study, each type of benchmarking can be carried out either internally or externally. The difference between these two procedures is that on the one hand reference values of an own portfolio are determined and compared with each other (internal benchmarking), and on the other benchmarks are provided by an external survey of facilities of another proprietor (external benchmarking). An external benchmarking therefore provides the opportunity to experience other facilities management strategies with regard to contracting or outsourcing, for in- stance, which could be promising for own implementation. An internal benchmarking offers the significant advantage though, that the facilities manager has a better knowledge of his own portfolio and can therefore often make a better evaluation of the calculation basis for the different facilities under consideration.[8] Occupancy consumption or cost analysis for different properties, as well as time-series analysis for a single portfolio or building type of one proprietor, can be named as examples of an internal facilities benchmarking study.

Each implementation of real estate benchmarking requires a diverse set of data that comprises cost data as well as property and usage-related information. According to GEFMA 300:1996-6, an appropriate basis for evaluating cost indicators and their underlying consumptions is established if the following three requirements are fulfilled for both the actual property under review and the reference source of data:

- Consistency in the compilation of consumption and cost data
- Consistency in the definition of reference values
- Provision of supplementary descriptions

In correspondence with the remarks on the determination of occupancy expenditure, a uniform compilation of cost data is aspired which can be achieved either by comparing the scope of individual cost postings or by disclosing the underlying cost classification or structural cost level under review in accordance with DIN 18960:2008-2, for instance. In addition, the appropriate reference quantity (such as m² GROFA or the number of pupils) shall be uniformly determined for the specific performance under examination to avoid distortion in measurement and to enable unbiased indicator comparisons. As with the identification of appropriate cost indicators for the purpose of occupancy cost prediction, further information is required to evaluate the level of comparability between the observed property and the benchmarking data as well as for the definition of an adequate indicator within a given distribution of reference values. With regard to this scope of information required for benchmarking occupancy consumptions and costs, the present study determines the appropriate reference areas and significant comparison criteria for the building type schools which are essential for valid benchmarking results. From the basis of a statistical investigation of various property and usage-related characteristics, the relevant key performance indicators for evaluating the physical performance and, in particular, the financial performance are provided that can be used for external benchmarking studies of the environmental and economic sustainability. In addition, an external benchmarking approach is exemplified for the financial performance of a concrete school building in Section 7.2.

---

[8]  Further types of benchmarking are described in the literature that can be seen as sub-categories of the internal and external benchmarking approach. They include competitive benchmarking (i.e. a direct comparison between competing organizations of the same business area), functional benchmarking in terms of comparing equal work processes across various business fields, and generic benchmarking that focuses on identifying analogies by analyzing process performance information of other business fields (cf. Watson 2001, p.11).

## Summary

Based on a description of both disciplines, it can be summarized that both occupancy cost planning and real estate benchmarking represent an iterative process of continuous cost approximation and evaluation performed throughout different life-cycle stages. Common to both approaches is that they can be carried out at various investigation levels on an individual building or portfolio for instance, whereby on the one hand reference is made to a single and highly comparable facility, and on the other hand the reference data required is provided by descriptive statistics regarding the distribution of sample data. In contrast, differences in the objectives of both procedures, their period of implementation and the respective data base required can be identified as being relevant distinctive characteristics. Whereas the determination of occupancy costs focuses on the approximation of total occupancy expenditure (such as € or $ p.a.) for a real estate under consideration by means of both cost prediction and cost compilation respectively, financial facilities benchmarking is an analytical technique to constantly determine and evaluate observed cost indicators (such as € or $ per m² reference area p.a.) of an operated real estate (cf. GEFMA 300:1996-6). With respect to the scope of individual proceedings concerned, occupancy cost planning comprises the entirety of all measures for total cost identification, monitoring and control, whereas, by definition, benchmarking serves to determine, monitor and assess an actual outlay by means of a cost indicator as basis for decision making and cost control.

Tab. 3:    Characteristics of the occupancy cost planning and benchmarking approach (own source)

| Common characteristics | Occupancy cost planning / benchmarking | |
|---|---|---|
| General approach | Iterative process | |
| Level of investigation | Real estate: Portfolio, property, building, etc. | |

| Distinctive charachteristics | Occupancy cost planning | Occupancy cost benchmarking |
|---|---|---|
| Object of investigation | Total costs (e.g. € or $ p.a.) | Cost indicators (e.g. €/m² reference area p.a., $/pupil p.a.) |
| Overall objective | Cost prediction and determination for an actual real estate under investigation | Evaluation of costs incurred for an actual real estate under review |
| Working stages | Cost determination, monitoring and control | Cost determination, monitoring and evaluation |
| Period of time | Construction planning and operation stage | Operation stage |
| Data base | Appropriate cost indicators of a reference source (with regard to determined reference quantities and influential factors) for the purpose of cost projection and estimation, or total costs incurred for a final cost statement of an actual real estate<br><br>Building quanitites of the planned or actual real estate<br><br>Descriptions of the planned or actual real estate | Appropriate cost indicators of a reference source (with regard to determined reference quantities and influential factors)<br><br>Observed cost indicators of the actual real estate (with regard to determined reference quantities and influential factors) |

A substantial challenge for both disciplines is the evaluation of adequate cost indicators for the purpose of occupancy cost prediction and comparison. The present study is addressed to this issue. It therefore determines the appropriate building reference areas and influential factors for the definition of unbiased and valid cost indicators for the operation and repair of schools i.e. individual and aggregate cost types according to DIN 18960:2008-2, cost group 300 to 400. Based on this, specific reference values for various factor levels are provided by way of descriptive statistics for sample data of around 130 properties. The distribution of significant cost indicators compiled in this study for different school utilization types, standards and characteristics, serves for various planning and benchmarking purposes as demonstrated by the examples in Section 7. An overview of the relevant characteristics of both approaches is given in Tab. 3.

## 1.5    Structure of the investigation

The investigation begins with describing the underlying theoretical basis in Section 2, followed by a presentation of the empirical occupancy cost analyses in Sections 3 to 6, and then proceeds to exemplify the practical application of the research findings in Section 7.

The theoretical principles of the analysis are introduced at the beginning from the point of view of the building types examined and the scope of consumption and cost data taken into consideration. Subsequently, the factor groups under analysis and their descriptive factors are differentiated and the relevant assumptions about the causal interrelations that theoretically exist between the occupancy consumptions and costs, and their underlying determinants are delineated. Based on a description of the data survey and processing carried out, the underlying data sample of this study as well as its statistical representativeness are described. In addition, an overview of the statistical research methods applied in the context of this analysis is given coupled with a presentation of the corres-ponding statistical measures used to analyze univariate and multivariate data.

The empirical investigation of occupancy costs is divided into three main sections which comprise the investigation of individual operating consumptions and costs, as well as the analysis of repair costs and the examination of the aggregate outlay for operating and repair. Here, a four-stage approach is performed for each analysis into the consumptions and costs of operating and repair. In the first step, the theoretical assumptions and empirical data base specifications are presented. This is followed by a presentation and discussion of the statistical models evaluated for continuous estimates of total consumptions and costs as well as for their indicators based on the respective theories. The magnitude and direction of the influences that exert by the impacting factors, i.e. by the empirically determined causes for measured differences in the consumptions and costs, are described and quantified. This also comprises the evaluation of the appropriate building reference areas for the normalization of the consumption and cost data concerned. Subsequently, a validation test is carried out and presented for each cost group under analysis based on five schools which were not included in the model development process before. A comparison between the predicted scores and the empirical mean and median values is drawn up, in order to assess whether the experimental design of a statistical model can be replicated, or not, and to evaluate the prediction accuracy of each cost model beyond the underlying data sample and framework of the statistical approach. In this way, a two-stage evaluation process is described that includes both a teststatistical and a practical assessment of estimated influences. Finally, specific indicators and their distributions are provided for individual and aggregate operating and repair costs for the practice of cost planning and as reference values for benchmarking purposes. A summarizing presentation of the empirical research findings is shown in Section 6. An overview is given of the relevant factor groups and cost determinants for which an independent impact on the operating and repair costs of different school types could be verified. The study then proceeds to exemplify the different application fields of the research findings for various occupancy cost planning and benchmarking purposes in an additional section. The investigation concludes with a summary statement in Section 8. The limitations inherently connected with the study are presented that arise, in particular, from the underlying data sample and the subject-matter considered. In addition, further research aspects in the context of cost planning and benchmarking are outlined in the form of a future outlook.

## 2       Theoretical basis of the investigation

An overview of the subject under investigation is given in the following sections and the central terms of the present research study are clarified. The level of investigation is delineated with regard to the scope of school utilization types that are included in the survey. Based on this, the underlying cost structure is determined and the extent of individual consumption and cost types is set out in more detail. The relevant factor groups of the investigation are determined and their descriptive variables from which cost influential effects are expected are presented. Subsequently, the procedure of the data collection and processing is described with respect to evaluated standards. This is followed by an overview of the empirical data sample, on the basis of which the representativity and validity of the research findings is designated. Finally, the research methods for evaluating the underlying data sample are described and the corresponding statistical measures that are applied are introduced.

### 2.1      Type of buildings under investigation

The present investigation focuses on public school complexes of the state capital Stuttgart (Germany), whereby a school complex is defined as a functional and spatial utilization unit that is represented on property level. This observation level was determined at the beginning of the study to correspond with real-built structures and to obtain representative data for the evaluation process. This applies in particular to the consumption and cost data concerned as well as to specific descriptions ascertained for the underlying school facilities and their usage, such as the extent of outbuildings and additional utilizations on site, the number of pupils or details of the school plots of land.

For benchmarking purposes at national level, building types are frequently classified according to the requirements of the German Building Assignment Catalogue[9] of Argebau (2010), see VDI 3807-2:1998-6[10] for utility supply for example. Performance indicators for schools are thus assigned to the category 4000 (education and culture) and subdivided for different school types, without making any distinction between further differences in utilization profiles and patterns. In contrast to this, DETR (1998) and Ages (2005) among others, explicitly point out the necessity to also take additional sports facilities as relevant distinguishing characteristics into account when comparing the different performance indicators of schools. The investigation follows this recommendation and therefore comprises a detailed survey of various school utilization profiles that can be classified by means of primary and secondary utilization types. Primary utilization describes the type of school usage, i.e. the main function of a real estate investigated in this study. The German school system hereby mainly consists of four different types of school education,

---

[9]  In German: Bauwerkszuordnungskatalog (BWZ-Katalog).

[10]  VDI: Verband Deutscher Ingenieure (in German), Association of German Engineers (in English).

i.e. elementary, secondary, special and vocational schools (cf. KMK, 2011).[11] Elementary school attendance is compulsory for all children of the age of six years. This school type comprises largely the first four years of school education in Germany and prepares the children for attending secondary schools. Secondary schools usually comprise the subsequent five to seven school years, i.e. grades 5-10 or 5-12. This type of school provides general education and includes secondary general schools (which offer basic general education), intermediate secondary schools (with extensive general education), grammar schools (for in-depth general education) as well as multiple school centers, whereby the latter school type incorporates various combinations of the other three types of secondary school. Special schools provide an adequate educational assistance for mentally or physically handicapped children. Vocational schools offer an educational concept at upper secondary level, i.e. grades 10-13, and are directed towards an extra occupational training (dual system) in the form of in-company training and part-time vocational schooling. Besides these educational functions, the present study also takes additional functions such as sports facilities, i.e. sports halls and indoor swimming pools for teaching purposes, into consideration that are located on site of a school property. Auxiliary nursery schools and underground parking garages are further types of secondary school utilization which are sporadically integrated in a school complex. Further descriptions of the underlying school properties which enable a more extensive presentation of the empirical data sample are outlined in Section 2.4.

## 2.2    Definition of key variables

### 2.2.1    Scope of cost data under investigation

Occupancy costs are the subject of the investigation that according to DIN 18960:2008-2 comprise 'all costs associated with buildings and the land on which such buildings stand, that recur regularly or irregularly from the moment these are available for use until their final demolition.' In preliminary analysis, the most appropriate cost structure for the investigation was determined. As the cost structure of the above mentioned standard has a clear three-stage structure, and is also widely used in Germany for the purpose of occupancy cost planning (see reference in the CEEC Code of Measurement for Cost Planning 2008-1, for instance), this cost structure is used as basis for defining the cost classification of the current study. By definition, the cost structure of DIN 18960:2008-2 covers the capital, management, operating and repair costs, 'whereby company and production-related personnel and equipment costs are not to be considered if they can be regarded separately'.

The study examines the annual outlay for operation and repair measures (costs including VAT, based on 2008 figures) for 16 individual cost types and, in addition, for five aggregate cost groups on higher structural cost level (first and second hierarchic level according to DIN 18960:2008-2). Tab. 4 depicts the cost structure and therefore the scope of costs

---

[11] The respective educational system comprises school education on primary and secondary level without those programs for tertiary education, such as colleges, universities or other educational institutions for adults.

investigated for the three hierarchic levels of DIN 18960:2008-2. It should be noted that the cleaning and care of grounds and outdoor facilities (cost group 340), in Germany comprises the cleaning and care of all surfaces outside of the building which are on the property site or adjacent to it and are being used or seen in connetion with a school's utilization (hard surfaces such as asphalt, sidewalks or green areas, for example). The respective sports areas under investigation consist of hard surfaces such as gravel or asphalted sport fields, football pitches, tracks or basketball courts.

The cost data available enables the annual expenses for operation, inspection and maintenance, as part of the operating costs (cost group 300), to be examined separately from the repair costs (cost group 400). Moreover, the investigation of the outlay for operation, inspection and maintenance[12] (cost group 350) as well as for utilities (cost group 310) is carried out for both the aggregate costs on second structural cost level, and more detailed for individual cost groups on third hierarchic level. In addition, the aggregate outlay for repair measures and their underlying costs for individual structural components are likewise investigated separately, which are presented by the building constructions, technical installations, grounds and outdoor facilities, and the fittings, furnishings and equipment (cost group 410 to 440 as defined by DIN 18960:2008-2).

The study only focuses on those occupancy costs that are directly influenced by the properties themselves, their buildings, plot of land and usage. The previously named capital and management costs are not part of this study, as these are particularly dependent on other basic conditions. With regard to the determination of capital costs (cost group 100), reference is made to the calculation of the building construction costs as described in DIN 276-1:2008-12, for example, that constitutes the basis for the estimation of this cost block. Management costs (cost group 200) are also not included in the analysis, as they are to a great extent independent of the buildings themselves. By contrast, these expenditures are rather influenced by the organizational structure of a building management department and the scope of facilities services performed respectively, which makes it difficult to compare those expenditures across different municipalities.[13] The same applies to labour costs for caretaker services. As municipalities also provide different services, those costs are also not included as a proportion to individual cost groups.

The statistical models that are presented in this study have been developed on this cost basis are denominated for individual cost groups in Tab. 4. The abbreviation A (for absolute) indicates those models specified for absolute costs, and B (for benchmarking) stands for model predictions that are carried out for cost indicators of a designated cost group. According to the strategic management objectives of a municipality, specific cost types and specified models gain importance.

---

[12] In accordance with DIN 18960:2008-2, the designation 'inspection, operation and maintenance' for cost group 350 is used for the aggregate outlay of the cost groups 352 to 355 under analysis.

[13] Among others, KGSt (2/2009, p.5) points out that those differences, existing in the extent of services provided by a building management, can mostly not be explained by any determination of certain legal forms for municipal building departments.

Tab. 4: Cost structure of the investigation

| Cost structure of the investigation according to DIN 18960:2008-2 | | | Statistical Models |
|---|---|---|---|
| 300 | **Aggregate operating costs** | | **Model 15.A and Model 15.B** |
| 310 | **Utilitties** | | **Model 4.A and Model 4.B** |
| | 311 Water | | Model 1.A.1 and Model 1.B.1, Model 1.A.2 and Model 1.B.2 |
| | 312 Oil<br>313 Gas<br>314 Solid fuels<br>315 District heating | Heating | Model 2.A.1 and Model 2.B.1, Model 2.A.2 and Model 2.B.2 |
| | 316 Electricity | | Model 3.A.1 and Model 3.B.1, Model 3.A.2 and Model 3.B.2 |
| 320 | **Waste disposal**<br>321 Sewage<br>322 Garbage<br>329 Waste disposal, other items | | **Model 5.A and Model 5.B** |
| 330 | **Cleaning and care of buildings**<br>331 Regular cleaning<br>332 Glass cleaning<br>333 Facade cleaning<br>334 Cleaning of technical installations<br>339 Cleaning and care of buildings, other items | | **Model 6.A and Model 6.B** |
| 340 | **Cleaning und care of grounds and outdoor facilities**<br>341 Hard surfaces<br>342 Green areas<br>343 Water area (incl. bank formation)<br>344 Outdoor constructions<br>345 Outdoor technical installations<br>346 Permanent outdoor fixtures<br>349 Cleaning und care of grounds and outdoor facilities, other items | | **Model 7.A and Model 7.B** |
| 350 | **Operation, inspection and maintenance** | | **Model 12.A and Model 12.B** |
| 352 | Inspection and maintenance of building constructions | | Model 8.A and Model 8.B |
| 353 | Inspection and maintenance of technical installations | | Model 9.A and Model 9.B |
| 354 | Inspection and maintenance of grounds and outdoor facilities | | Model 10.A and Model 10.B |
| 355 | Inspection and maintenance of fittings, furnishings and equipment | | Model 11.A and Model 11.B |
| 360 | **Security and surveillance services**<br>361 Monitoring according to public law regulations<br>362 Property and personal security<br>369 Security and surveillance services, other items | | **Model 13.A** |
| 370 | **Statutory charges and contributions**<br>371 Taxes<br>372 Insurance premiums<br>379 Statutory charges and contributions, other items | | **Model 14.A** |
| 400 | **Aggregate repair costs** | | **Model 20.A, Model 20.B.1 and Model 20.B.2** |
| 410 | **Repair of building constructions**<br>411 Foundation<br>412 External walls<br>413 Internal walls<br>414 Ceilings<br>415 Roofs<br>416 Permanent fixtures<br>419 Repair of building constructions, other items | | **Model 16.A and Model 16.B.2** |

(continued)

| Cost structure of the investigation according to DIN 18960:2008-2 | | Statistical Models |
|---|---|---|
| **420** | **Repair of technical installations** | |
| | 421    Sewage, water and gas supply systems | |
| | 422    Heat supply systems | |
| | 423    Air treatment systems | |
| | 424    Power installations | |
| | 425    Telecommunications and other communications systems | Model 17.A |
| | 426    Transport systems | |
| | 427    Function-related equipment | |
| | 428    Building automation | |
| | 429    Repair of technical installations, other items | |
| **430** | **Repair of grounds and outdoor facilities** | |
| | 431    Grounds | |
| | 432    Hard surfaces | |
| | 433    Outdoor constructions | Model 18.A |
| | 434    Outdoor technical installations | |
| | 435    Permanent outdoor fixtures | |
| | 439    Repair of grounds and outdoor facilities, other items | |
| **440** | **Repair of fittings, furnishings and equipment** | |
| | 441    Fittings, furnishings and equipment | |
| | 442    Works of art | Model 19.A |
| | 449    Repair of fittings, furnishings and equipment, other items | |
| Σ (300;400) | **Aggregate operating and repari costs** | Model 21.A, Model 21.B.1 and Model 21.B.2 |

In general, a comparison of outlays which are determined by various cost structures is often difficult, in particular on an international level. This is because of the differences existing in the definition and differentiation of individual cost groups and classifications. Furthermore, each cost structure is embedded in a particular context of standards, which often makes it hard to compare them with each other (see ÖNORM B1801-2:2011, pp.12-17, for instance). In demarcation to the underlying cost structure of this study, as defined by DIN 18960:2008-2, the cost classifications outlined below are frequently used for the purpose of occupancy cost planning and benchmarking on both the national and international level. The following overview emphasizes the main characteristics of these sources to support cost comparisons and the interpretation of the research findings in a wider context.

- *DIN 18960:1999-8: Running costs of buildings (Germany)*

   A comparison between the actual edition of the German standard from 2008 and the English version from 1999 shows a modification in the cost structure which has resulted from an update of this standard. In the cost group 100 (capital costs), the actual version contains, alongside the finance charges (i.e. costs of loan capital and capital resources), also the outlay for the wear and tear of an asset in the form of calculatory depreciation. In contrast to this, the English version does not contain this cost type. Specific reference areas for individual cost groups are not determined.

- *DIN 32736:2000-8: Building Management (Germany)*

  In Germany, this standard serves for structuring of building management performances by means of four categories: the technical, infrastructural and business building management, as well as the room allocation management. Although this standard does not explicitly contain a cost structure, the performance descriptions delineated in this standard are sporadically used for occupancy cost analyses. Compared to DIN 18960:2008-2, this standard includes some services, such as catering, romal services and internal post services. In general, however, this performance-related structure is coarser and the terminology used in this standard makes references to other standards such as DIN 276-1:2008-12 and DIN 31051:2003-6 more complicated. Reference areas for individual cost groups are not provided.

- *GEFMA 200:2004-7: Costs of Facilities Management (Germany)*

  This guideline contains a comprehensive and detailed cost structure with five classifying levels, which is directed towards both the building life-cycle and the spectrum of facilities management services. Reference is made to various standards, such as to DIN 18960:1999-8, for instance, in the operating and utilization phase. Further to this, building independent services are incorporated such as catering, romal or car pool services. Some reference values in the form of building reference areas or usage-related units are named for individual cost groups in GEFMA 300:1996-6.

- *ProLeMo (Switzerland)*

  The cost structure for occupancy costs of this guideline is based on three cost levels that are hierarchically structured. Besides building-related costs, this guideline also deals with building-independent support services such as catering, communication, post, forwarding and romal services. In addition, rental expenditures are considered separately. Reference areas for individual cost groups are not defined.

- *ÖNORM B1801-2:1997-6: Civil engineering and building construction costs (Austria)*

  This occupancy cost structure, widely used in Austria, comprises object-related occupancy costs including depreciation, whereby an object is defined in terms of civil engineering and building construction. The cost classification is organized over two levels and supplemented by various proposals for a cause-related depiction of occupancy costs in both public and private areas. Specific areas are given as reference values for benchmarking purposes of the operating and maintenance costs.

- *NS 3454:1998: Life cycle costs for building and civil engineering work (Norway)*

  This Norwegian standard is also addressed to building and civil engineering works in general. The cost structure introduced here distinguishes between standard and additional categories, whereby the standard categories comprise capital costs as well as the outlay for management, operation, maintenance and development (MOMD). Additional categories include servicing and support costs for core activities, such as canteen services, moving workplace and IT-services among others.

- *ISO 15686-5: 2008: Buildings and constructed assets (USA)*

  This international standard provides a cost structure for life-cycle costing (LCC) and whole-life costing (WLC) that also includes non-construction costs, income and externalities. The standard is compatible with a range of national and international cost codes, classifications and conventions. With regard to the occupancy costs, reference is made to building-related expenses for operation and maintenance (including management costs) by means of a slightly differentiated classification structure. Reference areas for individual cost groups are not explicitly specified.

- *BCIS 1991: Standard Form of Property Occupancy Cost Analysis (UK)*

  This cost structure is widely used throughout Great Britain. The underlying classification predominately comprises building-relevant occupancy costs, such as cleaning, maintenance and engineering services, which are supplemented by individual building-independent services, such as laundry and porterage. In total, the cost classification consists of seven cost groups organized over two hierarchic levels. Reference areas for individual cost groups are not discussed.

- *NEN 2632:1980-9: Working costs of buildings (The Netherlands)*

  This standard classifies building-related costs that arise during operation and usage of a building in three categories. Two of them comprise the outlay caused by the provision of real estate as well as its operation and maintenance, for which the property owner is responsible for. By contrast, occupancy expenditures that result from partial or complete object utilization and that can be passed on to the tenant, such as energy costs for heating and telecommunication, are differentiated from the others. Some reference values for comparing the cost indicator of specific types of buildings, such as offices, hospitals, hotels and schools, are disclosed.

## 2.2.2   Relevant factor groups and variables

In addition to the definition of the underlying occupancy cost types of this study described above, also the relevant factors which are taken into consideration are determined in this section. The German Standard DIN 18960:2008-2 designates in particular three factor groups from which influences on the outlay for occupancy expenditures may be expected. These are the user behaviour, the functional, technical and organizational system characteristics of a building, and external influences from the environment which cannot be influenced by local authorities. Within the international research context, several other investigations underline the importance of these factor groups from which various economic influences result. As an example, the Public Housing Operating Cost Study[14] of the GSD (2003) takes variables of all three of these factor groups into account, whereby the location, i.e. the urban and geographical location of a property, can be seen as being a predetermined characteristic for the respective sample examined, which cannot be influenced and thus represents an external influence. Agreement to this interpretation is also given by Kalusche (2008), for instance. According to him, quantities which cannot be influenced are composed in particular of external effects from the social, legal, fiscal or climatic environment that result from the location of a property. Contrary to those determinants predetermined by environmental conditions, Kalusche (2008) points out that the above mentioned system characteristics cover attributes like the year and type of construction as well as more detailed specifications on the building usage and operation.

BMI (2003) designates building functions and the intensity of use, building characteristics such as size, shape, layout, and the location as being relevant factors to explain variation in occupancy costs. JLL (2011) mainly takes functional characteristics into consideration for evaluating the deviation incurred for occupancy cost indicators of office buildings. Among others, these include the total building size and technical characteristics such as the standard of the building constructions and technical installations. Finally, in the field of economically sustainability of real estate and life-cycle costing, characteristics of the building, its usage and operation are often cited as being decisive parameters for measured differences in occupancy costs (cf. BMVBS, 2011; IFMA-Switzerland, 2011).

The present study includes all of the cost influential determinants outlined above, from which influences are expected from a theoretical point of view on the underlying costs, i.e. the individual and aggregate outlay for the operation and repair of the public schools examined. At the beginning of the survey, the individual factor groups were defined and subdivided into measurable factors for the purpose of a statistical investigation. This process of variable definition and evaluation was accompanied by an extensive literature review and discussions with experts form the building management of the state capital Stuttgart and other specialists. The participating experts (architects, facilities manager and property owner among others), who were involved and accompanied this evaluation process are named in Appendix A.

Tab. 5 gives an overview of the factor groups and their underlying subgroups as they have been defined for this study and been taken as a basis. The utilization is differentiated and examined into three categories of potential influences, i.e. the type, standard and intensity of usage. The type of school utilization (primary utilization) is described in accordance with the classification structure of the relevant German school system, presented in Section 2.1, that basically consists of four main types of schools, i.e. elementary, secondary, special and vocational schools. In addition, secondary utilizations such as sports functions and auxiliary nursery schools are also taken into consideration.

---

[14] The study comprises the sum of the total administrative expenses, operating and maintenance costs as well as the total outlay for taxes and insurances minus real estate taxes (cf. GSD, 2003, p.17).

With regard to the standard of school utilization, the municipal building management of the state capital Stuttgart names differences in the type of educational programs[15], canteen services and the number of computer workstations as particularly relevant factors for the data sample concerned that might help to explain variation in annual occupancy costs. These characteristics are therefore incorporated in the analysis to depict different utilization standards.

Tab. 5:    Factor groups of the investigation

| Factor groups | |
| --- | --- |
| Utilization | Type of utilization |
| | Standard of utilization |
| | Intensity of utilization |
| Characteristics | Functional characteristics |
| | Technical characteristics |
| Strategy and operation | Building Management |
| Location | Region, topography |

Furthermore, BMI (2003), DETR (1998) and GEFMA 300:1996-6 regard the usage intensity as being of interest, particularly due to the effects of this category on the degree of soiling, energy demand and the wear and tear of the interior, whereby this factor group is defined on the one hand in relation to the hours of usage per day, and on the other hand to the occupancy level, i.e. the level of public access and the space that is available per pupil. Both considerations are employed in this study in the form of temporal and spatial usage intensity and investigated by means of various factors to capture the individual utilization patterns of schools. The temporal usage intensity is measured in several ways, i.e. as the average operating time of a whole school complex, and of individual functional units (i.e. school and sports facilities) in hours per school week and also as the average number of schooldays per school week. The operating time of school buildings is made up of the number of hours that teaching takes place on working days and extracurricular use outside of the primary working hours. The operating time of sports facilities comprises physical education classes as well as afterschool recreation for non-school activities. The spatial usage intensity of the underlying schools is particularly described by the number of pupils and school classes respectively per m² reference area. In addition, the volume of water required for complete refillings of swimming pools per year is ascertained. For a school facility with integrated swimming pool, this variable constitutes the consumed volume of water (measured in m³ p.a.) used to refill the pool and therefore supplements the description of a school's usage intensity.

---

[15] In Germany, primary and secondary educational institutions vary in their operating times. Three main operating models can be distinguished that are for regular schools, from 8 a.m. until midday, for extended regular schools from 8 a.m. to early afternoon, which includes lunch and homework supervision, and for full-day schools, which also have teaching classes in the afternoon.

According to BMVBS (2001) and IFMA-Switzerland (2011), the factor group 'characteristics' named in Tab. 5 comprises functional and technical characteristics. The organizational characteristics additionally named in DIN 18960:2008-2 are considered separately in the factor group strategy and operation. The author makes this subdivision particularly because the strategy and operation are fundamentally subject to other possible influences and parameters, which are not associated with the facilities themselves, but moreover result from the operating and maintenance strategy determined by the building management department.

Functional characteristics comprise specifications on usage-dependent data (such as building floor areas) and thus serve for a more detailed determination of different utilization types and patterns. The variation that occurs in these building quantities is mainly influenced by functional-related circumstances. As an example, a comparison of different school utilization types dealt with here reveals that vocational schools represent, without exception, large properties, measured in $m^2$ gross floor area or $m^3$ building volume for instance. Furthermore, both the average storey height and the size of the sanitary area can also be named as variables, whose manifestations (measured in m or $m^2$) correlate in particular with the existence of sports facilities on a school property site. Among others, GEFMA 300:1996-6 refers to the importance of evaluating specific building floor areas and their supplementary inclusion for a more detailed classification of utilization types. This recommendation is followed here. In addition to a qualitative distinction of different utilization types, described in Section 2.1 by means of primary and secondary utilizations, various building reference areas and their representative proportions (such as the share of UFA 5 per $m^2$ NEFA) are therefore taken into account. Specific school and sports utilization areas, such as the gymnasium or swimming pool utilization area of a school complex, and their individual proportions to the total size of a school complex, are to be named for instance. In addition, consideration is given to other building floor areas, whose independent impact on the outlay for operation and repair measures is investigated. In compliance with the standardization of the cost data carried out with regard to the cost structure of DIN 18960:2008-2 (cost groups 300 and 400), the standard DIN 277:2005-2 (Part 1 and 2) and VDI 3807-1:2007-3, were made for use of the standardization of specific building floor areas and volumes. The respective standards are widely used for the classification of building quantities in the Germany speaking region, and therefore also taken as a basis for a uniform definition of the underlying building floor areas in this study. An extract of the relevant key definitions given in these norms for the purpose of standardization are listed in the glossary. In addition, Fig. 1 and Fig. 2 give an overview of the relevant building floor areas which are referred to in this study, and graphically depict the individual areas in proportion to both the gross floor area (GROFA) and the usable floor area (UFA) respectively.

Based on these definitions of building quantities, the investigation examines on the one hand, to which extent these building floor areas can be used for the normalization of individual cost data and the definition of cost indicators respectively, and on the other hand, in how far these building floor areas are additionally useful to explain the variation measured in occupancy cost indicator.

| Areas and volumes of buildings DIN 277-1:2005-2 | Gross floor area, GROFA (English) Brutto-Grundfläche, BGF (German) | | | |
| --- | --- | --- | --- | --- |
| | Net floor area, NEFA (English) Netto-Grundfläche, NGF (German) | | | Construction area, CONA (English) Konstruktions-Grundfläche, KGF (German) |
| | Usable floor area, UFA (English) Nutzfläche, NF (German) | Technical floor area, TEFA (English) Technische Funktionsfläche, TF (German) | Circulation area, CICA (English) Verkehrsfläche, VF (German) | |

Fig. 1:    Classification of building floor areas according to DIN 277-1:2005-2

| Usable floor area, UFA (English) Nutzfläche, NF (German) DIN 277-2:2005-2 | Living and recreation, UFA 1 (English) Wohnen und Aufenthalt, NF 1 (German) |
| --- | --- |
| | Office work, UFA 2 (English) Büroarbeit, NF 2 (German) |
| | Production, manual and machine work, experiments, UFA 3 (English) Produktion, Hand- und Maschinenarbeit, Experimente, NF 3 (German) |
| | Storage, distribution and sale, UFA 4 (English) Lagern, Verteilen und Verkaufen, NF 4 (German) |
| | Education, teaching and culture, UFA 5 (English) Bildung, Unterricht und Kultur, NF 5 (German) |
| | Convalescence and care, UFA 6 (English) Heilen und Pflegen, NF 6 (German) |
| | Other functions, UFA 7 (English) Sonstige Nutzflächen, NF 7 (German) |

Fig. 2:    Classification of the net floor area according to DIN 277-2:2005-2

Further to these building quantities, the following factors have also been specified and are taken into account for describing further functional characteristics of the school complexes examined:

- *Standard of floorings:* Qualitative and quantitative description of different flooring materials, i.e. wood, stone, carpet or synthetic materials in m² flooring area and as a percentage of the whole flooring area according to DIN 277-3:2005-4.

- *Standard of internal wall linings:* Qualitative and quantitative description of different lining materials, i.e. wood, ceramic, panels, paintwork or wallpaper in m² internal wall lining area and as a percentage of the whole internal wall lining area according to DIN 277-3:2005-4.

- *Standard of ceiling and roof linings:* Qualitative and quantitative description of different lining materials, i.e. wood, wallpaper, panels, paintwork or plaster in m² ceiling and roof lining area and as a percentage of the whole ceiling and roof lining area according to DIN 277-3:2005-4.

In addition, the technical characteristics are determined in relation to specific structural components as defined by the cost groups 300 to 600 of DIN 276-1:2008-12, i.e. the building constructions, technical installations, grounds and outdoor facilities, and the fittings, furnishings and equipment. The individual impacts of both the standard and the condition of these structural components are examined on both the amount of individual and aggregate operating and repair costs. In contrast to the functional building characteristics, outlined above, the variability of these technical characteristics is independent of specific utilization types. As examples of the technical characteristics of building constructions, the age of a school property or the condition of structural components according to DIN 276-1:2008-12 can be named, such as the condition of walls and ceilings, external glasses, roofs or permanent fixtures, which are included in the statistical analysis. The standard of insulation, the heat storage capacity or the existence of historic building conservation represent further factors, among others, which the examination is based on. In addition, the standard of grounds and outdoor facilities is defined with regard to specific proportions of the external property area[16], such as the share of sports grounds or green areas. This variable is considered in the investigation of those cost groups that concern the schools grounds and outdoor facilities, for example the cleaning and care, inspection and maintenance, as well as specific repair measures (i.e. cost groups 340, 354 and 430 according to the German standard DIN 18960:2008-2).

In this study, consideration is given to the possible influences of numerous partial sections of the property area. Those comprise the non-built up plot area, the water impermeable plot area and the external cleaning area in particular, which are subsequently described. The non-built up area of a plot is defined as that specific part of the overall property area that includes the entirety of all open areas. The overall area can be further subdivided into specifically designated sections, such as hard surfaces of school playground areas and sports areas (sports fields, football pitches, tracks or basketball courts) as well as green areas. According to this definition, those parts of the property area that are overbuilt by buildings are not part of the non-built up area of a plot.

The water impermeable area of a plot comprises all outdoor areas of a property which are covered by hard surfaces or buildings. Whereas this area represents a specific proportion of the overall property area, the outdoor cleaning area consists of those hard surfaces that directly belong to a school's property usage. It therefore includes those of school playground and sports areas, external grounds and roof areas, as well as those areas of public sidewalks adjacent to a property for which the occupant, i.e. a school, has cleaning responsibility in Germany.

Aspects of different building management strategies and operational concepts are also often additionally referred to as being decisive causes of occurring cost differences (see DIN 18960:2008-2; Stoy, 2005 or BMVBS, 2011, for example). Different maintenance strategies or service level agreements (SLA)[17] for the inspection and maintenance or the

---

[16] According to DIN 277-3:2005-4, the size of a property area is determined from the land register or by survey.

[17] Service level agreements (SLA) comply with the contractually agreed-upon quality standards with regard to timing, frequencies and the outlay for service performances which match the business need (cf. Pratt, 2003, p.254).

cleaning and care, for instance, are pointed out as relevant factors. An examination of the respective cost drivers requires an extensive inter-municipal comparison or, generally speaking, a consideration of various facilities management strategies, which is not subject of the present survey. As the schools examined here are all operated by a single municipality, this study can only take a few selected variables from this factor group into account. These are different disposal concepts and outsourcing-rates of caretaker services for security and surveillance, defined as being either complete in-house services or completely outsourced ones. In addition, consideration is given to differences in the SLAs for the cleaning and care services of buildings, which relate to different school types and functional building character-istics in the case of the underlying sample.

A corresponding limitation can also be formulated for the factor group location. The study incorporates regional and topographic characteristics with regard to the location of all of the various schools in the vicinity of the city of Stuttgart. The topography is hereby determined as the vertical dimension of the land surface, flat or sloped, and existing environmental pollution from external sources such as the atmosphere and noise are described. By con-trast, the investigation does not examine any inter-regional factors. All the factors described above are included in the present investigation of schools and are taken into account in terms of cost influential determinants within the statistical analysis of operating and repair costs that is described in Sections 3 to 5. The individual factors examined in a specific analysis of occupancy costs are presented at the beginning of each investigation with regard to the underlying factor groups introduced here i.e. the type, standard and intensity of utilization, functional and technical characteristics, the building management strategy and the operational concept as well as the location according to Tab. 5.

## 2.3    Data collection and processing

The relevant operating and repair costs and their influential factors under investigation which form the basis for the current analysis into schools are described in the preceding sections. Based on these definitions, an extensive data survey was carried out during the calendar year 2008. The scope of data compiled includes numerical information in the form of cost data and building quantities, as well as various descriptions of the underlying school facilities and their types of usage.

In general, difference can be made between two types of data collection, whereby for the one, the data required is particularly compiled for an actual examination purpose (primary statistical survey) and for the other, i.e. a secondary statistical survey, already existing data is utilized (see Bleymüller, p.2). Both types of data collection are incorporated in the performed real estate survey. Electronically data on occupancy costs and building quantities were made available by various offices and departments of the state capital Stuttgart and supplemented by additional information obtained from school visits on site supervised by the author. The information ascertained on operating and repair costs, building quantities and school descriptions was subsequently uniformly processed. An important aspect here was the standardization of the data obtained on the one hand, and the uniform preparation of the respective data on school property level, on the other. To this end, the data pools from various sources (such as MBD, SQL, Oracle, SAP, MS Excel) were processed and linked with various standard definitions, and the relevant factors as previously determined were compiled for the respective school complexes examined.

The preparation of the relevant operating and repair costs under analysis was performed on the basis of the underlying cost structure of this investigation as described in Section 2.2.1. The cost classification of the state capital Stuttgart was therefore cross tabulated with the cost breakdown of this study. The respective cost data include VAT and is based on 2008 figures. Besides the information that was available to assign each cash flow to an individual cost group and property, also the underlying consumption quantities for the utility supply could have been ascribed to individual cost groups and functional units, and thus uniformly prepared for the purpose of the statistical investigation. The grouping of individual consumption and cost postings, and their classification according to the cost groups 300 and 400 of DIN 18960:2008-2 were realized by a detailed inspection and categorization of documented booking texts that were made available by the proprietor for the respective calendar year. The data quality thereby allows the processing of the underlying consumption and cost data on second structural cost level according to DIN 18960:2008-2 across all the cost types taken into consideration. Furthermore, the individual consumption and cost data for utility supply, i.e. for water, heating and electricity, as well as the cost postings available for various inspection and maintenance measures that concern the different structural components, i.e. the building constructions, technical installations, grounds and outdoor facilities, as well as the fittings, furnishings and equipment, were classified in more detail and therefore broken down on the third structural cost level according to DIN 18960:2008-2, cost groups 310 and 350. Finally, the compilation of the relevant consumption and cost data was validated by means of visuel inspection of the respective data distributions. To this end, descriptive statistics and scatter plots were examined, and substantial deviations that were unveiled for individual scores (outliers) were eliminated from the data sample. The data plausibility tests were carried out with matching the survey of this study against other reference values published in the literature, for example by DGNB 2008; DAC-BW, 2005; KGSt, 2009; JLL, 2011; Pom+Consulting, 2008; VDI 3807-2:1998-6; VDI 3807-3:2000-7; Ages, 2005, among others. The empirical distributions of the underlying consumption and cost data uniformly prepared for this study are given in Appendix C.

In accordance with the collection and preparation of the operating and repair costs, also the real estate quantities, as defined in Section 2.2.2, were constantly prepared and standardized with regard to the definitions on spatial data, i.e. specific building floor areas and volumes, provided by DIN 277:2005-2 (Part 1 and 2) and VDI 3807-1:2007-3 in particular, as well as by means of determined surfaces of constructional components (such as the external cladding area) according to DIN 277-3:2005-4. In addition, specific areas of school usage and sports utilization were ascertained at both room level and at the level of building sections to be able to differentially evaluate the specific influences of existing utilizations. As an example, the survey performed at the level of building sections (measured in $m^2$ net floor area) allows, not only the influence of the original sports fields (measured in $m^2$ UFA 5 on room level) to be taken into consideration, but also those spaces belonging to a sports function (such as sanitary and changing rooms measured in m² UFA 7 according to DIN 277-2:2005-2) to be included, and thus to be examined in this study.

With the completion of the data survey on operating and repair costs as well as on the real estate quantities, the sample size of the present study is defined for 130 school complexes in total. Based on this compilation of electronically data, the primary statistical survey was carried out for the underlying cases on property level. The further data collection for theses cases comprised the collection of school property and usage-related descriptions in particular which were consistently ascertained by means of a questionnaire. The school visits included accompanied inspections of around 300 school buildings and 140 sports facilities and their respective plots of land along with interviews conducted with the school principals and caretakers. To enable a uniform examination each of the data sets, a standardized questionnaire was developed at the beginning of the data survey and taken as a basis for each of the school observations carried out. The author supervised all of the school visits to ensure consistency in data collection across all of the underlying properties.

The development process of this questionnaire was beforehand based on an extensive review of secondary literature (see Section 1.3). First drafts of the data entry form were evaluated and revised step-by-step in collaboration with experts of the building management department of the state capital Stuttgart as well as other specialists (see Appendix A). Afterwards, a preliminary version of the questionnaire was tested for ten representative school complexes of different sizes and utilization types (such as elementary, secondary or vocational schools with or without sports facilitieis). Within these pre-tests, the interviewed school principals and caretakers were also given the opportunity to evaluate the extent and level of detail, and also to make their remarkson the preliminary draft. Finally, the results of these test observations were evaluated and processed with regard to the subject and purpose of the intended data survey. A copy of the final version of the questionnaire which was developed for the underlying type of building usage (i.e. schools and sports facilities) and applied for a consistent data collection of the respective municipal school complexes in Germany is attached in Appendix B. This final version consists of five main parts comprising basic data of the property and its usage, information from on-site interviews, an extensive evaluation of the actual conditions, as well as additional details on planning documents which could not made available electronically. This approach of a condition-related facilities survey that takes the state of various structural components according to DIN 276-1:2006-11 (cost groups 300 to 600) into account refers in particular to the data entry forms and investigations carried out by IP Bau (1995) and Stoy (2005). The condition survey was basically performed within four predetermined categories, whereby the category A represents a good condition of a depicted structural component, and the category D designates a poor state of repair. The individual assessments of the observed conditions were uniformly prepared on property level and supplemented by aggregate condition categories, i.e. weighted factors that take both the condition of individual structural com-ponents and specified building reference areas into account.

The scope of these information uniformly compiled on property level, i.e. consumption and cost data as well as further characteristics, which form the basis for the present investigation is presented in Appendix C. Additional information is given on the underlying standard of data processing, with regard to the extent of data aggregation and weighting, that were carried out for all investigated factors, such as the standard of aggregated building quantities from room level or from the level of building sections respectively. In addition to the level of data processing, also the number of properties that are characterized by a specific variable or manifestiation (such as a specifc type of school or educational program) is outlined.

## 2.4    Presentation of the sample

The entire data sample of this study consists of 130 school complexes located in Stuttgart (Germany) that include around 300 school buildings and 140 sports facilities. The major part of these properties (111 schools) is built in a urban surrounding, i.e. either an inner-city or suburban region, whereas 19 schools are found in a rural environment. The building types under analysis comprise 31 elementary schools, 66 secondary schools, 15 special schools for mentally or physically handicapped children, and 18 vocational schools that provide an extra occupational training in the form of a dual education system (primary utilization, cf. Section 2.1). The underlying data sample of such vocational schools covers eleven schools which have a technical focus and seven with a business focus (cf. Tab. 105). It is found that in total, 107 of the 130 school complexes under investigation have additional sports facilities on site such as gymnasiums[18] of various sizes, or indoor swimming pools for teaching purposes (see Tab. 6). The respective swimming pools concerned differ to swimming baths in that they have relatively small pool volumes with a maximum water content of about 230 m³, and most of their bottoms can be lifted. Additional nursery schools are in 20 out of 130 cases integrated within a school complex.

Tab. 6:    Building types under investigation: Primary and secondary school utilization

| Primary utiization | Secondary utilization | N |
|---|---|---|
| Elementary schools (N = 31) | Without sports facilities | 5 |
| | With sports halls | 26 |
| Secondary schools (N= 66) | Without sports facilities | 5 |
| | With sports halls | 58 |
| | With sports halls and indoor swimming pool for teaching purposes | 3 |
| Special schools (N= 15) | Without sports facilities | 3 |
| | With sports halls | 7 |
| | With indoor swimming pool for teaching purpose | 1 |
| | With sports halls and indoor swimming pool for teaching purposes | 4 |
| Vocational schools (N = 18) | Without sports facilities | 10 |
| | With sports halls | 8 |
| Total | | 130 |

Regarding the absolute school sizes that are incorporated in the study, the empirical data sample is made up of properties between 1,400 to 9,799 m² gross floor area (GROFA), which provide space for around 48 up to almost 1,300 pupils. Further differences in the type

---

[18] Gymnasium in terms of sports hall (gym).

of utilization can also be described with regard to the kind of educational program and the individual operating times, for instance. Here, an 'extended regular school' is provided in 57 cases and thus represents the most frequently occurring form of school education (see Tab. 107). This educational concept offers school teaching, lunch as well as homework supervision from 8 a.m. to early afternoon. Whereas the overall distribution can be evaluated as being relatively equal in this instance, the operating times of the respective school complexes vary in a dimension (range) between 36 to 94 hours per school week. With regard to some technical characteristics of the properties outlined in Appendix C, 43 of the 130 schools that were constructed between 1873 and 2005 include historic buildings that are completely or in part listed for preservation. By comparing the conditions of individual structural components, i.e. of the building constructions, technical installations, grounds and outdoor school facilities, as well as of the fittings, furnishings and equipment, the majority of all properties examined is characterized without exception, by a good state of repair.

Details on further property and usage-related characteristics of the underlying school complexes are shown in Appendix C. In addition, an overview of the uniformly prepared consumption and cost data of the investigation and their distributions for individual and aggregate costs is given. The present sample has therefore a total average outlay of around 385,000 € for the operation and repair and is characterized by an interquartile range of around 246,500 €. The mean cost indicator for aggregate operation and repair amounts to almost 50 €/m² GROFA p.a. (costs including VAT, based on 2008 figures), with a corresponding interquartile deviation stated at 24 €/m² GROFA p.a. Here, the operating costs constitute, on average, a proportion of around 52% of the overall outlay under consideration.

## 2.5    Representativity of the sample

In general, the objective of a statistical approach is to make inferences from statistics of an empirical sample to parameters of the population (cf. Jurs, 1988, p.17). It is therefore important to specify the distinctive characteristics of the present data sample to ensure an appropriate implementation and exploitation of the research findings on both national and international level. Parameters which are found to be constant in this empirical survey cannot be evaluated and quantified, and thus restrict the level of generalization and validity to a certain degree for other municipalities.

With regard to the underlying data sample of the investigation described in the preceding sections, the population concerned comprises schools which are located in the south of Germany and operated by the state capital Stuttgart. The relatively restricted location of the properties substantially reduces the variation in regional and climatic conditions, whose influences can therefore not be examined here. As outlined in Section 2.2.2, this regional limitation also applies to the provision and operation of the underlying school complexes that are uniformly managed by a single proprietor. Differences existing in maintenance strategies and operating standards and concepts, which may arise from various service level agreements (SLAs) or outsourcing rates of facilities services for instance, can therefore not been specified and considered.

Another important aspect that needs to be emphasized is the scope of cost types that is taken into account in this study and which could lead to distorted occupancy cost prediction and benchmarking results in the case that other classification standards are employed in an inter-municipal comparison. This gains particularly in importance when referring to aggregate outlays as defined on higher structural cost level. The underlinyg cost groups of this study are determined in Sections 2.2.1 according to DIN 18960:2008-2. In addition, exising differences in the definition and classification of various cost breakdowns are named to support further occupancy cost comparisons and interpretations of the research findings in a wider context. In compliance with this, the practical application and transferability of the research findings are also reduced under fundamentally different basic conditions, such as deviations in the schools operating times, or divergent definitions of the relevant building floor areas for example.

A further restriction arises from the time period of data collection, i.e. the calendar year in which the date survey is performed. Each property is characterized by actual consumptions and costs incurred in 2008, as opposed to a calculation of mean values on the basis of time series analyses for instance. The representativity of an observed value is therefore relatively restricted for an individual school property, whose respective outlay varies significantly across different years of observation (i.e. accounting periods) and life-cycle stages (see Riegel, 2004; Bahr, 2008). For the current research of sample data, however, this limitation can be relativized. The underlying schools are found to be in an age between 3 to 171 years and their examination thus enables a large proportion of the overall life-cycle to be illustrated.

Finally, the sample size (N) is restricted for each cost group analysis carried out here. In general, it can be stated that the larger a sample size, the greater is the probability of identifying outliers more accurately, and to achieve more reliable and substantiated statistical measures, such as descriptive statistics for central tendency and dispersion for instance.

Taking the aforementioned restrictions into consideration, the properties are randomly selected out of the total school portfolio of the municipality Stuttgart and greatly differ in their utilization types and standards, construction years and states of repair. The survey comprises the majority of the local building stock and thus constitutes a representative cross-section, particularly for the project partner. Another advantage is that the investigation is performed at property level. This level of observation allows to take account of various basic conditions, such as the influences that result from main facilities, outbuildings, adjacent sports facilities and canteens for example.

Inductive conclusions, and thus an appropriate generalization of the research results, can be achieved when the sampling restrictions described above are interpreted in an adequate manner. As an example, regionally different wage levels can be assessed for inter-municipal results according to the indicators published by the statistical offices of the federal and state governments of Germany (2011).[19] [20] Destatis (2011b) furthermore provides various price indices for monetary time series analysis which allow an adjustment of the consumption and cost data presented in this study for inflation.

## 2.6   Research method

Descriptive and inferential statistics are applied for evaluating the underlying data sample from approximately 130 schools. Before presenting the prediction models for individual cost groups in the following sections, the research methods employed are initially described and an overview of the corresponding statistical measures is provided. At this point, reference is made to the relevant secondary literature on multivariate analyses (see Bakchaus, et al., 2008 or Bleymüller, et al., 2008, for example) for additional in-depth information on this subject.

### Deskriptive statistics

The underlying sample covers certain characteristics in the form of cost data and descriptions relating to the schools investigated in this study. Each school complex represents a specific case that is characterized by a certain observed value (manifestation $x_i$) which relates to a particular attribute (variable $X_i$). Descriptive statistics is a means of concentrating the information on individual cases in order to make assumptions for groups of cases with equal characteristics. For this purpose, a variety of different research methods and measures is available. Their field of application depends primarily on whether it is intended to describe individual variables separately (univariate distribution), or the focus is on the association existing between different variables (bivariate or multivariate distribution). Furthermore, it is possible to classify statistical measures into categorical (qualitative) and continuous (quantitative) variables in terms of their measurement level (see Benninghaus 2007, p.29, for instance). The corresponding measurement levels are the nominal scale and the ordinal scale for categorical variables to describe the type or quality of an attribute categorically. The nominal scale enables an attribute to be classified according to different manifestations, although it is not possible to arrange the individual categories in any order. The next higher level, the ordinal scale, also allows the classified elements to be arranged in order of priority (such as a structural component is found to be in a good or a poor condition). If it is also possible to measure and quantify the distance between different manifestations by way of a calculation, reference is made to continuous variables with a metric measurement level[21]. Examples of such metrically-scaled continuous variables used in this study include the total size of a school complex, the annual outlay or cost indicators. Within this study, the arithmetical mean $(\bar{x})$ and the median $(\tilde{x})$ are used to describe the

---

[19] In German: Statistische Ämter des Bundes und der Länder.

[20] According to GSD (2003), property location is one of the key drivers of labour costs.

[21] Metric variables can moreover be subdivided into interval-scaled and ratio-scaled variables in cases where there is an invariable zero point (the latter with a natural zero point). This study employs ratio-scaled variables which support the four elementary arithmetic operations for differentiated comparisons between the different cases (schools).

central tendency of metric variables, i.e. the univariate distribution of metrically-scaled attributes. The investigation relies on the measures range (R), interquartile range and standard deviation (s) to describe the dispersion (variability of univariate distributions) ascertained for a characteristic.

While the mean represents the average value of a sample (series of measured values), the median (lat. medianus = in the middle) indicates the central tendency of a row of measured values. By definition, the median (0.5-quartile, $Q_2$) is the score that divides the distribution into halves i.e. representing the central value below which not more than half of the observed cases of an attribute lie. The quartiles correspondingly split the data into four equal parts. The advantage of the median over the mean is that it is more resilient against outliers, i.e. extreme deviations in individual scores from the mean. The median is calculated as follows:

$$\tilde{x} = U + \left( \frac{\frac{1}{2}N - F_u}{F_m} \right) K_b \qquad\qquad \text{(Equation 1)}$$

Where:    $\tilde{x}$  :   Median

$U$  :   Lower exaxt limit of the class containing the median

$N$  :   Sample size

$F_u$ :   Cumulative frequency below the interval containing the median

$F_m$ :   Frequency in the interval containing the median

$K_b$ :   Width of the class intervall

The range (R) refers to the limits of a distribution and describes the variability of data calculated as the difference between the extreme values of an attribute ($R = x_{max} - x_{min}$). Similar to this statistical measure, the interquartile range defines the difference (interquartile deviation) between the upper and lower quartile ($Q_3 - Q_1$) that includes the middle 50% of the cases. The standard deviation is employed to determine the distribution within these limits, calculated on the basis of the squared deviations of all scores from their arithmetical mean and is expressed in the unit of the metric variable (such as € or m²). Frequency tables are used for describing bivariate distributions in which the common frequencies for combinations of multiple manifestations are depicted.

The aforementioned classification system for variables based on their respective measurement levels is widely used in the literature, and is of particular relevance for determining appropriate measures and methods for the statistical data analysis. At this stage, it should also be pointed out that an attribute, in correspondence with the underlying research objective, can be described or measured respectively by means of various scales. In research practice, this issue is also referred to as a theory-adequate operationalization of the subject under investigation. For instance, attributes ascertained on a higher measure-ment level can be transferred to, and depicted on, lower levels. Similarly, categorical variables can also be interpreted as dichotomous dummy variables (0,1), and used in the form of continuous variables from the point of view of the data evaluation.

## Inferential statistics

Based on a description and contextualization of some core values of descriptive statistics, which are employed in this study, the analytical techniques and methodological approach applied is described in the following in more detail. In order to assess the assumptions (i.e. theoretical and practical contemplations) presented in Section 2.2.2, regarding the causal interrelations between individual operating and repair costs and the characteristics of school complexes under investigation, this investigation uses structure-examining analyses.[22] This approach has already been employed successfully in numerous real estate cost analyses (see GSD, 2003 or Stoy, et al., 2009, for example).

For the purpose of this analysis, the individual outlay for operating and repair is defined as dependent variable (Y), whereas the various descriptions of school complexes represent the independent variables $(X_i)$.[23] In this way, it can be statistically examined, based on the data sample available, whether the assumption of an one-sided relationship between each independent variable $(X_1, X_2, X_3,..., X_n)$ and Y can be verified, or not. Based on this, the magnitude and direction of a significant influence can be quantified for each independent variable $(X_i)$ included in the analysis, by simultaneously keeping the variability of all other model variables constant. In this way, cost prognoses for each cost group (Y) under analysis as defined by DIN 18960:2008-2 are provided, whereby prediction is defined according to Jurs, et al. (1988, p.128) as a 'process of estimating scores on one variable from knowledge of scores on another variable.'

In the investigations presented here, the cost data (Y) is available metrically. The multivariate regression analysis is applied for data evaluation when all independent variables $(X_1, X_2, X_3,..., X_n)$ are also available on metric measurement level, or can be treated as metric variables via dummy variable coding respectively. In contrast, when all model variables are represented by categorical variables, the analysis of variance is employed. Both methods are implemented in a software-based manner based on SPSS.

The general statistical approach can be described as follows. Based on the collected sample data, the variables for each specific cost group of the operating and repair costs under analysis are described. These contemplations are accompanied by an array of statistical pre-analyses. In order to evaluate the fitness of the underlying data for the item to be investigated, for example, the Levene Test (F-test) is applied for a specific analysis of

---

[22] Structure-examining analyses are used to examine causal interrelations on the basis of determined variables a priori. Structure-discovery analyses are applied when descriptions of logical interrelations between variables are lacking a prior (cf. Backhaus, et al., 2008,p.11 et seqq.)

[23] Alternative designations for a dependent variable are regressand, endogenous or explained variable or forecast variable. The independent variables, from which the effects to be analyzed are derived, are also known as exogenous, explanatory variables or predictor (cf. Backhaus, et al., 2008, p.55).

variance and the t-test is used for mean value comparisons. The Kolmogorov-Smirnov Test (KS-test) is used to determine whether the underlying data of an investigation is nearly normally distributed. The results of these preliminary analyses are then employed to develop prediction models step-by-step and compare them with each other, before proceeding to examine and assess the entire prediction model as well as their individual parameters and underlying model assumptions. The best cost estimates are presented as the outcome of an analysis and described in more detail using statistical measures.

## Regression analysis

The theoretical basis behind regression analysis is the Gauss-Markov theorem[24], which states that the best possible estimates are achieved when the mean squared differences between the observed and the predicted values, as an expression of the error term, are kept as small as possible (see Bleymüller, et al., 2008, p.141 or Jurs, et al., 1988, p.461, for instance). This estimation method is called OLS estimation[25], which utilizes the classic (i.e. linear or linearized) regression analysis in order to estimate the unknown model parameters $\beta_0$ and $\beta_i$ as clearly as possible on the basis of the general multivariate regression model below:

$$Y_i = \beta_0 + \sum_{i=1}^{n} \beta_i X_i + \varepsilon_i \qquad \text{(Equation 2)}$$

Where:    $Y_i$ :    *Dependent variable (for an observation i where i=1,2,3,...n)*

         $\beta_0$ :    *Regression constant, intercept*

         $\beta_i$ :    *Regression coefficient, slope (i=1,2,3,...,n)*

         $X_i$ :    *Independent variable (i=1,2,3,...,n)*

         $\varepsilon$ :    *Error term*

This general form of the regression model contains the error term $\varepsilon$ as a random variable that can neither be observed nor accounted for in a regression analytical sense. In empirical analysis, this error term U is manifested by the deviations (residuals) between the measured and predicted values for the dependent variable Y under investigation. The residuals generally occur as a result of measurement and model design errors during the data collection and model analysis.

The individual estimation models and their parameters are uniformly described in Sections 3 to 5. This is backed up by details of the prediction quality, the significance and the fundamental hypotheses for each statistical model. The prediction quality determines how accurately a model estimation reflects the corresponding empirical data, i.e. goodness-of-fit. Significance tests are carried out to examine the probability with which the interrelations

---

[24] The Gauss-Markov theorem, named after the mathematicians Carl Friedrich Gauss and Andrei Andrejewitsch Markow, was first introduced as the Theory of Errors in 1823 (see Krengel, 2005, p.172).

[25] OLS stands for ordinary least squares.

revealed by the analyzed sample, not only occur incidentally but moreover can also be applied to the population in general, i.e. further school complexes not included in the underlying sample. Subsequently, the statistical measures employed in the analysis are presented in order to evaluate the prediction standards and describe the test statistics applied to draw up further conclusions regarding the population, i.e. inferences about the population:

- *Coefficient of determination (R² and R² adjusted):*

  The coefficient of determination ($R^2$) is a global measure for a prediction model that shows how well an estimate is aligned to, and reflects the empirical data. This measure denotes the ratio of the explained variation, i.e. the part of variation that can be attributed to the variation in the combined predictor variables, to the total variation [0;1]. It is a characteristic of $R^2$ to increase in proportion to the growing number of independent variables in a model. $R^2$ adjusted takes this circumstance into account by additionally taking the degrees of freedom (df) into account.

- *Standard error of estimate (SEE):*

  The standard error of estimate is another global measure for evaluating a prediction model which determines the mean error in prediction. This measure quantifies the deviations occurring between the observed and predicted scores of Y. In a similar way to $R^2$ adjusted, this measure also takes into consideration the number of degrees of freedom (df). As opposed to the coefficient of determination ($R^2$), lower values display a better goodness-of-fit between model predictions and the dependent variable Y.

- *Mean absolute percentage error (MAPE in %):*

  MAPE defines the mean absolute percentage error in prediction and indicates the forecast accuracy of a model as a percentage. If Y is the dependent variable and $\hat{Y}$ comprises the values predicted by the model, MAPE [0;+∞] is calculated by the equation below. In the context of this study, the mean absolute percentage errors are employed in particular in the context of validation tests, to compare and evaluate the prediction quality of a specified model with the absolute percentage errors of empirical mean and median values.

$$MAPE = \frac{1}{N}\sum_{i=1}^{n}\left|\frac{Y_i - \hat{Y}_i}{Y_i}\right| \times 100 \qquad \text{(Equation 3)}$$

Where:   $\hat{Y}_i$ :   Predicted value (for an observation i where i=1,2,3,…n)

$Y_i$ :   Dependent variable (for an observation i where i=1,2,3,…n)

$N$ :   Sample size

- *F-statistics:*

  This significance test examines the probability of making inferences about population parameters based on sample statistics ascertained for the overall model. Depending on the result of this test, it can be decided whether to generalize hypotheses about interrelations detected in the empirical data for the population. The empirical test statistic (F-value) takes into consideration the variance components of $R^2$ and the degrees of freedom (df). The significance test investigates the null hypothesis that the statistical model does not explain any interrelation between the variables under analysis, against the alternative hypothesis, that the prediction model reveals a causal interrelation at least between two variables. To this end, the study refers to a 95%-confidence interval and describes the empirical F-value and the empirical significance level of the test statistic.

- *Standardized partial regression coefficient (beta):*

  The standardized partial regression coefficient makes it possible to compare the magnitude of an influence across various independent variables ($X_i$) of a linear model on a standard scale. In contrast to the (unstandardized) partial regression coefficient $b_i$, estimated values for the standardized partial regression coefficient cannot be used for the purpose of empirical estimates.

- *t-statistics:*

  This significance test examines the probability, if each single regression coefficient $b_i$ that is estimated in a model exerts a significant impact on Y, in other words, whether the sample data provides reasonable grounds to generalize estimates on regression coefficients for the population (other schools). The significance test examines the null hypothesis $H_0(\beta_i = 0)$ that $b_i$ does not exert any influence on Y against the alternative hypothesis $H_1(\beta_i \neq 0)$ at a 5% significance level. To this end, the empirical test statistic (t-value) is calculated as a quotient of the partial regression coefficient ($b_i$) and the standard error of $b_i$ ($SE_b$: estimated distribution of $b_i$). The respective calculation parameters as well as the empirical significance level are given for each prediction model in Sections 3 to 5. In addition, also the confidence interval [Lower CL; Upper CL] is described that comprises the value of the real partial regression coefficient $\beta_i$ with a probability of 95%. The lower the confidence interval is, the more accurate the prediction of $\beta_i$ for a specific independent variable $X_i$ can be determined.

- *Multicollinearity:*

  In the case of multicollinearity, where the variances of different independent variables overlap within a multivariate model, the estimates of the separate partial regression coefficients $b_i$ become unstable and therefore unreliable. In general, a linear correlation between individual X-variables can be detected by means of a multivariate regression analysis, and thus the degree of multicollinearity with $R^2$ [0;1] can be determined. In the context of this study, the degree of existing multicollinearity is expressed by the two statistical measures, the tolerance (where $T_i = 1 - R_i^2$) and the variance inflation factor (where VIF=1/T). The tolerance [0;1] is calculated by means of a multiple regression of each independent variable $X_i$ on the other independent variables X. As an example, tolerance values near 0.00 indicate a high level of multicollinearity between the predictor variables and model estimates can be classified as inefficient. By contrast, tolerance values in the region of 1.00 signify that the independent variable $X_i$ possesses its own share of variance in the model. VIF corresponds to the reciprocal value of the tolerance.

In general, evaluated models introduced in this study for predicting consumption and costs values are the result of a single estimation that is based on sample observations. In this context, it is possible to investigate whether the relevant models fulfill the regression theoretical assumptions and allow for unbiased, efficient and consistent estimates, or not. The statistical models presented in Sections 3 to 5 correspond with the following four BLUE-assumptions[26] that can be specified on the basis of the empirical distribution of the error term U for linear, i.e. intrinsic-linear, prediction model estimates:

- *Assumption No.1:* $Var(U_i) = \sigma_i^2 = \sigma_k^2$

  This assumption means that the residuals (U) display to a great extent a constant variance $(\sigma^2)$. Besides the visual inspection of residual plots, a statistical analysis is conducted in order to investigate the assumption of homoscedasticity using the Levene Test (F-test for variance homogenity). Alternatively, it is also possible to verify heteroscedasticity using the Glesjer test or the Goldfeld/Quandt test, for example (cf. Backhaus, et al., 2008, p.86).

- Assumption No.2: $E(U) = 0$

  If the residuals of equal distances are symmetrically distributed to Y (within the positive and negative quadrants of scatter plot), the error term U has the expected value of 0.00. By contrast, violation of this assumption would result in biased estimates.

- *Assumption No.3:* $Cov(X_iU_i) = 0$

  This assumption means that there is no correlation between the independent variables and the error term. Both variables do not covariate with the other, and the residuals are independent of the scores of the predictor variable. Otherwise, i.e. if this assumption is not fulfilled and $Cov(X_iU_i) > 0$ is valid, the predicted values $\hat{Y}$ would be biased. In this case, $b_j$ would not only assume the impact of $X_i$, but also that of U, which would lead to specification errors.

---

[26] BLUE stands for the best linear unbiased estimation.

- *Assumption No.4:* $Cov(U_k, U_{k-1}) = 0$

  There is no correlation between consecutive residuals of a series of observations. The residuals are uncorrelated, i.e. no autocorrelation exists. Otherwise the residuals would no longer be incidental but moreover dependent in terms of their direction on the previous case. This study investigates this assumption using Durbin-Watson statistics based on the empirical test value of d [0;4].

**Analysis of variance**

While regression analysis is used for case-related consumption and cost predictions for individual school complexes, the analysis of variance supports group-oriented mean estimates based on categorical variables. In general, the various types of variance analyses are classified according to the number of factors included in a model. The statistical model used for the multivariate analysis of variance (MANOVA, two-factor design) with the two factors $\alpha$ and $\beta$ has the following form:

$$Y_{ghi} = \mu + \alpha_g + \beta_h + (\alpha\beta)_{gh} + \varepsilon_{ghi}$$

(Equation 4)

Where:     $Y_{ghk}$ :    *Dependent variable (for an observation i where i=1,2,3,...n)*

            $\mu$ :        *Grand mean of the population*

            $\alpha_g$ :       *Effect of belonging to group α (factor level g=1,2,3,...,k)*

            $\beta_h$ :       *Effect of belonging to group β (factor level h=1,2,3,...,k)*

            $(\alpha\beta)_{gh}$ :   *Interaction effect*

            $\varepsilon_{ghi}$ :      *Error term*

Each school complex is characterized as a particular case by certain factor levels (g, h) of the factors $\alpha$ and $\beta$ (such as the type of school or educational program). The random error $\varepsilon$ associated with a prediction, however, describes other incidental influences that are impossible to ascertain or explain. The interaction effect $(\alpha\beta)$ also makes it possible to take into account the simultaneous interaction among the two factors considered within the model. In the case of a single-factor analysis of variance (one-way ANOVA) this model is accordingly reduced to the factor $\alpha$. The analysis of variance is therefore based on the subdivision of the total variance into different parts and the subsequent evaluation of the explanatory part by means of the factors considered in model. The objective of such an approach is to analyze and estimate the effects of different factor levels to predict the dependent variable (Y), i.e. consumption and cost values. To this end, the total variance, defined as the mean sum of squared deviations around the grand mean, is divided into the different parts $MS_b$ and $MS_w$. Here, $MS_b$ describes the mean sum of the squares between the factor levels (deviation explained by the main effects and the interaction term) and $MS_w$ represents the mean sum of squares within the factor levels (non-explained deviation). By comparing these deviations with one another, the significance of the factors incorporated in the model can be evaluated and consequently the quality of a prediction model can be assessed. The F-test (test of significance) is again used to examine if generalized inferences can be formulated for the population regarding the sample examination and a 95%-confidence interval.

# 3    Investigation of operating costs

With reference to 2008, the calendar year in question, the aggregate operating costs averaging approximately 26 €/m² GROFA p.a. for the school complexes under investigation. These costs are relatively consistent, only varying with a standard deviation of around 5 €/m² GROFA p.a. (cf. Tab. 103, costs including VAT). Based on Tab. 4, the investigation of operating costs takes the following cost groups on the second structural cost level into consideration, as defined by DIN 18960:2008-2:

- Utilities (cost group 310)

- Waste disposal (cost group 320)

- Cleaning and care of buildings (cost group 330)

- Cleaning and care of grounds and outdoor facilities (cost group 340)

- Operation, inspection and maintenance (cost group 350)

- Security and surveillance services (cost group 360)

- Statutory charges and contributions (cost group 370)

The largest, and most substantial, part of operating costs is attributable primarily to utilities, and here in particular to heating, followed by costs for the cleaning and care of buildings and for the operation, inspection and maintenance. The empirical investigation not only examines the aforementioned cost groups as defined on second cost level but also allows for detailed estimates of utility consumptions and costs, as well as a more precise analysis of expenses for operation, inspection and maintenance on the third structural cost level according to DIN 18960:2008-2. In addition, the analysis of the aggregate outlay for operating schools is described in Section 3.8.

## 3.1    Utility supply

The investigation of utility supply takes into account the evaluation of the annual consumption and ancillary costs of 125 school complexes in 2008. The individual outlay for drinking water, heating and electricity is made up of the basic rate and the consumption-related costs, whereas the basic rate depends on the absolute annual supply quantity of a school complex. The theoretical basis for the initial investigation of individual utilities is particularly based on interviews conducted with experts in the field of energy planning and management and the study of secondary literature (see Section 2.2.2). The underlying variables of the investigation are defined according to these sources and the models for estimating total costs and specific cost indicators for water, heating and electricity that form the basis for the investigation of aggregated utility costs, are presented in detail. Based on validation tests carried out for 5 schools, the results of the statistical analysis of research are evaluated and utility cost indicators for the respective schools are presented.

### 3.1.1   Water

#### 3.1.1.1  Empirical and theoretical basis

The investigation includes both the drinking water consumption and costs for 125 school complexes in calendar year 2008 (see Appendix C). The basic condition of only referring to the properties form a single municipality allows the influences of various utilization patterns and also of the functional and technical characteristics of school complexes to be examined in the data evaluation.

Neil and Brümmer (2007) and Cheng and Hong (2004), among others, refer to the importance which is to be given to these factor groups, and the influential factors resulting from them, in the course of an evaluation of the water demand of schools (see also VDI 3807-1:2007-3 and Ages (2005). In a study of 64 public schools, Neil and Brümmer (2007) name particularly general facility influences and installed water saving technologies as being major influences on the water consumption of schools. With reference to their terminology, general facility influences comprise activities and patterns of facility occupancy, including the type of usage (classrooms, showers, etc.), the temporal intensity of operation, and the extent of exterior sports fields and landscaped gardens. Cheng and Hong (2004) additionally name the number of consumers, the existence and type of kitchens, the size of a swimming pool facility (in m²) and also the size of garden areas to be watered as especially significant factors that cause greatly divergent water consumptions. With regard to the watering of external grounds, the building management of the state capital Stuttgart assumes that irrigated sports fields can particularly influence the water usage of their operated properties. This factor has therefore been included in this investigation in the form of the size and proportions of irrigated green areas. Further characteristics which result from the aforementioned factor groups for the investigation of the underlying data sample are presented in the following overview. Additional information relating to the descriptive statistics and pertaining to each separate variable is given in Appendix C.

**Factor group: Utilization**

*Type of utilization:*

- Primary utilization: Elementary school, secondary school such as comprehensive school (secondary general school, intermediate secondary school, multiple school center) or grammar school, special school, vocational school with technical or business focus; qualitative description of different utilization types and quantitative description of the school utilization area in m² NEFA as well as its proportion per m² NEFA of the whole school property.

- Secondary utilization: Sports facilities such as gymnasiums or indoor swimming pools for teaching purposes, nursery school; qualitative and quantitative description of different utilization types with regard to their building reference areas and volumes respectively e.g. the net floor area of swimming pool utilization in m² and its proportion per m² NEFA, the area of a swimming pools base in m² and the water volume of swimming pools in m³.

*Standard of utilization:*

- Type of educational program: Regular school, extended regular school or full-day school.

- Type of canteen service: School based canteen, external catering or no canteen service.

*Intensity of utilization:*

- Temporal usage intensity:

  Average operating time of the whole school complex as well as individual operating times of both the primary and secondary utilizations, i.e. the school and its sports facilities, in hours per school week and with regard to the average number of schooldays per school week.

- Spatial usage intensity:

  - The total number of pupils, number of pupils per m² specific floor area according to DIN 277:2005-2 (Part 1 and 2) and the number of pupils with respect to other reference areas such as m² net floor area of school utilization e.g. the number of pupils per m² UFA.

  - The total number of school classes, number of school classes per m² specific floor area according to DIN 277:2005-2 (Part 1 and 2) and number of school classes with respect to other reference areas such as m² net floor area of school utilization e.g. the number of school classes per m² UFA.

  - Water volume of swimming pools in m³ of complete refillings per year.

**Factor group: Functional and technical characteristics**

*Functional characteristics:*

- Specific building floor areas according to DIN 277:2005-2 (Part 1 and 2) e.g. in m² NEFA, m² UFA, m² UFA 5 and their representative proportion to the total size of a property in m² GROFA or other specific building floor areas e.g. the share of UFA 5 per m² NEFA.

- The total sanitary area and its proportion to specific building floor areas according to DIN 277: 2005-2 (Part 1 and 2) e.g. the share of the sanitary area per m² UFA.

*Technical characteristics:*

- Standard of technical installations:

  Qualitative description of the standard of technical installations and in particular the standard of water supply systems.

- Condition of technical installations:

  Qualitative description of the condition of technical installations and in particular the condition of water supply systems.

- Standard of grounds and outdoor facilities:

  The total size of irrigated grounds of green areas in m² and its representative proportion to the non-built up plot area.

From a theoretical point of view, all of the factors outlined above exert an impact on water consumption and costs, and are therefore taken into account within the analytical framework of this study.

### 3.1.1.2 Model design and parameters

The statistical analysis of significant interrelationships between the factors outlined in Section 3.1.1.1 and the total annual water consumption and costs (Y) identifies significant effects from the predictive variables; usable floor area, the annual water volume required for complete pool refillings, the proportionate sanitary area, and the number of school classes per m² UFA respectively on Y. According to Models 1.A.1 and 1.A.2, the size of a school's usable floor area has a significant influence on Y and, in particular, causes variation in the total water consumption and costs. Detailed information on the model design and specifications of both models is shown in Tab. 7 and Tab. 8. A nonlinear relationship between the usable floor area and the total annual consumption and costs is identified on the basis of a sample of 125 schools. With R² around 0.79 and SEE around 0.312, both regression models verify reliable estimates. In addition, the mean absolute percentage error accounts for 26% (Model 1.A.1) and 24% (Model 1.A.2) respectively, verifying accurate predictions for both regression models. In the case of Model 1.A.2, a non-significant regression constant is accepted at a 5% significance level for predicting the total water costs $(\hat{Y})$. The confidence limits between -1.553 and 0.361, described in Tab. 8, indicate that this regression constant does not deviate significantly from zero in population, and therefore does not have an important practical relevance for the prediction of total costs.

Tab. 7:     Model description for estimating total water consumption

| Dependent variable | Transf. | R² | R² adj. | SEE | F-value | Sign. | Durbin-Watson-Statistic | | N |
|---|---|---|---|---|---|---|---|---|---|
| Water consumption (m³ p.a.) | LN | 0.781 | 0.773 | 0.326 | 106.859 | 0.000 | 2.010 | | 125 |

| Factors | Transf. | B | St. Error | Beta | t-value | Sign. | Lower CL | Upper CL | T | VIF |
|---|---|---|---|---|---|---|---|---|---|---|
| Constant | LN | -2.091 | 0.510 | | -4.096 | 0.000 | -3.102 | -1.080 | | |
| Usable floor area (UFA in m²) | LN | 0.999 | 0.053 | 0.876 | 18.675 | 0.000 | 0.893 | 1.105 | 0.831 | 1.204 |
| Water volume of complete pool refillings p.a. | - | 0.002 | 0.000 | 0.275 | 6.365 | 0.000 | 0.002 | 0.003 | 0.980 | 1.020 |
| Share of the sanitary area per m² UFA | - | 7.133 | 1.977 | 0.170 | 3.608 | 0.000 | 3.219 | 11.048 | 0.822 | 1.217 |
| Number of school classes per m² UFA | - | 41.141 | 11.596 | 0.153 | 3.548 | 0.001 | 18.181 | 64.101 | 0.982 | 1.018 |

**Dependent variable:** Water consumption (m³ p.a.), 2008

$$\hat{Y} = 0.124 \cdot X_1^{0.999} \cdot e^{0.002 X_2} \cdot e^{7.133 X_3} \cdot e^{41.141 X_4} \qquad \text{(Model 1.A.1)}$$

Where:     $\hat{Y}$ :   Water consumption (m³ p.a.)

$X_1$ :   Usable floor area (UFA in m²)

$X_2$ :   Water volume of swimming pools in m³ of complete refillings p.a.

$X_3$ :   Share of the sanitary area per m² UFA

$X_4$ :   Number of school classes per m² UFA

Tab. 8:   Model description for estimating total water costs

| Dependent variable | Transf. | R² | R² adj. | SEE | F-value | Sign. | Durbin-Watson-Statistic | | N |
|---|---|---|---|---|---|---|---|---|---|
| Water costs (€ p.a.) | LN | 0.794 | 0.787 | 0.309 | 115.437 | 0.000 | 2.040 | | 125 |

| Factors | Transf. | B | St. Error | Beta | t-value | Sign. | Lower CL | Upper CL | T | VIF |
|---|---|---|---|---|---|---|---|---|---|---|
| Constant | LN | -0.596 | 0.483 | | -1.234 | 0.220 | -1.553 | 0.361 | | |
| Usable floor area (UFA in m²) | LN | 0.981 | 0.051 | 0.881 | 19.372 | 0.000 | 0.881 | 1.081 | 0.831 | 1.204 |
| Water volume of complete pool refillings p.a. | - | 0.002 | 0.000 | 0.276 | 6.583 | 0.000 | 0.002 | 0.003 | 0.980 | 1.020 |
| Number of school classes per m² UFA | - | 39.795 | 10.979 | 0.152 | 3.625 | 0.000 | 18.057 | 61.533 | 0.982 | 1.018 |
| Share of the sanitary area per m² UFA | - | 6.518 | 1.872 | 0.159 | 3.482 | 0.001 | 2.812 | 10.224 | 0.822 | 1.217 |

**Dependent variable:** Water costs (€ p.a.), costs including VAT, based on 2008 figures

$$\hat{Y} = 0.551 \cdot X_1^{0.981} \cdot e^{0.002X_2} \cdot e^{39.795X_3} \cdot e^{6.518X_4} \qquad \text{(Model 1.A.2)}$$

Where:    $\hat{Y}$ :   Water costs (€ p.a.)

$X_1$ :   Usable floor area (UFA in m²)

$X_2$ :   Water volume of swimming pools in m³ of complete refillings p.a.

$X_3$ :   Number of school classes per m² UFA

$X_4$ :   Share of the sanitary area per m² UFA

$X_5$ :   Share of the sanitary area per m² NEFA

The following investigation of consumption and cost indicators is based on the Models 1.A.1 and 1.A.2 for estimating the total water consumption and costs described above, by taking into account the key factors identified therein. The schools' usable floor area is used to normalize total consumption and cost values, rather than the net floor area which also comprises technical floor and circulation areas and for which share no significant effect could be statistically proven. Tab. 9 and Tab. 10 give an overview of model estimates for water consumption and cost indicators (Model 1.B.1 and 1.B.2) regarding R², R² adjusted, SEE, outlier statistics and the empirical significance level for each model type.

As a result of step-by-step analysis, different models for estimating water consumption and cost indicators were carried out in order to compare and evaluate their predictive accuracy. If, for example, the total water capacity of swimming pools is considered as an alternative to the predictor $X_1$ (annual water volume of complete pool refilling p.a.) in Model 1.B.2, the coefficient of determination R²= 0.634 is reduced to R²=0.539. By contrast, to determine the water capacity of swimming pools as an independent variable, the predictor $X_1$ allows the number of pool refillings p.a. to be taken into account. Differences in the frequency of full refillings are influenced by the intensity of pool utilization, which particularly depends on the amount of pool cleaning and tank emptying required, due to repair measures.

Tab. 9:     Model description for estimating water consumption indicators

| Dependent variable | Transf. | R² | R² adj. | SEE | F-value | Sign. | Durbin-Watson-Statistic | | N |
|---|---|---|---|---|---|---|---|---|---|
| Water consumption (m³/m² UFA p.a.) | - | 0.620 | 0.610 | 0.074 | 65.686 | 0.000 | 1.973 | | 125 |

| Factors | Transf. | B | St. Error | Beta | t-value | Sign. | Lower CL | Upper CL | T | VIF |
|---|---|---|---|---|---|---|---|---|---|---|
| Constant | - | 0.047 | 0.028 | | 1.672 | 0.097 | -0.009 | 0.103 | | |
| Water volume of complete pool refillings p.a. | - | 0.001 | 0.000 | 0.690 | 12.220 | 0.000 | 0.001 | 0.001 | 0.986 | 1.014 |
| Share of the sanitary area per m² UFA | - | 2.067 | 0.415 | 0.282 | 4.981 | 0.000 | 1.245 | 2.888 | 0.982 | 1.018 |
| Number of school classes per m² UFA | - | 11.346 | 2.611 | 0.245 | 4.345 | 0.000 | 6.177 | 16.515 | 0.988 | 1.012 |

**Dependent variable**: Water consumption (m³/m² usable floor area p.a.), 2008

$$\hat{Y} = 0.047 + 0.001X_1 + 2.067X_2 + 11.346X_3 \qquad \text{(Model 1.B.1)}$$

Where:     $\hat{Y}$ :     Water consumption (m³/m² UFA p.a.)

$X_1$ :     Water volume of swimming pools in m³ of complete refillings p.a.

$X_2$ :     Share of the sanitary area per m² UFA

$X_3$ :     Number of school classes per m² UFA

Tab. 10:    Model description for estimating water cost indicators

| Dependent variable | Transf. | R² | R² adj. | SEE | F-value | Sign. | Durbin-Watson-Statistic | | N |
|---|---|---|---|---|---|---|---|---|---|
| Water costs (€/m² UFA p.a.) | - | 0.634 | 0.625 | 0.251 | 69.974 | 0.000 | 1.921 | | 125 |

| Factors | Transf. | B | St. Error | Beta | t-value | Sign. | Lower CL | Upper CL | T | VIF |
|---|---|---|---|---|---|---|---|---|---|---|
| Constant | - | 0.210 | 0.096 | | 2.182 | 0.031 | 0.019 | 0.400 | | |
| Water volume of complete pool refillings p.a. | - | 0.004 | 0.000 | 0.700 | 12.650 | 0.000 | 0.003 | 0.004 | 0.986 | 1.014 |
| Share of the sanitary area per m² UFA | - | 7.179 | 1.412 | 0.282 | 5.083 | 0.000 | 4.383 | 9.975 | 0.982 | 1.018 |
| Number of school classes per m² UFA | - | 39.484 | 8.887 | 0.246 | 4.443 | 0.000 | 21.889 | 57.078 | 0.988 | 1.012 |

**Dependent variable**: Water costs (€/m² usable floor area p.a.), costs including VAT, based on 2008 figures

$$\hat{Y} = 0.210 + 0.004X_1 + 7.179X_2 + 39.484X_3 \qquad \text{(Model 1.B.2)}$$

Where:     $\hat{Y}$ :     Water costs (€/m² UFA p.a.)

$X_1$ :     Water volume of swimming pools in m³ of complete refillings p.a.

$X_2$ :     Share of the sanitary area per m² UFA

$X_3$ :     Number of school classes per m² UFA

*Summary*

All of the introduced models for estimating water consumption and costs take the independent impacts of the variables; water volume required for complete pool refillings p.a., the number of school classes and the share of the sanitary area per m² UFA on water consumption and costs into account. In addition, the usable floor area is defined by Models 1.A.1 and 1.A.2 as being the relevant building reference area to explain variation in Y. All independent variables used to estimate and forecast water consumption and costs derive from the schools' utilization intensity and their functional building characteristics. In order to approximate the volume of water required for pool utilization throughout the year, the frequency with which pool refillings take place is also taken into consideration. The water volume employed is based on pool size multiplied by the number of times the pool is emptied and completely refilled. Regarding the number of school classes, schools with a greater number of classes per m² UFA consume, on average, more water per year. Within the context of 125 schools, this is particularly the case for vocational schools with a relatively large number of pupils and small class sizes. Other potential assumptions relating to the impact of different educational programs or school operating times on water consumption and costs could not be confirmed by means of regression analysis.

### 3.1.1.3  Validation of the model

The statistical investigation introcuded for water cost indicators (Model 1.B.2) takes the annual water volume required for complete pool refillings, the share of the sanitary area per m² UFA, and the number of school classes per m² UFA into account. These independent variables particularly verify significant cost differences between schools with additional sports facilities, vocational schools, and other utilization types (cf. Section 3.1.1.2).[27]

Based on sample data of five validation properties, the forecast quality of Model 1.B.2 is compared with empirical mean and median values by percentage errors. The validation test shown in Tab X. confirms these more precise model estimates by Model 1.B.2 for designated school types using the examples of a special school with gymnasium, a secondary school with gymnasium and indoor swimming pool, and a vocational school with technical focus and without any sports facility (samples No.2, 4 and 5, costs including VAT, based on 2008 figures). With reference to the other two validation properties, the empirical median at 0.78 €/m² UFA p.a., in particular, achieves better cost predictions.

Tab. 11:   Model validation for water cost indicators

| No. | Type of school | Observed value | Predicted value | Absolute error % of prediction | Absolute error % of mean | Absolute error % of median | Preference |
|---|---|---|---|---|---|---|---|
| 1 | Elementary school without sports facilities | 0.73 | 0.88 | 20 | 19 | 8 | Median |
| 2 | Special school with gymnasium | 0.56 | 0.77 | 38 | 56 | 41 | Prediction |
| 3 | Secondary school without sports facilities | 0.68 | 0.82 | 19 | 27 | 15 | Median |
| 4 | Secondary school with gymnasium and pool | 1.71 | 1.36 | 21 | 49 | 54 | Prediction |
| 5 | Vocational school without sports facilities | 1.21 | 0.98 | 19 | 28 | 35 | Prediction |
| Ø | **Mean Absolute percentage error** | | | 24 | 36 | 31 | Prediction |

**Observed value:** Water costs (€/m² usable floor area p.a.), costs including VAT, based on 2008 figures, N=125

---

[27] The underlying empirical data reveals that schools with sports facilities, such as indoor swimming pools or gymnasiums, have on average a higher proportion of the sanitary area per m² UFA (6%) than those schools without these sport functions and an associated proportionate sanitary area per m² UFA of around 4%.

Comparing the estimation methods presented in Tab. 11, and taking MAPE to be around 24% for the validation sample, the regression produces more accurate estimates by making use of the quantified factors described above. Summarizing, it can be concluded that estimating water cost indicators purely by averaging would appear to be risky/ (empirical data) appears risky. This is confirmed by the validation test on the one hand and underlined by an empirical standard deviation of 0.41 €/m² UFA p.a. for N=125 on the other (see Tab. 101).

### 3.1.1.4 Cost indicators for water

Regression Model 1.B.2 identifies a substantial increase in the annual costs per m² UFA regarding the predictor variable $X_1$ (water volume of complete pool refilling p.a.). With a standardized regression coefficient (beta) of 0.700, this variable represents the greatest effect on Y in multivariate analysis. In addition to continuous estimates for water consumption and costs, described in Section 3.1.1.2, specific cost values for a categorical distinction of school utilization types are presented in Tab. 12. For the purpose of cost planning and facilities management, designated cost indicators are described for schools with or without indoor swimming pool. Based upon sample data from 125 properties, reference is made to the predictor variable $X_1$, incorporated in Model 1.B.2. Underlying cost indicators in €/m² UFA p.a. include VAT and are based on 2008 figures. The comparison between the empirical mean values of schools with or without swimming pools reveals that those schools with swimming facilities have, with a mean of 1.80 €/m² UFA p.a., higher average costs of 1.40 €/m² UFA p.a. The subsample of schools with swimming pool utilization has a range of 2.29 €/m² UFA p.a. However, more accurate cost estimates can be made on the basis of the annual water consumption for pool refillings shown in Tab. 10. According to empirical sample data, described in Tab. 108, the category of water volume for complete pool refillings p.a. ≥ 200 m³ incorporates those schools with a maximum annual filling volume of almost 700 m³.

Tab. 12: Evaluated cost indicators for water

| Factor level | Minimum | Mean | Median | Maximum | Range |
|---|---|---|---|---|---|
| Schools without swimming pools | 0.23 | 0.80 | 0.77 | 1.61 | 1.39 |
| Schools with swimming pools | 0.85 | 1.80 | 1.75 | 3.14 | 2.29 |
| < 200 m³ water volume of complete pool refillings p.a. | 0.85 | 1.37 | 1.42 | 2.01 | 1.17 |
| ≥ 200 m³ water volume of complete pool refillings p.a. | 1.81 | 2.53 | 2.63 | 3.14 | 1.33 |

Dependent variable: Water costs (€/m² usable floor area p.a.), costs including VAT, based on 2008 figures, N=125

## 3.1.2   Heating

### 3.1.2.1 Empirical and theoretical basis

Based on the 2008 figures for the 125 school complexes, the costs for heating[28], which are on average 6.70 €/m² GROFA p.a. (costs including VAT), represent the largest share of the overall utility costs examined. Within the discussion of evaluating the heating energy demand of buildings, reference is in particular made to a building's size, volume, layout, the type and intensity of usage, as well as to detailed specifications regarding the building construction and technical installations (see Ages, 2005; VDI 3807-1:2007-3; DETR, 1998; Hasan, et al., 2008). This analysis accordingly includes a qualitative classification of different utilization types and quantitative descriptions of numerous school utilization areas, such as those defined by DIN 277:2005-2 (Part 1 and 2). In addition, the heatable gross floor area (H-GROFA) is considered, as defined by the German guideline VDI 3807-1:2007-3 to be the gross floor area (GROFA) of a building minus major non-heatable gross floor areas. Regarding the technical features of building constructions, particular details are given in the literature on the heat storage capacity, glazing standard and the insulation of external walls. These factors are taken to be influences on the energy saving potential and therefore to be essential in energy indicator comparisons (cf. Filippin, 2000; Depecker et al., 2001 or Becker et al., 2007).

The classification of different construction types in SIA 380/1:2009 is followed in this study, so that the heat storage capacity is represented as the thermal mass in the form of a dichotomous variable. The standard, size and condition of external glass areas are considered as three independent and continuous variables. With respect to the characteristic features of technical installations, previous studies have especially named the standard and condition of these components and the type of energy source as being relevant factors for the heating demand and its examination (cf. Balaras et al., 2007; DAC-BW, 2006 or Hernandez, et al., 2008). This study finally also considers the geographical location of a school within an urban, suburban or rural environment as, according to Corgnati et al., 2008 or DETR, 1997, among others, this has a direct effect on the energy performance of buildings. To summarize, the individual influences of the following theoretically relevant variables are taken into consideration in the analysis of heating consumption and costs:

**Factor group: Utilization**

*Type of utilization:*

*   Primary utilization: Elementary school, secondary school such as comprehensive school (secondary general school, intermediate secondary school, multiple school center) or grammar school, special school, vocational school with technical or business focus; qualitative description of different utilization types and quantitative description of the

---

[28] According to DIN 18960:2008-2, heat supply comprises expenses incurred for oil, gas, solid fuels and district heating. The majority of the schools investigated rely on gas as their main source of heating energy (N=85), the remainders (N=45) are supplied by district heating (cf. Appendix C).

school utilization area in m² NEFA as well as its proportion per m² NEFA of the whole school property.

- Secondary utilization: Sports facilities such as gymnasiums or indoor swimming pools for teaching purposes, nursery school, underground parking; qualitative and quantitative description of different utilization types with regard to their building reference areas and volumes respectively e.g. the net floor area of swimming pool utilization in m² or the net floor area of underground parking in m² and their representative proportion per m² NEFA, the water volume of swimming pools in m³.

*Standard of utilization:*

- Type of educational program: Regular school, extended regular school or full-day school.

*Intensity of utilization:*

- Temporal usage intensity:

  Average operating time of the whole school complex as well as individual operating times of both the primary and secondary utilizations, i.e. the school and its sports facilities, in hours per school week and with regard to the average number of schooldays per school week.

- Spatial usage intensity:

  Qualitative and quantitative description of the spatial standard e.g. the total size of specific floor areas according to DIN 277:2005-2 (Part 1 and 2) in relation to the number of pupils or school classes as well as other reference areas such as m² net floor area of school utilization or m² heatable gross floor area with respect to the number of pupils or school classes.

**Factor group: Functional and technical characteristics**

*Functional characteristics:*

- Specific building floor areas according to DIN 277:2005-2 (Part 1 and 2) e.g. in m² GROFA, m² UFA, m² UFA 5 and their representative proportion to the total size of a property in m² GROFA or other specific building floor areas e.g. the share of UFA 5 per m² GROFA.

- The total gross building volume and the average storey height as defined by DIN 277-1: 2005-2.

- Total heatable gross floor area according to VDI 3807-01:2007-03 and its representative proportion to the total size of a property in m² GROFA according to DIN 277-1: 2005-2.

*Technical characteristics:*

- Standard of building constructions:

  - Heat storage capacity: Light or heavy thermal mass.

  - Glass area of external walls and roofs according to DIN 277-3:2005-4 and its share in percentage of specific building floor areas according to DIN 277: 2005-2 (Part 1 and

2) or according to VDI 3807-01:2007-03 e.g. the share of glass areas of external walls and roofs per m² H-GROFA.

- Glazing standard: Qualitative and quantitative description of single, double and triple glazing in m² glass area of external walls and as a percentage of the whole glass area of external walls according to DIN 277-3:2005-4.

- Standard of insulation: Qualitative and quantitative description of modernized insulation e.g. as a percentage of the whole external wall and roof cladding area according to DIN 277-3:2005-4.

- Condition of building constructions:

  Qualitative and quantitative description of the condition of external glass areas e.g. the share of defective glass areas of external walls as a percentage of the whole glass area of external walls.

- Standard of technical installations:

  - Kind of energy source: Gas, district heating.

  - Qualitative and quantitative description of the standard of technical installations and in particular the standard of heat generators or heating control systems e.g. heat generators including or excluding central water heaters.

- Condition of technical installations:

  Qualitative and quantitative description of the condition of technical installations and in particular the condition of heat supply systems e.g. the percentage of defective heat supply systems.

**Factor group: Location**

- Region: Urban, suburban or rural.

### 3.1.2.2 Model design and parameters

Based on the factors described above, this survey defines the heatable gross floor area as being the effective building reference area for estimating the total heating energy consumption and costs. Models 2.A.1 and 2.A.2 take the extent of inefficient heat supply systems and defective external glass areas, as well as the existence of an indoor swimming pool, into account to explain variations in the total amount of annual heating energy consumption and costs for individual school complexes. With $beta_3$ set at around 0.127, this investigation clearly shows that the existence of an indoor swimming pool increases the energy demand for heating both the water and the space. In addition, Model 2.A.1, which estimates the total heating energy consumption, considers the independent effect of different energy sources with respect to the categorical variable $X_4$. For the purpose of the survey, the effects of different standards, conditions and proportions of external glass areas are tested as continuous variables. The proportion of glass areas of external walls and roofs is determined with respect to H-GROFA.

The glazing standard is defined as a percentage of single, double or triple glazing, with respect to the glass area of external walls and the condition is represented as a percentage of defective glass areas. Based on quantified determinants at a significance level of 5%, only the variable share of external glass areas per m² H-GROFA is incorporated in the multivariate regression model as being representative of the proportion of glass façades and roofs.

Tab. 13: Model description for estimating total heating consumption

| Dependent variable | Transf. | $R^2$ | $R^2$ adj. | SEE | F-value | Sign. | Durbin-Watson-Statistic | | N |
|---|---|---|---|---|---|---|---|---|---|
| Heating energy consumption (kWh p.a.) | LN | 0.888 | 0.883 | 0.227 | 188.622 | 0.000 | 1.997 | | 125 |

| Factors | Transf. | B | St. Error | Beta | t-value | Sign. | Lower CL | Upper CL | T | VIF |
|---|---|---|---|---|---|---|---|---|---|---|
| Constant | LN | 4.820 | 0.309 | | 15.599 | 0.000 | 4.208 | 5.432 | | |
| Heatable gross floor area (H-GROFA in m²) | LN | 0.940 | 0.034 | 0.881 | 27.343 | 0.000 | 0.872 | 1.008 | 0.907 | 1.103 |
| Share of defective heat supply systems (%) | LN | 0.013 | 0.003 | 0.143 | 4.481 | 0.000 | 0.008 | 0.019 | 0.931 | 1.075 |
| Indoor swimming pool for teaching purposes | - | 0.347 | 0.084 | 0.128 | 4.142 | 0.000 | 0.181 | 0.513 | 0.983 | 1.017 |
| Gas (energy source) | - | 0.169 | 0.043 | 0.122 | 3.883 | 0.000 | 0.083 | 0.254 | 0.951 | 1.051 |
| Share of glass areas of external walls and roofs per m² H-GROFA | - | 0.368 | 0.144 | 0.079 | 2.556 | 0.012 | 0.083 | 0.653 | 0.984 | 1.017 |

**Dependent variable:** Heating energy consumption (kWh p.a.), 2008

$$\hat{Y} = 123.965 \cdot X_1^{0.940} \cdot X_2^{0.013} \cdot e^{0.347 X_3} \cdot e^{0.169 X_4} \cdot e^{0.368 X_5}$$  (Model 2.A.1)

Where: $\hat{Y}$ : Heating energy consumption (kWh p.a.)

$X_1$ : Heatable gross floor area (H-GROFA in m²)

$X_2$ : Share of defective heat supply systems (%)

$X_3$ : Indoor swimming pool for teaching purposes

$X_4$ : Gas (energy source)

$X_5$ : Share of glass areas of external walls and roofs per m² H-GROFA

Tab. 14: Model description for estimating total heating costs

| Dependent variable | Transf. | $R^2$ | $R^2$ adj. | SEE | F-value | Sign. | Durbin-Watson-Statistic | | N |
|---|---|---|---|---|---|---|---|---|---|
| Heating energy costs (€ p.a.) | LN | 0.892 | 0.888 | 0.219 | 247.183 | 0.000 | 2.082 | | 125 |

| Factors | Transf. | B | St. Error | Beta | t-value | Sign. | Lower CL | Upper CL | T | VIF |
|---|---|---|---|---|---|---|---|---|---|---|
| Constant | LN | 2.584 | 0.286 | | 9.040 | 0.000 | 2.018 | 3.150 | | |
| Heatable gross floor area (H-GROFA in m²) | LN | 0.921 | 0.032 | 0.877 | 28.389 | 0.000 | 0.857 | 0.985 | 0.945 | 1.058 |
| Share of defective heat supply systems (%) | LN | 0.012 | 0.003 | 0.129 | 4.166 | 0.000 | 0.006 | 0.018 | 0.938 | 1.066 |
| Indoor swimming pool for teaching purposes | - | 0.335 | 0.080 | 0.126 | 4.170 | 0.000 | 0.176 | 0.495 | 0.989 | 1.011 |
| Share of glass areas of external walls and roofs per m² H-GROFA | - | 0.417 | 0.139 | 0.091 | 3.005 | 0.003 | 0.142 | 0.691 | 0.986 | 1.014 |

**Dependent variable:** Heating energy costs (€ p.a.), costs including VAT, based on 2008 figures

$$\hat{Y} = 13.250 \cdot X_1^{0.921} \cdot X_2^{0.012} \cdot e^{0.335X_3} \cdot e^{0.417X_4}$$  (Model 2.A.2)

Where:  $\hat{Y}$ :  Heating energy costs (€ p.a.)

$X_1$ :  Heatable gross floor area (H-GROFA in m²)

$X_2$ :  Share of defective heat supply systems (%)

$X_3$ :  Indoor swimming pool for teaching purposes

$X_4$ :  Share of glass areas of external walls and roofs per m² H-GROFA

Taking the analysis of total heating energy consumption and costs as a basis, the heatable gross floor area, as defined in the German guideline VDI 3807-1:2007:3, is identified as being the appropriate reference area for consistent estimates and the normalization of total values. In the following section, this building floor area is used to specify the dependent variable for investigating the consumption and cost indicators described by Models 2.B.1 and 2.B.2.

Tab. 15:  Model description for estimating heating consumption indicators

| Dependent variable | Transf. | R² | R² adj. | SEE | F-value | Sign. | Durbin-Watson-Statistic | | N |
|---|---|---|---|---|---|---|---|---|---|
| Heating energy consumption | - | 0.497 | 0.471 | 20.089 | 19.403 | 0.000 | 1.967 | | 125 |

| Factors | Transf. | B | St. Error | Beta | t-value | Sign. | Lower CL | Upper CL | T | VIF |
|---|---|---|---|---|---|---|---|---|---|---|
| Constant | - | 157.202 | 26.936 | | 5.836 | 0.000 | 103.862 | 210.542 | | |
| Indoor swimming pool for teaching purposes | - | 39.274 | 7.429 | 0.349 | 5.286 | 0.000 | 24.562 | 53.987 | 0.976 | 1.024 |
| Share of defective heat supply systems (%) | LN | 1.202 | 0.263 | 0.309 | 4.575 | 0.000 | 0.682 | 1.722 | 0.935 | 1.070 |
| Gas (energy source) | - | 13.975 | 3.847 | 0.243 | 3.633 | 0.000 | 6.357 | 21.592 | 0.957 | 1.045 |
| Share of glass areas of external walls and roofs per m² H-GROFA | - | 42.763 | 12.769 | 0.221 | 3.349 | 0.001 | 17.477 | 68.050 | 0.975 | 1.025 |
| Heavy thermal mass | - | -17.071 | 5.130 | -0.223 | -3.328 | 0.001 | -27.229 | -6.913 | 0.952 | 1.050 |
| Heatable gross floor area (H-GROFA in m²) | LN | -9.556 | 2.973 | -0.219 | -3.215 | 0.002 | -15.443 | -3.670 | 0.918 | 1.089 |

Dependent variable: Heating energy consumption (kWh/m² heatable gross floor area p.a.), 2008

$$\hat{Y} = 157.202 + 39.274X_1 + 1.202\ln(X_2) + 13.975X_3 + 42.763X_4 - 17.071X_5 - 9.556\ln(X_6)$$ (Model 2.B.1)

Where:  $\hat{Y}$ :  Heating energy consumption (kWh/m² H-GROFA p.a.)

$X_1$ :  Indoor swimming pool for teaching purposes

$X_2$ :  Share of defective heat supply systems (%)

$X_3$ :  Gas (energy source)

$X_4$ :  Share of glass areas of external walls and roofs per m² H-GROFA

$X_5$ :  Heavy thermal mass (heat storage capacity)

$X_6$ :  Heatable gross floor area (H-GROFA in m²)

With respect to the factors evaluated above, the investigation of heating energy consumption and costs indicators primarily refers to the same predictors. In compliance with

Model 2.A.2, the type of energy source is also determined as being a significant criterion for the differentiation of consumption indicators, whereby properties which are heated by gas have, on average, higher consumption values compared with those facilities that are connected to the district heating network. In addition, the heat storage capacity of buildings describes an independent effect on heating consumption and cost indicators, specified within the statistical investigation by the qualitative variable $X_5$.

The best model estimates show good compliance with the underlying sample as regards equations 2.B.1 and 2.B.2, the statistical measures of which are displayed in Tab. 15 and Tab. 16. In terms of underlying model assumptions, each model describes a nonlinear relationship between the two independent variables: the share of defective heat supply systems and the heatable gross floor area on Y. Using Model 2.B.2 as an example, this means that the condition of heat supply systems has a nonlinear effect on heating cost indicators, whose impact decreases with increasing deficiency in the heat supply systems. With respect to the variable heatable gross floor area, the estimation model reflects the fact that large-scale school complexes have greater savings in heating costs - due to the building's greater heat storage capacity, for instance. Both models allow efficient and consistent estimates for heating energy consumption and costs which are confirmed by $R^2=0.497$ and $R^2=0.444$ respectively and MEAN values between 18 to 19% (N = 125).

Tab. 16:   Model description for estimating heating cost indicators

| Dependent variable | Transf. | R² | R² adj. | SEE | F-value | Sign. | Durbin-Watson-Statistic | | N |
|---|---|---|---|---|---|---|---|---|---|
| Heating energy costs (€/m² H-GROFA p.a.) | - | 0.444 | 0.420 | 1.559 | 18.975 | 0.000 | 1.994 | | 125 |

| Factors | Transf. | B | St. Error | Beta | t-value | Sign. | Lower CL | Upper CL | T | VIF |
|---|---|---|---|---|---|---|---|---|---|---|
| Constant | - | 14.279 | 2.012 | | 7.096 | 0.000 | 10.295 | 18.264 | | |
| Indoor swimming pool for teaching purposes | - | 3.044 | 0.575 | 0.365 | 5.290 | 0.000 | 1.905 | 4.184 | 0.980 | 1.020 |
| Share of glass areas of external walls and roofs per m² H-GROFA | - | 3.737 | 0.990 | 0.261 | 3.774 | 0.000 | 1.776 | 5.699 | 0.977 | 1.024 |
| Share of defective heat supply systems (%) | LN | 0.086 | 0.020 | 0.299 | 4.240 | 0.000 | 0.046 | 0.127 | 0.938 | 1.066 |
| Heatable gross floor area (H-GROFA in m²) | LN | -0.867 | 0.227 | -0.268 | -3.825 | 0.000 | -1.315 | -0.418 | 0.952 | 1.051 |
| Heavy thermal mass | - | -1.352 | 0.397 | -0.238 | -3.405 | 0.001 | -2.139 | -0.566 | 0.956 | 1.046 |

**Dependent variable:** Heating energy costs (€/m² heatable gross floor area p.a.), costs including VAT, based on 2008 figures

$$\hat{Y} = 14.279 + 3.044X_1 + 3.737X_2 + 0.086\ln(X_3) - 0.867\ln(X_4) - 1.352X_5 \qquad \text{(Model 2.B.2)}$$

Where:   $\hat{Y}$ :   Heating energy costs (€/m² H-GROFA p.a.)

$X_1$ :   Indoor swimming pool for teaching purposes

$X_2$ :   Share of glass areas of external walls and roofs per m² H-GROFA

$X_3$ :   Share of defective heat supply systems (%)

$X_4$ :   Heatable gross floor area (H-GROFA in m²)

$X_5$ :   Heavy thermal mass (heat storage capacity)

*Summary*

The empirical investigation into total heating energy consumption and costs considers different building floor areas which, from a theoretical point of view, could be of relevance for unbiased estimates. The statistical analysis of 125 schools in Germany verifies the assumption that there is a causal relationship between the heatable gross floor area, as defined by the German guideline VDI 3807-1:2007:3, and heating energy consumption and costs at a 5% significance level. The study subsequently confirms that existing differences in heating consumption and cost indicators are related to the type of school utilization as well as to functional and technical building characteristics such as the standard of building constructions and the condition of the technical installations.

### 3.1.2.3  Validation of the model

Based on sample data for 125 schools in Germany, Model 2.B.2 identifies five factors at a 5% significance level for optimized estimates for heating cost indicators (costs including VAT, based on 2008 figures). Apart from a distinction made between schools with or without indoor swimming pools, differences in cost indicators are explained by regression analysis with regard to functional and technical building characteristics.

The following validation test evaluates the level of prediction accuracy achieved by multivariate analysis. Absolute percentage errors for five validation properties are shown for the estimation Model 2.B.2 and compared with empirical mean and median estimates in Tab. 17. The regression model achieves good prediction accuracy, with a MAPE of almost 16%, compared with empirical cost estimates based on average and median values, which is measured by a 7% reduction in the absolute percentage error. Comparing single prediction errors for the validated cost indicators of 5 schools, the most efficient model forecast, with a prediction error lower than 4%, is achieved for sample No.4 which represents a school with a gymnasium and an indoor swimming pool. In addition, the validation test verifies convincing cost estimates for schools without any additional sports facilities (samples No.1, 3 and 5).

Tab. 17:   Model validation for heating cost indicators

| No. | Type of school | Observed value | Predicted value | Absolute error % of prediction | Absolute error % of mean | Absolute error % of median | Preference |
|-----|----------------|----------------|-----------------|-------------------------------|--------------------------|----------------------------|------------|
| 1 | Elementary school without sports facilities | 13.94 | 8.27 | **41** | 46 | 47 | **Prediction** |
| 2 | Special school with gymnasium | 6.81 | 7.99 | 17 | 11 | 9 | Median |
| 3 | Secondary school without sports facilities | 7.98 | 7.17 | 10 | 5 | 7 | Mean |
| 4 | Secondary school with gymnasium and pool | 11.28 | 10.89 | **3** | 33 | 34 | **Prediction** |
| 5 | Vocational school without sports facilities | 6.40 | 6.92 | **8** | 18 | 16 | **Prediction** |
| Ø | **Mean Absolute percentage error** | | | **16** | 23 | 23 | **Prediction** |

**Observed value:** Heating energy costs (€/m² heatable gross floor area p.a.), costs including VAT, based on 2008 figures, N=125

### 3.1.2.4  Cost indicators for heating

The multivariate Model 2.B.2 allows continuous cost estimates for heating energy indicators based on five explanatory variables identified in Section 3.1.2.2. In addition, specific values are provided for the two independent variables $X_1$ and $X_3$, which have been statistically proved to exert a significant impact on heating costs, with beta values of 0.365 and 0.299 respectively. In the multivariate model, $X_1$ describes a classification of different school utilization types, whereas $X_3$ quantifies the inefficient condition of heat supply systems as a percentage. For the purpose of simplified presentation, variable $X_3$ is also included by way of a qualitative variable subdivided into two categories, as shown in Tab. 18. In comparing designated cost indicators, schools running on an inefficient heat supply system have, on average, between 1 to 2.50 €/m² H-GROFA in extra outlay p.a. than those schools with a good, efficient heat supply system. In terms of mean values, this shows that with annual costs of 10.64 €/m² H-GROFA p.a., schools with swimming pools have around 3 €/m² H-GROFA p.a. higher costs than those schools without these additional swimming pool facilities (costs including VAT, based on 2008 figures). The corresponding indexing table for annual price adjustments is provided by Destatis (2011b).

Tab. 18:  Evaluated cost indicators for heating

| Factor level | Minimum | Mean | Median | Maximum | Range |
|---|---|---|---|---|---|
| **Schools without swimming pools** | **2.42** | **7.35** | **7.35** | **12.09** | **9.67** |
| Heat supply systems in a good condition | 2.42 | 6.93 | 7.12 | 11.22 | 8.80 |
| Heat supply systems in a poor condition | 4.90 | 7.90 | 7.70 | 12.09 | 7.19 |
| **Schools with swimming pools** | **6.47** | **10.64** | **9.53** | **14.88** | **8.41** |
| Heat supply systems in a good condition | 6.47 | 9.06 | 8.49 | 12.21 | 5.74 |
| Heat supply systems in a poor condition | 9.24 | 11.59 | 9.69 | 14.88 | 5.64 |

**Dependent variable**: Heating energy costs (€/m² heatable gross floor area p.a.), costs including VAT, based on 2008 figures, N=125

### 3.1.3  Electricity

### 3.1.3.1  Empirical and theoretical basis

SIA 380/4:1995 relates the amount of electricity consumed to lighting, ventilation/air conditioning, electric heating and usage of diverse other technical components, the contributions of which are particularly influenced by usage-related factors as well as requirements of the building and technical installations. At 2.23 €/m² GROFA p.a., the average electricity costs for 2008 are 4.50 €/m² GROFA p.a. below the average outlay for heating. In comparison with office buildings, which in general have a higher standard of installations and equipment (air treatment systems, transport systems, computer workstations, etc.), the annual outlay for the electricity supply of the 125 schools investigated in this study is lower (cf. cost indicators published by JLL, 2011, for instance). Referring to the different types of school under investigation, in the opinion of experts, a greater consumption of electricity is to be expected for vocational schools and schools with additional sports facilities, as well as for full-day schools. To evaluate the variability in electricity consumption of individual schools at property level, the statistical analysis examines the theoretical influences of different usage patterns, including canteen services and the number of computer workstations, the functional characteristics derived from diverse utilization types and the technical features that Firth, et a. (2008), Stoy et al. (2009) and Zhang, et al. (2011), in particular, consider to have a considerably relevance from a theoretical point of view. The empirical distribution of the factors named in the following is additionally shown in Appendix C.

**Factor group: Utilization**

*Type of utilization:*

• Primary utilization: Elementary school, secondary school such as comprehensive school (secondary general school, intermediate secondary school, multiple school center) or grammar school, special school, vocational school with technical or business focus; qualitative description of different utilization types and quantitative description of the school utilization area in m² NEFA as well as its proportion per m² NEFA of the whole school property.

• Secondary utilization: Sports facilities such as gymnasiums or indoor swimming pools for teaching purposes, nursery school; qualitative and quantitative description of different utilization types with regard to their building reference areas and volumes respectively e.g. the net floor area of a gymnasium or swimming pool utilization in m² and their representative proportions per m² NEFA.

*Standard of utilization:*

• Type of educational program: Regular school, extended regular school or full-day school.

• Type of canteen service: School based canteen, external catering or no canteen service.

• Total number of computer workstations.

*Intensity of utilization:*

• Temporal usage intensity:

  Average operating time of the whole school complex as well as individual operating times of both the primary and secondary utilizations, i.e. the school and its sports facilities, in hours per school week and with regard to the average number of schooldays per school week.

• Spatial usage intensity:

  • The total number of pupils, number of pupils per m² specific floor area according to DIN 277:2005-2 (Part 1 and 2) and the number of pupils with respect to other reference areas such as m² net floor area of school utilization e.g. the number of pupils per m² NEFA.

  • The total number of school classes, number of school classes per m² specific floor area according to DIN 277:2005-2 (Part 1 and 2) and number of school classes with respect to other reference areas such as m² net floor area of school utilization e.g. the number of school classes per m² NEFA.

**Factor group: Functional and technical characteristics**

*Functional characteristics:*

- Specific building floor areas according to DIN 277:2005-2 (Part 1 and 2) e.g. in m² NEFA, m² UFA, m² UFA 5 and their representative proportion to the total size of a property in m² GROFA or other specific building floor areas e.g. the share of UFA 5 per m² NEFA.

*Technical characteristics:*

- Standard of technical installations:

  Number of lifts and average number of lift-stops.

- Condition of technical installations:

  Qualitative description of the condition of technical installations and in particular the condition of power installations.

### 3.1.3.2 Model design and parameters

The underlying factors for the statistical analysis of electricity consumption and costs (Y) are described above The investigation of significant factors impacting on Y at a 5% level of significance designates the net floor area which, according to DIN 2771:2005-2, also comprises the circulation area of buildings as being relevant to estimate and forecast total electricity consumption and costs.

In addition to this reference area, the two models presented in this survey for forecasting the total annual electricity consumption (Model 3.A.1) and costs (Model 3.A.2) include descriptions of the different school utilization types. In particular, both models indicate a distinction line between vocational schools and other school types, and take into account the proportionate areas of sports and swimming facilities in terms of continuous variables.

Tab. 19: Model description for estimating total electricity consumption

| Dependent variable | Transf. | R² | R² adj. | SEE | F-value | Sign. | Durbin-Watson-Statistic | | N |
|---|---|---|---|---|---|---|---|---|---|
| Electricity consumption (kWh p.a.) | LN | 0.880 | 0.876 | 0.294 | 220.817 | 0.000 | 2.021 | | 125 |

| Factors | Transf. | B | St. Error | Beta | t-value | Sign. | Lower CL | Upper CL | T | VIF |
|---|---|---|---|---|---|---|---|---|---|---|
| Constant | LN | 1.598 | 0.387 | | 4.128 | 0.000 | 0.832 | 2.364 | | |
| Net floor area (NEFA in m²) | LN | 1.109 | 0.045 | 0.844 | 24.386 | 0.000 | 1.019 | 1.199 | 0.831 | 1.203 |
| Share of the swimming pool utilization area per m² NEFA | - | 12.262 | 2.730 | 0.143 | 4.491 | 0.000 | 6.856 | 17.667 | 0.983 | 1.018 |
| Vocational schools | - | 0.452 | 0.093 | 0.181 | 4.833 | 0.000 | 0.267 | 0.637 | 0.711 | 1.407 |
| Share of the gymansium area per m² NEFA | - | 1.667 | 0.601 | 0.095 | 2.775 | 0.006 | 0.477 | 2.857 | 0.845 | 1.184 |

**Dependent variable:** Electricity consumption (kWh p.a.), 2008

$$\hat{Y} = 4.943 \cdot X_1^{1.109} \cdot e^{12.262 X_2} \cdot e^{0.452 X_3} \cdot e^{1.667 X_4}$$  (Model 3.A.1)

Where:  $\hat{Y}$ :  *Electricity consumption (kWh p.a.)*

$X_1$ :  *Net floor area (NEFA in m²)*

$X_2$ :   Share of the swimming pool utilization area (UFA 5 on room level) per m² NEFA

$X_3$ :   Vocational schools (type of school)

$X_4$ :   Share of the gymnasium area (UFA 5 on room level) per m² NEFA

Tab. 20:   Model description for estimating total electricity costs

| Dependent variable | Transf. | R² | R² adj. | SEE | F-value | Sign. | Durbin-Watson-Statistic | | N |
|---|---|---|---|---|---|---|---|---|---|
| Electricity costs (€ p.a.) | LN | 0.874 | 0.870 | 0.294 | 207.933 | 0.000 | 1.982 | | 125 |

| Factors | Transf. | B | St. Error | Beta | t-value | Sign. | Lower CL | Upper CL | T | VIF |
|---|---|---|---|---|---|---|---|---|---|---|
| Constant | LN | 0.048 | 0.386 | | 0.124 | 0.901 | -0.716 | 0.812 | | |
| Net floor area (NEFA in m²) | LN | 1.078 | 0.045 | 0.845 | 23.757 | 0.000 | 0.988 | 1.167 | 0.831 | 1.203 |
| Share of the swimming pool utilization area per m² NEFA | - | 12.237 | 2.722 | 0.147 | 4.495 | 0.000 | 6.847 | 17.627 | 0.983 | 1.018 |
| Vocational schools | - | 0.417 | 0.093 | 0.172 | 4.472 | 0.000 | 0.232 | 0.602 | 0.711 | 1.407 |
| Share of the gymansium area per m² NEFA | - | 1.549 | 0.599 | 0.091 | 2.585 | 0.011 | 0.363 | 2.735 | 0.845 | 1.184 |

**Dependent variable**: Electricity costs (€ p.a.), costs including VAT, based on 2008 figures

$$\hat{Y} = 1.049 \cdot X_1^{1.078} \cdot e^{12.237 X_2} \cdot e^{0.417 X_3} \cdot e^{1.549 X_4} \tag{Model 3.A.2}$$

Where:      $\hat{Y}$ :   Electricity costs (€ p.a.)

$X_1$ :   Net floor area (NEFA in m²)

$X_2$ :   Share of the swimming pool utilization area (UFA 5 on room level) per m² NEFA

$X_3$ :   Vocational schools (type of school)

$X_4$ :   Share of the gymnasium area (UFA 5 on room level) per m² NEFA

The estimation of electricity consumption and cost indicators is based on the analysis of total annual consumption and costs, and outlined below with respect to the linear regression Model 3.B.1 ($R^2=0.351$, SEE=4.547) and Model 3.B.2 ($R^2=0.316$, SEE=0.719). The normalization of consumption and cost indicators is conducted with reference to the schools' net floor areas, as defined in DIN 277-1:2005-2. According to Models 3.A.1 and 3.A.2, the analyses of indicators for consumption and costs (Y) confirm significant correlations between $X_1$, the share of the swimming pool utilization area per m² NEFA, and $X_3$, the proportionate gymnasium area per m² NEFA, respectively on Y.

Compared with schools without any additional sport facility, those schools which have gymnasiums or indoor swimming pools generally verify to have higher electricity indicators in terms of both consumption and costs, resulting primarily from large-scale panel heating and ventilation systems but also from the operation of water circulation pumps and floor-lifting mechanisms for swimming pools. In addition, both models confirm the assumption that cost differences exist between the electricity indicators of vocational schools with a technical or a business focus, thus allowing differentiated estimates for both types of vocational schools with respect to the predictors $X_2$ and $X_4$ in Models 3.B.2 and 3.B.2.

Tab. 21: Model description for estimating electricity consumption indicators

| Dependent variable | Transf. | $R^2$ | $R^2$ adj. | SEE | F-value | Sign. | Durbin-Watson-Statistic | | N |
|---|---|---|---|---|---|---|---|---|---|
| Electricity consumption (kWh/m² NEFA p.a.) | - | 0.351 | 0.329 | 4.547 | 16.194 | 0.000 | 2.148 | | 125 |

| Factors | Transf. | B | St. Error | Beta | t-value | Sign. | Lower CL | Upper CL | T | VIF |
|---|---|---|---|---|---|---|---|---|---|---|
| Constant | - | 12.980 | 0.805 | | 16.121 | 0.000 | 11.386 | 14.575 | | |
| Share of the swimming pool utilization area per m² NEFA | - | 244.037 | 41.977 | 0.430 | 5.814 | 0.000 | 160.925 | 327.149 | 0.991 | 1.009 |
| Vocational schools with technical focus | - | 9.399 | 1.613 | 0.461 | 5.828 | 0.000 | 6.206 | 12.593 | 0.864 | 1.157 |
| Share of the gymansium area per m² NEFA | - | 23.131 | 9.253 | 0.198 | 2.500 | 0.014 | 4.810 | 41.452 | 0.859 | 1.164 |
| Vocational schools with business focus | - | 4.488 | 1.934 | 0.174 | 2.320 | 0.022 | 0.658 | 8.317 | 0.968 | 1.033 |

**Dependent variable**: Electricity consumption (kWh/m² net floor area p.a.), 2008

$$\hat{Y} = 12.980 + 244.037X_1 + 9.399X_2 + 23.131X_3 + 4.488X_4 \qquad \text{(Model 3.B.1)}$$

Where: $\hat{Y}$ : Electricity consumption (kWh/m² NEFA p.a.)

$X_1$ : Share of the swimming pool utilization area (UFA 5 on room level) per m² NEFA

$X_2$ : Vocational schools with technical focus (type of school)

$X_3$ : Share of the gymnasium area (UFA 5 on room level) per m² NEFA

$X_4$ : Vocational schoos with business focus (type of school)

Alternatively, a distinction is also conceivable between these two types of vocational schools with respect to the continuous variable share of UFA 3 per m² UFA, which usually indicates higher values for vocational schools with a technical focus. Within statistical pre-analysis, the categorical variables ($X_2$ and $X_4$) and the continuous variable (share of UFA 3 per m² UFA) were evaluated and verified efficient and unbiased model estimates. However, with $R^2=0.238$, the cost model specified by the continuous variable achieves a reduced estimation quality of almost 25%. Consequently, in order to obtain better results, a categorical distinction between the different types of vocational schools is retained (cf. Models 3.B.1 and 3.B.2.).

Tab. 22: Model description for estimating electricity cost indicators

| Dependent variable | Transf. | $R^2$ | $R^2$ adj. | SEE | F-value | Sign. | Durbin-Watson-Statistic | | N |
|---|---|---|---|---|---|---|---|---|---|
| Electricity costs (€/m² NEFA p.a.) | - | 0.316 | 0.293 | 0.719 | 13.837 | 0.000 | 2.145 | | 125 |

| Factors | Transf. | B | St. Error | Beta | t-value | Sign. | Lower CL | Upper CL | T | VIF |
|---|---|---|---|---|---|---|---|---|---|---|
| Constant | - | 2.100 | 0.127 | | 16.483 | 0.000 | 1.848 | 2.352 | | |
| Share of the swimming pool utilization area per m² NEFA | - | 38.459 | 6.642 | 0.439 | 5.791 | 0.000 | 25.309 | 51.609 | 0.991 | 1.009 |
| Vocational schools with technical focus | - | 1.258 | 0.255 | 0.401 | 4.930 | 0.000 | 0.753 | 1.763 | 0.864 | 1.157 |
| Share of the gymansium area per m² NEFA | - | 3.514 | 1.464 | 0.196 | 2.400 | 0.018 | 0.616 | 6.413 | 0.859 | 1.164 |
| Vocational schools with business focus | - | 0.620 | 0.306 | 0.156 | 2.027 | 0.045 | 0.014 | 1.226 | 0.968 | 1.033 |

**Dependent variable**: Electricity costs (€/m² net floor area p.a.), costs including VAT, based on 2008 figures

$$\hat{Y} = 2.100 + 38.459X_1 + 1.258X_2 + 3.514X_3 + 0.620X_4 \qquad \text{(Model 3.B.2)}$$

Where:     $\hat{Y}$ :   Electricity costs ($€/m^2$ H-GROFA p.a.)

            $X_1$ :   Share of the swimming pool utilization area (UFA 5 on room level) per $m^2$ NEFA

            $X_2$ :   Vocational schools with technical focus (type of school)

            $X_3$ :   Share of the gymnasium area (UFA 5 on room level) per $m^2$ NEFA

            $X_4$ :   Vocational schoos with business focus (type of school)

*Summary*

The preceding investigation of total electricity consumption and costs identifies the net floor area as being the relevant reference area to analyze and compare electricity indicators for schools. According to DIN 277-2:2005-2, this area comprises the usable floor area, the technical floor area, and the circulation area of a building. The regression models verify the hypothesis that the electricity consumption of a school does not depend on the usable floor area alone. They clearly demonstrate that the variation in Y is also influenced by the total size of the technical floor and circulation area, comprising the operation of machines or lighting systems of these areas, among other factors. Moreover, the statistical analysis of 125 schools indicates that significant differences in consumption and costs are directly related to functional differences in usage, in particular the differences between primary and secondary school utilization. Consequently, schools with an indoor swimming pool and vocational schools with a technical focus (both variables based on beta >0.4), particularly have a higher electricity indicators than other school types and should be considered separately within a benchmarking.

### 3.1.3.3 Validation of the model

Tab. 23 gives an overview of the validation test conducted to compare percentage errors of the prediction Model 3.B.2 with empirical mean and median values. The underlying cost indicators in $€/m^2$ NEFA p.a. include VAT and are based on 2008 figures.

Compared with mean absolute percentage errors for empirical average and median values, both of which are around 41%, the regression Model 3.B.2 verifies a considerable improvement in the estimated electricity cost indicators across most of the validated schools, based on a MAPE of approximately 24%. In addition, the percentage error of prediction (24%) obtained for the validated properties confirms the stability of assumptions postulated by means of regression analysis, which are statistically tested in Section 3.1.3.2 on the basis of sample data pertaining to 125 school complexes, with a MAPE of 27%. In four out of five cases, the validation test verifies differences detected in electricity cost indicators with respect to functional descriptions of school utilization. Based on this validation, specific cost indicators are presented in the following section for different types of school utilization.

Tab. 23:  Model validation for electricity cost indicators

| No. | Type of school | Observed value | Predicted value | Absolute error % of prediction | Absolute error % of mean | Absolute error % of median | Preference |
|---|---|---|---|---|---|---|---|
| 1 | Elementary school without sports facilities | 1.87 | 2.10 | 12 | 36 | 34 | Prediction |
| 2 | Special school with gymnasium | 2.73 | 2.41 | 12 | 7 | 8 | Mean |
| 3 | Secondary school without sports facilities | 1.44 | 2.10 | 46 | 77 | 74 | Prediction |
| 4 | Secondary school with gymnasium and pool | 3.77 | 3.46 | 8 | 32 | 34 | Prediction |
| 5 | Vocational school without sports facilities | 5.67 | 3.36 | 41 | 55 | 56 | Prediction |
| Ø | Mean Absolute percentage error | | | 24 | 41 | 41 | Prediction |

Observed value: Electricity costs (€/m² net floor area p.a.), costs including VAT, based on 2008 figures, N=125

### 3.1.3.4  Cost indicators for electricity

Based on sample data from 125 school complexes, four independent variables are identified to explain a relevant part of the variation in electricity cost indicators (Y). According to Model 3.B.2, the variables with the greatest partial explanatory impact (beta > 0.400) are the continuous variables $X_1$ (share of swimming pool utilization area per m² NEFA) and the categorical variable $X_2$ (vocational school with a technical focus). Step-by-step analysis, moreover, revealed significant differences in the cost indicators evaluated for vocational schools with a business focus. All designated factors describe differences in the type of school utilization and these are taken into account when providing specific cost indicators. This approach takes all possible combinations of school utilization types within the empirical data sample into consideration and uses these particulars for classifying the cost data concerned. As a result, Tab. 24 shows that the mean value for vocational schools (3.19 €/m² NEFA p.a.) is 0.74 €/m² NEFA p.a. higher than the average cost indicator for all other school types, with or without the swimming pool facilities. Differentiating between the different types of vocational schools, those with a business focus have the lowest electricity cost indicator at 1.33 €/m² NEFA p.a., and those with a technical focus have the highest outlay at 4.49 €/m² NEFA p.a. (costs including VAT, based on 2008 figures).

Tab. 24:  Evaluated cost indicators for electricity

| Factor level | Minimum | Mean | Median | Maximum | Range |
|---|---|---|---|---|---|
| Vocational schools (without swimming pools) | 1.33 | 3.19 | 3.16 | 4.49 | 3.16 |
| Vocational schools with technical focus | 2.38 | 3.39 | 3.26 | 4.49 | 2.11 |
| Vocational schools with business focus | 1.33 | 2.86 | 3.05 | 3.73 | 2.40 |
| Other school types | 0.78 | 2.45 | 2.39 | 5.35 | 4.57 |
| Without swimming pools | 0.78 | 2.34 | 2.36 | 4.23 | 3.45 |
| With swimming pools | 2.47 | 3.78 | 3.79 | 5.35 | 2.88 |

Dependent variable: Electricity costs (€/m² net floor area p.a.), costs including VAT, based on 2008 figures, N=125

### 3.1.4    Aggregate utilities

#### 3.1.4.1  Empirical and theoretical basis

The empirical investigation of utility costs for 125 schools in Germany analyzes the aggregate costs for water, heating and electricity (cost groups 311 to 316 according to DIN 18960:2008-2) during the calendar year 2008. The analysis primarily takes into account those variables whose independent influence, at a 5% significance level, is statistically proven in the analytical models presented in Sections 3 to 5. Additionally, other factors are considered that literature review or interviews with experts have determined as relevant parameter for this examination, or which have been identified during the course of individual analyses described above. With respect to the last item, this includes interrelations arising from the ratio of evaluated reference areas for water, electricity or heating, i.e. the share of UFA or H-GROFA per m² NEFA, for instance. Regarding additional factors that are named by literature, particularly property- and usage-specific aspects, are deemed relevant and included in the analysis (cf. VDI 3807-1:2007-3 or Ages, 2005 for instance). The average operating time of a property (measured in hours per school week) or the condition of technical installations, for example, can be named for an investigation of these aspects with regard to the respective schools.

#### 3.1.4.2  Model design and parameters

Heating costs represent approximately 70% of the total utility costs with a standard deviation of 32,452 (see Tab. 99). Thus, the heating costs account for the biggest proportion and variation of overall utility costs within the sample under investigation, followed by the costs for electricity. According to the analysis of total heating energy consumption and costs and the definition of an appropriate reference area in Section 3.1.2.2, the following aggregate cost analysis also takes into account the heatable gross floor area for estimating the total utility costs and normalizing the cost data. In addition, the proportionate area of swimming pool utilization per m² H-GROFA, the share of external glass areas per m² H-GROFA, as well as the percentage of defective heat supply systems are also taken into account. Tab. 25 presents an overview of the variables and their statistical measures used in Model 4.A to estimate total utility costs. All variables included in regression Model 4.A were considered in the investigation of heating energy and electricity costs that preceded this survey. This underlines the significance of the interrelationships that exist between the driving factors of these two cost groups for investigating the total utility costs.

Tab. 25:  Model description for estimating aggregate utility costs

| Dependent variable | Transf. | R² | R² adj. | SEE | F-value | Sign. | Durbin-Watson-Statistic | | N |
|---|---|---|---|---|---|---|---|---|---|
| Utility costs (€ p.a.) | LN | 0.931 | 0.928 | 0.182 | 401.880 | 0.000 | 2.005 | | 125 |

| Factors | Transf. | B | St. Error | Beta | t-value | Sign. | Lower CL | Upper CL | T | VIF |
|---|---|---|---|---|---|---|---|---|---|---|
| Constant | LN | 2.321 | 0.233 | | 9.964 | 0.000 | 1.860 | 2.782 | | |
| Heatable gross floor area (H-GROFA in m²) | LN | 0.995 | 0.026 | 0.926 | 37.838 | 0.000 | 0.943 | 1.048 | 0.966 | 1.035 |
| Share of the swimming pool utilization area per m² H-GROFA | - | 9.250 | 1.554 | 0.144 | 5.951 | 0.000 | 6.173 | 12.327 | 0.983 | 1.017 |
| Share of defective heat supply systems (%) | LN | 0.009 | 0.002 | 0.093 | 3.734 | 0.000 | 0.004 | 0.014 | 0.943 | 1.060 |
| Share of glass areas of external walls and roofs per m² H-GROFA | - | 0.262 | 0.116 | 0.055 | 2.261 | 0.026 | 0.033 | 0.491 | 0.976 | 1.024 |

**Dependent variable:** Utility costs (€ p.a.), costs including VAT, based on 2008 figures

$$\hat{Y} = 10.186 \cdot X_1^{0.995} \cdot e^{9.250 X_2} \cdot X_3^{0.009} \cdot e^{0.262 X_4} \qquad\qquad \text{(Model 4.A)}$$

Where:   $\hat{Y}$ :   Utility costs (€ p.a.)

$X_1$ :   Heatable gross floor area (H-GROFA in m²)

$X_2$ :   Share of the swimming pool utilization area (UFA 5 on room level) per m² H-GROFA

$X_3$ :   Share of defective heat supply systems (%)

$X_4$ :   Share of glass areas of external walls and roofs per m² H-GROFA

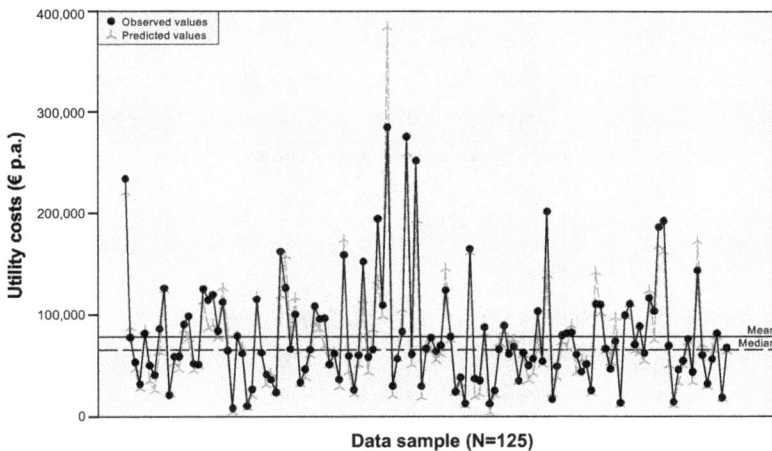

Fig. 3:    Comparison between observed and predicted utility costs (costs including VAT, based on 2008 figures)

The subsequent investigation of utility cost indicators is based on Model 4.A and refers to a large extent to the same continuous variables used to estimate total utility costs.[29] The linear Model 4.B for estimating and forecasting utility cost indicators is described with respect to

---

[29] The heatable gross floor area is used to normalize the dependent variable Y (€/m² H-GROFA p.a., costs including VAT, based on 2008 figures).

the partial regression coefficients $b_j$, shown in Tab. 26. With $R^2$ =0.446 and a mean absolute percentage error (MAPE) of 15%, the regression model displays a convincing goodness of fit. Compared with a standard deviation of 2.55 €/m² H-GROFA p.a. for utility costs pertaining to the analyzed sample data, the standard error of estimate (SEE=1.924) verifies a greater level of accuracy using the regression model for prediction purposes. A graphical comparison between the observed values (Y) and predicted values ($\hat{Y}$) calculated by the regression Model 4.B for N=122 is illustrated in Fig. 3. Theoretically, all of the factors examined have an impact on utility costs. Those factors that are included in the specified Model 4.B explain a significant proportion of the variation in utility cost indicators. Their partial regression coefficients $b_j$ represent realizations of the real parameters ($\beta$-coefficients) that occur with a probability of 95% between confidence limits (CL) outlined in Tab. 26. Other designated factors, such as the number of school classes or the share of the sanitary area per m² reference area, fail at a 5% significance level and are not included in the regression model for this reason.

Tab. 26:  Model description for estimating aggregate utility cost indicators

| Dependent variable | Transf. | $R^2$ | $R^2$ adj. | SEE | F-value | Sign. | Durbin-Watson-Statistic | | N |
|---|---|---|---|---|---|---|---|---|---|
| Utility costs (€/m² H-GROFA p.a.) | - | 0.446 | 0.432 | 1.924 | 32.471 | 0.000 | 2.020 | | 125 |

| Factors | Transf. | B | St. Error | Beta | t-value | Sign. | Lower CL | Upper CL | T | VIF |
|---|---|---|---|---|---|---|---|---|---|---|
| Constant | - | 9.818 | 0.393 | | 24.964 | 0.000 | 9.040 | 10.597 | | |
| Share of the swimming pool utilization area per m² H-GROFA | - | 131.063 | 16.399 | 0.545 | 7.992 | 0.000 | 98.596 | 163.530 | 0.983 | 1.017 |
| Share of defective heat supply systems (%) | LN | 0.088 | 0.025 | 0.244 | 3.564 | 0.001 | 0.039 | 0.137 | 0.976 | 1.025 |
| Share of glass areas of external walls and roofs per m² H-GROFA | - | 3.214 | 1.223 | 0.180 | 2.629 | 0.010 | 0.794 | 5.634 | 0.976 | 1.024 |

**Dependent variable**: Utility costs (€/m² heatable gross floor area p.a.), costs including VAT, based on 2008 figures

$$\hat{Y} = 9.818 + 131.063 X_1 + 0.088 \ln(X_2) + 3.214 X_3 \qquad \text{(Model 4.B)}$$

Where:    $\hat{Y}$ :  Utility costs (€/m² H-GROFA p.a.)

$X_1$ :  Share of the swimming pool utilization area (UFA 5 on room level) per m² H-GROFA

$X_2$ :  Share of defective heat supply systems (%)

$X_3$ :  Share of glass areas of external walls and roofs per m² H-GROFA

*Summary*

The empirical investigation of utility costs for 125 schools in Germany is based on a statistical evaluation of factors influencing the annual outlay for water, heating and electricity outlined in Sections 3.1.1 to 3.1.3. The analysis shows that the major part of the variation in utility costs can be ascribed to heating costs. Accordingly, the heatable gross floor area, which has previously been identified as the appropriate reference area for heating cost indicators, is also taken into consideration for normalizing utility costs. The subsequent analysis of relevant factors impacting on utility cost indicators (€/m² H-GROFA p.a.) refers predominantly to those independent variables which have statistically proven, with beta between 0.261 to 0.365 in Model 2.B.2, to constitute the greatest influence on heating energy costs indicators in multivariate analysis.

Whereas Model 2.B.2 considers a qualitative description of different utilization types (schools with or without indoor swimming pools), Model 4.B refers to a quantitative description of the proportionate swimming pool utilization area for the purpose of estimating utility costs, in accordance with model 3.B.2. Summing up, it can be concluded that the variation between the utility cost indicators ascertained for 125 schools included in the survey can be specifically explained by the key factor groups, type of utilization, standard of constructions and the condition of the technical installations in the buildings concerned.

### 3.1.4.3  Validation of the model

Regression Model 4.B, which is used for estimating utility cost indicators, incorporates a selection of causal determinants which have already been identified within the multivariate analysis of the heating and electricity costs (Models 2.B.2 and 3.B.2 respectively). The validation test conducted for aggregate utility costs confirms a high forecasting standard for the prediction model, largely in agreement with corresponding test results for individual costs (water, heating and electricity) on the third structural cost level according to DIN 18960:2008-2.

Tab. 27:  Model validation for aggregate utility cost indicators

| No. | Type of school | Observed value | Predicted value | Absolute error % of prediction | Absolute error % of mean | Absolute error % of median | Preference |
|---|---|---|---|---|---|---|---|
| 1 | Elementary school without sports facilities | 16.73 | 9.44 | 44 | 35 | 36 | Mean |
| 2 | Special school with gymnasium | 9.70 | 10.76 | 11 | 11 | 10 | Median |
| 3 | Secondary school without sports facilities | 9.79 | 9.64 | 2 | 10 | 9 | Prediction |
| 4 | Secondary school with gymnasium and pool | 15.73 | 14.40 | 8 | 31 | 32 | Prediction |
| 5 | Vocational school without sports facilities | 12.90 | 10.72 | 17 | 16 | 17 | Mean |
| Ø | Mean Absolute percentage error | | | 16 | 21 | 21 | Prediction |

Observed value: Aggregate utility costs (€/m² heatable gross floor area p.a.), costs including VAT, based on 2008 figures, N=125

Tab. 27 compares various estimation methods and associated percentage errors with respect to five validated school properties. The underlying cost indicators in €/m² H-GROFA p.a. include VAT and are based on 2008 figures. Additional information on parameters, evaluated in Section 3.1.4.2, improves the mean absolute percentage error for the overall validation sample on average by 5% compared with estimates based on the empirical mean or median, both of which achieve a MAPE of 21%.

### 3.1.4.4  Cost indicators for aggregate utilities

With reference to 2008, the calendar year in question, Tab. 101 shows that utility costs averaging 10.82 €/m² H-GROFA p.a. have a range of 15.28 €/m² H-GROFA p.a. for 125 investigated schools (costs including VAT, based on 2008 figures). Based on quantified and validated factors, which have been determined by means of a statistical approach in Section 3.1.4.2, the empirical variability of sampling distribution can be reduced to an average range of around 10 €/m² H-GROFA p.a. classified according to the type of schools outlined in Tab. 28. As regards the underlying data sample, a maximum value of around 21 €/m² H-GROFA p.a. is observed for a school with an indoor swimming pool and a declared inefficient condition of heat supply systems, whereby a minimum cost value of almost 5.94 €/m² H-GROFA p.a. is described for a school property without a swimming pool facility and a declared efficient condition of heat supply systems. The average difference in costs between schools with and without swimming pools amounts to 5.50 €/m² H-GROFA p.a., whereby more accurate cost estimates can be made for the subcategories described with regard to the heat supply systems designated in Tab. 28. Based on corresponding categories described for heating cost indicators in Tab. 18, it is possible to make comparisons between the indicators for utility costs shown here, in particular. All costs described are based on 2008 figures and include VAT. The corresponding indexing table for annual price adjustments is provided by Destatis (2011b).

Tab. 28:   Evaluated cost indicators for aggregate utilities

| Factor level | Minimum | Mean | Median | Maximum | Range |
|---|---|---|---|---|---|
| Schools without swimming pools | 5.94 | 10.46 | 10.52 | 15.33 | 9.39 |
| Heat supply systems in a good condition | 5.94 | 10.01 | 9.82 | 14.92 | 8.98 |
| Heat supply systems in a poor condition | 7.78 | 11.06 | 10.80 | 15.33 | 7.55 |
| Schools with swimming pools | 10.77 | 15.94 | 15.95 | 21.22 | 10.45 |
| Heat supply systems in a good condition | 10.77 | 13.71 | 11.79 | 18.58 | 7.81 |
| Heat supply systems in a poor condition | 12.40 | 17.27 | 16.65 | 21.22 | 8.81 |

Dependent variable: Aggregate utility costs (€/m² heatable gross floor area p.a.), costs including VAT, based on 2008 figures, N=125

## 3.2     Waste disposal

### 3.2.1     Empirical and theoretical basis

With an average of 0.51 €/m² GROFA p.a., waste disposal accounts for a relatively small proportion of the entire operating and repair costs in 2008 (cf. Tab. 103). Costs investigated include VAT and comprise expenses for garbage and sewage such as waste water and non-seeping rainwater. The latter outlay incurs for municipal rainwater charges calculated in Germany as a proportion to the water impermeable surface of a plot. Those disposal costs that arise in connection with construction work for new buildings, renovation or modernization according to DIN 276-1:2008-12 are not included in the survey. The same applies to the disposal costs incurred for hazardous waste in conjunction with repair measures; these are assigned to the appropriate cost group 400 on the second structural cost level as defined by DIN 18960:2008-2.

Similarly to water costs, it is assumed that the outlay for waste disposal is to a great extent usage dependent and that therefore the sewage and garbage costs of a school can be directly influenced by usage-related factors such as the type of school (elementary vs. vocational school, for instance), the number of pupils and the existence of a swimming pool or of canteen services. In addition, the area of the water impermeable surface of a plot is taken into consideration to represent the regularly occurring rates for municipal rainwater for properties in Germany. Technical characteristics are also taken into account in a similar way to the analysis of utility expenses, such as descriptions of the condition of technical installations or the size of irrigated green areas. In total, the investigation of waste disposal cost is theoretically based on the following list of factors:

### Factor group: Utilization

*Type of utilization:*

- Primary utilization: Elementary school, secondary school such as comprehensive school (secondary general school, intermediate secondary school, multiple school center) or grammar school, special school, vocational school with technical or business focus; qualitative description of different utilization types and quantitative description of the school utilization area in m² NEFA as well as its proportion per m² NEFA of the whole school property.

- Secondary utilization: Indoor swimming pool for teaching purposes, nursery school; qualitative and quantitative description of different utilization types with regard to their building reference areas and volumes respectively e.g. the water volume of swimming pools in m³.

*Standard of utilization:*

- Type of educational program: Regular school, extended regular school or full-day school.

- Type of canteen service: School based canteen, external catering or no canteen service.

*Intensity of utilization:*

- Temporal usage intensity:

  Average operating time of the whole school complex as well as individual operating times of both the primary and secondary utilizations, i.e. the school and its sports facilities, in hours per school week and with regard to the average number of schooldays per school week.

- Spatial usage intensity:

  - The total number of pupils, number of pupils per m² specific floor area according to DIN 277:2005-2 (Part 1 and 2) and the number of pupils with respect to other reference areas such as m² net floor area of school utilization.

  - The total number of school classes, number of school classes per m² specific floor area according to DIN 277:2005-2 (Part 1 and 2) and number of school classes with respect to other reference areas such as m² net floor area of school utilization.

  - Water volume of swimming pools in m³ of complete refillings per year.

**Factor group: Functional and technical characteristics**

*Functional characteristics:*

- Specific building floor areas according to DIN 277:2005-2 (Part 1 and 2) e.g. in m² NEFA, m² UFA or m² UFA 5 and their representative proportion to the total size of a property in m² GROFA or other specific building floor areas.

- The total sanitary area and its proportion to specific building floor areas according to DIN 277: 2005-2 (Part 1 and 2) e.g. the share of the sanitary area per m² UFA.

*Technical characteristics:*

- Standard of technical installations:

  Number of press containers (waste disposal facilities).

- Condition of technical installations:

  Qualitative description of the condition of sewage systems: Higher or lower standard.

- Standard of grounds and outdoor facilities:

  - The total size of irrigated grounds of green areas in m² and its representative proportion to the non-built up plot area.

  - The total size of water impermeable surfaces in m² and its proportion to the total non-built up area of the plot.

**Factor group: Strategy and operation**

- Disposal concept: Efficient or inefficient.

### 3.2.2   Model design and parameters

The statistical analysis of waste disposal costs takes all factors outlined above into account and is performed for sample data from 125 schools at a 5% significance level. Based on statistical pre-analysis, the best prediction of total costs for waste disposal is achieved by the multivariate regression Model 5.A. In accordance with Model 1.A.2, for estimating the amount of water costs, the specified Model 5.A primarily incorporates the independent impacts of the variables: the usable floor area, the annual water volume required for complete pool refilling p.a., and the share of the sanitary area per m² UFA. The analyses of drinking water and waste disposal costs accordingly verify that the usable floor area is the appropriate building reference area for both cost groups. Based on equally normalized cost data, overall cost indicators for drinking water and waste disposal can easily be ascertained. In addition, the annual water consumption due to pool utilization ($X_2$) and the proportionate size of the sanitary area per m² UFA ($X_3$ in Model 5.A) are identified as relevant determinants on the outlay for drinking and waste water, whereby the waste water expenses are taken into consideration for aggregate waste disposal costs within the scope of this study (cost group 320 according to DIN 18960:2008-2). Whereas the variable $X_3$ (number of school classes per m² UFA) is included in the analysis of water costs in Model 1.B, no influence is statistically confirmed using regression analysis for estimating total waste disposal costs.

Tab. 29: Model description for estimating total waste disposal costs

| Dependent variable | Transf. | R² | R² adj. | SEE | F-value | Sign. | Durbin-Watson-Statistic | | N |
|---|---|---|---|---|---|---|---|---|---|
| Waste disposal costs (€ p.a.) | LN | 0.788 | 0.783 | 0.289 | 150.175 | 0.000 | 1.909 | | 125 |

| Factors | Transf. | B | St. Error | Beta | t-value | Sign. | Lower CL | Upper CL | T | VIF |
|---|---|---|---|---|---|---|---|---|---|---|
| Constant | LN | -0.009 | 0.438 | | -0.020 | 0.984 | -0.876 | 0.858 | | |
| Usable floor area (UFA in m²) | LN | 0.943 | 0.047 | 0.903 | 20.041 | 0.000 | 0.849 | 1.036 | 0.862 | 1.160 |
| Water volume of complete pool refillings p.a. | - | 0.001 | 0.000 | 0.157 | 3.746 | 0.000 | 0.001 | 0.002 | 0.991 | 1.009 |
| Share of the sanitary area per m² UFA | - | 4.159 | 1.774 | 0.106 | 2.345 | 0.021 | 0.648 | 7.671 | 0.857 | 1.167 |

**Dependent variable:** Waste disposal costs (€ p.a.), costs including VAT, based on 2008 figures

$$\hat{Y} = 0.991 \cdot X_1^{0.943} \cdot e^{0.001 X_2} \cdot e^{4.159 X_3} \qquad \text{(Model 5.A)}$$

Where: $\hat{Y}$ : Waste disposal costs (€ p.a.)

$X_1$ : Usable floor area (UFA in m²)

$X_2$ : Water volume of swimming pools in m³ of complete refillings p.a.

$X_3$ : Share of the sanitary area per m² UFA

The statistical investigation of significant factors impacting on waste disposal cost indicators is in line with the analysis of total annual costs outlined above (Model 5.A) and is described below by the multivariate Model 5.B with respect to sample data from 125 school complexes. The regression model specified for estimating waste disposal cost indicators refers to a large extent to the same continuous variables used in Model 5.A. The normalization of waste disposal costs is therefore conducted in terms of the usable floor area, as defined in DIN 277-1:2005-2, and the independent influences of the two continuous variables water volume of complete pool refilling p.a., and the share of the sanitary area per m² UFA are determined for efficient cost predictions. In addition, the absolute size of the water impermeable area of a school's plot ($X_3$) is incorporated in Model 5.B as a positive effect, (with beta₃ of 0.236), that refers to this specific share of cost variation which is caused by municipal charges for non-seeping rainwater.

In particular, these model specifications allow explaining the variation in waste water expenses, as part of waste disposal costs. At the same time it was not possible to confirm any further assumption for the cost differences in garbage disposal by means of regression analysis, i.e. in consideration of the number of school classes, or the waste disposal concept practiced by the schools under investigation. It can be assumed, that this lack of explanation reduces the goodness-of-fit to a certain extent described by a coefficient of determination ($R^2$) of 0.298 and a standard error of estimate (SEE) of 0.224 (see Tab. 30).

Tab. 30:   Model description for estimating waste disposal cost indicators

| Dependent variable | Transf. | R² | R² adj. | SEE | F-value | Sign. | Durbin-Watson-Statistic | | N |
|---|---|---|---|---|---|---|---|---|---|
| Waste disposal costs (€/m² UFA p.a.) | - | 0.289 | 0.272 | 0.224 | 16.419 | 0.000 | 1.913 | | 125 |

| Factors | Transf. | B | St. Error | Beta | t-value | Sign. | Lower CL | Upper CL | T | VIF |
|---|---|---|---|---|---|---|---|---|---|---|
| Constant | - | -0.318 | 0.304 | | -1.046 | 0.298 | -0.920 | 0.284 | | |
| Water volume of complete pool refillings p.a. | - | 0.001 | 0.000 | 0.397 | 5.163 | 0.000 | 0.001 | 0.002 | 0.993 | 1.007 |
| Share of the sanitary area per m² UFA | - | 4.360 | 1.283 | 0.263 | 3.399 | 0.001 | 1.821 | 6.899 | 0.985 | 1.015 |
| Water impermeable surface of the plot (m²) | LN | 0.101 | 0.033 | 0.236 | 3.065 | 0.003 | 0.036 | 0.166 | 0.991 | 1.009 |

**Dependent variable:** Waste disposal costs (€/m² usable floor area p.a.), costs including VAT, based on 2008 figures

$$\hat{Y} = -0.318 + 0.001X_1 + 4.360X_2 + 0.101\ln(X_3)$$                                         (Model 5.B)

Where:        $\hat{Y}$ :   Waste disposal costs (€/m² UFA p.a.)

$X_1$ :   Water volume of swimming pools in m³ of complete refillings p.a.

$X_2$ :   Share of the sanitary area per m² UFA

$X_3$ :   Water impermeable surface of the plot (m²)

*Summary*

Besides quantifying relevant factors, the investigation of waste disposal costs for 125 schools in Germany also documents the congruities that exist between those determinants identified for predicting both waste disposal costs (Model 5.A) as well as drinking water (Model 1.A.2). On the one hand, this becomes apparent through the definition of the same appropriate reference area (UFA) for both cost groups. On the other hand, this congruity is underlined by a wide consensus in identified factors impacting both on the annual amount of drinking water and waste disposal costs. Using three independent variables, the regression Model 5.A particularly explains differences in sewage costs, that occur for waste water and non-seeping rainwater for the schools in question, by taking into account the annual water volume required for complete pool refilling ($X_1$), the share of the sanitary area per m² UFA ($X_2$), and the size of the impermeable surface of a school's grounds ($X_3$). Summarizing, the investigation confirms that existing differences in cost indicators for waste disposal are related to the intensity of an indoor swimming pool usage, as well as to functional and technical characteristics pertaining to the standard of a school's grounds and outdoor facilities.

## 3.2.3   Validation of the model

The following validation test is conducted on the basis of sample data from 5 school complexes in Stuttgart (Germany). Underlying cost indicators for waste disposal estimated by the regression Model 5.B are described in Tab. 31 and compared with individual observed values along with empirical mean and median estimates. Cost indicators designated in €/m² UFA p.a. include VAT and are based on 2008 figures.

Comparing the estimation quality achieved by the multivariate analysis, the introduced regression Model 5.B produces adequate predictions across both the underlying random sample of 125 schools investigated in Section 3.2.2 (MAPE of 24%) and the validation sample of 5 schools (MAPE of 22%). The comparison between the mean absolute percentage errors of prediction, mean and median shown below reveals that the regression model achieves a relatively small error reduction, lower than 1%, so that the regression Model 5.B (with $R^2=0.289$) does not allow much better cost predictions for the schools forming the object of this survey. In three out of five validated cases the empirical average provides more accurate estimates. By contrast, the median shows the largest deviation from the observed values across all properties taken into account.

Tab. 31:   Model validation for waste disposal cost indicators

| No. | Type of school | Observed value | Predicted value | Absolute error % of prediction | Absolute error % of mean | Absolute error % of median | Preference |
|-----|----------------|----------------|-----------------|--------------------------------|--------------------------|----------------------------|------------|
| 1 | Elementary school without sports facilities | 1.25 | 0.64 | 49 | **34** | 34 | Mean |
| 2 | Special school with gymnasium | 1.04 | 0.81 | 22 | **20** | 21 | Mean |
| 3 | Secondary school without sports facilities | 0.84 | 0.80 | 5 | **2** | 3 | Mean |
| 4 | Secondary school with gymnasium and pool | 1.30 | 1.11 | **15** | 36 | 37 | **Prediction** |
| 5 | Vocational school without sports facilities | 0.69 | 0.82 | **18** | 20 | 19 | **Prediction** |
| Ø | **Mean Absolute percentage error** | | | **22** | 22 | 23 | **Prediction** |

**Observed value:** Waste disposal costs (€/m² usable floor area p.a.), costs including VAT, based on 2008 figures, N=125

## 3.2.4   Cost indicators for waste disposal

In accordance with the analysis of water costs in Section 3.1.1, the usable floor area is also evaluated as the appropriate reference area for defining specific cost indicators for waste disposal. Moreover, the analyses of water and waste disposal cost indicators (Models 1.B.2 and 5.B, N=125) both reveal that the presence of swimming facilities in a school complex accounts for significant differences in the cost indicators for both the water supply and waste disposal. Therefore, specified cost indicators for waste disposal designated in Tab. 32 below can easily be related to those categories described for water, set out in Tab. 12. When compared to schools without swimming pools, those with swimming facilities have, on average, almost an higher outlay of 0.40 €/m² UFA p.a. based on a mean value of 1.17 €/m² UFA p.a. (costs including VAT, based on 2008 figures). The validation test conducted in the preceding section verifies that the efficiency of those mean estimates for waste disposal costs, as opposed to empirical median predictions. As regards schools with swimming pools, the outlay for sewage, as a relevant part of disposal costs, depends in particular on the water volume required for complete pool emptying and refilling p.a. (cf. $X_1$ in Model 5.B). According to the subcategories for water cost indicators described above in Section 3.1.1.4, the water volume category for complete pool refillings p.a. $\geq 200$ m³ covers those schools with a maximum annual filling volume of almost 700 m³.

Tab. 32:   Evaluated cost indicators for waste disposal

| Factor level | Minimum | Mean | Median | Maximum | Range |
|---|---|---|---|---|---|
| Schools without swimming pools | 0.37 | 0.80 | 0.81 | 1.43 | 1.06 |
| Schools with swimming pools | 0.51 | 1.17 | 1.05 | 1.69 | 1.18 |
| < 200 m³ water volume of complete pool refillings p.a. | 0.51 | 0.85 | 0.91 | 1.05 | 0.54 |
| ≥ 200 m³ water volume of complete pool refillings p.a. | 1.47 | 1.60 | 1.62 | 1.69 | 0.22 |

**Dependent variable:** Waste disposal costs (€/m² usable floor area p.a.), costs including VAT, based on 2008 figures, N=125

## 3.3     Cleaning and care of buildings

### 3.3.1     Empirical and theoretical basis

Apart from the costs for utility supplies, the outlay for cleaning and care of school buildings, averaging 8.50 €/m² GROFA p.a., represents one of the largest operating cost groups (costs including VAT, based on 2008 figures). In detail, the costs for the cleaning and care of buildings include personnel and material costs of the following cost groups according to the German standard DIN 18960:2008-2:

- Regular cleaning (cost group 331)
- Glass cleaning (cost group 332)
- Facade cleaning (cost group 333)
- Cleaning of technical installations (cost group 334)
- Cleaning and care of buildings, other items (cost group 339)

Construction cleanings as defined by REFA (2004, p.15), for instance, are not included in the aforementioned expenditures for the cleaning and care of buildings that occur regularly during operation. Those cleaning costs associated with building constructions according to DIN 276-1:2008-12, for new buildings, renovation or modernization measures for example, belong to the category of additional work, i.e. cost group 397 (other construction-related activites) or cost group 497 (other service-related work), and are therefore not included in the investigation of costs for the cleaning and care, described below.

Factors that are relevant to the investigation are in particular described by BMI (2003) and REFA (2004). According to these, the intensity of utilization is decisive for the degree of soiling and therefore for the time required for the cleaning and care of a building. Further to this, BMI (2003) underlines the importance of the size of a building and the total glazed area of it with regard to both its functional and technical characteristics.

Contrary to this, REFA (2004) stresses the significance of various service level agreements. The requirement of various cleaning services and differing cleaning frequencies is illustrated, for example, by consideration of the relative proportions of specific utilization areas, such as teaching, sports and sanitary areas, and also of the condition of a building itself and the furnishings and equipping of it (see also GEFMA 300:1996-6). The share of the sanitary area is often taken to be an important influential factor on the overall outlay a school for cleaning and care (see BMI, 2000 or Stadt Zürich, 2006, for example). It is additionally pointed out that the time expenditure for the necessary waste disposal services can greatly vary and so lead to a corresponding variation in the costs.

Regarding the SLAs described in the tender documents for the cleaning of the schools taken as the sample, differences in the frequency of cleaning mainly occur between different types of schools, but also between the sizes of specific building and cleaning floor areas, such as the gross floor area (GROFA) of the ground floor, for instance. The type of cleaning to be made is additionally dependent on the standard of floorings and other internal surfaces, such as floorings and linings. To summarize, this investigation takes various descriptions which refer to a school utilization type and its functional and technical characteristics as well as influencing factors from the factor group strategy and operation into consideration. The individual qualitative and quantitative variables subsequently described are incorporated within the statistical analysis. Further details on the empirical data base of each individual variable are given in Appendix C.

## Factor group: Utilization

*Type of utilization:*

- Primary utilization: Elementary school, secondary school such as comprehensive school (secondary general school, intermediate secondary school, multiple school center) or grammar school, special school, vocational school with technical or business focus; qualitative description of different utilization types and quantitative description of the school utilization area in m² NEFA as well as its proportion per m² NEFA of the whole school property.

- Secondary utilization: Sports facilities such as gymnasiums or indoor swimming pools for teaching purposes, nursery school, underground parking; qualitative and quantitative description of different utilization types with regard to their building reference areas e.g. the net floor area of a gymnasium in m² and its representative proportion per m² NEFA , net floor area of swimming pool utilization in m² and its proportion per m² NEFA, net floor area of underground parking in m² and its proportion per m² NEFA.

*Standard of utilization:*

- Type of educational program: Regular school, extended regular school or full-day school.
- Type of canteen service: School based canteen, external catering or no canteen service.

*Intensity of utilization:*

- Temporal usage intensity:

   Average operating time of the whole school complex as well as individual operating times of both the primary and secondary utilizations, i.e. the school and its sports facilities, in hours per school week and with regard to the average number of schooldays per school week.

- Spatial usage intensity:

  Qualitative and quantitative description of the spatial standard e.g. the total size of specific floor areas according to DIN 277:2005-2 (Part 1 and 2) in relation to the number of pupils or school classes as well as other reference areas such as m² net floor area of school utilization with respect to the number of pupils or school classes.

### Factor group: Functional and technical characteristics

*Functional characteristics:*

- Specific building floor areas according to DIN 277:2005-2 (Part 1 and 2) e.g. in m² NEFA, m² UFA, m² CICA or m² UFA 5 and their representative proportion to the total size of a property in m² GROFA or other specific building floor areas e.g. the share of UFA 5 per m² NEFA.

- The total gross building volume and the average storey height as defined by DIN 277-1: 2005-2.

- Total gross floor area (GROFA) of the ground floor and its proportion to the total size of a property in m² GROFA according to DIN 277-1: 2005-2.

- The total sanitary area and its proportion to specific building floor areas according to DIN 277: 2005-2 (Part 1 and 2) e.g. the share of the sanitary area per m² NEFA.

- Total cleaning floor area and its proportion to specific building floor areas according to DIN 277: 2005-2 (Part 1 and 2) e.g. the share of cleaning floor area per m² NEFA.

- Standard of flooring: Qualitative and quantitative description of different flooring materials i.e. wood, stone, carpet or synthetic materials in m² flooring area and as a percentage of the whole flooring area according to DIN 277-3:2005-4.

- Standard of internal wall linings: Qualitative and quantitative description of different lining materials i.e. wood, ceramic, panels, paintwork or wallpaper in m² internal wall lining area and as a percentage of the whole internal wall lining area as defined by DIN 277-3:2005-4.

- Standard of ceiling and roof linings: Qualitative and quantitative description of different lining materials i.e. wood, wallpaper, panels, paintwork or plaster in m² ceiling and roof lining area and as a percentage of the whole ceiling and roof lining area according to DIN 277-3:2005-4.

*Technical characteristics:*

- Standard of building constructions:

  - Standard of external claddings: Qualitative and quantitative description of different cladding materials i.e. wood, stone, concrete, plaster or panels in m² external cladding area and as a percentage of the whole external wall cladding area according to DIN 277-3:2005-4.

- Glass area of external walls and roofs according to DIN 277-3:2005-4 and its share in percentage of specific building floor areas according to DIN 277: 2005-2 (Part 1 and 2) e.g. the share of glass areas of external walls and roofs per m² NEFA.

- Glazing standard: Qualitative and quantitative description of single, double and triple glazing in m² glass area of external walls and as a percentage of the whole glass area of external walls according to DIN 277-3:2005-4.

- Condition of technical installations:

  Qualitative description of the condition of sanitary installations: Good or poor condition.

- Standard of fittings, furnishings and equipment: Higher or lower standard.

- Condition of fittings, furnishings and equipment: Good or poor condition.

**Factor group: Strategy and operation**

- Disposal concept: Efficient or inefficient.

### 3.3.2 Model design and parameters

Based on the factors outlined above and statistical pre-analyses, different models for estimating costs for the cleaning and care of schools have been developed and compared step-by-step. In the following section the models evaluated for predicting total costs and cost indicators by means of Models 6.A and 6.B respectively are introduced.

The statistical analysis of total costs for the cleaning and care of buildings (Model 6.A) refers to a schools' net floor area for estimating and forecasting total costs. According to the German standard DIN 277-1:2005-1, the net floor area also comprises the circulation area, whose variability is also taken into account when predicting annual costs (Y). With $R^2=0.940$, SEE=0.153 and a MAPE of 12%, the multivariate model shows excellent compatibility with the underlying sample of 122 schools (see Tab. 33).

Moreover, Model 6.A quantifies the independent influences that exert by the variables $X_2$ (the swimming pool utilization area measured in m² UFA 5 on room level), $X_3$ (the share of the sanitary area per m² NEFA) and $X_4$ (the share of the gross floor area of the ground floor per m² GROFA) [30] on the overall costs for cleaning and care of buildings. Detailed information on the collinearity statistics, the coefficient estimates and the empirical significance for each variable, tested at a 5% level, are presented in Tab. 33.

---

[30] In this instance, the variable X4 is specified in terms of the total building floor area (m² GROFA) because the total area of the ground floor is also given in m² GROFA.

Tab. 33:   Model description for estimating total costs for the cleaning and care of buildings

| Dependent variable | Transf. | R² | R² adj. | SEE | F-value | Sign. | Durbin-Watson-Statistic | | N |
|---|---|---|---|---|---|---|---|---|---|
| Costs for the cleaning and care of buildings | LN | 0.940 | 0.938 | 0.153 | 461.368 | 0.000 | 2.034 | | 122 |

| Factors | Transf. | B | St. Error | Beta | t-value | Sign. | Lower CL | Upper CL | T | VIF |
|---|---|---|---|---|---|---|---|---|---|---|
| Constant | LN | 2.548 | 0.219 | | 11.661 | 0.000 | 2.115 | 2.981 | | |
| Net floor area (NEFA in m²) | LN | 0.929 | 0.023 | 0.975 | 41.208 | 0.000 | 0.885 | 0.974 | 0.911 | 1.098 |
| Swimming pool utilization area (m²) | - | 0.001 | 0.000 | 0.104 | 4.452 | 0.000 | 0.001 | 0.002 | 0.940 | 1.064 |
| Share of the sanitary area per m² NEFA | - | 4.338 | 1.384 | 0.079 | 3.133 | 0.002 | 1.596 | 7.079 | 0.796 | 1.257 |
| Share of the gross floor area of the ground floor per m² GROFA | - | 0.361 | 0.118 | 0.074 | 3.052 | 0.003 | 0.127 | 0.595 | 0.875 | 1.143 |

**Dependent variable:** Costs for the cleaning and care of buildings (€ p.a.), costs including VAT, based on 2008 figures

$$\hat{Y} = 12.782 \cdot X_1^{0.929} \cdot e^{0.001 X_2} \cdot e^{4.338 X_3} \cdot e^{0.361 X_4}$$                                        (Model 6.A)

Where:     $\hat{Y}$ :   Costs for the cleaning and care of buildings (€ p.a.)

           $X_1$ :   Net floor area (NEFA in m²)

           $X_2$ :   Swimming pool utilization area (UFA 5 on room level in m²)

           $X_3$ :   Share of the sanitary area per m² NEFA

           $X_4$ :   Share of the gross floor area of the ground floor per m² GROFA

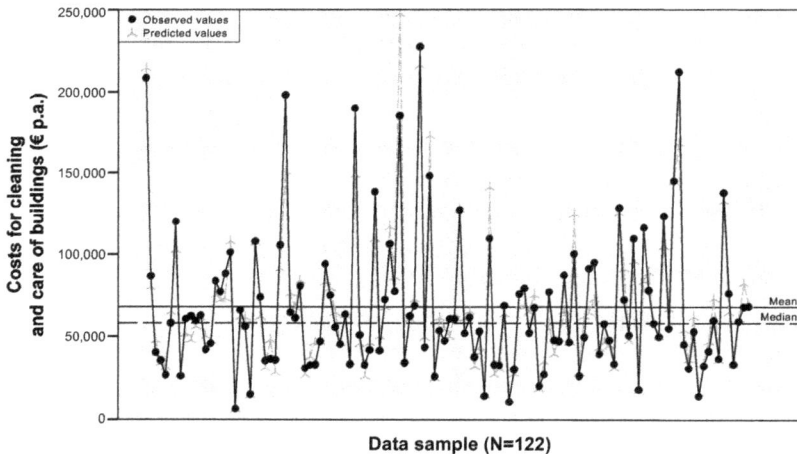

Fig. 4:    Comparison between observed and predicted costs for the cleaning and care of buildings
           (costs including VAT, based on 2008 figures)

As an alternative to the predictor variable $X_1$ (net floor area), the cleaning area of a school can also considered and tested by means of multivariate analysis. When the cleaning area of a school is taken into account by way of a predictor and otherwise constant model assumptions, a merely slightly better estimation quality is achieved with $R^2$=0.942 and SEE=0.151. However, the practical application of the prediction is reduced. The reason for this is that different regulations apply inter-municipally to the definition and calculation of the respective cleaning area, so that the comparability and transferability which the study strived for is reduced in such a prediction model (see also Naber, 2002, p.180). Across different municipalities, the respective reference area is calculated on the basis of different calculation rules which include underground parking areas or other building surfaces such as vertical surfaces, for instance, or the cleaning area is calculated as a weighted factor (see KGSt, 2009). With the target of providing a transferable estimation model available for use in practice, therefore, this study accordingly gives preference to the net floor area as defined by DIN 277-1:2005-1 and uses this reference area for predicting the total costs for the cleaning and care for school buildings.

The subsequent examination of significant factors impacting on cost indicators for the cleaning and care of buildings (€/m² NEFA p.a.) is based on the regression Model 6.A specified above. To a large extent the same independent factors are taken into account as those included in the regression model for estimating the total costs. In concrete terms, the following factors represent three independent influences in the multivariate model: the swimming pool utilization area ($X_2$), the proportionate sanitary area per m² NEFA ($X_3$), and the share of the gross floor area of the ground floor per m² GROFA ($X_4$). In addition, specific types of utilization, determined by the predictor variable $X_1$ (elementary or special school) with $beta_1 = 0.273$, are positively evaluated at a 5% significance level and therefore included for the estimation of cost indicators. The specific impact of each of the predictors is presented by partial regression coefficient $b_j$ for Model 6.B in Tab. 34.

Tab. 34: Model description for estimating cost indicators for the cleaning and care of buildings

| Dependent variable | Transf. | $R^2$ | $R^2$ adj. | SEE | F-value | Sign. | Durbin-Watson-Statistic | | N |
|---|---|---|---|---|---|---|---|---|---|
| Costs for the cleaning and care of buildings | - | 0.433 | 0.413 | 1.493 | 22.323 | 0.000 | 2.021 | | 122 |

| Factors | Transf. | B | St. Error | Beta | t-value | Sign. | Lower CL | Upper CL | T | VIF |
|---|---|---|---|---|---|---|---|---|---|---|
| Constant | - | 6.562 | 0.568 | | 11.556 | 0.000 | 5.438 | 7.687 | | |
| Elementary schools or special schools | - | 1.108 | 0.309 | 0.273 | 3.586 | 0.000 | 0.496 | 1.719 | 0.839 | 1.191 |
| Swimming pool utilization area (m²) | - | 0.011 | 0.002 | 0.338 | 4.735 | 0.000 | 0.007 | 0.016 | 0.954 | 1.048 |
| Share of the sanitary area per m² NEFA | - | 41.069 | 13.403 | 0.238 | 3.064 | 0.003 | 14.526 | 67.612 | 0.802 | 1.247 |
| Share of the gross floor area of the ground floor per m² GROFA | - | 2.584 | 1.181 | 0.168 | 2.187 | 0.031 | 0.244 | 4.924 | 0.825 | 1.212 |

**Dependent variable:** Costs for the cleaning and care of buildings (€/m² net floor area p.a.), costs including VAT, based on 2008 figures

$$\hat{Y} = 6.562 + 1.108X_1 + 0.011X_2 + 41.069X_3 + 2.584X_4 \qquad \text{(Model 6.B)}$$

Where:     $\hat{Y}$ :   Costs for the cleaning and care of buildings (€/m² NEFA p.a.)

$X_1$ :   Elementary schools or special schools (type of school)

$X_2$ :   Swimming pool utilization area (UFA 5 on room level in m²)

$X_3$ :   Share of the sanitary area per m² NEFA

$X_4$ :   Share of the gross floor area of the ground floor per m² GROFA

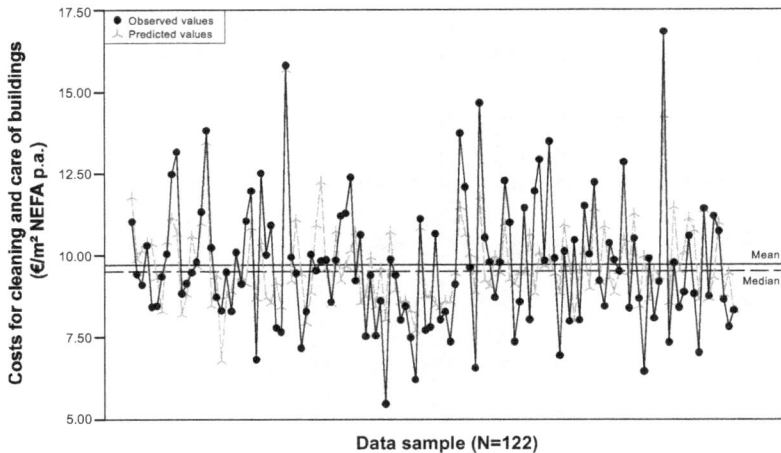

Fig. 5:     Comparison between observed and predicted cost indicators for the cleaning and
            care of buildings (costs including VAT, based on 2008 figures)

To sum up, Model 6.B ($R^2$ =0.433, adjusted $R^2$ =0.413) proves that about 40% of the total variation in costs per m² NEFA p.a. can be explained using the statistical approach. Additional information, such as a standard error of estimate (SEE) of 1.493 and a MAPE of 13%, also displays a good estimation quality for the regression model introduced in this section. Deviations between observed and predicted values visualized in Fig. 5 are the result of such factors that were not taken into consideration, such as the number of special cleanings within the calendar year in question.

*Summary*

Based on an analysis of the variation in total costs, the net floor area is identified as being the relevant reference area for calculating the annual outlay for the cleaning and care of school buildings. The subsequent investigation into the cost indicators (€/m² NEFA p.a.) predominantly verifies the influence of area-related factors.

In the case of the 122 schools which are the subject of this survey, this outcome is illustrated by three independent variables: the size of the swimming pool utilization area and specific proportionate areas of the sanitary area, and of the gross floor area of the ground floor. According to the tender documents issued by Stuttgart city council, the last mentioned building area is defined as part of the entrance cleaning zone of analyzed schools.

Differences revealed between the cost indicators of the facilities under comparison, in particular, result from the more frequent cleaning schedule per school week for the designated building areas. In addition, wet rooms, represented as both swimming pool utilization and sanitary areas in the statistical models, have higher service-levels, which is manifested by the nature of cleaning tasks. Besides these area-related factors, Model 6.B confirms the assumption that elementary and special schools have, on average, higher annual costs per m² NEFA than other types of schools under investigation. This is due to the higher degree of covered floor space of the buildings, leading to a greater time investment per square meter of area to be cleaned in these two kinds of school.

Based on sample data from 122 schools, the examination concludes that statistics confirm that there are significant differences in the costs of cleaning and caring for school buildings from the point of view of the type of school utilization and functional building characteristics.

### 3.3.3 Validation of the model

The validation test considers cost indicators predicted for the cleaning and care of buildings (€/m² NEFA p.a. according to Model 6.B) and compares their accuracy with empirical estimates based on mean and median calculations relating to the observed cost values of five validation properties. All measures are based on cost indicators from 2008 figures and include VAT. The corresponding indexing table for annual price adjustments is provided by Destatis (2011b).

With a MAPE of 19%, the mean absolute percentage error achieved by Model 6.B indicates the lowest prediction error, and consequently an overall high prediction level, compared with a MAPE of 27% for mean and a MAPE of 28% for median respectively. Comparing observed values across all assessed properties, higher cost indicators are confirmed for a validated school with an indoor pool facility (sample No.4), an elementary school and a special school (samples No.1 and 2), in particular. With an observed cost outlay in the region of 14-18 €/m² NEFA p.a. for these school types, compared with 8-10 €/m² NEFA p.a. for a secondary and vocational school (samples No.3 and 5), previous assumptions that were postulated for functional related differences in the costs of cleaning and caring for school buildings by means of regression analysis are also substantiated (cf. $X_1$ and $X_2$ in Model 6.B).

Tab. 35: Model validation for cost indicators of the cleaning and care of buildings

| No. | Type of school | Observed value | Predicted value | Absolute error % of prediction | Absolute error % of mean | Absolute error % of median | Preference |
|---|---|---|---|---|---|---|---|
| 1 | Elementary school without sports facilities | 13.86 | 10.53 | 24 | 30 | 32 | Prediction |
| 2 | Special school with gymnasium | 17.50 | 11.30 | 35 | 45 | 46 | Prediction |
| 3 | Secondary school without sports facilities | 10.23 | 9.39 | 8 | 5 | 7 | Mean |
| 4 | Secondary school with gymnasium and pool | 15.68 | 11.91 | 24 | 38 | 39 | Prediction |
| 5 | Vocational school without sports facilities | 8.29 | 8.56 | 3 | 17 | 14 | Prediction |
| Ø | Mean Absolute percentage error | | | 19 | 27 | 28 | Prediction |

Observed value: Costs for the cleaning and care of buildings (€/m² net floor area p.a.), costs including VAT, based on 2008 figures, N=122

### 3.3.4 Cost indicators for the cleaning and care of buildings

Based on an underlying sample of 122 schools in Germany, empirical measures for central tendency and dispersion of cost indicators for the cleaning and care of school buildings are described in Tab. 101. The overall data sample can accordingly be described in terms of an empirical mean value of 9.70 €/m² NEFA p.a. and a interquartile range of around 2.31 €/m² NEFA p.a. (costs including VAT, based on 2008 figures). Turning to the quantified and subsequently validated determinants investigated in the preceding sections, the cost indicators presented below refer to those factors which have statistically proved to constitute the greatest impact on costs for the cleaning and care of school buildings. According to Model 6.B, these factors are the total size of the swimming pool utilization area ($X_2$ with $beta_2$=0.338) and a categorical distinction between different types of school utilization according to the variable $X_1$ ($beta_1$=0.273). Specific cost indicators for schools with and without indoor swimming pools are shown in Tab. 36 and a distinguishing is made between elementary and special schools in contrast to other schools types. With a mean value of 12.57 €/m² NEFA p.a., schools with an indoor swimming pool have around 3 €/m² NEFA higher costs p.a. compared to those schools without these additional swimming pool facilities. In comparing cost differences within the latter category, the mean cost indicator for elementary or special schools, based on 10.56 €/m² NEFA p.a., is about 1.60 €/m² NEFA p.a. higher than the average costs incurred by other school types, such as secondary or vocational schools (costs based on 2008 figures including, VAT). In addition to presented measures, classified according to the type of school utilization, continuous cost indicators are provided by Model 6.B based on four independent variables, introduced in Section 3.3.2.

Tab. 36:   Evaluated cost indicators for the cleaning and care of buildings

| Factor level | Minimum | Mean | Median | Maximum | Range |
|---|---|---|---|---|---|
| Schools without swimming pools | 5.47 | 9.52 | 9.44 | 14.66 | 9.19 |
| Elementary schools or special schools | 8.01 | 10.56 | 10.09 | 14.66 | 6.65 |
| Other school types | 5.47 | 8.99 | 8.73 | 13.48 | 8.01 |
| Schools with swimming pools | 8.43 | 12.57 | 12.27 | 16.82 | 8.39 |
| Elementary schools or special schools | 9.83 | 14.07 | 14.82 | 16.82 | 6.99 |
| Other school types | 8.43 | 10.58 | 11.03 | 12.27 | 3.84 |

Dependent variable: Costs (€/m² net floor area p.a.), costs including VAT, based on 2008 figures, N=122

## 3.4     Cleaning and care of grounds and outdoor facilities

### 3.4.1   Empirical and theoretical basis

The investigation of annual costs for cleaning and care of grounds and outdoor facilities is based on a sample of 125 school properties in Stuttgart (Germany) and comprises according to DIN 18960:2008-2 the following operating costs:

- Hard surfaces (cost group 341)
- Green areas (cost group 342)
- Water area including bank formation (cost group 343)
- Outdoor constructions (cost group 344)

- Outdoor technical installations (cost group 345)
- Permanent outdoor fixtures (cost group 346)
- Cleaning and care of grounds and outdoor facilities, other items (cost group 349)

According to the Department of Asset and Construction of Baden-Württemberg (DAC-BW, 2005), the extent of the measures required to maintain outdoor grounds is primarily dependent on the standard of cleaning and care and the size of the individuals grounds. The standard of cleaning and care is hereby oriented to the need of care of each of the separate grounds on the one hand and the standard of grounds and outdoor facilities on the other hand. According to DAC-BW (2005), further marginal conditions, such as the degree of soiling or the topography, can be determined which influence the possibility of mechanical cleaning and thus the time and cost expenditures for cleaning and care. This study incorporates these thoughts by evaluation of the standard of grounds and outdoor facilities in addition to the size and quality of specific outdoor areas, such as the outdoor cleaning area and the non-built up area of a plot including specific sections of hard surfaces and green areas. Experts involved in the survey are interested in the possibility of formulating a general statement on the annual outlay for cleaning and care of grounds and outdoor facilities for specific types of school. They hereby presume higher average costs for elementary schools, for example, with extensive sports areas and school playgrounds than for the often more monotonous arranged vocational school areas, which frequently consist to a great extent of parking lots. The following variables were defined together with those responsible of the building management and taken as basis for the statistical analysis:

**Factor group: Utilization**

*Type of utilization:*

- Primary and secondary utilization: Qualitative description of different utilization types such as elementary school, secondary school, special school, vocational school or nursery school.

*Standard of utilization:*

- Type of educational program: Regular school, extended regular school or full-day school.

*Intensity of utilization:*

- Temporal usage intensity:
  Average operating time of the whole school comples in hours per school week and with regard to the average number of schooldays per school week.

**Factor group: Functional and technical characteristics**

*Technical characteristics:*

- Standard of grounds and outdoor facilities:
  - Standard of grounds and outdoor facilities: Higher or lower standard.

- Total size of property area in m²

- Non-built up area of the plot in m² and its designated sections such as school playground area, sports area or green area in m² and their representative proportion to the non-built up area of the plot.

- Total external cleaning area in m² (including public sidewalks adjacent to plot of land) and its proportion to the total non-built up area of the plot.

- Condition of grounds and outdoor facilities:

Qualitative description of the condition of grounds and outdoor facilities and in particular the condition of hard surfaces, outdoor constructions, permanent outdoor fixtures or green areas: Good or poor condition.

**Factor group: Location:**

- Region: Urban, suburban or rural.

- Topography: Flat, sloped.

### 3.4.2    Model design and parameters

The empirical investigation into total costs for the cleaning and care of grounds and outdoor school facilities is based on sample data from 122 schools and takes into account all factors outlined above, which have to be incorporated theoretically into the statistical analysis. The survey identifies a definite interrelation between the absolute size of the non-built up plot area and the relevant outlay. As revealed by Model 7.A, this specific part of the property area, as defined in Section 2.2.2, constitutes the appropriate reference area for the estimation of overall costs and the normalization of cost data, based on beta$_1$ of 0.701. In addition to this continuous variable, Model 7.A determines the standard of grounds and outdoor facilities, and the presence of an elementary, special or nursery school within a school complex, in terms of two categorical variables, which both have an independent impact on the total annual outlay

Within this study, different descriptions of school utilization types, specified as independent variables, are taken into consideration and step-by-step evaluated by a statistical approach (see Appendix C). Whereas previous analysis, for electricity costs (Model 3.A.2) or for the outlay for the cleaning and care of buildings (Model 6.A), for instance, indicated that the amount of underlying costs (Y) differs across different types of primary school utilization, this factor, the primary utilization, does not represent a relevant effect on the underlying costs for the cleaning and care of grounds and outdoor facilities. By contrast, Model 7.B shows that just the existence of specific school types on site, i.e. an elementary, special or nursery school ($X_3$), generally exerts a significant influence, whether these school types occur as a primary or secondary utilization within a school complex. As regard content, those averaging higher cost indicators can be partly explained by a higher proportion of particularly cleaning-intensive playground areas for elementary, special or nursery school utilizations, as opposed to the average outlay for purely secondary or vocational schools without the other school functions.

Detailed information on the model design and specifications of both models are shown in Tab. 37. Based on $R^2$=0.566 and SEE=0.588, the nonlinear regression model achieves a convincing estimation quality. Other theoretical assumptions relating to the independent influences other property areas have on total costs for the cleaning and care of grounds and outdoor facilities, such as the size of the playground area, the sports grounds, or the outdoor cleaning area of a school's property, for example, are not confirmed at a 5% significance level using regression analysis.

Tab. 37:   Model description for estimating total costs for the cleaning and care of grounds and outdoor facilities

| Dependent variable | Transf. | R² | R² adj. | SEE | F-value | Sign. | Durbin-Watson-Statistic | | N |
|---|---|---|---|---|---|---|---|---|---|
| Costs for the cleaning and care of grounds and outdoor facilities (€ p.a.) | LN | 0.566 | 0.555 | 0.588 | 52.614 | 0.000 | 2.074 | | 125 |

| Factors | Transf. | B | St. Error | Beta | t-value | Sign. | Lower CL | Upper CL | T | VIF |
|---|---|---|---|---|---|---|---|---|---|---|
| Constant | LN | 2.138 | 0.527 | | 4.057 | 0.000 | 1.095 | 3.181 | | |
| Non-built up plot area (m²) | LN | 0.673 | 0.059 | 0.701 | 11.431 | 0.000 | 0.557 | 0.790 | 0.955 | 1.047 |
| Higher standard of grounds and outdoor facilities | - | 0.269 | 0.120 | 0.137 | 2.236 | 0.027 | 0.031 | 0.507 | 0.949 | 1.054 |
| Existence of elementary, special or nursery school on site | - | 0.217 | 0.109 | 0.119 | 1.983 | 0.050 | 0.000 | 0.433 | 0.993 | 1.007 |

**Dependent variable**: Costs for cleaning and care of grounds and outdoor facilities (€ p.a.), costs including VAT, based on 2008 figures

$$\hat{Y} = 8.482 \cdot X_1^{0.637} \cdot e^{0.269 X_2} \cdot e^{0.217 X_3} \qquad \text{(Model 7.A)}$$

Where:    $\hat{Y}$ :   Costs for the cleaning and care of grounds and outdoor facilities (€ p.a.)

   $X_1$ :   Non-built up area of the plot (part of the property area in m²)

   $X_2$ :   Higher standard of grounds and outdoor facilities

   $X_3$ :   Existence of elementary, special or nursery school on site

The subsequent survey on cost indicators, normalized by the non-built up plot area, is based on the estimation of total costs for the cleaning and care of grounds and outdoor facilities. In compliance with Model 7.A, the best model prediction is achieved by Model 7.B, which initially distinguishes between different types of school utilization and individual standards of grounds and outdoor facilities. As outlined above, the independent predictor $X_2$ allows a categorical distinction between those school complexes that comprise an elementary, special or nursery school as their primary or secondary utilization, as opposed to other school complexes without these school functions.

In addition, the proportionate size of the outdoor cleaning area per m² non-built up area of a school's plot is incorporated as the continuous variable $X_1$ in Model 7.B. In the multivariate model, the variable describes a nonlinear effect on cost indicators (Y), corresponding to a less pronounced increase in Y upwards of a certain proportionate outdoor cleaning area due to mechanical outdoor cleaning methods of extended school grounds hard surfaces.

Tab. 38:   Model description for estimating cost indicators for the cleaning and care of grounds and outdoor facilities

| Dependent variable | Transf. | R² | R² adj. | SEE | F-value | Sign. | Durbin-Watson-Statistic | | N |
|---|---|---|---|---|---|---|---|---|---|
| Costs for the cleaning and care of grounds and outdoor facilities | LN | 0.331 | 0.314 | 0.549 | 19.936 | 0.000 | 2.152 | | 125 |

| Factors | Transf. | B | St. Error | Beta | t-value | Sign. | Lower CL | Upper CL | T | VIF |
|---|---|---|---|---|---|---|---|---|---|---|
| Constant | LN | -0.461 | 0.115 | | -4.015 | 0.000 | -0.689 | -0.234 | | |
| Share of the outdoor cleaning area per m² non-built up plot area | LN | 0.724 | 0.100 | 0.555 | 7.272 | 0.000 | 0.527 | 0.921 | 0.949 | 1.054 |
| Existence of elementary, special or nursery school on site | - | 0.333 | 0.103 | 0.243 | 3.234 | 0.002 | 0.129 | 0.537 | 0.976 | 1.025 |
| Higher standard of grounds and outdoor facilities | - | 0.266 | 0.111 | 0.181 | 2.392 | 0.018 | 0.046 | 0.487 | 0.964 | 1.037 |

**Dependent variable:** Costs (€/m² non-built up plot area p.a.), costs including VAT, based on 2008 figures

$$\hat{Y} = 0.630 \cdot X_1^{0.724} \cdot e^{0.333 X_2} \cdot e^{0.266 X_3} \qquad\qquad \text{(Model 7.B)}$$

Where:   $\hat{Y}$ :   Costs for cleaning and care of grounds and outdoor facilities (€/m² non-built up plot area p.a.)

$X_1$ :   Share of the outdoor cleaning area per m² non-built up plot area

$X_2$ :   Existence of elementary, special or nursery school on site

$X_3$ :   Higher standard of grounds and outdoor facilities

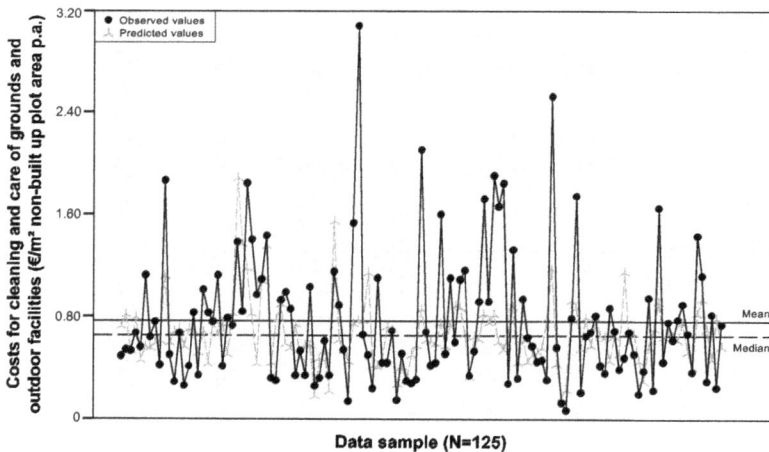

Fig. 6:   Comparison between observed and predicted cost indicators for the cleaning and care of grounds and outdoor facilities (costs including VAT, based on 2008 figures)

The relevant factors of Model 7.B are described in Tab. 38 along with details of coefficient estimates and empirical significance levels. With $R^2=0.331$ and a MAPE of 49%, the specified Model 7.B explains a relatively small proportion of the total variation of investigated cost indicators for the object under investigation. Compared with an empirical standard deviation of 0.52 €/m² non-built up plot area p.a. (costs including VAT, based on 2008 figures for N=125), the regression model slightly improves predictions with a standard error of estimate (SEE) of 0.549.

Factors not taken into account in the survey, such as the number of special cleanings p.a., or existing differences in the quality of partial green areas, and in particular the cost of mechanical outdoor cleaning equipment over the course of the calendar year in question, lower Model 7.B's estimation quality and imply uncertainties associated with cost estimates for the cleaning and care of grounds and outdoor facilities by regression. Fig. 6 particularly reflects these uncertainties for some observations with higher values, where aberrations occur when using the regression model for prediction purposes.

*Summary*

The investigation of total costs for the cleaning and care of grounds and outdoor facilities (Model 7.A) defines the non-built up plot area as the appropriate part of a school's property area for explaining variation in total costs at a 5% significance level. Subsequently, the relevant factors impacting on the costs indicators (€/m² non-built plot up area p.a.) are identified on the basis of 125 school complexes. According to Model 7.B, significant factors emerge from the two categories: the type of school utilization and the standard of the grounds and outdoor facilities and are primarily responsible for cost differences between the schools under comparison. The model shows an adequate standard of estimation. However, with $R^2$ of 0.331, a calculated MAPE of 49% and particularly higher aberrations for some observations depicted in Fig. 6, the cost model achieves a slightly lower prediction quality.

### 3.4.3    Validation of the model

With a standard error of estimate (SEE) of 0.539, Model 7.B, introduced in Section 3.4.2, initially documents several discrepancies in the estimation of cost indicators for the cleaning and care of grounds and outdoor facilities. With reference to an empirical mean of 0.76 €/m² non-built up plot area p.a. (costs including VAT, based on 2008 figures) for the overall distribution of 125 schools, the standard error of estimate accounts for a value of 71%, which cannot be assessed as good to begin with. Comparing the mean absolute percentage errors of prediction with those resulting from empirical estimates based on mean and median, however, the regression model verifies a considerable improvement in the standard of prediction when additional information is taken into account for individual school properties.

With a MAPE of almost 32%, the prediction model falls below the mean absolute percentage error of median and mean at 6 to17%, confirming better results for model predictions for the overall validation sample of 5 school properties. Comparing single prediction errors for the underlying cost indicators, the validation test shows more accurate estimates in three out of five cases. Based on these results, the regression Model 7.B is evaluated as being a satisfactory statistical tool for forecasting cost indicators of grounds and outdoor school facilities. The following section presents specific cost indicators regarding the outcome of the multivariate analysis process.

Tab. 39:   Model validation for cost indicators of the cleaning and care of grounds and outdoor facilities

| No. | Type of school | Observed value | Predicted value | Absolute error % of prediction | Absolute error % of mean | Absolute error % of median | Preference |
|-----|----------------|----------------|-----------------|-------------------------------|--------------------------|----------------------------|------------|
| 1 | Elementary school without sports facilities | 0.76 | 0.70 | 8 | 1 | 14 | Mean |
| 2 | Special school with gymnasium | 0.87 | 0.37 | 58 | 12 | 25 | Mean |
| 3 | Secondary school without sports facilities | 0.46 | 0.58 | 26 | 66 | 41 | Prediction |
| 4 | Secondary school with gymnasium and pool | 0.35 | 0.54 | 54 | 119 | 86 | Prediction |
| 5 | Vocational school without sports facilities | 0.53 | 0.60 | 14 | 44 | 23 | Prediction |
| Ø | Mean Absolute percentage error | | | 32 | 48 | 38 | Prediction |

Observed value: Costs (€/m² non built up plot area p.a.), costs including VAT, based on 2008 figures, N=125

### 3.4.4   Cost indicators for the cleaning and care of grounds and outdoor facilities

The non-built up area of the plot is identified in Model 7.A as the appropriate reference area for defining cost indicators for the cleaning and care of grounds and outdoor facilities. Furthermore, the most efficient cost estimates for indicators (€/m² non-built up area of the plot p.a.) are evaluated by means of multivariate regression analysis, with respect to the continuous variable $X_1$ (share of outdoor cleaning area per m² non-built up plot area). This variable is deemed as a significant criterion for differentiating cost indicators for the cleaning and care of school grounds and outdoor facilities, with a standardized regression coefficient $beta_1$ of 0.555 (cf. Section 3.4.2). Based on this evaluation, Tab. 40 displays cost values for distinguishing between three categories set up for the predictor variable $X_1$, comprising the manifestations $X_1 < 0.5$, $0.5 < X_1 < 1.0$, $X_1 > 1.0$.[31] Cost data includes VAT and has been compiled for an underlying data sample of 125 school complexes, based on 2008 figures. By comparing the empirical mean values, it is depicted that those schools with $X_1 > 1.0$ have, with average costs of 1.18 €/m² non-built up plot area p.a., around twice the average outlay for cleaning and care of grounds and outdoor facilities per m² reference area and year than those schools with $X_1 < 0.5$ and accordingly a relatively small outdoor cleaning area in proportion to the non-built up plot area.

Tab. 40:   Evaluated cost indicators for the cleaning and care of grounds and outdoor facilities

| Factor level | Minimum | Mean | Median | Maximum | Range |
|--------------|---------|------|--------|---------|-------|
| Share of the outdoor cleaning area per m² non-built up plot area < 0.5 | 0.07 | 0.52 | 0.50 | 1.12 | 1.05 |
| Share of the outdoor cleaning area per m² non-built up plot area between 0.5 and 1.0 | 0.14 | 0.86 | 0.74 | 3.08 | 2.94 |
| Share of the outdoor cleaning area per m² non-built up plot area > 1.0 | 0.23 | 1.18 | 1.14 | 2.52 | 2.29 |

Dependent variable: Costs (€/m² non built up plot area p.a.), costs including VAT, based on 2008 figures, N=125

---

[31] With reference to the designated categories, the proportion of the outdoor cleaning area per m² non-built up plot area may be higher than 1.00, because the external cleaning area not only comprises the hard surfaces of a school property but also public sidewalks, adjacent to the school grounds, which the school is responsible for cleaning in Germany (see Section 2.2.2 for further details).

## 3.5    Operation, inspection and maintenance

Apart from the utility costs and the outlay for the cleaning and care of buildings, the costs for the operation, inspection and maintenance, given as an average of 3.44 €/m² GROFA p.a. (costs including VAT, based on 2008 figures), also account for a substantial share of the overall operating costs amounting to about 13%. This survey takes the annual outlay for the following cost types within the calendar year 2008 into consideration, as specified on the third structural cost level in DIN 18960-2008-2:

- Inspection and maintenance of building constructions (cost group 352)
- Inspection and maintenance of technical installations (cost group 353)
- Inspection and maintenance of grounds and outdoor facilities (cost group 354)
- Inspection and maintenance of fittings, furnishings and equipment (cost group 355)

The scope of individual inspection and maintenance measures is defined according to DIN 31051:2003-6, where maintenance denotes measures to delay wear and tear on an operating system and inspection is defined as all measures employed to determine and assess the current condition of an operating system including the identification of the causes for wear and tear and the consequences required for further operation.

As regards the data base of the investigation, differences in the underlying sample size of individual analyses are due to fewer cost postings being available for the cost groups 354 and 355 according to DIN 18960-2008-2.

BMI (2003) and Bahr (2008) name the scope of usage and in particular the intensity of use as being relevant influencing factors that affect the wear and tear of buildings. On the basis of an evaluation of cost drivers for routine inspection, maintenance and repair measures, Bahr (2008) also gives decisive importance to technical characteristics in terms of age and the technical installation standard of a property and subsequently to the quality of planning and construction. The quality of planning can be evaluated with regard to the type of construction, the dimension of structural components and the building material used, for example. These also influence the necessary extent of regularly recurring inspection and maintenance measures and their respective costs. With regard to the standard of technical installations mentioned above, particularly vocational schools have a higher standard across the schools examined. In addition, auxiliary swimming pools, sports facilities and lifts can be named as further elements that require a higher standard of regular maintenance for the properties of the underlying sample. The corresponding characteristics are also named in other research carried out on the outlay for regularly recurring maintenance costs. El-Haram and Horner (2002), for instance, analyzed the outlay for maintaining building characteristics and point out, that alongside usage-related factors, in particular the type of a structure, the age and location, constructional methods and materials, as well as the height of buildings with reference to scaffolding requirements for maintenance measures can be responsible for varying maintenance costs. In this study, consideration is given to specifications of primary and secondary school utilization, the standard and intensity of usage, the functional building characteristics derived from these, such as the share of UFA 5 or TEFA per m² NEFA, the location and detailed information on technical descriptions, such as those for the standard and condition of building constructions, grounds and outdoor facilities.

Starting from a description of the underlying variables of the survey, the models evaluated for estimating total costs and specific cost indicators for individual structural components are presented. In detail, the investigation into schools comprises separate analyses of the inspection and maintenance costs for building constructions, technical installations, grounds and outdoor facilities, fittings, furnishings and equipment as well as for aggregate costs. Based on quantified determinants for cost predictions and comparisons, the estimation standard achieved by the statistical approach is evaluated separately for each cost group by means of a validation test conducted for 5 schools. Finally, cost indicators determined for specific categories are presented for individual and aggregate expenses.

### 3.5.1    Inspection and maintenance of building constructions

### 3.5.1.1    Empirical and theoretical basis

Besides the costs for the inspection and maintenance of technical installations, those for the inspection and maintenance of the building constructions, averaging 1.38 €/m² GROFA p.a. (costs including VAT, based on 2008 figures), also constitute a large share of the overall operation, inspection and maintenance costs for the 125 schools under consideration. From a theoretical perspective, the following factors have an impact on the outlay analyzed for the inspection and maintenance of building constructions and accordingly are taken into consideration within the statistical analysis. Additional information on each factor is given in Appendix C.

### Factor group: Utilization

*Type of utilization:*

- Primary utilization: Elementary school, secondary school such as comprehensive school (secondary general school, intermediate secondary school, multiple school center) or grammar school, special school, vocational school with technical or business focus; qualitative description of different utilization types and quantitative description of the school utilization area in m² NEFA as well as its proportion per m² NEFA of the whole school property.

- Secondary utilization: Sports facilities such as gymnasiums or indoor swimming pools for teaching purposes, nursery school; qualitative and quantitative description of different utilization types with regard to their building reference areas e.g. the net floor area of a gymnasium or swimming pool utilization in m² and their representative proportions per m² NEFA.

*Standard of utilization:*

- Type of educational program: Regular school, extended regular school or full-day school.

- Type of canteen service: School based canteen, external catering or no canteen service.

*Intensity of utilization:*

- Temporal usage intensity:

  Average operating time of the whole school complex as well as individual operating times of both the primary and secondary utilizations, i.e. the school and its sports facilities, in hours per school week and with regard to the average number of schooldays per school week.

- Spatial usage intensity:

  - The total number of pupils, number of pupils per m² specific floor area according to DIN 277:2005-2 (Part 1 and 2) and the number of pupils with respect to other reference areas such as m² net floor area of school utilization e.g. the number of pupils per m² GROFA.

  - The total number of school classes, number of school classes per m² specific floor area according to DIN 277:2005-2 (Part 1 and 2) and number of school classes with respect to other reference areas such as m² net floor area of school utilization e.g. the number of school classes per m² GROFA.

**Factor group: Functional and technical characteristics**

*Functional characteristics:*

- Specific building floor areas according to DIN 277:2005-2 (Part 1 and 2) e.g. in m² GROFA, m² UFA, m² UFA 5 and their representative proportion to the total size of a property in m² GROFA or other specific building floor areas e.g. the share of UFA 5 per m² GROFA.

- The average storey height according to DIN 277-1: 2005-2.

- Standard of flooring: Qualitative and quantitative description of different flooring materials i.e. wood, stone, carpet or synthetic materials in m² flooring area and as a percentage of the whole flooring area according to DIN 277-3:2005-4.

- Standard of internal wall linings: Qualitative and quantitative description of different lining materials i.e. wood, ceramic, panels, paintwork or wallpaper in m² internal wall lining area and as a percentage of the whole internal wall lining area as defined by DIN 277-3:2005-4.

- Standard of ceiling and roof linings: Qualitative and quantitative description of different lining materials i.e. wood, wallpaper, panels, paintwork or plaster in m² ceiling and roof lining area and as a percentage of the whole ceiling and roof lining area according to DIN 277-3:2005-4.

*Technical characteristics:*

• Standard of building constructions:

  • Age of a school property

  • Standard of external claddings: Qualitative and quantitative description of different cladding materials i.e. wood, stone, concrete, plaster or panels in m² external cladding area and as a percentage of the whole external wall cladding area according to DIN 277-3:2005-4.

  • Glass area of external walls and roofs according to DIN 277-3:2005-4 and its share in percentage of specific building floor areas according to DIN 277:2005-2 (Part 1 and 2) e.g. the share of glass areas of external walls and roofs per m² GROFA.

• Condition of building constructions:

  Qualitative and quantitative description of the condition of building constructions and in particular the condition of single structural components according to DIN 276-1:2008-12 such as the condition of walls and ceilings, external glass areas or permanent fixtures e.g. the share of defective glass areas of external walls as a percentage of the whole glass area of external walls.

## 3.5.1.2 Model design and parameters

Based on the factors outlined in the preceding section, the statistical analysis of total costs for the inspection and maintenance of building constructions indicates causal interrelations between the predictor variables; the absolute sizes of the gross floor, and swimming pool utilization area ($X_1$ and $X_2$), the number of pupils per m² GROFA ($X_3$) and the total outlay during the calendar year in question (Y). The gross floor area is therefore deemed to be appropriate for forecasting and normalizing cost data, based on a 5% significance level.

The variable $X_3$ (number of pupils per m² GROFA) describes the spatial usage intensity of a school as a continuous variable that has an effect on the wear margin of building constructions, such as flooring and permanent fixtures, among other factors that impact on the outlay for maintenance of building constructions. Tab. 41 presents an overview of the variables and their statistical measures used in Model 8.A to estimate total costs for the inspection and maintenance of schools' building constructions. The tolerance and VIF values given in Tab. 41, reveal that there is no interrelation between the individual predictors (multicollinearity), so the predicted regression coefficients can be regarded as stable. The Durbin-Watson statistic, moreover shows, based on a value of 2.187, that there is no autocorrelation between the consecutive residuals of 125 school complexes forming the basis of this survey. As regards the confidence limits indicated for individual regression parameters, the estimation for the constant does not hold true at a significance level of 5%, but this can be disregarded.

Tab. 41:   Model description for estimating total costs for the inspection and maintenance of building constructions

| Dependent variable | Transf. | R² | R² adj. | SEE | F-value | Sign. | Durbin-Watson-Statistic | | N |
|---|---|---|---|---|---|---|---|---|---|
| Costs for the inspection and maintenance of building constructions (€ p.a.) | LN | 0.610 | 0.600 | 0.503 | 63.035 | 0.000 | 2.187 | | 125 |

| Factors | Transf. | B | St. Error | Beta | t-value | Sign. | Lower CL | Upper CL | T | VIF |
|---|---|---|---|---|---|---|---|---|---|---|
| Constant | LN | 0.422 | 0.655 | | 0.644 | 0.521 | -0.875 | 1.720 | | |
| Gross floor area (GROFA in m²) | LN | 0.935 | 0.071 | 0.755 | 13.116 | 0.000 | 0.794 | 1.076 | 0.974 | 1.026 |
| Swimming pool utilization area (m²) | - | 0.001 | 0.000 | 0.208 | 3.506 | 0.001 | 0.000 | 0.001 | 0.915 | 1.092 |
| Number of pupils per m² GROFA | - | 5.461 | 2.096 | 0.156 | 2.606 | 0.010 | 1.312 | 9.610 | 0.901 | 1.110 |

**Dependent variable:** Costs (€ p.a.), costs including VAT, based on 2008 figures

$$\hat{Y} = 1.525 \cdot X_1^{0.953} \cdot e^{0.001X_2} \cdot e^{5.461X_3} \qquad\qquad\qquad \text{(Model 8.A)}$$

Where:    $\hat{Y}$ :   Costs for the inspection and maintenance of building constructions (€ p.a.)

$X_1$ :   Gross floor area (GROFA in m²)

$X_2$ :   Swimming pool utilization area (NEFA of building sections in m²)

$X_3$ :   Number of pupils per m² GROFA

The estimation of the cost indicators for the inspection and maintenance of building constructions is based on the analysis of total costs, as set out below for the linear regression Model 8.B with R²=0235 and SEE=0.617. The normalization of cost indicators is conducted according to the total size of a school, measured in m² gross floor area, as defined in DIN 277-1:2005-1.

Based on Model 8.A, the estimation of cost indicators takes into account the continuous variables: number of pupils per m² GROFA, and the absolute size of both the swimming pool and gymnasium area, tested at a 5% significance level. The step-by-step developed model complies with all statistical assumptions of unbiased and efficient estimates. The statistical measures of Model 8.B are displayed in Tab. 42.

As opposed to Model 8.A, the regression Model 8.B, specified for cost indicators, also incorporates the gymnasium utilization area of a school as an independent variable. Because both types of sports facilities are included in the statistical model by way of two independent variables, with individual partial regression coefficients $b_j$, specific maintenance costs can be estimated and compared for different combinations of sports utilizations.

Both kinds of sports areas included in the model are measured as net floor area on the level of building-sections comprising original sports and adjacent areas. This reference area is particularly meaningful, as it not only covers the inspection and maintenance tasks connected with the sports facilities, like measures for fixed sports equipments and internal linings, but also those maintenance tasks connected with permanent fixtures like the cubicles in changing rooms or the tiled surfaces in showers, for example.

In total, Model 8.B shows that those of the 125 schools covered by the survey that have sports facilities and a large number of pupils per m² GROFA generally have higher maintenance costs per m² GROFA.

Tab. 42: Model description for estimating cost indicators for the inspection and maintenance of building constructions

| Dependent variable | Transf. | R² | R² adj. | SEE | F-value | Sign. | Durbin-Watson-Statistic | N |
|---|---|---|---|---|---|---|---|---|
| Costs for the inspection and maintenance of building constructions | - | 0.235 | 0.216 | 0.617 | 12.409 | 0.000 | 1.965 | 125 |

| Factors | Transf. | B | St. Error | Beta | t-value | Sign. | Lower CL | Upper CL | T | VIF |
|---|---|---|---|---|---|---|---|---|---|---|
| Constant | - | 0.558 | 0.184 | | 3.038 | 0.003 | 0.194 | 0.921 | | |
| Swimming pool utilization area (m²) | - | 0.002 | 0.000 | 0.410 | 4.931 | 0.000 | 0.001 | 0.002 | 0.914 | 1.094 |
| Number of pupils per m² GROFA | - | 9.100 | 2.582 | 0.293 | 3.524 | 0.001 | 3.988 | 14.212 | 0.914 | 1.095 |
| Gymnasium area (m²) | - | 1.784 | 0.628 | 0.226 | 2.840 | 0.005 | 0.540 | 3.027 | 0.998 | 1.002 |

Dependent variable: Costs (€/m² gross floor area p.a.), costs including VAT, based on 2008 figures

$$\hat{Y} = 0.558 + 0.002X_1 + 9.100X_2 + 1.784X_3 \quad\quad\quad\quad\quad\text{(Model 8.B)}$$

Where:  $\hat{Y}$ : Costs for inspection and maintenance of building constructions (€/m² GROFA p.a.)

$X_1$ : Swimming pool utilization area (NEFA of building sections in m²)

$X_2$ : Number of pupils per m² GROFA

$X_3$ : Area of gymnasium utilization (NEFA of building sections in m²)

*Summary*

The empirical investigation of the total costs for the inspection and maintenance of building constructions reveals that the absolute size of a school, in terms of the gross floor area, explains the greatest part of the variation in the overall costs for the 125 schools under investigation. Consequently, the gross floor area, as defined in DIN 277-1:2005-1, is identified as the appropriate reference area for cost estimates upon which the subsequent analysis of cost indicators is based. The following study of cost indicators in particular demonstrates that existing differences in costs are to a certain extent related to usage-related parameters and can therefore be explained according to the type and intensity of a school's utilization. The spatial intensity of a school is represented by the continuous variable $X_2$ (number of pupils per m² GROFA), and the differences existing in the type of school utilization are designated by both the total size of the swimming pool and gymnasium utilization area.

All variables considered within the multivariate analysis constitute a positive effect on the outlay for the inspection and maintenance of building constructions and reflect a higher level of wear and tear on building constructions on the one hand, as well as a higher degree of inspection and maintenance work required for schools with sports utilizations.

### 3.5.1.3  Validation of the model

The validation test conducted for cost indicators for the inspection and maintenance of building constructions is based on 5 randomly selected school complexes which had not been part of the previous model development process. The underlying cost indicators in €/m² GROFA p.a. include VAT and are based on 2008 figures. Tab. 43 gives an overview of the validation test conducted to compare percentage errors of the prediction Model 8.B with empirical mean and median values. Model 8.B reveals prediction errors ranging from 13% to 37% across all of the underlying schools with different types of utilization, whether they possess extra sports facilities, or not. On the whole, the regression model shows a considerable improvement (in the region of 11%) in the overall prediction reliability for analyzed cost indicators, based on a mean absolute percentage error of 24% and compared with empirical mean and median estimates. Based on these results, the specific cost indicators for the inspection and maintenance of building constructions are presented in the following section for different types of school utilization.

Tab. 43:   Model validation for cost indicators of the inspection and maintenance of building constructions

| No. | Type of school | Observed value | Predicted value | Absolute error % of prediction | Absolute error % of mean | Absolute error % of median | Preference |
|---|---|---|---|---|---|---|---|
| 1 | Elementary school without sports facilities | 2.67 | 1.67 | 37 | 49 | 53 | Prediction |
| 2 | Special school with gymnasium | 1.54 | 1.16 | 25 | 11 | 18 | Mean |
| 3 | Secondary school without sports facilities | 0.80 | 0.97 | 20 | 71 | 57 | Prediction |
| 4 | Secondary school with gymnasium and pool | 1.84 | 2.26 | 23 | 25 | 31 | Prediction |
| 5 | Vocational school without sports facilities | 1.12 | 0.98 | 13 | 23 | 12 | Median |
| Ø | Mean Absolute percentage error | | | 24 | 36 | 34 | Prediction |

Observed value: Costs (€/m² gross floor area p.a.), costs including VAT, based on 2008 figures, N=125

### 3.5.1.4  Cost indicators for the inspection and maintenance of building constructions

Based on sample data from 125 school complexes, the gross floor area, as defined in DIN 277-1:2005-1, is identified as the relevant reference area for defining cost indictors for the inspection and maintenance of building constructions (cf. Model 8.A). The cost indicators outlined in Tab. 44 refer to this building floor area and are given for different types of school usage. Particular reference is made to the predictor variables $X_1$ (swimming pool utilization area) and $X_3$ (gymnasium utilization area), incorporated in Model 8.B, because both variables have been statistically proved to account for a considerable percentage of the variation in cost indicators revealed by multivariate analysis. For the sake of simplicity, both variables are used to determine different categories of school utilization types, with or without sports facilities, designated below. This comparison between the empirical values described for schools with or without sports facilities reveals that schools with sports facilities generally have a higher outlay, with an average costs of 1.44 €/m² GROFA p.a. for the inspection and maintenance of building constructions. In addition, cost indicators are given for a subsample of 95 school complexes that include gymnasiums only. In contrast, it is not possible to allocate empirical measures on the basis of this survey for schools that only comprise swimming pools. More accurate cost predictions can be described by making use of the variable $X_2$ (number of pupils per m² GROFA) of Model 8.B, which allows the intensity of a school's utilization also taking into account.

Tab. 44:   Evaluated cost indicators for the inspection and maintenance of building constructions

| Factor level | Minimum | Mean | Median | Maximum | Range |
|---|---|---|---|---|---|
| Schools without sport facilities | 0.29 | 1.11 | 1.09 | 2.39 | 2.10 |
| Schools with sport facilities | 0.04 | 1.44 | 1.28 | 3.61 | 3.57 |
| Schools with gymnasiums | 0.04 | 1.38 | 1.27 | 3.45 | 3.41 |

Dependent variable: Costs ($€/m^2$ gross floor area p.a.), costs including VAT, based on 2008 figures, N=125

## 3.5.2    Inspection and maintenance of technical installations

### 3.5.2.1  Empirical and theoretical basis

With an average of 1.83 $€/m^2$ GROFA p.a. (costs including VAT, based on 2008 figures), the costs for the inspection and maintenance of technical installations represent the greatest share of the overall annual outlay for operation, inspection and maintenance examined for 125 public schools over the calendar year in question. The following factors have been compiled and form the basis for the statistical analysis:

**Factor group: Utilization**

*Type of utilization:*

•   Primary utilization: Elementary school, secondary school such as comprehensive school (secondary general school, intermediate secondary school, multiple school center) or grammar school, special school, vocational school with technical or business focus; qualitative description of different utilization types and quantitative description of the school utilization area in $m^2$ NEFA as well as its proportion per $m^2$ NEFA of the whole school property.

•   Secondary utilization: Sports facilities such as gymnasiums or indoor swimming pools for teaching purposes, nursery school; qualitative and quantitative description of different utilization types with regard to their building reference areas e.g. the net floor area of a gymnasium or swimming pool utilization in $m^2$ and their representative proportions per $m^2$ NEFA.

*Standard of utilization:*

•   Type of educational program: Regular school, extended regular school or full-day school.

•   Type of canteen service: School based canteen, external catering or no canteen service.

•   Total number of computer workstations.

*Intensity of utilization:*

•   Temporal usage intensity:

    Average operating time of the whole school complex as well as individual operating times of both the primary and secondary utilizations, i.e. the school and its sports facilities, in hours per school week and with regard to the average number of schooldays per school week.

- Spatial usage intensity:

  Qualitative and quantitative description of the spatial standard e.g. the total size of specific floor areas according to DIN 277:2005-2 (Part 1 and 2) in relation to the number of pupils or school classes as well as other reference areas such as m² net floor area of school utilization with respect to the number of pupils or school classes.

**Factor group: Functional and technical characteristics**

*Functional characteristics:*

- Specific building floor areas according to DIN 277:2005-2 (Part 1 and 2) e.g. in m² GROFA, m² NEFA, m² UFA, m² TEFA, m² UFA 5 and their representative proportion to the total size of a property in m² GROFA or other specific building floor areas e.g. the share of TEFA per m² NEFA.

- Total heatable gross floor area according to VDI 3807-01:2007-03 and its representative proportion to the total size of a property in m² GROFA according to DIN 277-1:2005-2.

- The total sanitary area and its proportion to specific building floor areas according to DIN 277:2005-2 (Part 1 and 2) e.g. the share of the sanitary area per m² UFA.

*Technical characteristics:*

- Standard of building constructions:

  - Age of a school property.

- Standard of technical installations:

  - Qualitative and quantitative description of the standard of technical installations and in particular the standard of water supply systems, heat generators and heating control systems e.g. the number of decentralized water heaters, heat generators including or excluding central water heaters.

  - Number of lifts and average number of lift-stops.

- Condition of technical installations:

  Qualitative and quantitative description of the condition of technical installations and in particular the condition of sewage systems, water supply systems, sanitary installations, heat supply systems or power installations e.g. the percentage of defective heat supply systems.

### 3.5.2.2 Model design and parameters

The statistical analysis of causal interrelationships existing between the factors outlined above and the total amount of annual costs for the inspection and maintenance of technical installations (Y) reveals significant effects arising from three predictive variables described in Model 9.A. Within the scope of the survey, this regression model displayed the best compliance with the underlying random sample of 125 school complexes and is therefore detailed below with reference to Tab. 45. The best model prediction is achieved by the two continuous variables $X_1$ (net floor area of a school complex) and $X_3$ (share of technical floor area per m² NEFA) and a distinction made between different types of school classified according to usage and described by the independent variable $X_2$. The categorical variable $X_2$ distinguishes between vocational schools and other school types (i.e. primary, special or secondary schools), generally indicating higher cost values for vocational schools with either a technical or a business focus. According to Model 9.A, the size of a school's net floor area ($X_1$) has a significant impact on Y and, in particular, with beta$_1$=0.714, largely accounts for the variation in total outlay. This area comprises the usable floor area, the technical floor area and the circulation area of a building, as defined in DIN 277-2:2005-2.

The significance of the technical floor area for estimating the costs incurred for inspecting and maintaining the technical installations is also expressed by the variable $X_3$, that defines the ratio of this area to the overall net floor area. The technical floor area of the schools under investigation not only covers the space taken up by the utility supply and waste disposal facilities but also the space occupied by such high-maintenance equipment as the air treatment systems, lifts or swimming facilities, for example (see DIN 277-2:2005-2). The ratio of the technical floor area to the overall net floor area can be regarded as an indicator for the degree of technology installed in the school concerned, which is depicted in the form of the quantitative variables $X_3$ in Model 9.A.

With R² of 0.802, MAPE of 30% and a standard error of estimate (SEE) of 0.360, the regression model outlined above allows reliable estimates and is taken as a basis for the following analysis of cost indicators for the inspection and maintenance of technical installations.

Tab. 45: Model description for estimating total costs for the inspection and maintenance of technical installations

| Dependent variable | Transf. | R² | R² adj. | SEE | F-value | Sign. | Durbin-Watson-Statistic | | N |
|---|---|---|---|---|---|---|---|---|---|
| Costs for the inspection and maintenance of technical installations | LN | 0.802 | 0.797 | 0.360 | 163.355 | 0.000 | 1.947 | | 125 |

| Factors | Transf. | B | St. Error | Beta | t-value | Sign. | Lower CL | Upper CL | T | VIF |
|---|---|---|---|---|---|---|---|---|---|---|
| Constant | LN | 1.137 | 0.497 | | 2.289 | 0.024 | 0.153 | 2.120 | | |
| Net floor area (NEFA in m²) | LN | 0.918 | 0.060 | 0.714 | 15.420 | 0.000 | 0.800 | 1.036 | 0.763 | 1.310 |
| Vocational schools | - | 0.685 | 0.108 | 0.279 | 6.347 | 0.000 | 0.471 | 0.898 | 0.844 | 1.185 |
| Share of the technical floor area per m² NEFA | - | 3.354 | 1.329 | 0.108 | 2.524 | 0.013 | 0.723 | 5.986 | 0.894 | 1.119 |

Dependent variable: Costs (€ p.a.), costs including VAT, based on 2008 figures

$$\hat{Y} = 3.117 \cdot X_1^{0.918} \cdot e^{0.685 X_2} \cdot e^{3.354 X_3}$$

(Model 9.A)

Where:    $\hat{Y}$ :   Costs for inspection and maintenance of technical installations (€ p.a.)

$X_1$ :   Net floor area (NEFA in m²)

$X_2$ :   Vocational schools (type of school)

$X_3$ :   Share of the technical floor area per m² NEFA

Tab. 46:   Model description for estimating cost indicators for the inspection and maintenance of technical installations

| Dependent variable | Transf. | R² | R² adj. | SEE | F-value | Sign. | Durbin-Watson-Statistic | | N |
|---|---|---|---|---|---|---|---|---|---|
| Costs for the inspection and maintenance of technical installations | - | 0.348 | 0.337 | 0.828 | 32.514 | 0.000 | 1.952 | | 125 |

| Factors | Transf. | B | St. Error | Beta | t-value | Sign. | Lower CL | Upper CL | T | VIF |
|---|---|---|---|---|---|---|---|---|---|---|
| Constant | - | 1.543 | 0.160 | | 9.617 | 0.000 | 1.225 | 1.860 | | |
| Vocational schools | - | 1.698 | 0.222 | 0.560 | 7.656 | 0.000 | 1.259 | 2.137 | 0.998 | 1.002 |
| Share of the technical floor area per m² NEFA | - | 6.473 | 2.914 | 0.163 | 2.221 | 0.028 | 0.704 | 12.243 | 0.998 | 1.002 |

**Dependent variable:** Costs (€/m² net floor area p.a.), costs including VAT, based on 2008 figures

$$\hat{Y} = 1.543 + 1.698 X_1 + 6.473 X_2 \qquad\qquad\qquad\qquad\text{(Model 9.B)}$$

Where:   $\hat{Y}$ :   Costs for the inspection and maintenance of technical installations (€/m² NEFA p.a.)

$X_1$ :   Vocational schools (type of school)

$X_2$ :   Share of the technical floor area per m² NEFA

A minimum outlay of 0.43 €/m² NEFA p.a. is observed for the inspection and maintenance of technical installations over the course of the calendar year in question and the maximum outlay is identified for a school with costs of 6.71 €/m² NEFA p.a. (costs including VAT, based on 2008 figures). In total, this defines an overall range of around 6.30 €/m² NEFA p.a. for the inspection and maintenance costs of the technical installations for the 125 schools forming the subject of this survey. The objective of the following statistical approach is to reduce the uncertainties in cost predictions associated with the variation in cost data under inspection and to draw up more precise cost estimates for practical planning purposes in lieu of predicting scores based on the aforementioned empirical values.

The investigation of cost indicators for the inspection and maintenance of technical installations is based on Model 9.A for estimating the total costs, by taking into account the key factors identified above. To begin with, the schools' net floor area is identified as being the appropriate building reference area for this analysis and is accordingly employed to normalize the underlying cost data. As with Model 9.A, the prediction model described for cost indicators (Model 9.B) refers to the same independent variables as outlined above. Again, a categorical distinction is made between vocational schools and other school types using the variable $X_2$ in the regression Model 9.B and the share of a school's technical floor area per m² NEFA is similarly incorporated as the predictor variable $X_3$.

The evaluation accordingly confirms that the same assumptions about causal interrelations that were outlined above for total cost estimates also apply to the prediction of cost indicators, at a significance level of 5%. On average, a higher outlay for the inspection and maintenance of technical installations is expected for vocational schools. In addition, the statistical analysis reveals that the variable $X_2$ has a positive effect on the annual costs, which means that the assumption the higher the share of a school's technical floor area per m² NEFA, the higher the inspection and maintenance costs for the technical installations, is borne out by the regression Model 9.B. Detailed information on coefficient estimates, their empirical significance tested at a level of 5% and their collinearity statistics are set out in

Tab. 46. In the context of the study, Model 9.B achieves a convincing goodness of fit with R²=0.348, SEE=0.828 and a MAPE of 35%.

*Summary*

Within the scope of the study, different models were developed for estimating the inspection and maintenance costs for technical installations in order to compare and evaluate their predictive accuracy. The models employed distinguish between vocational schools and other school types and take the proportion of a school's technical floor are per m² NEFA into account. In addition, the net floor area is defined by Model 9.A as being the appropriate building reference area to explain variation in Y and is subsequently taken as a basis for normalizing cost values. All independent variables considered for the purpose of estimating and forecasting costs describe a school's type of usage and its functional building characteristics. In contrast, the statistical analysis of 125 properties could not verify other potential influences related to differences in the standard of schools' technical installations, such as the standard of the heat generators or the heating control systems.

### 3.5.2.3  Validation of the model

The regression Model 9.B described above statistically proved to provide reliable estimates on cost indicators for the inspection and maintenance of technical installations based on sample data of 125 school complexes. The following validation test compares the forecasting efficiency of the regression Model 9.B with empirical mean and median estimates achieved by means of percentage errors for five validation properties. To this end, the model predictions refer to two aspects of the underlying five properties, i.e. the type of usage of a validated school and the ratio of the technical floor area per m² NEFA

Tab. 47:  Model validation for cost indicators of the inspection and maintenance of technical installations

| No. | Type of school | Observed value | Predicted value | Absolute error % of prediction | Absolute error % of mean | Absolute error % of median | Preference |
|---|---|---|---|---|---|---|---|
| 1 | Elementary school without sports facilities | 3.32 | 1.65 | 50 | **38** | 43 | Mean |
| 2 | Special school with gymnasium | 1.56 | 1.72 | **10** | 33 | 23 | **Prediction** |
| 3 | Secondary school without sports facilities | 2.42 | 2.16 | **11** | 14 | 21 | **Prediction** |
| 4 | Secondary school with gymnasium and pool | 3.51 | 1.75 | 50 | **41** | 46 | Mean |
| 5 | Vocational school without sports facilities | 4.98 | 3.55 | **29** | 58 | 62 | **Prediction** |
| Ø | **Mean Absolute percentage error** | | | **30** | 37 | 39 | **Prediction** |

**Observed value**: Costs (€/m² net floor area p.a.), costs including VAT, based on 2008 figures, N=125

Tab. 47 gives an overview of both the percentage errors for each individual estimation method and validated case, as well as for the mean absolute percentage error of a specific estimation approach. The underlying cost indicators in €/m² NEFA p.a. include VAT and are based on 2008 figures. Comparing the test results, and taking MAPE to be around 30% for the validation sample, the regression Model 9.B is shown to produce estimates that are about 7-9% more accurate by making use of the quantified factors described above. Based on this validation, specific cost indicators are presented in the following section with respect to evaluated factors of Model 9.B.

### 3.5.2.4  Cost indicators for the inspection and maintenance of technical installations

The trivariate regression Model 9.B identifies a substantial increase in the annual costs for the inspection and maintenance of technical installations per m² NEFA relating to vocational schools in contrast to other school types, as defined by the predictor variable $X_1$, and relating to the proportion of a school's technical floor area per m² NEFA based on the continuous variable $X_2$. Both variables were determined by means of a statistical approach based on a significance level of 5% and an underlying sample of 125 school complexes. In addition to continuous cost estimates, described in Section 3.5.2.2, specific cost indicators and their distribution are presented in Tab. 48 below for different categories of both variables $X_1$ and $X_2$. Based on the variable $X_1$, with $beta_1$ set at 0.560 in Model 9.B, the first differentiation in cost indicators is described by the type of school utilization. This is followed by a further sub-differentiation derived from the variable $X_2$ (share of the technical floor area per m² NEFA), whereby a simplified division is made according to values < 7% and ≥ 7% respectively. All cost values described are based on 2008 figures and include VAT. The corresponding indexing table for annual price adjustments is provided by Destatis (2011b).

Tab. 48:   Evaluated cost indicators for the inspection and maintenance of technical installations

| Factor level | Minimum | Mean | Median | Maximum | Range |
|---|---|---|---|---|---|
| **Vocational schools** | **1.32** | **3.57** | **3.23** | **6.71** | **5.38** |
| Share of the technical floor area per m² NEFA < 7% | 1.32 | 2.94 | 2.65 | 5.48 | 4.16 |
| Share of the technical floor area per m² NEFA ≥ 7% | 4.40 | 5.47 | 5.40 | 6.71 | 2.31 |
| **Other school types** | **0.43** | **1.85** | **1.81** | **4.13** | **3.71** |
| Share of the technical floor area per m² NEFA < 7% | 0.43 | 1.82 | 1.81 | 3.53 | 3.10 |
| Share of the technical floor area per m² NEFA ≥ 7% | 1.19 | 2.03 | 1.95 | 4.13 | 2.94 |

**Dependent variable:** Costs (€/m² net floor area p.a.), costs including VAT, based on 2008 figures, N=125

In comparing designated cost indicators for vocational schools with those indicators for other school types, and taking a mean value of 3.57 €/m² NEFA p.a. for vocational schools as a basis, an average extra annual outlay of 1.72 €/m² NEFA is indicated for these school types as opposed to other school types, such as elementary or secondary schools. As regards the underlying data sample, a maximum value of 6.71 €/m² NEFA p.a. is observed for a vocational school whose technical floor area per m² NEFA accounts for ≥ 7%, whereas a minimum cost value of 0.43 €/m² NEFA p.a. is described for a non-vocational school with a technical floor area per m² NEFA lower than 7%.

### 3.5.3    Inspection and maintenance of grounds and outdoor facilities

### 3.5.3.1 Empirical and theoretical basis

With regard to the cost postings available for the calendar year in question, the analysis of the inspection and maintenance of grounds and outdoor facilities is based on a sample of 114 school complexes, whose average outlay amounts to 0.29 €/m² GROFA p.a. (costs including VAT, based on 2008 figures). The following compilation provides an overview of the factors under investigation, which are regarded to exert an influence on the costs for the inspection and maintenance of grounds and outdoor facilities from a theoretical point of view.

**Factor group: Utilization**

*Type of utilization:*

• Primary and secondary utilization: Qualitative description of different utilization types such as elementary school, secondary school, special school, vocational school or nursery school.

*Standard of utilization:*

• Type of educational program: Regular school, extended regular school or full-day school.

*Intensity of utilization:*

• Temporal usage intensity:

• Average operating time of the whole school complex in hours per school week.

**Factor group: Functional and technical characteristics**

*Technical characteristics:*

• Standard of grounds and outdoor facilities:

  • Standard of grounds and outdoor facilities: Higher or lower standard.

  • The total size of property area in m².

  • The non-built up area of the plot in m² and designated sections of hard surfaces such as the school playground area or the sports area in m² and their representative proportions to the non-built up area of the plot (e.g. share of the school playground area per m² non-built up plot area).

• Condition of grounds and outdoor facilities:

  Qualitative description of the condition of grounds and outdoor facilities and in particular the condition of hard surfaces, outdoor constructions, permanent outdoor fixtures or green areas: Good or poor condition.

**Factor group: Location:**

- Region: Urban, suburban or rural.

- Topography: Flat or sloped.

### 3.5.3.2 Model design and parameters

The survey into the outlay for the inspection and maintenance of grounds and outdoor facilities is based on 114 school properties and takes numerous areas of the plot into account, such as the total size of a property area and the non-built up plot area, for example. Here, the latter reference area is defined as a specific part of the overall property in Section 2.2.2. An overview of all the plot surfaces that theoretically might be of relevance for the current investigation is shown above. Using a step-by-step approach for the assessment of different plot areas at a 5% significance level, Model 10.A defines the non-built up area as the appropriate reference area for efficient predictions into total costs. In addition, the regression model takes the proportion of outdoor sports areas per m² of the non-built up plot area into account, specified by the continuous variable $X_2$, and identifies, furthermore, a categorical classification between primary and special schools on the one hand, and other school types, such as secondary or vocational schools, on the other hand. According to Section 2.2.2, sports areas under investigation consist of hard surfaces such as gravel or asphalted sport fields, football pitches, tracks or basketball courts. In total, the statistical analysis ascribes a relevant part of the variation in overall costs to three independent variables. However, statistical measures shown in Tab. 49, i.e. $R^2=0.373$ and SEE=1.101, reveal that a certain level of uncertainty remains.

Tab. 49:  Model description for estimating total costs for the inspection and maintenance of grounds and outdoor facilities

| Dependent variable | Transf. | R² | R² adj. | SEE | F-value | Sign. | Durbin-Watson-Statistic | N |
|---|---|---|---|---|---|---|---|---|
| Costs for the inspection and maintenance of grounds and outdoor facilities | LN | 0.373 | 0.356 | 1.101 | 21.824 | 0.000 | 1.901 | 114 |

| Factors | Transf. | B | St. Error | Beta | t-value | Sign. | Lower CL | Upper CL | T | VIF |
|---|---|---|---|---|---|---|---|---|---|---|
| Constant | LN | 0.114 | 1.258 | | 0.090 | 0.928 | -2.380 | 2.607 | | |
| Non-built up plot area (m²) | LN | 0.763 | 0.130 | 0.469 | 5.887 | 0.000 | 0.506 | 1.020 | 0.897 | 1.115 |
| Share of outdoor sports areas per m² non-built up plot area | LN | 0.040 | 0.013 | 0.243 | 3.060 | 0.003 | 0.014 | 0.065 | 0.901 | 1.110 |
| Elementary schools or special schools | - | 0.674 | 0.222 | 0.237 | 3.032 | 0.003 | 0.234 | 1.115 | 0.934 | 1.071 |

**Dependent variable:** Costs (€ p.a.), costs including VAT, based on 2008 figures

$$\hat{Y} = 1.120 \cdot X_1^{0.763} \cdot X_2^{0.040} \cdot e^{0.674X_3} \qquad \text{(Model 10.A)}$$

Where:     $\hat{Y}$ :   Costs for the inspection and maintenance of grounds and outdoor facilities (€ p.a.)

$X_1$ :   Non-built up area of the plot (part of the property area in m²)

$X_2$ :   Share of outdoor sports areas per m² non-built up plot area

$X_3$ :   Elementary schools or special schools (type of school)

Tab. 50:   Model description for estimating cost indicators for the inspection and maintenance of grounds and outdoor
           facilities

| Dependent variable | Transf. | R² | R² adj. | SEE | F-value | Sign. | Durbin-Watson-Statistic | | N |
|---|---|---|---|---|---|---|---|---|---|
| Costs for the inspection and maintenance of grounds and outdoor facilities | LN | 0.211 | 0.190 | 1.087 | 9.831 | 0.000 | 1.926 | | 114 |

| Factors | Transf. | B | St. Error | Beta | t-value | Sign. | Lower CL | Upper CL | T | VIF |
|---|---|---|---|---|---|---|---|---|---|---|
| Constant | LN | -2.724 | 0.307 | | -8.865 | 0.000 | -3.333 | -2.115 | | |
| Elementary school or special schools | - | 0.813 | 0.216 | 0.324 | 3.770 | 0.000 | 0.386 | 1.241 | 0.968 | 1.034 |
| Share of outdoor sports areas per m² non-built up plot area | LN | 0.039 | 0.012 | 0.271 | 3.105 | 0.002 | 0.014 | 0.063 | 0.944 | 1.060 |
| Share of the school playground area per m² non-built up plot area | - | 1.317 | 0.525 | 0.218 | 2.511 | 0.014 | 0.277 | 2.357 | 0.951 | 1.052 |

**Dependent variable**: Costs (€/m² non-built plot area p.a.), costs including VAT, based on 2008 figures

$$\hat{Y} = 0.066 \cdot e^{0.813 X_1} \cdot X_2^{0.039} \cdot e^{1.317 X_3}$$         (Model 10.B)

Where:   $\hat{Y}$ :   Costs for inspection and maintenance of grounds and outdoor facilities (€ p.a.)

$X_1$ :   Elementary schools or special schools (type of school)

$X_2$ :   Share of outdoor sports areas per m² non-built up plot area

$X_3$ :   Share of the school playground area per m² non-built up plot area

The analysis of cost indicators for the inspection and maintenance of grounds and outdoor facilities set out below is based on Model 10.A described above for estimating total costs. Cost data (Y) is normalized according to the non-built up area of a school's plot. As with Model 10.A, the best estimates of cost indicators, described by Model 10.B, are achieved on the basis of the explanatory variables: the share of the sports area per m² non-built up plot area, and a classification of different school types, both of which have been previously identified by multivariate regression. In addition, the continuous variable $X_3$ (share of a school's playground area per m² non-built up plot area) is also incorporated in Model 10.B, determined to be statistically significant with an empirical significance level of 1.4% at an underlying 95%-confidence interval.

Summing up, the statistical evaluation shows firstly that the underlying cost indicators for the inspection and maintenance of grounds and outdoor facilities are dependent on the share of the sports area and the school playground area (both of which are hard surfaces). The outlay for maintaining the proportionate share of the non-built up plot area reserved for green areas is, by definition, not included in the cost group under investigation and therefore not taken into account within this analysis, as the cleaning and care of these areas are part of the cost group 340 according to DIN 18960:2008-2. Both models, moreover, verify the assumption that elementary and special schools generally have a higher annual outlay for the inspection and maintenance of the grounds and outdoor facilities, which can be explained by the higher standard of permanent outdoor fixtures for sports areas and school playgrounds, among other factors. This circumstance is depicted by the categorical variable $X_1$ in Model 10 B. With tolerance values between 0.944 and 0.968, and VIF scores ranging from 1.034 to 1.060 respectively, none of the model variables indicate a multicollinearity problem, so all three variables are used for forecasting purposes. Detailed information on the overall model as well as for individual coefficient estimates and their empirical significance tested at a 5% level are presented in Tab. 50. With $R^2$ of 0.211 and SEE of 1.087 uncertainties still remain when using the overall model for cost predictions.

*Summary*

As with the investigation of costs for the cleaning and care of grounds and outdoor schools' facilities, the statistical investigation described above for the respective inspection and maintenance costs reveals that the non-built up area of the plot has a significant influence on the annual outlay and is accordingly taken into consideration when defining cost indicators. The property area is defined as a specific part of the plot which is not overbuilt by buildings (cf. Section 2.2.2). The multivariate Model 10.B, introduced for estimating cost indicators, verifies that elementary and special schools generally have a higher outlay compared with other schools types and that the independent impacts of both the proportions of the sports and school playground areas per m² non-built area of the plot are taken into account. All independent variables used to estimate and forecast cost indicators derive from the type of school usage and the specific standard of its grounds and outdoor facilities. The analysis of 114 school complexes reveals that these variables explain a major part of the variation in annual costs for the inspection and maintenance of school grounds and outdoor facilities. Other theoretical assumptions such as the impact exerted by the condition of hard surfaces, outdoor constructions or permanent outdoor fixtures could not me confirmed by regression analysis.

### 3.5.3.3  Validation of the model

The estimation model for cost indicators for the inspection and maintenance of grounds and outdoor school facilities (Model 10.B) takes the proportion of both the relevant school's sports and playground areas per m² of non-built up plot area into account, and verifies substantial differences in the annual outlay for elementary and special schools, in contrast to other school types. Based on these model specifications, the predictive accuracy of Model 10.B is compared with empirical mean and median values based on percentage errors set out below.

The lower number of cost postings that were available for the statistical data evaluation presented above also makes itself felt in the validation test described in this section. The number of cases analyzed by this test is limited to 3 schools because there are no entries available for two out of five validation properties. The mean absolute percentage error of the prediction Model 10.B amounting to roughly 78% reflects existing inaccuracies in prediction and is evidence of the uncertainties that occur when using the prediction model, as mentioned in Section 3.5.3.2. By comparison, with a MAPE of around 297% for the mean estimates and a MAPE of 190% for the median estimates that were carried out, the prediction described by the regression Model 10.B is nevertheless preferable to the empirical estimates. Similar to the variable $X_1$ of the regression model, sample No.1 (an elementary school without sports facilities) and sample No.2 (a special school with gymnasium) both reveal a higher outlay in costs. The model prediction for sample No.1 shows an excellent goodness of fit with the observed cost indicator of 0.14 €/m² non-built up plot area p.a., which lowers the overall MAPE relating to the 3 validation schools under analysis (costs including VAT, based on 2008 figures). Based on these test results, the estimation Model 10.B, introduced in the preceding section, for forecasting cost indicators for the inspection and maintenance of grounds and outdoor school facilities, is taken as a basis for providing cost indicators.

Tab. 51:   Model validation for cost indicators of the inspection and maintenance of grounds and outdoor facilities

| No. | Type of school | Observed value | Predicted value | Absolute error % of prediction | Absolute error % of mean | Absolute error % of median | Preference |
|-----|----------------|----------------|-----------------|-------------------------------|--------------------------|----------------------------|------------|
| 1 | Elementary school without sports facilities | 0.14 | 0.15 | 4 | 32 | 14 | Prediction |
| 2 | Special school with gymnasium | 0.28 | 0.09 | 70 | 34 | 57 | Mean |
| 3 | Secondary school without sports facilities | 0.02 | 0.05 | 161 | 825 | 500 | Prediction |
| 4 | Secondary school with gymnasium and pool | - | - | - | - | - | - |
| 5 | Vocational school without sports facilities | - | - | - | - | - | - |
| Ø | Mean Absolute percentage error | | | 78 | 297 | 190 | Prediction |

Observed value: Costs (€/m² non built up plot area p.a.), costs including VAT, based on 2008 figures, N=114

### 3.5.3.4  Cost indicators for the inspection and maintenance of grounds and outdoor facilities

The multivariate Model 10.B identifies substantial differences in the annual outlay for inspecting and maintaining grounds and outdoor schools' facilities per m² non-built up plot area (Y) with regard to three predictor variables based on sample data from 114 school properties. With standardized partial regression coefficients of $beta_1=0.324$ and $beta_2=0.271$ respectively, the type of school utilization specified by the categorical variable $X_1$, and the proportion of the sports area per m² non-built up plot area ($X_2$), exert the greatest effects on Y within the specified regression model. The following presentation of cost indicators refers to this evaluation of relevant factors impacting on Y by taking into account different categories for each of the two predictor variables presented in Tab. 52.

The comparison between the empirical mean values of elementary and special schools with other school types, such as secondary or vocational schools, reveals that the former have an extra annual outlay of almost 0.10 €/m² non-built up plot area, based on an average of 0.24 €/m² non-built up plot area p.a. (costs including VAT, based on 2008 figures).

However, the overall distribution of all the cost indicators depicted below cannot be completely explained using the designated categories. So the cost indicator of 1.29 €/m² non-built up plot area, which is high in relation to the overall sample data, is probably due to other causes that are unrelated to the predictions made by Model 10.B. Due to the relatively small proportion of the outlay (1% of the overall operating costs), less significance is attached to this cost group in general and the level of accuracy achieved for the inspection and maintenance costs of school grounds and outdoor facilities can be assessed as good/sufficient.

Tab. 52:   Evaluated cost indicators for the inspection and maintenance of grounds and outdoor facilities

| Factor level | Minimum | Mean | Median | Maximum | Range |
|---|---|---|---|---|---|
| **Elementary schools or special schools** | **0.05** | **0.24** | **0.16** | **0.92** | **0.87** |
| Schools with outdoor sports areas | 0.05 | 0.31 | 0.20 | 0.92 | 0.87 |
| Schools without outdoor sports areas | 0.05 | 0.19 | 0.14 | 0.78 | 0.73 |
| **Other school types** | **0.00** | **0.15** | **0.09** | **1.29** | **1.29** |
| Schools with outdoor sports areas | 0.01 | 0.15 | 0.12 | 0.72 | 0.71 |
| Schools without outdoor sports areas | 0.00 | 0.15 | 0.08 | 1.29 | 1.29 |

**Dependent variable:** Costs (€/m² non built up plot area p.a.), costs including VAT, based on 2008 figures, N=114

## 3.5.4    Inspection and maintenance of fittings, furnishings and equipment

### 3.5.4.1  Empirical and theoretical basis

The outlay for inspection and maintenance of fittings, furnishings and equipment represents the lowest cost block for the overall operation, inspection and maintenance costs, with a mean value of 0.14 €/m² GROFA p.a. (costs including VAT, based on 2008 figures), as investigated for an underlying data sample of 100 school complexes within the calendar year in question. The statistical analysis is based on the following factors describing different types, standards and intensities of school utilization, as well as functional characteristics of school buildings, and technical features of fittings, furnishings and equipment:

**Factor group: Utilization**

*Type of utilization:*

- Primary utilization: Elementary school, secondary school such as comprehensive school (secondary general school, intermediate secondary school, multiple school center) or grammar school, special school, vocational school with technical or business focus; qualitative description of different utilization types and quantitative description of the school utilization area in m² NEFA as well as its proportion per m² NEFA of the whole school property.

- Secondary utilization: Sports facilities such as gymnasiums or indoor swimming pools for teaching purposes, nursery school; qualitative and quantitative description of different utilization types with regard to their building reference areas e.g. the net floor area of a gymnasium or swimming pool utilization in m² and their representative proportions per m² UFA.

*Standard of utilization:*

- Type of educational program: Regular school, extended regular school or full-day school.

*Intensity of utilization:*

- Temporal usage intensity:

  Average operating time of the whole school complex as well as individual operating times of both the primary and secondary utilizations, i.e. the school and its sports facilities, in hours per school week and with regard to the average number of schooldays per school week.

- Spatial usage intensity:

  - The total number of pupils, number of pupils per m² specific floor area according to DIN 277:2005-2 (Part 1 and 2) and the number of pupils with respect to other reference areas such as m² net floor area of school utilization e.g. the number of pupils per m² GROFA.

  - The total number of school classes, number of school classes per m² specific floor area according to DIN 277:2005-2 (Part 1 and 2) and number of school classes with respect to other reference areas such as m² net floor area of school utilization e.g. the number of school classes per m² GROFA.

**Factor group: Functional and technical characteristics**

*Functional characteristics:*

- Specific building floor areas according to DIN 277:2005-2 (Part 1 and 2) e.g. in m² NEFA, m² UFA, m² UFA 5 and their representative proportion to the total size of a property in m² GROFA or other specific building floor areas e.g. the share of UFA 5 per m² UFA.

*Technical characteristics:*

- Standard of fittings, furnishings and equipment: Higher or lower standard.
- Condition of fittings, furnishings and equipment: Good or poor condition.

**3.5.4.2  Model design and parameters**

Similar to the evaluation of the costs for the inspection and maintenance of school grounds and outdoor facilities, the analysis into the outlay for schools' fittings, furnishings and equipment set out below is likewise based on a small number of cost postings for 100 school complexes, which accounts for a comparatively low percentage of the overall operating costs, which average 0.14 €/m² GROFA p.a. (costs including VAT, based on 2008 figures). The underlying factors for the statistical analysis of total costs (Y) are described above. The investigation of significant factors impacting on Y at a 5% significance level names the usable floor area, as defined by DIN 277-1:2005-2, as being relevant for efficient estimates of the total costs. In addition to this building floor area, Model 11.A, introduced in this section for forecasting the total annual outlay for schools, includes two proportionate areas in terms of continuous variables. These include the proportion of the floor area used for education, teaching and culture (UFA 5) per m² UFA ($X_3$ with $beta_3$=0.337), and the share of a the gym utilization are, in cases where a gymnasium is available, per m² of the overall school's usable floor area (UFA), $X_1$ with $beta_1=0.216$ (see Tab. 53). Here, the size of the gym corresponds to the net floor area on the level of building sections and comprises the space for physical education plus the the the space for sanitary and changing rooms etc. belonging to the gym hall. In total, the regression Model 11.A incorporates with its two continuous variables $X_1$ and $X_3$ the relevant areas of a school complex used for education and sports purposes respectively and therefore makes use of these functional characteristics to estimate the outlay for the inspection and maintenance of fittings, furnishings and equipment.

Tab. 53: Model description for estimating total costs for the inspection and maintenance of fittings, furnishings and equipment

| Dependent variable | Transf. | R² | R² adj. | SEE | F-value | Sign. | Durbin-Watson-Statistic | N |
|---|---|---|---|---|---|---|---|---|
| Costs for the inspection and maintenance of fittings, furnishings and equipment | LN | 0.206 | 0.181 | 1.163 | 8.316 | 0.000 | 1.950 | 100 |

| Factors | Transf. | B | St. Error | Beta | t-value | Sign. | Lower CL | Upper CL | T | VIF |
|---|---|---|---|---|---|---|---|---|---|---|
| Constant | LN | -0.456 | 1.853 | | -0.246 | 0.806 | -4.133 | 3.222 | | |
| Share of the gymnasium area per m² UFA | - | 2.148 | 0.929 | 0.216 | 2.313 | 0.023 | 0.305 | 3.991 | 0.952 | 1.050 |
| Usable floor area (UFA in m²) | LN | 0.900 | 0.232 | 0.395 | 3.874 | 0.000 | 0.439 | 1.361 | 0.795 | 1.259 |
| Share of UFA 5 per m² UFA | LN | 2.416 | 0.743 | 0.337 | 3.253 | 0.002 | 0.942 | 3.890 | 0.769 | 1.301 |

**Dependent variable:** Costs (€ p.a.), costs including VAT, based on 2008 figures

$$\hat{Y} = 0.634 \cdot e^{2.148 X_1} \cdot X_2^{0.900} \cdot X_3^{2.416} \qquad \text{(Model 11.A)}$$

Where:   $\hat{Y}$ :   Costs for the inspection and maintenance of fittings, furnishings and equipment (€ p.a.)

   $X_1$ :   Share of gymnasium area per m² UFA

   $X_2$ :   Usable floor area (UFA in m²)

   $X_3$ :   Share of the usable floor area for education, teaching and culture (UFA 5) per m² UFA

The estimation of cost indicators for the inspection and maintenance of fittings, furnishings and equipment is based on the analysis of total costs outlined above. Reference is made to regression Model 11.A by normalizing cost data with respect to a school's usable floor area. The best model prediction of cost indicators, where $R^2=0.207$ and SEE=1.157, is provided by Model 11.B based on sample data from 100 school complexes (see Tab. 54). The analyses verifies significant correlations between Y and the share of the usable floor area for education, teaching and culture (UFA 5) per m² UFA ($X_1$), and the share of the gym hall utilization area calculated as the net floor area for physical education and sports at the level of building sections per m² UFA ($X_2$) respectively.

The regression Model 11.B accordingly confirms the assumptions postulated for the relevant model parameters, such as those already included in the multivariate Model 11.A. The best goodness of fit between the actual outlay for the inspection and maintenance of fittings, furnishings and equipment and the estimated cost indicators is achieved when the area of the gym hall ($beta_1=0.357$) and the proportionate share of the usable floor area for education, teaching and culture of a school complex ($beta_2=0.216$) are taken into account.

Therefore, the estimation model covers those parts of the building complex that largely account for a school's overall outlay for the inspection and maintenance of fittings, furnishings and equipment, such as the general furnishings of classrooms and changing rooms, or special fittings indented for a school's class or sports education, as specified in cost group 610 of DIN 276-1:2008-12. However, with $R^2$ set at 0.207, the regression Model 11.B explains just a relatively small proportion of the total variation in the cost indicators under investigation and still reveals uncertainties associated with the cost estimates described in this section.

Tab. 54:   Model description for estimating cost indicators for the inspection and maintenance of fittings, furnishings and equipment

| Dependent variable | Transf. | $R^2$ | $R^2$ adj. | SEE | F-value | Sign. | Durbin-Watson-Statistic | | N |
|---|---|---|---|---|---|---|---|---|---|
| Costs for the inspection and maintenance of fittings, furnishings and equipment | LN | 0.207 | 0.191 | 1.157 | 12.699 | 0.000 | 1.958 | | 100 |

| Factors | Transf. | B | St. Error | Beta | t-value | Sign. | Lower CL | Upper CL | T | VIF |
|---|---|---|---|---|---|---|---|---|---|---|
| Constant | LN | -1.226 | 0.457 | | -2.681 | 0.009 | -2.133 | -0.318 | | |
| Share of UFA 5 per m² UFA | LN | 2.557 | 0.664 | 0.357 | 3.851 | 0.000 | 1.239 | 3.874 | 0.953 | 1.049 |
| Share of the gymnasium area per m² UFA | - | 2.160 | 0.924 | 0.216 | 2.338 | 0.021 | 0.326 | 3.994 | 0.953 | 1.049 |

**Dependent variable:** Costs (€/m² usable floor area p.a.), costs including VAT, based on 2008 figures

$$\hat{Y} = 0.293 \cdot X_1^{2.557} \cdot e^{2.160 X_2}$$                                    (Model 11.B)

Where:      $\hat{Y}$ :   Costs for the inspection and maintenance of fittings, furnishings and equipment (€/m² UFA p.a.)

$X_1$ :   Share of the usable floor area for education, teaching and culture (UFA 5) per m² UFA

$X_2$ :   Share of the gymnasium area (NEFA of building sections) per m² UFA

*Summary*

The preceding investigation of total costs for the inspection and maintenance of fittings, furnishings and equipment identifies the usable floor area as being relevant to analyze and compare cost indicators. According to DIN 277-2:2005-2, this floor area does not include either the technical floor or circulation area of a building. Based on a sample of 100 school complexes, the statistical analysis shows that the best estimates of cost indicators can be conducted by means of two continuous variables: the share of the usable floor area for education, teaching and culture (UFA 5) per m² UFA, and the proportionate area of the gymnasium per m² UFA. The gym area is measured as the net floor area of a school sports unit also comprising the changing rooms, showers and toilets. The analysis of costs for the inspection and maintenance of fittings, furnishings and equipment indicates that significant differences in the annual outlay are directly related to two factor groups; the functional building characteristics and the scope of usages within a school complex, and the influence of both aspects should be taken into account in any school benchmarking process.

### 3.5.4.3  Validation of the model

Tab. 55 gives an overview of the validation test performed to compare percentage errors of the trivariate prediction Model 11.B, with mean and median values of the empirical sample data from 100 schools. The underlying cost indicators in €/m² UFA p.a. include VAT and are based on 2008 figures. As with the model development process, there are fewer cost postings available for the validation test. No records were available for two of the five validation properties, so the practical test presented below had to be restricted to just three schools. In total, the regression model yields much better forecasting results for the three validated schools with sports facilities than the empirical estimates by mean and median (cf. MAPE for each estimation method in Tab. 55). The statistical model achieves a higher level of prediction accuracy across all 3 validated schools because it takes additional information into account relating to both the functional building characteristics, specified by the predictor variable $X_1$ in Model 11.B, and in particular regarding a quantification of the gym hall utilization area per m² UFA ($X_2$). Based on these test results, specific cost indicators are subsequently presented for different categories of significant factors described above.

Tab. 55:   Model validation for cost indicators of the inspection and maintenance of fittings, furnishings and equipment

| No. | Type of school | Observed value | Predicted value | Absolute error % of prediction | Absolute error % of mean | Absolute error % of median | Preference |
|-----|----------------|----------------|-----------------|-------------------------------|--------------------------|----------------------------|------------|
| 1 | Elementary school without sports facilities | - | - | - | - | - | - |
| 2 | Special school with gymnasium | 0.06 | 0.14 | **123** | 262 | 130 | **Prediction** |
| 3 | Secondary school without sports facilities | - | - | - | - | - | - |
| 4 | Secondary school with gymnasium and pool | 0.20 | 0.17 | **12** | 17 | 26 | **Prediction** |
| 5 | Vocational school without sports facilities | 0.01 | 0.02 | **133** | 2186 | 1348 | **Prediction** |
| Ø | **Mean Absolute percentage error** | | | 89 | 822 | 501 | **Prediction** |

Observed value: Costs (€/m² usable floor area p.a.), costs including VAT, based on 2008 figures, N=100

### 3.5.4.4  Cost indicators for the inspection and maintenance of fittings, furnishings and equipment

The statistical analysis of cost indicators for the inspection and maintenance of fittings, furnishings and equipment (Y) identifies two continuous variables that both serve to explain a relevant part of the variation in Y. According to the trivariate regression Model 11.B, these variables are the proportion of the usable floor area designated for education, teaching and culture (UFA 5) per m² UFA ($X_1$ with $beta_1$=0.357), and the area of a school's gym facilities per m² UFA ($X_2$ with $beta_2$=0.216). In this case, the gymnasium utilization area is calculated as the net floor area of a property reserved for physical education also including the changing rooms, showers and restrooms. The cost indicators presented in Tab. 56 refer to both variables, the cost data being classified for schools with or without a gym hall ($X_1$) on the one hand, and for schools with a share of UFA 5 per m² UFA ($X_2$) that is higher or lower than a threshold value of 60%, on the other. As regards the underlying data sample of 100 school complexes, this threshold value is determined in accordance with an empirical median of 62%, where a minimum of 32% and a maximum value of 87% is observed for $X_2$.

Differentiating between the scope of utilization types within a school complex, Tab. 56 shows that the mean value for schools without gymnasiums (0.15 €/m² UFA p.a.) is about 0.10 €/m² UFA p.a. lower than the average cost indicator for schools with gym facilities. Within the calendar year in question, a mean value of 0.04 €/m² UFA p.a.is recorded for schools without a gym and a share of UFA 5 per m² UFA lower than 60%, and an average cost indicator of 0.29 €/m² UFA p.a. is declared for schools with gymnasiums and a share of UFA 5 per m² UFA that is higher than 60% (costs including VAT, based on 2008 figures).

Tab. 56:   Evaluated cost indicators for the inspection and maintenance of fittings, furnishings and equipment

| Factor level | Minimum | Mean | Median | Maximum | Range |
|---|---|---|---|---|---|
| **Schools without gymnasiums** | **0.00** | **0.15** | **0.03** | **0.69** | **0.69** |
| Share of UFA 5 per m² UFA < 60% | 0.00 | 0.04 | 0.01 | 0.17 | 0.17 |
| Share of UFA 5 per m² UFA ≥ 60% | 0.02 | 0.28 | 0.14 | 0.69 | 0.67 |
| **Schools with gymnasiums** | **0.01** | **0.24** | **0.16** | **2.21** | **2.20** |
| Share of UFA 5 per m² UFA < 60% | 0.01 | 0.17 | 0.12 | 0.56 | 0.55 |
| Share of UFA 5 per m² UFA ≥ 60% | 0.01 | 0.29 | 0.22 | 2.21 | 2.20 |

**Dependent variable:** Costs (€/m² usable floor area p.a.), costs including VAT, based on 2008 figures, N=100

## 3.5.5    Aggregate operation, inspection and maintenance costs

### 3.5.5.1  Empirical and theoretical basis

The empirical investigation of costs for the operation, inspection and maintenance (cost group 350 according to DIN 18960:2008-2) is based on 105 schools in Germany and takes the aggregate amount of inspection and maintenance costs incurred for building constructions, technical installations, grounds and outdoor facilities, as well as for fittings, furnishings and equipment into account (cost groups 352 to 355 as defined by DIN 18960:2008-2). The empirical distribution of underlying cost data with reference to the calendar year 2008 is shown in Appendix C.

The multivariate analysis incorporates those variables that are deemed to explain a substantial part of the variation in the individual cost groups 352 to 355, at a 5% significance level, while simultaneously investigating the independent impact of other variables that either result from the ratio of identified factors and building reference areas in Sections 3.5.1 to 3.5.4, such as the share of the non-built up area of a plot per m² NEFA, or which are additionally defined by secondary literature and interviews with experts as relevant factors impacting on the level of wear and tear of buildings from a theoretical perspective. Among other factors, the temporal usage intensity, in terms of the average operating time of a property (in hours per school week), or the standard of technical installations, such as the standard of heat generators, heating control systems or the number of lifts, are found to be appropriate for examining the variation in the annual outlay considered here (cf. BMI 2003, p.9 or Naber 2002, p.155 et seq.).

### 3.5.5.2 Model design and parameters

Within the sample under investigation, the costs for the inspection and maintenance of technical installations account for the biggest proportion and variation of the overall operation, inspection and maintenance costs, with an average of 16,522 € p.a. and a standard deviation of 18,675 (costs including VAT, based on 2008 figures). According to the analysis of total costs for the inspection and maintenance of technical installations depicted by Model 9.A, the net floor area is also identified as the appropriate building reference area for the overall cost estimates set out below. Model 12.A presents the results of the step-by-step analysis conducted to statistically examine the annual outlay for the operation, inspection and maintenance of schools. A comparison between the observed and predicted costs for aggregate operation, inspection and maintenance is visualized in Fig. 7.

Tab. 57:   Model description for estimating total costs for aggregate operation, inspection and maintenance

| Dependent variable | Transf. | $R^2$ | $R^2$ adj. | SEE | F-value | Sign. | Durbin-Watson-Statistic | | N |
|---|---|---|---|---|---|---|---|---|---|
| Costs for the operation, inspection and maintenance (€ p.a.) | LN | 0.883 | 0.877 | 0.263 | 149.536 | 0.000 | 1.942 | | 105 |

| Factors | Transf. | B | St. Error | Beta | t-value | Sign. | Lower CL | Upper CL | T | VIF |
|---|---|---|---|---|---|---|---|---|---|---|
| Constant | LN | 0.750 | 0.436 | | 1.719 | 0.089 | -0.116 | 1.615 | | |
| Net floor area (NEFA in m²) | LN | 1.030 | 0.047 | 0.858 | 21.848 | 0.000 | 0.936 | 1.123 | 0.765 | 1.307 |
| Vocational schools | - | 0.452 | 0.087 | 0.206 | 5.186 | 0.000 | 0.279 | 0.625 | 0.751 | 1.332 |
| Swimming pool utilization area (m²) | - | 0.001 | 0.000 | 0.165 | 4.474 | 0.000 | 0.000 | 0.001 | 0.870 | 1.149 |
| Number of pupils per m² NEFA | - | 2.987 | 1.170 | 0.097 | 2.552 | 0.012 | 0.665 | 5.310 | 0.819 | 1.221 |
| Share of the non-built up plot area per m² NEFA | LN | 0.078 | 0.037 | 0.077 | 2.102 | 0.038 | 0.004 | 0.152 | 0.871 | 1.148 |

**Dependent variable:** Costs for the operation, inspection and maintenance (€ p.a.), costs including VAT, based on 2008 figures

$$\hat{Y} = 2.117 \cdot X_1^{1.030} \cdot e^{0.452 X_2} \cdot e^{0.001 X_3} \cdot e^{2.987 X_4} \cdot X_5^{0.078}$$   (Model 12.A)

Where:   $\hat{Y}$ :   Aggregate costs for operation, inspection and maintenance (€ p.a.)

$X_1$ :   Net floor area (NEFA in m²)

$X_2$ :   Vocational schools (type of school)

$X_3$ :   Swimming pool utilization area (NEFA of building sections in m²)

$X_4$ :   Number of pupils per m² NEFA

$X_5$ :   Share of the non-built up plot area on per m² NEFA

Besides the impact of the net floor area, other factors are identified within the scope of the study that also affect the overall costs, describing a categorical distinction between vocational schools and other school types (i.e. elementary, secondary or special schools) in conjunction with three continuous variables: the size of a school's swimming pool utilization area measured as net floor area at the level of building sections ($X_2$), the number of pupils per m² NEFA ($X_3$) and the share of the non-built up plot area per m² NEFA ($X_4$). Tab. 57 gives an overview of the variables incorporated in Model 12.A and their statistical measures.

All variables considered within the multivariate regression Model 12.A have already been taken into account in earlier investigations into the individual costs for the inspection and maintenance of the building constructions, technical installations or grounds and outdoor facilities (cf. Sections 3.5.1 to 3.5.4).

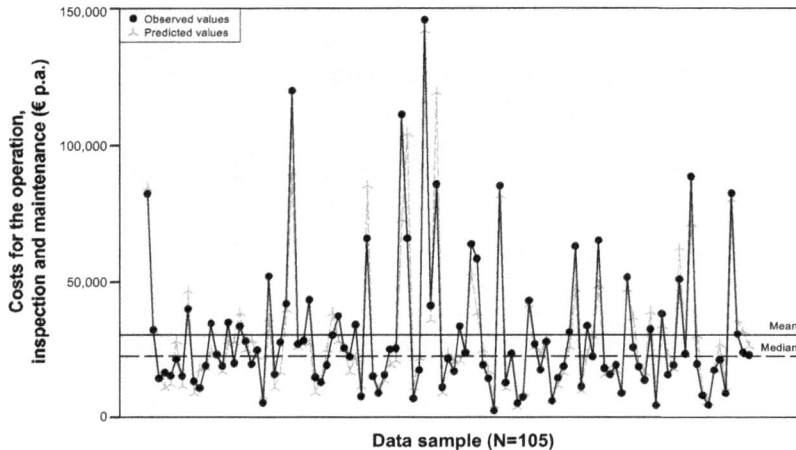

Fig. 7:     Comparison between observed and predicted costs for aggregate operation,
            inspection and maintenance (costs including VAT, based on 2008 figures)

The following investigation into the indicators [32] for aggregate operation, inspection and maintenance costs is based on Model 12.A and mainly considers the same independent variables used to predict total costs. In reference to Model 8.B for estimating cost indicators for the inspection and maintenance of building constructions, the swimming pool utilization area ($X_2$ with $beta_2=0.439$) and the number of pupils per m² NEFA ($X_4$ with $beta_4=0.176$) are taken into account for estimating overall cost indicators. In accordance with Model 9.B, for estimating cost indicators for the inspection and maintenance of technical installations, a distinction between the respective outlay for vocational schools and other types of school is identified and represented by the categorical variable $X_1$ ($beta_1=0.546$), whereby higher cost values generally being described for vocational schools. In addition, the predictor variable $X_3$, defined as the non-built up plot area in proportion to the net floor area, is incorporated in the multivariate regression Model 12.B ($beta_3=0.203$). The analysis of the inspection and maintenance costs for grounds and outdoor facilities already identified the non-built up area of a school's plot as a relevant factor to explain variation in costs and normalize the respective cost data of grounds and outdoor facilities. According to the investigation of individual inspection and maintenance costs, the analysis of aggregate cost also refers to this specific part of a school's property area.

---

[32] The net floor area is used to normalize the dependent variable Y (€/m² NEFA p.a., costs including VAT, based on 2008 figures).

Tab. 58 shows the partial regression coefficients $b_j$ used for estimating cost indicators for the overall inspection and maintenance of schools, together with the statistical measures for each variable $X_1$ to $X_4$. With $R^2$ =0.402, SEE=1.042 and a mean absolute percentage error (MAPE) of 22%, the regression model verifies an adequate compliance with the underlying sample of 105 schools. The specified model complies with all statistical assumptions of unbiased and efficient estimates and displays consistent predictions in Fig. 8.

Tab. 58:  Model description for estimating cost indicators for aggregate operation, inspection and maintenance

| Dependent variable | Transf. | $R^2$ | $R^2$ adj. | SEE | F-value | Sign. | Durbin-Watson-Statistic | | N |
|---|---|---|---|---|---|---|---|---|---|
| Costs for the operation, inspection and maintenance (€/m² NEFA p.a.) | - | 0.402 | 0.378 | 1.042 | 16.817 | 0.000 | 1.937 | | 105 |

| Factors | Transf. | B | St. Error | Beta | t-value | Sign. | Lower CL | Upper CL | T | VIF |
|---|---|---|---|---|---|---|---|---|---|---|
| Constant | - | 2.745 | 0.320 | | 8.580 | 0.000 | 2.110 | 3.380 | | |
| Vocational school | - | 2.110 | 0.320 | 0.546 | 6.587 | 0.000 | 1.474 | 2.745 | 0.871 | 1.147 |
| Swimming pool utilization area (m²) | - | 0.003 | 0.001 | 0.439 | 5.335 | 0.000 | 0.002 | 0.004 | 0.881 | 1.134 |
| Share of the non-built up plot area per m² NEFA | LN | 0.359 | 0.147 | 0.203 | 2.448 | 0.016 | 0.068 | 0.650 | 0.871 | 1.148 |
| Number of pupils per m² NEFA | - | 9.367 | 4.376 | 0.176 | 2.140 | 0.035 | 0.684 | 18.049 | 0.888 | 1.126 |

**Dependent variable:** Costs for the operation, inspection and maintenance (€/m² NEFA p.a.), costs including VAT, based on 2008 figures

$$\hat{Y} = 2.745 + 2.110X_1 + 0.003X_2 + 0.359\ln\left(X_3\right) + 9.367X_4 \qquad\qquad \text{(Model 12.B)}$$

Where:  $\hat{Y}$ :  *Aggregate cost indicators for operation, inspection and maintenance (€/m² NEFA p.a.)*

$X_1$ :  *Vocational schools (type of school)*

$X_2$ :  *Swimming pool utilization area (NEFA of building sections in m²)*

$X_3$ :  *Share of the non-built up plot area on per m² NEFA*

$X_4$ :  *Number of pupils per m² NEFA*

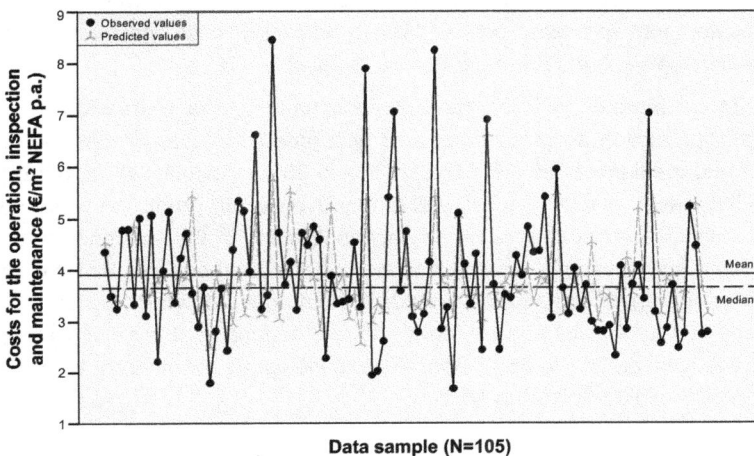

Fig. 8:  Comparison between observed and predicted cost indicators for aggregate operation, inspection and maintenance (costs including VAT, based on 2008 figures)

*Summary*

The statistical analysis of overall operation, inspection and maintenance costs ascertained for 105 schools is based on individual cost data for the inspection and maintenance of building constructions, technical installations, grounds and outdoor facilities, as well as fittings, furnishings and equipment (cost groups 352 to 355 as defined by DIN 18960:2008-2). The investigation reveals that the greatest part of the variation in aggregate costs can be ascribed to the inspection and maintenance of technical installations, followed by the outlay for the inspection and maintenance of building constructions. Accordingly, the net floor area, which has previously been declared appropriate for defining cost indicators for the inspection and maintenance of technical installations, is also used for normalizing the aggregate costs taken into account in this instance. The best prediction results for cost indicators are obtained with the multivariate regression Model 12.B on the basis of four independent variables. All of these variables have been included in earlier cost analyses carried out for the inspection and maintenance of building constructions, technical installations or the grounds and outdoor facilities. Summing up, the variation in underlying cost indicators for the operation, inspection and maintenance of schools can be particularly explained by the key factor groups; the type and spatial intensity of usage, and the standard of the grounds and outdoor facilities.

### 3.5.5.3  Validation of the model

The regression Model 12.B, specified for estimating cost indicators for the overall operation, inspection and maintenance of schools, incorporates a selection of causal determinants which have previously been considered for individual predictions of costs incurred for the inspection and maintenance of building constructions, technical installations, as well as the grounds and outdoor facilities. The following validation test evaluates the prediction accuracy achieved by multivariate analysis. Tab. 59 compares the percentage errors of different estimation methods with regard to five validated schools that were not included in the model development process before. The underlying cost indicators defined in €/m² NEFA p.a. include VAT and are based on 2008 figures.

Taking MAPE to be around 16% for the validation sample, the regression Model 12.B achieves a higher prediction accuracy compared with mean absolute percentage errors for empirical mean and median values (MAPE of 28% and 30% respectively). In four out of five cases, the validation test reveals a considerable improvement in prediction when additional information on individual schools is taken into account, such as the existence of an indoor swimming pool in case of sample No.4. It can be concluded, therefore, that the validation test conducted for aggregate costs describes adequate model predictions comparable to the test results presented for individual costs on the third structural cost level according to DIN 18960:2008-2 (cost groups 352 to 355). Specific cost indicators for different types of school usage are are depicted in the following section.

Tab. 59:   Model validation for cost indicators of aggregate operation, inspection and maintenance

| No. | Type of school | Observed value | Predicted value | Absolute error % of prediction | Absolute error % of mean | Absolute error % of median | Preference |
|---|---|---|---|---|---|---|---|
| 1 | Elementary school without sports facilities | 6.68 | 4.36 | 35 | 42 | 45 | Prediction |
| 2 | Special school with gymnasium | 4.64 | 3.70 | 20 | 16 | 21 | Mean |
| 3 | Secondary school without sports facilities | 3.42 | 3.55 | 4 | 14 | 7 | Prediction |
| 4 | Secondary school with gymnasium and pool | 5.76 | 5.68 | 1 | 32 | 37 | Prediction |
| 5 | Vocational school without sports facilities | 6.24 | 4.94 | 21 | 37 | 42 | Prediction |
| Ø | **Mean Absolute percentage error** | | | **16** | **28** | **30** | **Prediction** |

**Observed value:** Costs (€/m² net floor area p.a.), costs including VAT, based on 2008 figures, N=105

## 3.5.5.4  Cost indicators for aggregate operation, inspection and maintenance

Tab. 101 shows the empirical cost indicators for the overall operation, inspection and maintenance ascertained for 105 schools included in the survey. A mean outlay of 3.91 €/m² NEFA p.a. is indicated for the calendar year in question by a range of 6.77 €/m² NEFA p.a. (costs including VAT, based on 2008 figures). The statistical analysis in Section 3.5.5.2 particularly revealed significant differences in the cost indicators for the variables $X_1$ (vocational school) and $X_2$ (swimming pool utilization area), both with beta>0.400. For a simplified presentation of cost indicators in Tab. 60, both variables are used to classify different school utilization types whereby the underlying data sample allows a distinction to be made between vocational schools and other school types (i.e. primary, secondary or special schools) with or without indoor swimming pool facilities.

The comparison between the empirical values designated for vocational schools and other school types reveals that, with a mean value of 5.35 €/m² NEFA p.a., vocational schools have a higher average outlay of 1.66 €/m² NEFA p.a. (costs including VAT, based on 2008 figures). If the presence of a swimming pool within a school complex is also taken into account, the distribution of cost indicators described for those schools with swimming facilities shows a considerable compatibility with those indicators of vocational schools. Both of these distributions can be clearly separated from the empirical measures of central tendency and dispersion depicted for other school types (i.e. primary, secondary or special schools) without indoor swimming pools, whose cost indicators for the operation, inspection and maintenance are much lower than those of the two reference categories. The corresponding indexing table for annual price adjustments is provided by Destatis (2011b).

Tab. 60:   Evaluated cost indicators for aggregate operation, inspection and maintenance

| Factor level | Minimum | Mean | Median | Maximum | Range |
|---|---|---|---|---|---|
| **Vocational schools** | **3.18** | **5.35** | **5.16** | **8.25** | **5.07** |
| **Other school tpyes** | **1.68** | **3.69** | **3.49** | **8.45** | **6.77** |
| Schools without swimming pools | 1.68 | 3.55 | 3.44 | 5.41 | 3.74 |
| Schools with swimming pools | 2.99 | 5.14 | 4.43 | 8.45 | 5.46 |

**Dependent variable:** Costs (€/m² net floor area p.a.), costs including VAT, based on 2008 figures, N=105

## 3.6     Security and surveillance services

This analysis deals with all kinds of operating costs, as defined by DIN 18960:2008-2, on the second structural cost level. The costs for security and surveillance services (cost group 360, according to DIN 18960:2008-2) addressed in this section take the following cost groups into account:

- Monitoring according to public law regulations (cost group 361)
- Property and personal security (cost group 362)
- Security and surveillance services, other items (cost group 369)

With an average outlay of almost 0.40 €/m² GROFA p.a. (costs including VAT, based on 2008 figures) the costs investigated account for a relatively small proportion of the entire operating costs considered within the calendar year in question (cf. Tab. 103). The analysis takes the individual cost postings for a total of 122 school complexes into consideration.

With regard to the outlay for monitoring according to public law regulations for school buildings and their grounds (cost group 361), regular fees are particularly incurred for fire inspections, technical monitoring services, health and safety (such as the inspection of playground equipment and surfaces as per DIN EN 1176-1:2008-8), as well as for hygiene controls at all-day schools. Regarding the costs for property and personal security (cost group 362), expenses in general regularly occur for security and surveillance services that are required for school activities as well as for extra-curricular supervision, such as the use of gymnasiums and sports grounds for afterschool recreation etc. carried out by caretaker services, for example. In case of the state capital Stuttgart, those caretaker services are provided internally for the majority of municipal schools. The respective properties are to a great extent organized in groups and only rely on external service providers by way of an exception. In contrast, some rural schools are not included in the municipal caretaker system due to their isolated location. Property and personal security services incurred for rural properties are usually outsourced and therefore provided externally.

In a first step, the empirical analysis of the total costs for security and surveillance services designates the gross floor area as the appropriate building reference area for defining cost indicators. It is not possible to validate other influence exerted by other differentiated floor areas, such as the usable floor area or UFA 5, as defined by DIN 277:2005-2 (Parts 1 and 2), at a significance level of 5%. The prediction Model 13.A, moreover, distinguishes between schools where the caretaker services are completely outsourced and those that only occasionally rely on independent property security and surveillance service providers, or not at all. Generally speaking, the former category of schools incurs higher total costs than the latter-named group. Tab. 61 gives additional details concerning the prediction Model 13.A.

Tab. 61: Model description for estimating total costs for security and surveillance services

| Dependent variable | Transf. | R² | R² adj. | SEE | F-value | Sign. | Durbin-Watson-Statistic | | N |
|---|---|---|---|---|---|---|---|---|---|
| Costs for security and surveillance services | LN | 0.329 | 0.318 | 1.055 | 29.194 | 0.000 | 2.013 | | 122 |

| Factors | Transf. | B | St. Error | Beta | t-value | Sign. | Lower CL | Upper CL | T | VIF |
|---|---|---|---|---|---|---|---|---|---|---|
| Constant | LN | 1.045 | 1.427 | | 0.732 | 0.466 | -1.781 | 3.871 | | |
| Caretaker services for security and surveillance services completely outsourced | - | 2.399 | 0.314 | 0.619 | 7.629 | 0.000 | 1.776 | 3.021 | 0.855 | 1.169 |
| Gross floor area (GROFA in m²) | LN | 0.531 | 0.161 | 0.269 | 3.308 | 0.001 | 0.213 | 0.849 | 0.855 | 1.169 |

Dependent variable: Costs for security and surveillance services (€ p.a.), costs including VAT, based on 2008 figures

$$\hat{Y} = 2.843 \cdot e^{2.399 X_1} \cdot X_2^{0.531} \qquad \text{(Model 13.A)}$$

Where:    $\hat{Y}$ :   Costs for security and surveillance services (€ p.a.)

          $X_1$ :   Caretaker services for security and surveillance services completely outsourced

          $X_2$ :   Gross floor area (GROFA in m²)

Based on Model 13.A, it is not possible to confirm any further assumptions that might explain certain differences in the outlay for individual schools, such as vocational, all-day schools or properties with sports facilities, as formulated in the interviews with specialists. Nor does the analysis into cost indicators give any clues as to the impacts on the annual costs for security and surveillance services per m² GROFA in the form of stable cost estimates. The diversity of services contained in this cost group, which apply to both the grounds and the buildings (including diverse structural components and reference areas) fail to reveal any definite patterns for predicting detailed costs. Based on the evaluation of sample data from 113 school complexes, however, it can be concluded that a deviation from the empirical mean or median values depicted in Tab. 101, particularly occurs in regard to the level of outsourcing caretaker services.

## 3.7 Statutory charges and contributions

The empirical investigation of statutory charges and contributions is based on sample data from 122 school complexes and comprises the following three cost groups according to DIN 18960:2008-2:

- Taxes (cost group 371)
- Insurance premiums (cost group 372)
- Statutory charges and contributions, other items (cost group 379)

According to Tab. 103, the average cost indicator for statutory charges and contributions is 1.56 €/m² GROFA p.a. with a total range of 3.42 €/m² GROFA p.a. (costs including VAT, based on 2008 figures). Accordingly, cost group 370, described in this section, represents a relatively small portion and dispersion of the overall outlay within the second structural cost level of operating costs as per DIN 18960:2008-2. As regards this cost group, a lower rate for public schools forming the subject of this survey is determined by the German property tax act[33], which regulates tax exemptions for real estate belonging to certain legal entities. According to § 3 para.1 (3a) of this act, municipalities[34] in Germany are exempt from property taxes. Therefore, the following evaluation of statutory charges and contributions focuses mainly on costs incurred for insurance premiums cover for the buildings and special fittings, furnishings and equipment, during the calendar year in question as well as general charges for land and buildings, without taking taxes (cost group 371) into consideration.

The statistical analysis of 122 schools defines the gross floor area as being the appropriate building reference area for predicting total costs and normalizing cost data. In terms of content, this reference area is largely explained by the buildings' insurance values (cost group 372) for whose calculation the gross floor area is taken into account. Tab. 62 shows the bivariate regression Model 14.A which verifies a diminished estimation quality based on $R^2$=0.354 and a calculated MAPE of 50% for predicting the total outlay for statutory charges and contributions.

Tab. 62:   Model description for estimating total costs for statutory charges and contributions

| Dependent variable | Transf. | $R^2$ | $R^2$ adj. | SEE | F-value | Sign. | Durbin-Watson-Statistic | | N |
|---|---|---|---|---|---|---|---|---|---|
| Costs for statutory charges and contributions | LN | 0.354 | 0.349 | 0.529 | 65.726 | 0.000 | 2.142 | | 122 |

| Factors | Transf. | B | St. Error | Beta | t-value | Sign. | Lower CL | Upper CL | T | VIF |
|---|---|---|---|---|---|---|---|---|---|---|
| Constant | LN | 3.672 | 0.672 | | 5.468 | 0.000 | 2.343 | 5.002 | | |
| Gross floor area (GROFA in m²) | LN | 0.619 | 0.076 | 0.595 | 8.107 | 0.000 | 0.468 | 0.770 | 1.000 | 1.000 |

**Dependent variable:** Costs for statutory charges and contributions (€ p.a.), costs including VAT, based on 2008 figures

$$\hat{Y} = 39.33 \cdot X_1^{0.619} \qquad\qquad\qquad \text{(Model 14.A)}$$

Where:      $\hat{Y}$ :   Costs for statutory charges and contributions (€ p.a.)

            $X_1$ :   Gross floor area (GROFA in m²)

Based on Model 14.A, it is possible to estimate the cost indicators for statutory charges and contributions (Y) by means of a nonlinear regression model that includes a negative effect of the gross floor area ($X_1$ with beta$_1$= -0.268) on the outlay concerned. This bivariate model supports the assumption that large-scale schools, which often comprise extensions and outbuildings from the 1970s or 1980s, generally have a lower cost indicator for statutory charges and contributions than smaller schools that may only consist of a main building, for instance. Both prediction models outlined above for the absolute and normalized costs correspond to assumptions based on regression theory but simultaneously do not produce

---

[33] Grundsteuergesetz, GrStG (in German).

[34] Municipalities are the funding bodies for state schools in Germany and, in their capacity as regional authorities, count as corporate entities of public law.

conclusive cost forecasts. The bivariate prediction model explains less than 10% of the overall variation in Y. Due to the low percentage of costs incurred for statutory charges and contributions of municipal schools, and the instable parameter estimates on property level, the study refrains from presenting this model in detail in favour of the empirical cost indicators outlined in Tab. 101.

Summing up, it can be stated that the insurance premiums (cost group 372) represent a substantial share of the statutory charges and contributions for public schools in Germany that form the subject of this investigation. With regard to the underlying cost data available, it was possible to ascertain a school's gross floor area as the appropriate reference area for normalizing cost data, and to discuss differences in measured cost indicators. In addition, it is pointed out that the lower outlay for statutory charges and contributions (cost group 370) in the case of municipal buildings has to be taken into consideration in any benchmarking undertaken for various property owners.

## 3.8     Aggregate operating costs

### 3.8.1     Empirical and theoretical basis

The scope of the cost data investigated is outlined in Section 2.2.1 and described for individual costs groups having been itemized in previous sections. Therefore, the empirical analysis of aggregate operating costs includes the sum of all costs incurred on lower structural level (cost groups 310 to 370 according to DIN 18960:2008-2) throughout the calendar year 2008. Preliminary analysis have verified that it is possible to draw up a representative sample as an appropriate basis for this statistical approach based on 125 school complexes.

The statistical analysis of substantial causal interrelations includes all independent variables this study has identified to exert a significant influence on the outlay on lower structural levels. In addition, certain ratios of previously determined predictors and building reference areas that have been examined by means of individual analysis, such as the proportion of the usable floor area per m² NEFA, the share of the non-built up plot area per m² NEFA, or the proportionate heatable gross floor area per m² GROFA, are incorporated in the investigation. Other factors that literature review or interviews with experts reveal to be suitable criteria are also included in the empirical investigation. BMI (2003) and DETR (1998), for example, cites the intensity of utilization, from the point of view of both temporal and spatial, as a cause for existing differences in the annual outlay for operating costs. Measurable factors are defined for these theoretically relevant factors, and their independent influence is likewise analyzed as part of the evaluation of aggregate operating costs.

### 3.8.2     Model design and parameter

The statistical analysis proceeds to examine the influential factors on the amount of total operating costs in order to substantiate cost estimates for the annual outlay and to determine an appropriate building reference area for the subsequent analysis into cost indicators. The multivariate regression Model 15.A provides the best prediction results based on the net floor area of a school complex and four other independent variables (see Tab. 63). According to DIN 277-1:2005-2, the net floor area comprises the usable floor area, technical floor area and circulation area, but not the construction area. Among others, the relevant net floor area has already been used to define the cost indictors for the cleaning and care of buildings (cost group 330), as well as for the operation, inspection and maintenance (cost group 350 according to DIN 18960:2008-2). As these two cost groups account for roughly 46% of the total operating costs, it is clearly illustrated how important these two proportional costs are for the aggregate outlay under analysis and consequently for determining an appropriate reference area.

Tab. 63:   Model description for estimating aggregate operating costs

| Dependent variable | Transf. | R² | R² adj. | SEE | F-value | Sign. | Durbin-Watson-Statistic | | N |
|---|---|---|---|---|---|---|---|---|---|
| Aggregate operating costs (€ p.a.) | LN | 0.947 | 0.945 | 0.138 | 424.979 | 0.000 | 1.936 | | 125 |

| Factors | Transf. | B | St. Error | Beta | t-value | Sign. | Lower CL | Upper CL | T | VIF |
|---|---|---|---|---|---|---|---|---|---|---|
| Constant | LN | 3.347 | 0.271 | | 12.356 | 0.000 | 2.810 | 3.883 | | |
| Net floor area (NEFA in m²) | LN | 0.922 | 0.021 | 1.002 | 43.887 | 0.000 | 0.881 | 0.964 | 0.855 | 1.169 |
| Share of the non-built up plot area per m² NEFA | LN | 0.065 | 0.017 | 0.087 | 3.730 | 0.000 | 0.030 | 0.099 | 0.819 | 1.221 |
| Share of the swimming pool utilization area per m² NEFA | - | 6.519 | 1.303 | 0.110 | 5.004 | 0.000 | 3.940 | 9.099 | 0.920 | 1.087 |
| Share of the heatable gross floor area per m² GROFA | - | 0.575 | 0.195 | 0.069 | 2.943 | 0.004 | 0.188 | 0.962 | 0.813 | 1.230 |
| Share of the sanitary area per m² NEFA | - | 3.641 | 1.390 | 0.063 | 2.619 | 0.010 | 0.888 | 6.394 | 0.773 | 1.293 |

Dependent variable: Aggregate operating costs (€ p.a.), costs including VAT, based on 2008 figures

$$\hat{Y} = 28.417 \cdot X_1^{0.922} \cdot X_2^{0.065} \cdot e^{6.519 X_3} \cdot e^{0.575 X_4} \cdot e^{3.641 X_5}$$   (Model 15.A)

Where:     $\hat{Y}$ :   Aggregate operating costs (€ p.a.)

$X_1$ :   Net floor area (NEFA in m²)

$X_2$ :   Share of the non-built up plot area per m² NEFA

$X_3$ :   Share of the swimming pool utilization area per m² NEFA

$X_4$ :   Share of the heatable gross floor area per m² GROFA

$X_5$ :   Share of the sanitary area per m² NEFA

Based on a step-by-step approach, Model 15.A includes specific proportions of the non-built up plot area ($X_2$), the swimming pool utilization area ($X_3$), the heatable gross floor area ($X_4$) and the sanitary area ($X_5$) per m² NEFA and m² GROFA respectively. The gross floor area (GROFA) is applied for normalizing the heatable gross floor area in terms of $X_4$, as tha latter (H-GROFA) also comprises the construction area and is measured in m² GROFA. Previous analysis into the individual operating costs already attributed a certain explanatory share to each of the areas outlined above, based on an underlying significance level of 5%. Apart from the net floor area, the evaluated reference areas, in particular, describe characteristics of school facilities and their plots, used to predict the total operating costs in simple terms.

Tab. 63 outlines details of model design and specifications. With $R^2=0.947$ and a calculated MAPE of 11%, the multivariate regression Model 15.A produces an excellent standard of prediction, which can also be backed up by means of a visual inspection of scatter plot (see Fig. 9).

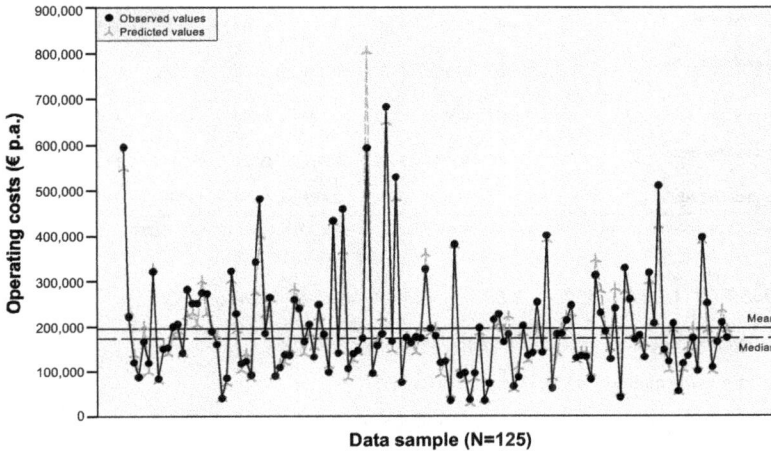

Fig. 9:    Comparison between observed and predicted operating costs (costs including VAT, based on 2008 figures)

The following investigation of cost indicators for the aggregate operating costs (Y) is described by Model 15.B and refers to the same five continuous variables used to estimate the total operating costs. The analysis accordingly underlines the relevance of previously quantified proportions of specific building and plot-related reference areas.

While a positive effect is also retained in the case of four out of five continuous variables, a negative and nonlinear influence on the operating cost indicators (Y) is revealed for the net floor area ($X_3$) in Model 15.B (cf. Tab. 64). Comparing school complexes of varying sizes (measured in m² NEFA), and assuming that the other model assumptions remain constant, the regression model accordingly verifies the assumption that the bigger the school, the lower the anticipated outlay for the operating cost indicators. (cf. BMI, 2008 or JLL, 2011, for instance). The specified Model 15.B displays accurate cost estimates with $R^2=0.525$, SEE=4.158 and a MAPE of 12%. Fig. 10 follows this up by visualizing the distribution of examined cost indicators and a convincing goodness-of-fit for the statistical model.

Tab. 64:   Model description for estimating aggregate operating cost indicators

| Dependent variable | Transf. | R² | R² adj. | SEE | F-value | Sign. | Durbin-Watson-Statistic | | N |
|---|---|---|---|---|---|---|---|---|---|
| Aggregate operating costs (€/m² NEFA p.a.) | - | 0.525 | 0.505 | 4.158 | 26.283 | 0.000 | 1.995 | | 125 |

| Factors | Transf. | B | St. Error | Beta | t-value | Sign. | Lower CL | Upper CL | T | VIF |
|---|---|---|---|---|---|---|---|---|---|---|
| Constant | - | 28.998 | 8.148 | | 3.559 | 0.001 | 12.863 | 45.132 | | |
| Share of the non-built up plot area per m² NEFA | LN | 1.965 | 0.523 | 0.262 | 3.757 | 0.000 | 0.930 | 3.001 | 0.819 | 1.221 |
| Share of the swimming pool utilization area per m² NEFA | - | 234.98 | 39.194 | 0.395 | 5.995 | 0.000 | 157.376 | 312.593 | 0.920 | 1.087 |
| Net floor area (NEFA in m²) | LN | -2.338 | 0.632 | -0.253 | -3.698 | 0.000 | -3.590 | -1.086 | 0.855 | 1.169 |
| Share of the heatable gross floor area per m² GROFA | - | 17.405 | 5.879 | 0.208 | 2.961 | 0.004 | 5.765 | 29.046 | 0.813 | 1.230 |
| Share of the sanitary area per m² NEFA | - | 102.58 | 41.825 | 0.176 | 2.453 | 0.016 | 19.766 | 185.402 | 0.773 | 1.293 |

**Dependent variable**: Aggregate operating costs (€/m² net floor area p.a.), costs including VAT, based on 2008 figures

$$\hat{Y} = 28.998 + 1.965\ln(X_1) + 234.985 X_2 - 2.338\ln(X_3) + 17.405 X_4 + 102.584 X_5 \qquad \text{(Model 15.B)}$$

Where:   $\hat{Y}$ :   Aggregate operating cost indicators (€/ m² net floor area p.a.)

$X_1$ :   Share of the non-built up plot area per m² NEFA

$X_2$ :   Share of the swimming pool utilization area per m² NEFA

$X_3$ :   Net floor area (NEFA in m²)

$X_4$ :   Share of the heatable gross floor area per m² GROFA

$X_5$ :   Share of the sanitary area per m² NEFA

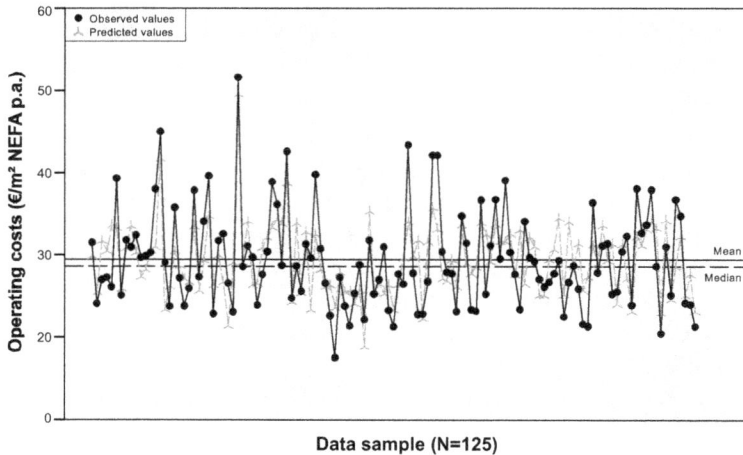

Fig. 10:   Comparison between observed and predicted operating cost indicators
(costs including VAT, based on 2008 figures)

*Summary*

Based on sample data from 125 school complexes, estimation models are presented for the aggregate outlay of operating costs. The preceding investigation of total costs identifies the net floor area as being relevant for analyzing and comparing the cost data concerned. This building reference area was already applied in previous cost analyses, such as those carried out to define the cost indictors for the cleaning and care of buildings (cost group 330), as well as for the operation, inspection and maintenance (cost group 350 according to DIN 18960:2008-2). Moreover, the statistical data evaluation also defines four independent variables that describe certain proportions of building and plot-related reference areas. Designated factors can be used to realize simple cost estimates relating to the absolute amount of operating costs.

The estimation Model 15.B that is subsequently introduced for estimating operating cost indicators incorporates the same five independent sources of influence as were previously specified for total costs predictions. All independent variables used to estimate the outlay for aggregate costs arise from the type of school usage as well as functional and technical characteristics. In addition, more detailed cost estimates for individual cost groups on lower structural level according to DIN 18960:2008-2 are provided in previous investigations, outlined above, which not only take area-related values into account but also other factors.

### 3.8.3    Validation of the model

The best estimation of cost indicators for aggregate operating costs is provided by the multivariate regression Model 15.B outlined above. The regression model takes account of additional descriptions by way of specific proportions of school buildings and plot-related reference areas. By contrast, the overall mean and median values, as described in Tab. 101, represent such cost estimates, as they are conducted when no further information is available or used on any causal interrelations that exist. Tab. 65 compares these three prediction methods for five observed values of different school types. Both individual and mean absolute percentage errors are presented to make it possible to compare the forecast quality of the prediction model with the empirical mean and median estimates. With regard to individual cases, the specified prediction Model 16.B produces more accurate estimates in three out of five cases under comparison, whereas the overall mean only provides a better result for sample No.5 (vocational school without sports facilities), and the median is preferable only in the case of sample No.3 (secondary school without sports facilities). Comparing the average prediction quality of all five cases, estimation Model 15.B reveals the lowest mean absolute percentage error with a MAPE of just under 16%, thus verifying the best approximation to the observed values. By contrast, the deviations in the estimates for both central values are in the region of 18% to 19%. The specific cost indicators given below are based on this test result with respect to evaluated factors of Model 15.B.

Tab. 65:  Model validation for aggregate operating cost indicators

| No. | Type of school | Observed value | Predicted value | Absolute error % of prediction | Absolute error % of mean | Absolute error % of median | Preference |
|---|---|---|---|---|---|---|---|
| 1 | Elementary school without sports facilities | 42.15 | 33.16 | 21 | 30 | 32 | Prediction |
| 2 | Special school with gymnasium | 38.93 | 33.35 | 14 | 24 | 26 | Prediction |
| 3 | Secondary school without sports facilities | 27.97 | 31.60 | 13 | 5 | 2 | Median |
| 4 | Secondary school with gymnasium and pool | 42.74 | 38.79 | 9 | 31 | 33 | Prediction |
| 5 | Vocational school without sports facilities | 29.58 | 23.36 | 21 | 1 | 3 | Mean |
| Ø | **Mean Absolute percentage error** | | | **16** | **18** | **19** | **Prediction** |

**Observed value:** Aggregate operating costs (€/m² net floor area p.a.), costs including VAT, based on 2008 figures, N=125

## 3.8.4  Cost indicators for aggregate operation

Based on sample data from 125 school complexes, the regression Model 15.B identifies considerable differences in the annual amount of aggregate operating cost indicator (Y). Within the multivariate context, the variable $X_2$ (share of the swimming pool utilization area per m² NEFA) represents the greatest effect on Y with $beta_2$=0.395. Subsequently, a substantial impact is verified on the annual operating costs per m² GROFA by means of the two variables $X_1$ (share of the non-built up plot area per m² NEFA) and $X_3$ (net floor area).

The following presentation of cost indicators in Tab. 66 refers to this evaluation of relevant factors impacting on Y by taking into account different categories for each of these three predictor variables. A categorical distinction between schools with and without swimming pools is described on the first stage, which is followed by further classifications of the cost indicators in terms of the two continuous variables and their underlying subcategories respectively. With regard to the empirical distribution of the underlying sample data, a threshold value of 6,000 m² (empirical median is 6.103 m²) is taken as a distinguishing criterion for the variable $X_3$ (net floor area). For the variable $X_1$ (share of the non-built up plot area per m² NEFA), however, a classification system based on the value of 1.4 (empirical median is 1.37) is drawn up. Designated cost indicators are given in €/m² GROFA p.a. They include VAT and are based on 2008 figures. The corresponding indexing table for annual price adjustments is provided by Destatis (2011b).

The impact certain variables exert on Y can be accounted for by comparing given reference values within designated categories in Tab. 66. An average cost indicator of just under 29 €/m² GROFA p.a. is generally ascertained for schools with swimming pools, for example, whereas the comparable cost value for schools with swimming pools is approximately 8 €/m² GROFA p.a. higher. The same applies to other and more detailed cost indicator comparisons. The average cost indicator for school complexes without swimming pools that have a net floor area lower than 6,000 m² amounts to approximately 31 €/m² GROFA p.a., whereas the corresponding cost indicator for the reference group with a net floor area that exceeds 6,000 m² is about 4 €/m² GROFA p.a. lower. If differentiated estimates for operating cost indicators are also required, with regard to the proportionate swimming pool utilization, or sanitary areas, for instance, these cost indicators can be additionally determined using regression Model 15.B.

Tab. 66:   Evaluated cost indicators for aggregate operating costs

| Factor level | Minimum | Mean | Median | Maximum | Range |
|---|---|---|---|---|---|
| **Schools without swimming pools** | **17.53** | **28.92** | **27.93** | **43.42** | **25.89** |
| Total NEFA < 6,000 m² | 21.35 | 30.79 | 30.32 | 43.42 | 22.07 |
| Share of the non-built up plot area per m² NEFA < 1.4 | 21.35 | 28.73 | 28.57 | 38.13 | 16.78 |
| Share of the non-built up plot area per m² NEFA ≥ 1.4 | 23.41 | 32.35 | 31.09 | 43.42 | 20.01 |
| Total NEFA ≥ 6,000 m² | 17.53 | 27.09 | 26.57 | 39.12 | 21.59 |
| Share of the non-built up plot area per m² NEFA < 1.4 | 17.53 | 25.60 | 25.12 | 36.74 | 19.21 |
| Share of the non-built up plot area per m² NEFA ≥ 1.4 | 23.08 | 29.43 | 29.22 | 39.12 | 16.04 |
| **Schools with swimming pools** | **26.13** | **36.81** | **35.44** | **51.64** | **25.51** |
| Total NEFA < 6.000 m² | 36.15 | 43.85 | 43.80 | 51.64 | 15.50 |
| Total NEFA ≥ 6.000 m² | 26.13 | 29.77 | 29.11 | 34.74 | 8.60 |

**Dependent variable:** Aggregate operating costs (€/m² net floor area p.a.), costs including VAT, based on 2008 figures, N=125

## 4      Investigation of repair costs

At an average rate of 23 €/m² GROFA p.a., the costs for repairs in the calendar year under assessment are slightly lower than the mean operating costs. Due to the wide variety of different repair tasks that were carried out on the schools investigated as part of this survey, moreover, the empirical distribution of cost indicators is spread over almost 66 €/m² GROFA p.a. The repair costs investigated include VAT and were incurred during the course of the calendar year 2008 for the following type of measures, as defined by DIN 18960:2008-2:

- Repair of building constructions (cost group 410)
- Repair of technical installations (cost group 420)
- Repair of grounds and outdoor facilities (cost group 430)
- Repair of fittings, furnishings and equipment (cost group 440)

The scope of individual measures covered by the cost group 400, as per DIN 18960:2008-2, can be described as being in compliance with DIN 31051:2003-6, whereas this German standard makes a conceptual distinction between repair measures and improvements. According to DIN 31051:2003-6, therefore, the statistical analysis not only comprises all the repair measures required to put an operating system back into working order but also the improvements, comprising technical, administrative or managerial tasks, designed to increase the functional reliability of an operating system or unit, without changing its original function. Investment costs that are incurred for construction work for new buildings, renovations or modernizations according to DIN 276-1:2008-12 are not included in the survey. Nor are structural measures that are part of the Federal and State Government's capital investment program, such as the Program for the Future of Education and Care[35] or Education for sustainable development[36], for example, included in cost group 400, as specified in DIN 18960:2008-2. In generel, the maintenance performance as defined by EN 15341:2005-9 'is dependent upon both external and internal influencing factors such as: location, culture, transformation and service processes, size, utilization rate and age.'[37]

For the investigation of repair costs presented in this section, particular restrictions are associated with the data sample concerned. Factors relating to the factor group strategy and operation are not incorporated in the analysis of repair costs because the representative properties are managed by a single proprietor (municipality of Stuttgart) and all school complexes are subject to a uniform maintenance strategy (cf. Section 2.5). At the same

---

[35] In German: Investitionsprogram Zukunft, Bildung und Betreuung (IZBB).

[36] In German: Chancen durch Bildung (CdB).

[37] The terms 'maintenance' and 'maintenance strategy' respectively are used to reflect the terminology contained in EN 15341:2005-9 and DIN EN 13306:2010-12 as defined by the European Committee for Standardization (CEN) which, according to the German Standard DIN 31051:2003-6, covers all maintenance, inspection, repair and im-provement measures and refers here to repair costs covered by cost group 400 according to DIN 18960:2008-2.

time, however, to determine the maintenance strategy is of relevance to facilitate comparing the cost indicators evaluated in this study with published reference values or cost indicators of other municipalities. Stoy (2005) and Bahr (2008), for example, emphasize that repair costs are dependent on a chosen maintenance strategy, whereby, due to the sample at their availability, they could only partially evaluate the impact of a strategy. As regards the scarcity of funds at the disposal of municipalities the designation corrective maintenance according to DIN EN 13306:2010-12 is most appropriate for the underlying schools, as it comprises the "maintenance carried out after fault recognition and intended to put an item into a state in which it can perform a required function."

The analysis of repair costs, as based on this definition of the applied maintenance strategy, includes those factors that provide information on differences in school utilization and their functional, technical and local characteristics (see Section 2.2.2). Numerous qualitative and quantitative analyses underline the significance of these factor groups and point out that they must be taken into consideration in an analysis of repair costs. From a theoretical perspective, among others, the user behaviour is to be named in terms of the type and intensity of usage, the kind of design and construction, the quality of component parts used and their building material characteristics, together with environmental influences, that effect on the degradation or susceptibility of individual structural components and their economic life span (cf. Kalusche, 2004; Bahr, 2008; Stoy, 2005; Naber, 2002; Ashworth, 1996; Flores-Colen and Brito, 2010).[38] According to Ashworth (1996, p.8): 'There are wide variations in the life expectancies of building component data...due to the many vagaries associated with design, construction, use and management of buildings.' Kalusche (2004) states that, wear and tear due to utilization can be particularly measured according to the condition of the structural components adjacent to interior space and surfaces, such as floorings, linings, doors and windows.

In collaboration with the municipality of the state capital Stuttgart and experts from the technical building management, the condition of certain selected parts of building constructions, technical installations, the grounds and outdoor facilities, as well as fittings, furnishings and equipment, were defined as having a crucial impact on the repair costs. The corresponding data across all the school complexes were collected using the questionnaire depicted in Appendix B. Regarding the standard of structural components, it is difficult to conclusively answer, in how far a specific standard, such as the standard of glazing, insulation or external claddings, has a positive or negative effect on the repair costs. According to Ashworth (1996, p.5), for example, 'a high quality building might also require higher costs in use in order to maintain its high quality in use and aesthetics.' With regard to the overall maintenance costs (according to DIN 31051:2003-6) of building constructions and technical installations, Bahr (2008) defines a series of technical characteristics, such as age and technical building standard. She further names the total size of a property to be a relevant factor, whereby this size is believed to exert a substantial influence on the outlay of

---

[38] According to Kalusche (2008, p.6 et seqq.), the technical life span of structural components, within which a component can physically perform as required without limitation, is to be disassociated from an economic life span of buildings, whereby the latter is particularly determined by market-relevant factors, such as the demand for, and attractiveness of, a real estate.

extraordinary repair measures. Moreover, the location, or rather, the external environmental pollution emanating from it, is seen as a critical factor for the technical life span of structural components and correspondingly taken into consideration within this analysis (cf. Naber, 2002, p.158 or Kalusche, 2004, for example).

The present study takes all factors outlined above into account and examines their independent influence for schools based on the underlying data sample. Since the age of a school can only be determined on property level for some of the school complexes under investigation, the following analysis into repair costs comprises data collected from a sample of maximum 113 schools. In terms of the repair costs investigated for the grounds and out-door facilities, and those for fittings, furnishings and equipment (cost groups 430 and 440 according to DIN 1896:2008-2), the scope of the sample is again restricted, as cost postings of repair costs were not available for all school complexes included in the survey for the calendar year concerned.

To begin with, the following sections deals with the statistical evaluation of school repair costs for individual repair measures described above and then proceeds to the aggregate repair costs. The theoretical basis and underlying factors of each analysis (cost group 410 to 440 according to DIN 18960:2008-2) are described by way of an introduction. This will be followed by the presentation of the prediction models investigated for both the total repair costs and specific cost indicators. Subsequently, a validation test carried out for each cost group is presented to assess the prediction accuracy of model estimates and finally, specific cost indicators are presented for the respective types of repairs costs for practical planning purposes.

## 4.1    Repair of building constructions

### 4.1.1    Empirical and theoretical basis

With almost 16 €/m² GROFA (costs including VAT, based on 2008 figures), the average amount of the repair costs for building constructions not only represents by far the largest amount across all operating and repair costs considered on the second structural cost level, but at the same time also has the highest standard deviation (cf. Tab. 103). By comparing the empirical cost indicators of the underlying data sample, the average outlay for the inspection and maintenance of building constructions is slightly lower than those expendi-tures for the technical installations, whereas the average costs for the repair of building constructions lie well above the outlay for the technical installations. The repair costs under investigation accordingly arise primarily from measures carried out on the structural building components, as defined by the cost groups 411 to 416 according to DIN 18960:2008-2:

- Foundation (cost group 411)
- External walls (cost group 412)
- Internal walls (cost group 413)
- Ceilings (cost group 414)

- Roofs (cost group 415)
- Permanent fixtures (cost group 416)
- Repair of building constructions, other items (cost group 419)

The present analysis examines numerous factors that arise from a school's usage, functional and technical characteristics of buildings constructions as well as a property's location, mentioned in literature, or which experts believe exert a crucial impact on the annual outlay for repairs of building constructions. Designated factors considered within the statistical analysis of schools are described in the following overview:

**Factor group: Utilization**

*Type of utilization:*

- Primary utilization: Elementary school, secondary school such as comprehensive school (secondary general school, intermediate secondary school, multiple school center) or grammar school, special school, vocational school with technical or business focus; qualitative description of different utilization types and quantitative description of the school utilization area in m² NEFA as well as its proportion per m² NEFA of the whole school property.
- Secondary utilization: Sports facilities such as gymnasiums or indoor swimming pools for teaching purposes, nursery school; qualitative and quantitative description of different utilization types with regard to their building reference areas e.g. the net floor area of a gymnasium or swimming pool utilization in m² and their representative proportions per m² NEFA.

*Standard of utilization:*

- Type of educational program: Regular school, extended regular school or full-day school.
- Type of canteen service: School based canteen, external catering or no canteen service.

*Intensity of utilization:*

- Temporal usage intensity:

    Average operating time of the whole school complex as well as individual operating times of both the primary and secondary utilizations, i.e. the school and its sports facilities, in hours per school week and with regard to the average number of schooldays per school week.

- Spatial usage intensity:

    - Spatial standard: Higher or lower standard.
    - The total number of pupils, number of pupils per m² specific floor area according to DIN 277:2005-2 (Part 1 and 2) and the number of pupils with respect to other reference areas such as m² net floor area of school utilization e.g. the number of pupils per m² GROFA.

- The total number of school classes, number of school classes per m² specific floor area according to DIN 277:2005-2 (Part 1 and 2) and number of school classes with respect to other reference areas such as m² net floor area of school utilization e.g. the number of school classes per m² GROFA.

**Factor group: Functional and technical characteristics**

*Functional characteristics:*

- Specific building floor areas according to DIN 277:2005-2 (Part 1 and 2) e.g. in m² GROFA, m² UFA, m² UFA 5and their representative proportion to the total size of a property in m² GROFA or other specific building floor areas e.g. the share of UFA 5 per m² GROFA.

- The average storey height according to DIN 277-1:2005-2.

- The total sanitary area and its proportion to specific building floor areas according to DIN 277:2005-2 (Part 1 and 2) e.g. the share of the sanitary area per m² UFA.

- Standard of flooring: Qualitative and quantitative description of different flooring materials i.e. wood, stone, carpet or synthetic materials in m² flooring area and as a percentage of the whole flooring area according to DIN 277-3:2005-4.

- Standard of internal wall linings: Qualitative and quantitative description of different lining materials i.e. wood, ceramic, panels, paintwork or wallpaper in m² internal wall lining area and as a percentage of the whole internal wall lining area as defined by DIN 277-3:2005-4.

- Standard of ceiling and roof linings: Qualitative and quantitative description of different lining materials i.e. wood, wallpaper, panels, paintwork or plaster in m² ceiling and roof lining area and as a percentage of the whole ceiling and roof lining area according to DIN 277-3:2005-4.

*Technical characteristics:*

- Standard of building constructions:

  - Age of a school property.

  - Existence of historic building conservation regulations.

  - Standard of external claddings: Qualitative and quantitative description of different cladding materials i.e. wood, stone, concrete, plaster or panels in m² external cladding area and as a percentage of the whole external wall cladding area according to DIN 277-3:2005-4.

  - Glass area of external walls and roofs according to DIN 277-3:2005-4 and its share in percentage of specific building floor areas according to DIN 277:2005-2 (Part 1 and 2) e.g. the share of glass areas of external walls and roofs per m² GROFA.

  - Type of roof structures: Qualitative and quantitative description of flat or sloped roofs e.g. as a percentage of the whole roof structure area according to DIN 277-3:2005-4.

- Condition of building constructions:

   Qualitative and quantitative description of the condition of building constructions and in particular the condition of single structural components according to DIN 276-1:2008-12 such as the condition of walls and ceilings, external glass areas, roofs or permanent fixtures e.g. the share of defective glass areas of external walls as a percentage of the whole glass area of external walls.

**Factor group: Location:**

- Existence of external environmental pollution

## 4.1.2    Model design and parameters

The empirical analysis of 113 school complexes takes into account various aspects, outlined above, regarding descriptions of a school's utilization, its functional and technical building characteristics, as well as its location which theoretically constitute a substantial impact on the repair costs of building constructions. Different models for estimating the outlay have been developed step-by-step and compared within statistical pre-analyses. As a result, the trivariate regression Model 16.A achieves the best approximation of the empirical data ascertained for the total repair costs of building constructions ($Y$) with respect to a school's gross floor area ($X_2$) and the interaction variable $X_1^*$ (poor condition of building construc-tions*m² GROFA) introduced in this study for estimating the total repair costs of municipal schools (see also Urban & Mayerl, 2008). As a multiplicative term, this interaction variable allows to use the size of the gross floor area and the condition of the building constructions for predicting the annual outlay. Fig. 11 displays this circumstance separately for two different situations representing the building constructions either found to be in a good condition or in a poor state of repair, showing the different increase rates of $b_2$=9.088 and $b_{1,2}$=26.114 respectively for cost estimates determined by Model 16.A on the basis of 113 school complexes.[39] As depicted in scatter plot, the gap between the two regression lines is continually widening, so determining the condition of the building constructions is becoming increasingly important for drawing up efficient cost estimates, particularly in the case of large-scale school complexes (measured in gross floor area). If a bivariate or trivariate model was specified with an additive dummy variable, for example, instead of including this interaction term, the cost predictions achieved in this way would increasingly display cases of underestimation or overestimation at certain intervals and in certain constellations, as shown by Fig. 11. This would lead to variance inhomogeneity (hetero-scedasticity) in the residuals, resulting in inefficient cost estimates for the municipal sample under analysis. In contrast, the interaction variable $X_1^*$ allows to clearly specify the effect of different conditions of the building constructions in the statistical model, i.e. whether the building constructions are found in a good state or a bad one, and consequently to take

---

[39] The regression equation is $\hat{Y} = -65.448 + 9.088X_2$ in the case of an assumed good condition of the building construc-tions, and $\hat{Y} = -65.448 + 26.114X_2$ in the case the respective structural components are found to be in a poor state.

different increase rates in Y into account when estimating the repair costs. The overall state of repair is determined according to the conditions of the walls and ceilings, glass areas of external walls and roofs, as well as of the permanent fixtures, in particular, that concerns the cost groups 330 to 370 according to DIN 276:1.2006-11. Over the course of the data survey, the condition of each of these structural components was consistently ascertained for individual school and sports facilities and then aggregated by means of a weighting factor for the present analysis carried out at property level (see Tab. 112). The weighting factor includes a qualitative grading of the individual conditions and the respective size of a school's gross floor area that is affected by a poor state of repair in order to give each condition assessment a dimension. An overall poor condition of the building constructions is particularly indicated if either the condition of the external glass surfaces or the condition of the roofs is found to be in a poor state (indicated by the category C or D according to the questionnaire shown in Appendix B) for a significant proportion of the total size of a school complex, and if simultaneously the survey also revealed considerable damages for at least one of the remaining structural components mentioned above.

Based on $R^2=0.795$, Model 16.A reveals an excellent compliance with the empirical sample of 113 schools. Detailed information on model specifications is shown in Tab. 67. Given confidence limits between -18.129 and 17.998, a non-significant regression constant is accepted at a 95% confidence interval, which can be disregarded based on an underlying empirical distribution of total costs with a range of 648.970 €.

Tab. 67:   Model description for estimating total repair costs of building constructions

| Dependent variable | Transf. | R² | R² adj. | SEE | F-value | Sign. | Durbin-Watson-Statistic | | N |
|---|---|---|---|---|---|---|---|---|---|
| Repair costs of building constructions | - | 0.795 | 0.791 | 55364 | 213.44 | 0.000 | 2.059 | | 113 |

| Factors | Transf. | B | St. Error | Beta | t-value | Sign. | Lower CL | Upper CL | T | VIF |
|---|---|---|---|---|---|---|---|---|---|---|
| Constant | - | -65.448 | 9114.86 | | -0.007 | 0.994 | -18129 | 17998 | | |
| Poor condition of building constructions* m² GROFA | - | 17.026 | 1.134 | 0.672 | 15.010 | 0.000 | 14.778 | 19.274 | 0.929 | 1.076 |
| Gross floor area (GROFA in m²) | - | 9.088 | 0.938 | 0.434 | 9.686 | 0.000 | 7.228 | 10.947 | 0.929 | 1.076 |

**Dependent variable:** Repair costs of building constructions (€ p.a.), costs including VAT, based on 2008 figures

$$\hat{Y} = -65.448 + 17.026 X_1^* + 9.088 X_2 \qquad\qquad \text{(Model 16.A)}$$

Where:       $\hat{Y}$ :   Repair costs of building constructions (€ p.a.)

$X_1^*$ :   Poor condition of building constructions*m² gross floor area

$X_2$ :   Gross floor area (GROFA in m²)

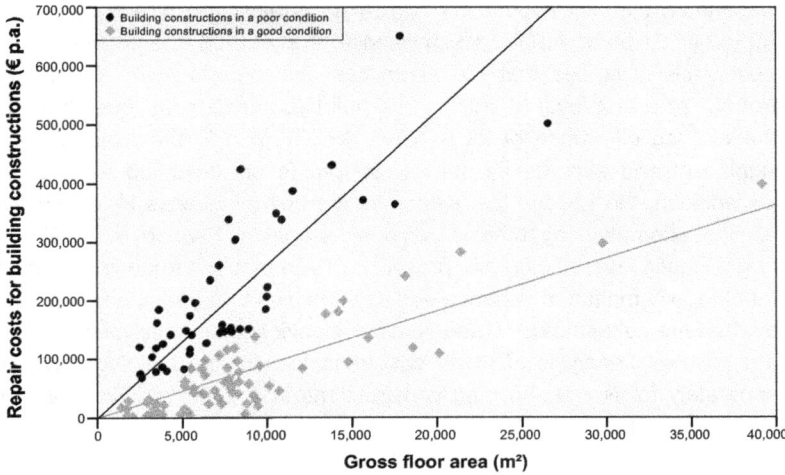

Fig. 11:    Comparison between observed and predicted repair costs of building constructions
            (costs including VAT, based on 2008 figures)

In accordance with Model 16.A, the gross floor area is used to normalize the repair costs of the building constructions. Since this particular building reference area has already been used for defining cost indicators for the inspection and maintenance of building construc-tions, it is possible to ascertain the overall maintenance cost indicators for these structural components, as defined by DIN 13306:2010-12.

The following analysis of the causal interrelations that exist between the factors outlined in the preceding section and the repair cost indicators for building constructions ($€/m^2$ GROFA p.a.) is not particularly convincing using a single model across all observations (N=113) at an underlying significance level of 5%. For this reason, the study will now proceed to present the results of preliminary statistical investigations, which form the basis for the evaluation of cost indicators.

Model 16.A identified significant differences in the annual repair costs investigated with regard to the condition of the building constructions. This will be followed by an analysis designed to ascertain whether substantial differences in the mean cost indicators are due to different conditions of the relevant components or occur randomly. At the same time, the study also examines whether different levels of condition reflect differences in the variance of Y. Both aspects are investigated using significance tests based on sample data for $N_1=44$ (building constructions in a good condition) and $N_2=69$ (building constructions in a poor condition). The t-test is applied for mean value comparisons and the Levene test (F-test) is used for the analysis of variance. Both tests are based on nearly normally distributed cost indicators, which is confirmed by the Kolmogorov-Smirnov test (KS-test) in terms of a statistical test with an empirical significance level of 0.757 for $N_1$ and 0.252 for $N_2$ respec-tively based on an 5% significance level.

The T-Test investigates the null hypothesis $H_0(\mu_1 = \mu_2)$ against the directional alternative hypothesis $H_1(\mu_1 < \mu_2)$. Given an empirical significance level of 0.00 (the empirical t-value is -15.798), the test statistic verifies that the mean cost indicator of $N_2$ is larger than the average value of $N_1$. At a test level of $\alpha = 5\%$ the null hypothesis consequently has to be rejected and the existing difference of 21.10 €/m² GROFA p.a. in the average values is regarded as significant and accordingly not as random (costs including VAT, based on 2008 figures). In addition, the Levene test examines the null hypothesis $H_0(\sigma_1 = \sigma_2)$ versus $H_1(\sigma_1 \neq \sigma_2)$, i.e. the alternative hypothesis. With an empirical F-value of 38.580 and a corresponding significance level of 0.00, the presence of variance heterogeneity is indicated, which means that the assumption of variance equality has also to be rejected. The results of both tests reveal that the subsamples $N_1$ and $N_2$ differ significantly in their mean values and variances, so the following analysis of repair cost indicators for the building constructions is performed separately for $N_1$=44 (building constructions in a good condition) and $N_2$=69 (building constructions in a poor condition).

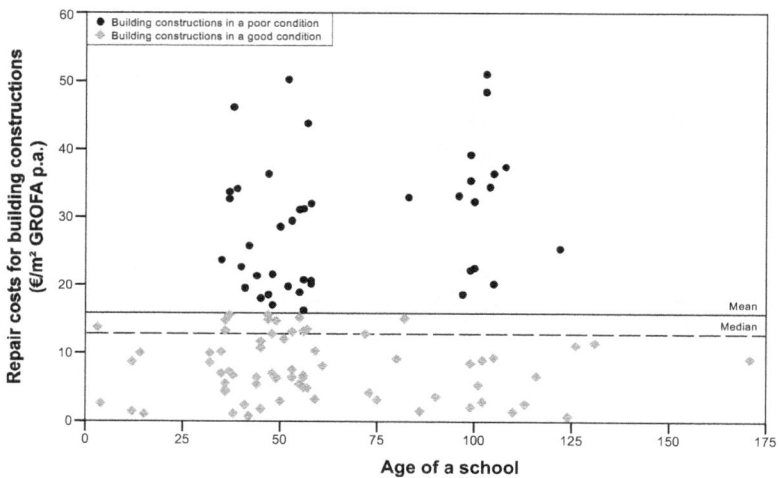

Fig. 12:   Empirical repair cost indicators for building constructions (costs including VAT, based on 2008 figures)

In case a good condition of building constructions is stated, the investigation into the cost indicators for the municipal outlay for repair measures on building constructions (Y) is conducted on the basis of sample data from 44 school complexes depicted in Fig. 12. The best estimates are achieved by a bivariate model, taking the type of school usage into account. Previous studies likewise point to differences existing in the repair costs depending on the type of usage, which supports the content of the assumption that a causal effect exists between both parameters (cf. Bahr, 2008). In the context of this study, elementary and special schools particularly have, on average, higher cost values, as opposed to the underlying reference categories (i.e. secondary and vocational schools). However, based on the sample data available it is not possible to determine stable predictions by use of the bivariate model. The influence of the utilization type accounts for less than 10% of the overall variation in Y which, at the same time, is only slightly significant at 0.048. It is therefore not recommended to use the model for prediction purposes. Instead, it is suggested to use the condition of the building constructions as a distinguishing feature for empirical cost indicators and therefore refer to the empirical values (such as mean or median) described for public school buildings with a good condition of the building constructions.

The following analysis of repair cost indicators (€/m² GROFA p.a.) performed for public schools buildings with a poor state of building constructions succeeds for $N_2=69$ and is described by Model 16.B.2. The multivariate analysis incorporates the independent influences of three independent variables: the average storey height ($X_1$), a poor condition of walls, ceilings and roofs ($X_2$), and the share of the usable floor area for education, teaching and culture (UFA 5) per m² GROFA ($X_3$).

Tab. 68:  Model description for estimating repair cost indicators of building constructions in a poor condition

| Dependent variable | Transf. | R² | R² adj. | SEE | F-value | Sign. | Durbin-Watson-Statistic | | N |
|---|---|---|---|---|---|---|---|---|---|
| Repair costs of building constructions | - | 0.427 | 0.384 | 7.276 | 9.918 | 0.000 | 1.950 | | 44 |

| Factors | Transf. | B | St. Error | Beta | t-value | Sign. | Lower CL | Upper CL | T | VIF |
|---|---|---|---|---|---|---|---|---|---|---|
| Constant | - | -13.843 | 8.815 | | -1.570 | 0.124 | -31.659 | 3.973 | | |
| Average storey height (in m) | - | 5.372 | 1.284 | 0.505 | 4.184 | 0.000 | 2.777 | 7.967 | 0.986 | 1.014 |
| Walls, ceilings and roofs in a poor condition | - | 7.368 | 2.284 | 0.395 | 3.226 | 0.003 | 2.752 | 11.983 | 0.955 | 1.048 |
| Share of UFA 5 per m² GROFA | - | 48.310 | 17.483 | 0.337 | 2.763 | 0.009 | 12.976 | 83.645 | 0.967 | 1.034 |

**Dependent variable**: Repair costs of building constructions (€/m² gross floor area p.a.), costs including VAT, based on 2008 figures

$$\hat{Y} = -13.843 + 5.372X_1 + 7.368X_2 + 48.310X_3 \qquad \text{(Model 16.B.2)}$$

Where:  $\hat{Y}$ :  Repair costs of building constructions (€/m² gross floor area p.a.)

$X_1$ :  Average storey height (in m)

$X_2$ :  Walls, ceilings and roofs in a poor condition

$X_3$ :  Share of UFA 5 per m² GROFA

As outlined in Tab. 68, the linear regression Model 16.B.2 supports the assumption, that, in general, a higher outlay for the repair costs of the building constructions is expected for schools with an above-average storey height and a large proportionate area of UFA 5. With regard to the underlying data sample, this is the case for schools with sports facilities, for example. In addition, those structural components of a building (walls, ceilings and roofs) are included in the estimation model, for which it is likely that higher repair costs per m² GROFA and year incur in case of an evaluated poor condition. These generally higher cost values are largely due to more extensive and costly repair measures required for these components, as opposed to permanent fixtures, for instance. Model 16.B.2 accordingly designates the strategic components whose repair costs should be taken into account in particular in order to predict or compare the likely outlay efficiently.[40]

*Summary*

The investigation takes all the factors outlined in Section 4.1.1 into account for estimating the repair costs of the building constructions based on sample data from 113 public school complexes and an underlying significance level of 5%. The statistical approach initially indicates the gross floor area as the relevant building reference area for estimating the total outlay under investigation and defining cost indicators. In addition, the significance of an underlying good or poor condition of the building constructions for estimating and bench-marking the corresponding repair costs is also addressed, taking the impact of different states of the building constructions in the form of an interaction variable in Model 16.A into account and depicting the level of influence in an appropriate manner. This is followed by arguments in favour of distinguishing between the different cases according to their con-dition in order to estimate the respective cost indicators accurately. While the consideration of additional information produces little improvement in estimating the repair costs investiga-ted for school buildings in a poor state of building constructions, Model 16.B.2 provides the means for achieving better cost predictions when three continuous variables are taken into consideration.

The evaluation of the repair costs of the building constructions not only takes the quantified factor of the general condition of the building constructions but also the age of a school into account as having a possible impact on the outlay. As shown by Fig. 12, a poor state of the respective structural component is particularly common in the case of school buildings that are in the age of 50 (40-60) or 100 (90-110) years, which partly attributes the higher cost indicators to the age. At the same time, this survey of 113 school complexes also shows that a property dating back to 1951-1971 and 1901-1921, only has a 50% probability of incurring higher repair costs of the building constructions due to an age-related poor condition. This percentage may be even lower if standardized categories given in the literature are considered with regard to the relevant years of construction. According to designated categories published by IFB (2006), for example, the construction years between 1850-1918 and 1949-1968 are of theoretical relevance and therefore constitute an alternative to the empirically ascertained age groups described above. If the properties built during these maintenance-intensive periods are taken into account, only 46% of the schools under investigation have building constructions found to be in a poor state of repair. This comparison reveals more precise forecasts for the annual outlay for repairs of the building constructions based on the regression analysis presented above. By taking the condition of building construction into consideration, it is possible to realize more efficient prognoses for the municipal repair outlay likely to be incurred than more general estimates based on the age of the school or the year it was built. To summarize, the statistical analysis into public schools verifies that significant differences in the annual repair costs of building construc-

---

[40] According to Balck (2002, p.363 et seqq.), strategic components are those structural elements which require an in-tensive maintenance throughout their life-cycle.

tions derive from functional and technical characteristics and, in particular, from the condition of the building constructions.

## 4.1.3    Validation of the model

In Section 4.1.2 a distinguishing is made between different conditions of the building constructions for the purpose of predicting the expected outlay for repair measures of the respective structural components. This was followed by a mean value estimate formulated for properties whose building constructions are found to be in a good condition, based on sample data from 44 school complexes ($N_1$). In addition, preference was given to regression Model 16.B.2 for estimating the annual repair costs for municipal schools with a stated poor condition of the building constructions.

With regard to the five validation properties presented in Tab. 69, sample Nos. 1 to 3 show school complexes that have a poor state of repair, and sample Nos. 4 and 5 represent those that have a good condition of building constructions. The estimated outlay for the repairs under investigation is accordingly based on the mean value of 7.62 €/m² GROFA p.a. for sample Nos. 4 and 5 (costs including VAT, based on 2008 figures, $N_1$=44). The predicted cost indicators for sample Nos. 1 to 3 were ascertained using the regression Model 16.B.2, taking the following variables into account: the average storey height, the share of the usable floor area for education, teaching and culture (UFA 5) per m² GROFA as well as the condition of the walls, ceilings and roofs.

Tab. 69:   Model validation for repair cost indicators of building constructions

| No. | Type of school | Observed value | Predicted value | Absolute error % of prediction | Absolute error % of mean | Absolute error % of median | Preference |
|---|---|---|---|---|---|---|---|
| 1 | Elementary school without sports facilities | 28.86 | 33.03 | 14 | 45 | 55 | Prediction |
| 2 | Special school with gymnasium | 27.49 | 40.69 | 48 | 42 | 53 | Mean |
| 3 | Secondary school without sports facilities | 21.60 | 24.74 | 15 | 27 | 41 | Prediction |
| 4 | Secondary school with gymnasium and pool | 5.79 | 7.62 | 31 | 173 | 122 | Prediction |
| 5 | Vocational school without sports facilities | 15.53 | 7.62 | 51 | 2 | 17 | Mean |
| Ø | **Mean Absolute percentage error** | | | **32** | **58** | **58** | **Prediction** |

**Observed value:** Repair costs of building constructions (€/m² gross floor area p.a.), costs including VAT, based on 2008 figures, N=113

The predicted values are listed in Tab. 69 for individual properties and compared with the observed values, as well as with the mean and median estimates of the overall empirical data sample. In total, the cost estimates specified in Section 4.1.2, based on a MAPE of almost 32%, display a good level of accuracy, which is roughly 26% better than the results of both the empirical mean and the median estimates. Whereas for none of the five schools included in the validation test preference can be given to median estimates, the cost models previously presented produce conclusive results with the lowest percentage errors for three out of five properties. Comparing the individual percentage errors, only one estimation error is apparent (sample No.5), which also may be the result of a measuring error. On the whole, the validation test reveals convincing results for the research findings stated above. The practical assessment verifies the reliability of mean value estimates based on $N_1=44$ for schools with a good condition of the building constructions and the significance of quantified impact factors with regard to $N_2$ (building constructions in a poor condition).

## 4.1.4    Cost indicators for the repair of building constructions

Corresponding to the assumptions made in Section 4.1.2 and an evaluation of different conditions of the building constructions, specific cost indicators are presented in Tab. 70 for the annual repair costs per m² GROFA. Empirical measures for central tendency and dispersion are displayed separately for the repair costs of 113 school complexes, depending on whether the building constructions of the underlying properties are found in an overall good or poor condition. Annual cost values uniformly prepared for practical planning and benchmarking purposes include VAT and are based on 2008 figures. Comparing the cost indicators stated below, the average outlay of almost 29 €/m² GROFA p.a. that is indicated for municipal schools whose building constructions are found in a poor condition exceeds the annual outlay for the reference group on average by approximately 21 €/m² GROFA. The corresponding mean repair cost indicator for schools that have their overall building constructions in a good state of repair and thus involved less extensive repair works during the period of observation amounts to just under 8 €/m² GROFA p.a.

Further factors account for other differences in costs, some of which are comprehensible using regression Model 16.B.2 for the determination of an appropriate repair cost indicator for public schools with an assumed poor state of the building constructions within the empirical distribution depicted below. With respect to previous contemplations, reference can particularly be made to the influential variable $X_1$ (average storey height) that has the largest partial regression coefficient ($beta_1=0.505$) in the multivariate Model 16.B.2. This variable can thus be used to define an adequate cost indicator between the stated limits of 16.30 and 51.01 €/m² GROFA p.a., particularly for repair measures on upright components. In this way, a further grading of repair cost indicators can be carried out on the basis of the distributions presented here which acquires a greater significance for the purpose of occupancy cost planning and benchmarking.

Tab. 70:    Evaluated cost indicators for the repair of building constructions

| Factor level | Minimum | Mean | Median | Maximum | Range |
|---|---|---|---|---|---|
| Building constructions in a good condition | 0.70 | 7.62 | 6.94 | 15.59 | 14.90 |
| Building constructions in a poor condition | 16.30 | 28.71 | 27.20 | 51.01 | 34.71 |

Dependent variable: Costs (€/m² gross floor area p.a.), costs including VAT, based on 2008 figures, N=113

## 4.2    Repair of technical installations

### 4.2.1    Empirical and theoretical basis

With reference to 2008, the calendar year in question, the repair costs for technical installations account at an average of 6.50 €/m² GROFA p.a. (costs including VAT) for a considerable proportion of the overall repair costs, which are only exceeded by the repair costs of building constructions.

Compared to the empirical cost indicators for the inspection and maintenance of technical installations, which are generally slightly higher than those for building constructions, the average costs for the repair of technical installations are substantially lower than the building repair costs. The underlying repair costs of technical installations for 113 school complexes were incurred for the following structural components and cost groups respectively, as defined in DIN 18960:2008-2:

- Sewage, water and gas supply systems (cost group 421)

- Heat supply systems (cost group 422)

- Air treatment systems (cost group 423)

- Power installations (cost group 424)

- Telecommunications and other communications systems (cost group 425)

- Transport systems (cost group 426)

- Function-related equipment (cost group 427)

- Building automation (cost group 428)

- Repair of technical installations, other items (cost group 429)

Besides the annual outlay for the repair of technical installations, various information on the type, standard and intensity of usage as well as on the functional and technical characteristics of 113 school properties were collected, and analyzed within the context of this study. The underlying factors of the examination are presented in the overview set out below.

**Factor group: Utilization**

*Type of utilization:*

- Primary utilization: Elementary school, secondary school such as comprehensive school (secondary general school, intermediate secondary school, multiple school center) or grammar school, special school, vocational school with technical or business focus; qualitative description of different utilization types and quantitative description of the school utilization area in m² NEFA as well as its proportion per m² NEFA of the whole school property.

- Secondary utilization: Sports facilities such as gymnasiums or indoor swimming pools for teaching purposes, nursery school; qualitative and quantitative description of different utilization types with regard to their building reference areas e.g. the net floor area of a gymnasium or swimming pool utilization in m² and their representative proportions per m² NEFA.

*Standard of utilization:*

- Type of educational program: Regular school, extended regular school or full-day school.

- Type of canteen service: School based canteen, external catering or no canteen service.

- Total number of computer workstations.

*Intensity of utilization:*

- Temporal usage intensity:

  Average operating time of the whole school complex as well as individual operating times of both the primary and secondary utilizations, i.e. the school and its sports facilities, in hours per school week and with regard to the average number of schooldays per school week.

- Spatial usage intensity:

  Qualitative and quantitative description of the spatial standard e.g. the total size of specific floor areas according to DIN 277:2005-2 (Part 1 and 2) in relation to the number of pupils or school classes as well as other reference areas such as m² net floor area of school utilization with respect to the number of pupils or school classes.

**Factor group: Functional and technical characteristics**

*Functional characteristics:*

- Specific building floor areas according to DIN 277:2005-2 (Part 1 and 2) e.g. in m² GROFA, m² NEFA, m² UFA, m² TEFA, m² UFA 5 and their representative proportion to the total size of a property in m² GROFA or other specific building floor areas e.g. the share of TEFA per m² NEFA.

- The average storey height according to DIN 277-1: 2005-2.

- Total heatable gross floor area according to VDI 3807-01:2007-03 and its representative proportion to the total size of a property in m² GROFA according to DIN 277-1:2005-2.

- The total sanitary area and its proportion to specific building floor areas according to DIN 277:2005-2 (Part 1 and 2) e.g. the share of the sanitary area per m² UFA.

*Technical characteristics:*

- Standard of building constructions:

  - Age of a school property.

- Standard of technical installations:

  - Qualitative and quantitative description of the standard of technical installations and in particular the standard of water supply systems, heat generators and heating control systems e.g. the number of decentralized water heaters, heat generators including or excluding central water heaters.

  - Number of lifts and average number of lift-stops.

- Condition of technical installations:

  Qualitative and quantitative description of the condition of technical installations and in particular the condition of sewage systems, water supply systems, sanitary installations, heat supply systems or power installations e.g. the percentage of defective heat supply systems.

### 4.2.2    Model design and parameters

The best forecast for the total costs to be incurred for the repair of technical installations (Y) is achieved by Model 17.A, described below, by taking the net floor area of a school complex into account. As in the corresponding investigation into the outlay for the inspection and maintenance of technical installations (Model 9.A), this building reference area is deemed to exert a significant influence on the annual expenses and therefore used for defining cost indicators. In accordance with the German Standard DIN 277-1:2005-1, the net floor area also includes the technical floor area, and their variation between the schools under analysis is therefore also taken into account for total cost estimates.

Apart from the effect of this continuous variable, the trivariate regression Model 17.A also incorporates differences in the condition of the technical installations. Here, the overall state of the respective 113 school complexes is defined as a weighted factor that particularly takes the individual conditions of the sewage and water supply systems (inclusive the sanitary installations), the heat supply systems as well as the state of the power installations into account (i.e. cost groups 410, 420 and 440 according to DIN 276-1:2006-11, see Tab. 112). Based on this survey, the technical installations of a school complex are deter-mined to represent a poor condition if at least two out of these aforementioned structural components considered on lower structural cost are simultaneously found in an ineffective state of repair and, in addition, if these components supply a representative proportion of a school's total size, i.e. a supplied share above 75% of a school's net floor area.

In compliance with Model 16.A, a distinction between a school's condition (i.a. an overall good or poor state of repair) is expressed in the form of an interaction term, which is specified by the variable $X_1^{\cdot}$ (poor condition of technical installations*m² NEFA) for the cost group under analysis. Taking this multiplicative term $X_1^{\cdot}$ into account, it is possible to estimate the outlay for municipal repair measures based on different condition categories of the technical installations concerned, which are depicted in Model 17.A by varied increase rates in Y. Fig. 13 illustrates these costs estimates for technical installations in a good con-dition on the basis of $b_2=5.164$ and, in the case of those described to be in a poor state of repair, based on $b_{1,2}=18.726$ (cf. Tab. 71). The regression model described above verifies accurate predictions, with R²=0.882, for the underlying sample of 113 school complexes. As described in previous analysis for total cost estimates, a non-significant constant may be disregarded for this purpose.

Tab. 71:   Model description for estimating total repair costs of technical installations

| Dependent variable | Transf. | R² | R² adj. | SEE | F-value | Sign. | Durbin-Watson-Statistic | | N |
|---|---|---|---|---|---|---|---|---|---|
| Repair costs of technical installations | - | 0.882 | 0.880 | 23424 | 410.474 | 0.000 | 1.963 | | 113 |

| Factors | Transf. | B | St. Error | Beta | t-value | Sign. | Lower CL | Upper CL | T | VIF |
|---|---|---|---|---|---|---|---|---|---|---|
| Constant | - | -7160 | 3768 | | -1.900 | 0.060 | -14628 | 307.461 | | |
| Poor condition of technical installations* m² NEFA | - | 13.562 | 0.608 | 0.759 | 22.288 | 0.000 | 12.356 | 14.768 | 0.927 | 1.079 |
| Net floor area (NEFA in m²) | - | 5.164 | 0.457 | 0.385 | 11.305 | 0.000 | 4.259 | 6.069 | 0.927 | 1.079 |

**Dependent variable**: Repair costs of technical installations (€ p.a.), costs including VAT, based on 2008 figures

$$\hat{Y} = -7,160 + 13.562X_1^* + 5.164X_2$$                     (Model 17.A)

Where:     $\hat{Y}$ :   Repair costs of technical installations (€ p.a.)

$X_1^*$ :   Poor condition of technical installations*m² net floor area

$X_2$ :   Net floor area (NEFA in m²)

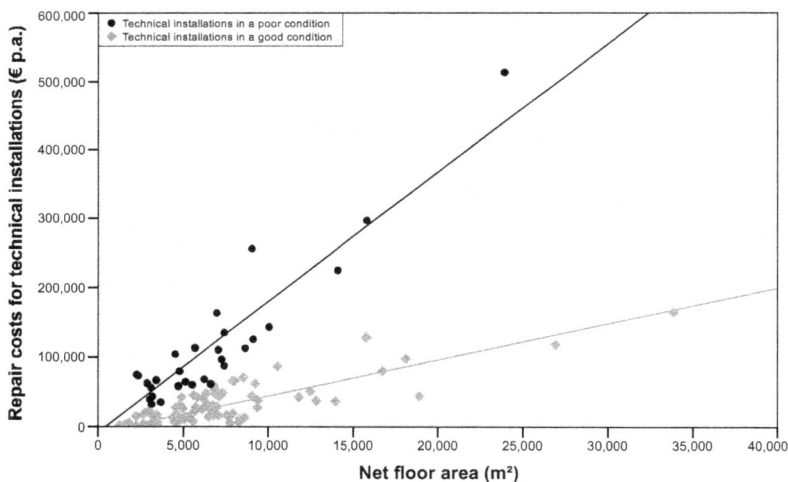

Fig. 13:   Comparison between observed and predicted repair costs of technical installations (costs including VAT, based on 2008 figures)

The investigation into the repair cost indicators for technical installations set out below is based on the aforementioned analysis of total repair costs and therefore uses the net floor area as for determining indicators in accordance with Model 17.A.

According to the approach described in Section 4.1.2 for the statistical evaluation of repair cost indicators for building constructions, the first step is to examine whether the analysis of the repair costs for technical installations can be implemented for the entire sample of 113 school complexes or whether it is necessary to create subsamples with regard to individual conditions. For this purpose, the t-test for mean value comparisons and the Levene Test (F-test) for the analysis of variance is again carried out. Both aspects are examined for an underlying sample data based on $N_1=84$ (technical installations in good condition) and $N_2=29$ (technical installations in poor condition), on the basis of an empirical cost distribution which is approximately normalized. The latter assumption of normalized costs can be statistically verified using the Kolmogorov-Smirnov test for both subsamples. This is followed by a t-test with an empirical significance level of 0.00 (the empirical t-value is -15.943), which shows that the difference in the mean values of the two subsamples amounting to 12.96 €/m² NEFA p.a. (costs including VAT, based on 2008 figures) does not appear random. Instead, the significance test confirms that the mean cost indicator of $N_2$ lies systematically above the mean value of $N_1$ so the null hypothesis $H_0(\mu_1 = \mu_2)$ is rejected in favour of the alternative hypothesis $H_1(\mu_1 < \mu_2)$ at a significance level of 5%. At an empirical F-value of 40.726 and a significance level of 0.00, moreover, the Levene Test confirms that the assumption of equal variances likewise has to be discarded. Both tests accordingly prove that the samples $N_1=84$ (technical installations in good condition) and $N_2=29$ (technical installations in poor condition) differ considerably in terms of their mean values and variances, and it is for this reason that the analysis of repair costs indicators set out below has been carried out separately for technical installations in a good condition and those in a poor condition.

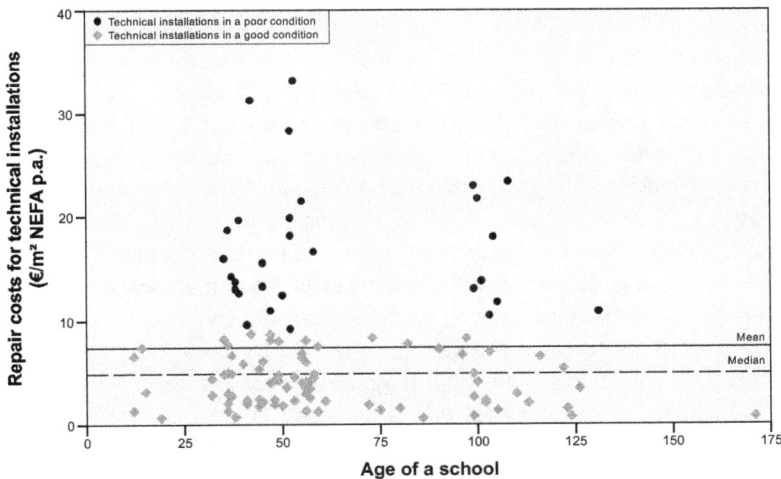

Fig. 14:    Empirical repair cost indicators for technical installations (costs including VAT, based on 2008 figures)

In the case of technical installations ascertained to be in a good state of repair, the best estimation model for $N_1$ is achieved by taking the continuous variable gross building volume, as defined in DIN 277-1:2005-2, into account. Since the specified bivariate regression model only explains a small part of the overall variation in the underlying repair costs of technical installations ($R^2$ <10%), and the impact of this variable (gross building volume) is shown to be just slightly significant by a sample of 84 school complexes, this model is rejected for the purpose of estimating the repair costs concerned.

The analysis of cost indicators in the case of technical installations in a poor condition produced similar results. The investigation shows that higher cost indicators generally occur for the underlying 29 school complexes over the course of the year 2008 whenever the survey reveals that the sanitary installations were in a poor condition. Accordingly, the univariate variance analysis reveals that, where the sanitary installations are found to be in a poor state, this has an influence on the outlay for repairs on technical installations. At a $R^2$ of 0.150, however, this model is likewise regarded as highly unreliable and is consequently not presented more detailed within this analysis. Neither the underlying data for technical installations in a good condition nor the data for those in a bad condition allow a reliable function to be formulated for estimating the municipal repair costs for technical installations. The residuals, i.e. differences between the observed and predicted values, delineate uncertainties in estimates, making the results unsuitable for a detailed prognosis on property level. On the basis of different condition categories, evaluated above, it is therefore recommended to base forecasts for the repair cost indicators of technical installations on the empirical mean values.

*Summary*

The empirical investigation of repair costs for the technical installations of 113 schools in Germany evaluates theoretically relevant factors described in Section 4.2.1. The statistical analysis of total costs reveals that the most efficient cost estimates are achieved by the trivariate regression Model 17.A taking into account a school's net floor area as a continuous variable, and the condition of the technical installations specified as an interaction variable. As a multiplicative term, this interaction variable denotes the mutual influence of the size of a school complex, measured in $m^2$ net floor area, and the actual condition of the technical installations, thus allowing different rates of increase in the underlying repair costs to be depicted satisfactorily in the statistical model. This consequently leads to specify that a statistical evaluation of the respective repair costs should be carried out separately for the technical installations found to be either in a good or poor condition. In order to obtain consistent and unbiased cost estimates, this requirement is implemented in the form of a case distinction for the different states of technical installations in the subsequent analysis of the repair cost indicators. In view of the sample data at disposal, however, no further assumptions can be statistically verified with respect to the causal interrelations at a significance level of 5% so the empirical measures of central tendency (mean and median values) for the aforementioned subsamples $N_1$ and $N_2$ remain the best possible means of estimating the cost indicators.

As an alternative to the cost estimates presented here, the age of a building or its technical installations are frequently used to delineate cost indicators. The uncertainties in those estimates that inevitably occur with more general predictions of this kind, are outlined in the comparison set out below. For the empirical sample concerned, 50 (40-60) and 100 (90-110) years respectively can be regarded as the critical age for the technical installations, when a school occasionally incurs a higher outlay for repair measures (see Fig. 14). Only approximately 29% of the 113 school complexes under investigation that belong in these age groups reveal higher repair cost indicators, however.[41] In terms of the empirical sample data, this means that the predicted annual outlay for repairs would be set too high for roughly 71% of the schools that were built between 1951-1971 or 1901-1921.

Beyond this case distinction, the procedure outlined above would also have far-reaching consequences for occupancy cost planning and benchmarking, however. If the two prediction methods are compared with one another, the mean cost indicator for the two age groups (construction years between 1951-1971 and 1901-1921 respectively) amounts to 8.22 €/m² NEFA p.a., which is about 8.82 €/m² NEFA p.a. lower than the cost indicator estimated here for technical installations found to be in a poor condition (costs including VAT, based on 2008 figures). This comparison illustrates the more precise cost estimates, described according to different conditions of the technical installations in question, versus the more unreliable cost prognoses based on the estimated outlay for repairs depending on the age of a school or the year it was built.

### 4.2.3    Validation of the model

Tab. 72 depicts the validation test for the repair cost of technical installations conducted across 5 school complexes that were not included in the model development process before. Based on an evaluation of the condition of technical installations, the validation test shows outstanding results for assumptions postulated above for defining the cost indicators for the repair of technical installations.

Tab. 72:   Model validation for repair cost indicators of technical installations

| No. | Type of school | Observed value | Predicted value | Absolute error % of prediction | Absolute error % of mean | Absolute error % of median | Preference |
|-----|----------------|----------------|-----------------|-------------------------------|--------------------------|----------------------------|------------|
| 1 | Elementary school without sports facilities | 1.45 | 4.08 | 181 | 411 | 239 | Prediction |
| 2 | Special school with gymnasium | 4.13 | 4.08 | 1 | 79 | 19 | Prediction |
| 3 | Secondary school without sports facilities | 3.62 | 4.08 | 13 | 105 | 36 | Prediction |
| 4 | Secondary school with gymnasium and pool | 5.99 | 4.08 | 32 | 24 | 18 | Median |
| 5 | Vocational school without sports facilities | 16.64 | 17.04 | 2 | 55 | 70 | Prediction |
| Ø | **Mean Absolute percentage error** | | | **46** | 135 | 76 | **Prediction** |

Observed value: Repair costs of technical installations (€/m² net floor area p.a.), costs including VAT, based on 2008 figures, N=113

[41] Taking into account age groups for buildings published in the literature, such as 1850-1918 or 1949-1968 as per IFB (2006), this corresponds to roughly 27% of the schools under analysis.

Based on the evaluation of technical installations in a good or poor state of repair, the mean absolute percentage error of prediction, stated at 46%, is roughly 89% lower than the MAPE of the mean estimate and about 31% lower than the MAPE of the median of all the sample data from 113 school complexes under investigation. Samples Nos. 1 to 4 were found to be in a good condition, whereas the technical installations in sample No.5 were in a poor state of repair. This information forms the basis for the validation test of this cost group. The underlying cost indicators given in €/m² NEFA p.a. include VAT and are based on 2008 figures. The corresponding indexing table for annual price adjustments is provided by Destatis (2011b).

By comparing the three prediction methods described above for estimating the repair costs of technical installations, it is evident that the mean value estimate yields a poor approximation to the observed values. Conversely, no preference could be given to the median estimate for any of the 5 cases taken into consideration in the validation test for the repair costs of building constructions.

### 4.2.4    Cost indicators for the repair of technical installations

For the repair of technical installations, an overall average of 7.41 €/m² NEFA p.a., coupled with a range of 32.51 €/m² NEFA p.a., is given in Tab. 101 for 113 school complexes (costs including VAT, based on 2008 figures). These empirical cost indicators were examined within a statistical examination in an attempt to provide more precise cost estimates to support the practical cost planning of repairs. In the process, a substantial difference in the annual outlay for repairs is discovered and validated according to the condition of technical installations. Tab. 73 accordingly displays the specific cost indicators provided for repair planning purposes, taking two different categories into account (technical installations in a good or a poor condition). Together with the cost indicators for the inspection and maintenance of technical installations, as shown in Tab. 48, the cost indicators given here in €/m² NEFA p.a. for the repair costs of technical installations (costs including VAT, based on 2008 figures) can be added to the overall maintenance costs for technical installations.

Tab. 73 shows that, at about 17 €/m² NEFA p.a., the mean cost indicator for those schools whose technical installations are found to be in poor condition is, on average, about 13 €/m² NEFA p.a. higher than the cost indicator in the reference category (technical installations in a good condition). Where the technical installations are declared to be in a good state of repair, the gross building volume according to DIN 277-1:2005-2 is additionally named in Section 4.2.2 by way of an independent variable for the purpose of estimating costs. Conversely, in cases where the state of the technical installations is assumed to be poor, differences in outlay are in particular related to the condition of sanitary installations. Both influential factors can be additionally used, when establishing the repair costs for a specific planning purpose, in order to determine an appropriate cost indicator in the categories outlined below more precisely.

Tab. 73:   Evaluated cost indicators for the repair of technical installations

| Factor level | Minimum | Mean | Median | Maximum | Range |
|---|---|---|---|---|---|
| Technical installations in a good condition | 0.64 | 4.08 | 3.63 | 8.77 | 8.13 |
| Technical installations in a poor condition | 9.27 | 17.04 | 15.56 | 33.15 | 23.88 |

Dependent variable: Costs (€/m² net floor area p.a.), costs including VAT, based on 2008 figures, N=113

## 4.3     Repair of grounds and outdoor facilities

### 4.3.1    Empirical and theoretical basis

Cost bookings from 71 school complexes are available for the year in question for examining the annual repair costs for the grounds and outdoor facilities, so the statistical analysis falls back on this database. With an average outlay of 0.44 €/m² GROFA p.a. (costs including VAT, based on 2008 figures) this cost group represents the lowest rate on the second cost level according to DIN 18960:2008-2 in the year under analysis. The statistical evaluation of the annual outlay for the repair of school grounds and outdoor facilities takes into account the measures undertaken on the following positions, as defined by DIN 18960:2008-2 on the third structural cost level:

* Grounds (cost group 431)
* Hard surfaces (cost group 432)
* Outdoor constructions (cost group 433)
* Outdoor technical installations (cost group 434)
* Permanent outdoor fixtures (cost group 435)
* Repair of grounds and outdoor facilities, other items (cost group 439)

On the basis of outlined factors above, the following descriptions of school utilization, their functional, technical as well as local characteristics area included in the statistical evaluation of the annual outlay for the repairs of school grounds and outdoor facilities.

**Factor group: Utilization**

*Type of utilization:*

* Primary and secondary utilization: Qualitative description of different utilization types such as elementary school, secondary school, special school, vocational school or nursery school.

*Standard of utilization:*

* Type of educational program: Regular school, extended regular school or full-day school.

*Intensity of utilization:*

• Temporal usage intensity:

  Average operating time of the whole school complex in hours per school week.

• Spatial usage intensity:

  • Total number of pupils, number of pupils per m² non-built up area of the plot and number of pupils with respect to the school playground area.

  • The total number of school classes, number of school classes per m² non-built up area of the plot and number of school classes with respect to the school playground area.

**Factor group: Functional and technical characteristics**

*Technical characteristics:*

• Standard of grounds and outdoor facilities:

  • Standard of grounds and outdoor facilities: Higher or lower standard.

  • Total size of property area in m².

  • Non-built up area of the plot in m² and its designated sections such as school playground area, sports area, green area and irrigated grounds in m² and their representative proportion to the non-built up area of the plot.

• Condition of grounds and outdoor facilities:

  Qualitative description of the condition of grounds and outdoor facilities and in particular the condition of hard surfaces, outdoor constructions, permanent outdoor fixtures or green areas: Good or poor condition.

**Factor group: Location:**

• Region: Urban, suburban or rural.

• Topography: Flat or sloped.

**4.3.2   Model design and parameters**

The investigation conducted into the repair costs of the grounds and outdoor facilities (Y) takes into account the costs incurred in 2008 for the aforementioned repair measures carried out at 71 school complexes. Apart from the available information on the type and intensity of a school's usage and its functional and technical characteristics, the statistical data evaluation also comprises descriptions of the location of a school complex (region and typography) which may exert an influence on the outlay for the repair of school grounds and outdoor facilities from a theoretical point of view.

In accordance with previous remarks on predicting municipal repair costs of specific structural components, Model 18.A produces the best estimates for the total repair costs of grounds and outdoor facilities, forming the subject of this investigation, taking a suitable reference area ($X_2$) and an evaluation of the condition of the underlying school grounds and outdoor facilities into account, by means of an interaction variable ($X_1^*$). Whereas a good condition of the grounds and outdoor school facilities is determined by the condition categories A (good) and B (rather good) for the respective structural components taken into account in the questionnaire, the grounds and outdoor school facilities are found to be in a poor state of repair, if the data survey revealed considerable damages for hard surfaces, such as sports grounds and playgrounds, paths, squares or courtyards, outdoor constructions, in terms of walls, ramps or stairs, as well as for permanent outdoor fixtures such as sports grounds or playgrounds, i.e. cost groups 520, 530 and 550 according to DIN 276-1:2006-11 (see Tab. 112). This is particularly the case, if the condition category D (i.e. a poor state of repair) is simultaneously ascertained for either the cost groups 520 and 530 or the cost groups 520 and 550 respectively.

The non-built up area of a plot, which has already been employed for predicting the total costs for the inspection and maintenance of grounds and outdoor facilities is again used as the appropriate reference area ($X_2$) for drawing up absolute cost estimates. This makes it easy to compare both indicators and determine the overall maintenance costs for school grounds and outdoor facilities (according to DIN 31051:2003-6). Further details on the regression Model 18.A designated in this section are shown in Tab. 74. In line with Models 16.A and 17.A, used for estimating the total repair costs for building constructions and technical installations respectively, Model 18.A represents another linear model for continuous costs estimates based on an appropriate reference area ($X_2$). Fig. 15 illustrates the quality of the defined prediction model. Based on $R^2=0.648$ (SEE=1.997), the model shows a satisfactory forecasting standard for total cost estimates regarding this cost group. In addition, no substantial influence on Y can be statistically verified for any of the other factors under investigation, based on an underlying significance level of 5%.

Tab. 74:  Model description for estimating total repair costs of grounds and outdoor facilities

| Dependent variable | Transf. | $R^2$ | $R^2$ adj. | SEE | F-value | Sign. | Durbin-Watson-Statistic | | N |
|---|---|---|---|---|---|---|---|---|---|
| Repair costs of grounds and outdoor facilities | - | 0.648 | 0.638 | 1997 | 62.692 | 0.000 | 2.199 | | 71 |

| Factors | Transf. | B | St. Error | Beta | t-value | Sign. | Lower CL | Upper CL | T | VIF |
|---|---|---|---|---|---|---|---|---|---|---|
| Constant | - | 1005 | 372.143 | | 2.700 | 0.009 | 262.22 | 1747.43 | | |
| Poor condition of grounds and outdoor facilities*m² non-built up plot area | - | 0.610 | 0.056 | 0.786 | 10.926 | 0.000 | 0.499 | 0.722 | 1.000 | 1.000 |
| Non-built up plot area (m²) | - | 0.056 | 0.023 | 0.177 | 2.461 | 0.016 | 0.011 | 0.101 | 1.000 | 1.000 |

**Dependent variable:** Repair costs of grounds and outdoor facilities (€ p.a.), costs including VAT, based on 2008 figures

$$\hat{Y} = 1,005 + 0.610X_1^* + 0.056X_2 \qquad \text{(Model 18.A)}$$

Where:  $\hat{Y}$ :  Repair costs of grounds and outdoor facilities (€ p.a.)

$X_1^*$ :  Poor condition of grounds and outdoor facilities*m² non-built up plot area

$X_2$ :  Non-built up area of the plot (part of the property area in m²)

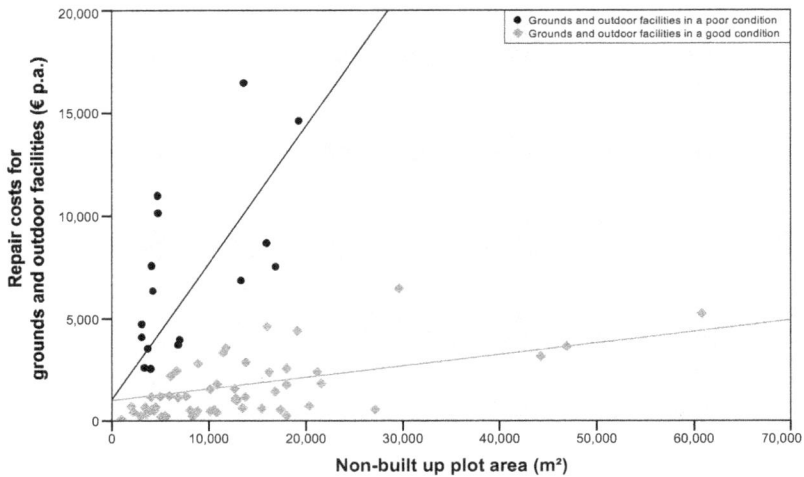

Fig. 15:   Comparison between observed and predicted repair costs of grounds and outdoor
           facilities (costs including VAT, based on 2008 figures)

The investigation into repair cost indicators for school grounds and outdoor facilities set out below is based on the estimation Model 18.A described above, and takes the non-built up area of a plot into consideration for the normalization of cost data. In order to clarify the uncertainty of subdivided reference samples according to the condition of grounds and outdoor facilities, a t-test is carried out, in accordance with the explanations in Section 4.1.2, to detect any discrepancies in the mean values. In addition, the Leven test is applied, by way of a F-Test to check the homogeneity of variance. Both issues are based on an empirical data sample of $N_1=55$ (grounds and outdoor facilities in a good condition) and $N_2=16$ (grounds and outdoor facilities in a poor condition), whose empirical cost distribution is approximately normal in each case. The assumption of normally distributed data is statistically verified by the Kolmogorov-Smirnov test with an empirical significance level of 0.134 for $N_1$ or 0.818 for $N_2$ respectively. The t-Test employed for this purpose tests the null hypothesis of equal average values, $H_0(\mu_1 = \mu_2)$, versus the assumption that the mean value of the data sample of $N_2$ is systematically higher than the average cost indicator of $N_1$, i.e. $H_1(\mu_1 < \mu_2)$. The result of the t-test corroborates the alternative hypothesis $H_1$ with an empirical significance level of 0.00 (empirical t-value is -15.943), so the hypothesis of equal average values is rejected at a 5% significance level. Furthermore, the Levene test is conducted to test the null hypothesi $H_0(\sigma_1 = \sigma_2)$ against the undirected alternative hypothesis $H_1(\sigma_1 \neq \sigma_2)$ and, with an empirical F-value of 110.275 and a corresponding significance level of 0.00, verifies that the assumption of variance equality likewise has to be rejected. Both test statistics accordingly endorse the assumptions that the two subsamples concerned differ significantly from one another, both in their mean outlay and in their relevant distribution, so the following analysis of cost indicators is conducted separately for $N_1$ and $N_2$ respectively.

While the evaluation of the data sample of $N_1$, where the grounds and outdoor facilities are found to be in a good condition, gives no clues to any influential factors, it is possible to reveal a negative and nonlinear correlation between the size of a school's non-built up plot area and the underlying repair cost indicators for the grounds and outdoor facilities (€/m² non-built up plot area p.a.) in the case of $N_2$ (grounds and outdoor facilities in a poor condition). From the point of view of content, this means that the mean cost indicator for the repair costs of grounds and outdoor facilities continuously decreases in inverse direction to an increase of a property's size, measured in m² of the non-built up plot area of a school. In regard to the small sample size ($N_2$=16) under investigation, however, this regression analysis contains estimation uncertainties that may be due to outliers, for example, and which might have a significant or incidental impact on the partial regression coefficients $b_j$ to be estimated. The bivariate regression model is accordingly assessed as unstable in favor of those estimates formulated by the empirical mean value for $N_1$ and $N_2$.

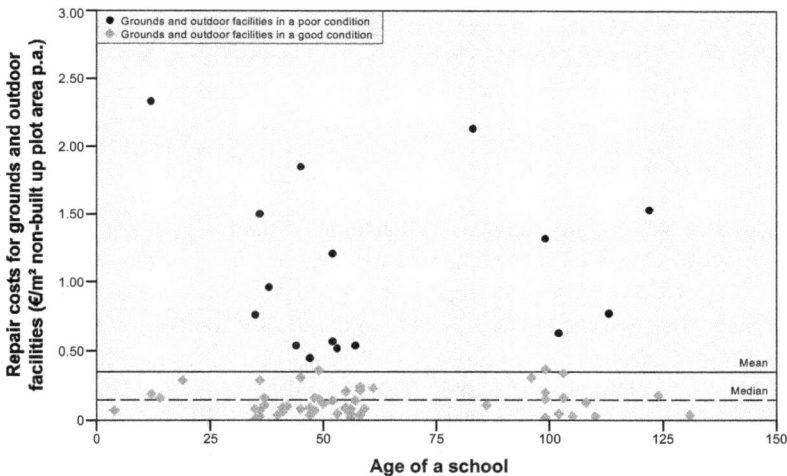

Fig. 16:   Empirical repair cost indicators for grounds and outdoor facilities (costs including VAT, based on 2008 figures)

*Summary*

The statistical analysis of relevant factors impacting on the repair costs for grounds and outdoor facilities is based on sample data of 71 public schools in Germany and takes the year of construction and the condition of grounds and outdoor facilities into account, among other factors. Based on an evaluation of the underlying total repair costs for grounds and outdoor facilities (Model 18.A), a significant influence of the non-built up area of a school's plot is established, so this specific part of the property area is used for defining the respective cost indicators. Additionally, the independent impact of the condition of grounds and outdoor facilities on the total repair outlay for technical installations is verified, specified in the form of an interactive variable. This factor is calculated multiplicatively from the evaluation of the condition examined and a school's non-built up plot area by way of a weighting factor. Both factors, the non-built up plot area as well as the condition of grounds and outdoor facilities, describe specific technical characteristics of a school complex.

The following examination of the cost indicators for the grounds and outdoor facilities (€/m² non-built up plot area p.a.) likewise confirms the need to distinguish between different condition categories. Comparing the empirical cost indicators for schools whose grounds and outdoor facilities are in a poor state it also becomes obvious that schools with a larger area of the non-built up plot generally have lower cost indicators. This can be partly explained by the often larger expanse of green areas in bigger school complexes. Taking the data sample and size into account, however, the mean value estimates are considered to produce more reliable prognoses for the annual outlay of municipal repair costs under analysis, in either a good or a poor state of the grounds and outdoor facilities. The quality of the estimates described here (by taking different condition categories into consideration) can also be contrasted with those cost indicators specified according to the age of a property in question. As outlined in Fig. 16, only 24% of the school complexes that were built around 45 (35-55) and 105 (95-115) years ago respectively have grounds and outdoor facilities that are found to be in a poor state, which shows that forecast based solely on age are again more risky than the estimates conducted here on the basis of different condition categories.

### 4.3.3    Validation of the model

Section 4.3.2 above set out the variation in the repair costs for municipal school grounds and outdoor facilities depending on whether the grounds and outdoor facilities are in a good or poor state of repair. Within a next step, mean value estimates were defined based on empirical data for the two subsamples $N_1=55$ (grounds and outdoor facilities in a good condition) and $N_2=16$ (grounds and outdoor facilities in a poor condition). In this way, the investigation identifies a characteristic value of 0.13 €/m² non-built up plot area p.a. for the repair costs of grounds and outdoor facilities found to be in a good condition and contrasts this assumption with an average cost indicator of 1.10 €/m² non-built up plot area p.a. in the reference group (poor condition). The underlying costs are based on 2008 figures and include VAT.

Tab. 75:   Model validation for repair cost indicators of grounds and outdoor facilities

| No. | Type of school | Observed value | Predicted value | Absolute error % of prediction | Absolute error % of mean | Absolute error % of median | Preference |
|-----|----------------|----------------|-----------------|--------------------------------|--------------------------|----------------------------|------------|
| 1 | Elementary school without sports facilities | 0.70 | 1.10 | 57 | 50 | 79 | Mean |
| 2 | Special school with gymnasium | 0.03 | 0.13 | 341 | 1068 | 400 | Prediction |
| 3 | Secondary school without sports facilities | - | - | - | - | - | - |
| 4 | Secondary school with gymnasium and pool | 0.02 | 0.13 | 561 | 1652 | 650 | Prediction |
| 5 | Vocational school without sports facilities | 0.23 | 0.13 | 43 | 52 | 35 | Median |
| Ø | Mean Absolute percentage error | | | 268 | 706 | 291 | Prediction |

Observed value: Costs (€/m² non-built up plot area p.a.), costs including VAT, based on 2008 figures, N=71

Based on these estimates, Tab. 75 compares the absolute percentage errors of prediction with the percentage errors resulting from overall mean and median predictions. The applied validation test comprises 4 schools, as there are no cost bookings available for sample No.3 and the calendar year in question. With regard to the remaining 4 cases, sample No.1 indicates grounds and outdoor facilities in a poor condition, whereas the respective state of the other 3 validated properties were found to be in a good condition from the point of view of the collated data. On average, all three estimation methods produced fairly large deviations from the observed values. By comparison, the estimates for $N_1$ and $N_2$ described above, those reveal the smallest percentage error, however, thus confirming the considerations set out in Section 4.3.2.

## 4.3.4    Cost indicators for the repair of grounds and outdoor facilities

The provision of cost indicators for the repair of grounds and outdoor facilities relies primarily on the empirical sampling distribution of the two subsamples $N_1$ (grounds and outdoor facilities in a good condition) and $N_2$ (grounds and outdoor facilities in a poor condition), which were defined in Section 4.3.2 on the basis of 71 school complexes. The corresponding cost indicators in €/m² non-built up plot area p.a. are displayed in Tab. 76 and, in particular, can be compared with the cost indicators given for the inspection and maintenance of school grounds and outdoor facilities (see Tab. 52).

Where the grounds and outdoor facilities are found to be in a good condition, the empirical cost data collected from 55 school complexes particularly reveals a comparatively small range of 0.36 €/m² non-built up plot area p.a. (costs including VAT, based on 2008 figures), as shown in Tab. 76. In the case, the grounds and outdoor facilities are stated to be in a poor condition, empirical measures are described more detailed for two subcategories. In consistency with the correlation previously revealed between a school's total size of the non-built up plot area and its annual outlay, differentiated indicators for the subcategories of the non-built up plot area grater or equal to and smaller than 5,000 m² respectively are provided. The empirical median of 4,740 m² non-built up plot area is applied as the distinguishing criterion in this case. The cost indicators constituted for the two subcategories support the assumption formulated in Section 4.3.2 that the total size of the non-built up plot area has a negative influence on the municipal repair costs of grounds and outdoor facilities. It is not possible to give any further explanations for the dispersion of observed cost indicators, based on the analysis conducted and the underlying sample data compiled on property level.

Tab. 76:   Evaluated cost indicators for the repair of grounds and outdoor facilities

| Factor level | Minimum | Mean | Median | Maximum | Range |
|---|---|---|---|---|---|
| Grounds and outdoor facilities in a good condition | 0.01 | 0.13 | 0.10 | 0.37 | 0.36 |
| Grounds and outdoor facilities in a poor condition | 0.45 | 1.10 | 0.87 | 2.33 | 1.88 |
| Non-built up plot area  < 5,000 m² | 0.63 | 1.45 | 1.50 | 2.33 | 1.70 |
| Non-built up plot area  ≥ 5,000 m² | 0.45 | 0.66 | 0.54 | 1.21 | 0.76 |

Dependent variable: Costs (€/m² non-built up plot area p.a.), costs including VAT, based on 2008 figures, N=71

## 4.4    Repair of fittings, furnishings and equipment

### 4.4.1    Empirical and theoretical basis

With 0.60 €/m² GROFA, the annual repair costs for fittings, furnishings and equipment in 2008 represent a minor portion of the overall repair costs (costs including VAT). The empirical analysis is based on the repair costs that were ascertained for the cost groups below, according to DIN 18960:2008-2:

- Fittings, furnishings and equipment (cost group 441)
- Works of art (cost group 442)
- Repair of fittings, furnishings and equipment, other items (cost group 449)

The underlying factors for the statistical evaluation of the municipal repair costs for fittings, furnishings and equipment are presented by the following list of independent variables that form the basis of this survey:

**Factor group: Utilization**

*Type of utilization:*

- Primary utilization: Elementary school, secondary school such as comprehensive school (secondary general school, intermediate secondary school, multiple school center) or grammar school, special school, vocational school with technical or business focus; qualitative description of different utilization types and quantitative description of the school utilization area in m² NEFA as well as its proportion per m² NEFA of the whole school property.
- Secondary utilization: Sports facilities such as gymnasiums or indoor swimming pools for teaching purposes, nursery school; qualitative and quantitative description of different utilization types with regard to their building reference areas e.g. the net floor area of a gymnasium or swimming pool utilization in m² and their representative proportions per m² NEFA.

*Standard of utilization:*

- Type of educational program: Regular school, extended regular school or full-day school.
- Total number of computer workstations.

*Intensity of utilization:*

- Temporal usage intensity:

  Average operating time of the whole school complex as well as individual operating times of both the primary and secondary utilizations, i.e. the school and its sports facilities, in hours per school week and with regard to the average number of schooldays per school week.

- Spatial usage intensity:

  - The total number of pupils, number of pupils per m² specific floor area according to DIN 277:2005-2 (Part 1 and 2) and the number of pupils with respect to other reference areas such as m² net floor area of school utilization e.g. the number of pupils per m² GROFA.

  - The total number of school classes, number of school classes per m² specific floor area according to DIN 277:2005-2 (Part 1 and 2) and number of school classes with respect to other reference areas such as m² net floor area of school utilization e.g. the number of school classes per m² GROFA.

**Factor group: Functional and technical characteristics**

*Functional characteristics:*

- Specific building floor areas according to DIN 277:2005-2 (Part 1 and 2) e.g. in m² NEFA, m² UFA, m² UFA 5 and their representative proportion to the total size of a property in m² GROFA or other specific building floor areas e.g. the share of UFA 5 per m² UFA.

*Technical characteristics:*

- Standard of fittings, furnishings and equipment: Higher or lower standard.

- Condition of fittings, furnishings and equipment: Good or poor condition.

### 4.4.2    Model design and parameters

To investigate the factors that have a substantial influence on the annual outlay for the repair of fittings, furnishings and equipment, all the factors mentioned above are taken into account and analyzed for a data sample of 108 school complexes. Model 19 A reveals the best estimates ($R^2$=0.618) for total costs. Tab. 77 shows detailed figures relating to the validity of the model and the underlying parameters used for this forecast. As with Model 11.A for estimating the outlay for the inspection and maintenance of fittings, furnishings and equipment, the usable floor area is incorporated in the statistical model for estimating the total repair costs of the respective structural components. At $beta_1$=0.736, the major part of the variation in Y is attributed to the interaction variable $X_1$ (poor condition of fittings, furnishings and equipment*m² UFA) incorporated in the linear regression Model 19.A. This variable makes it possible to distinguish between different states of a school's fittings, furnishings and equipment and to depict the level of influence in an appropriate manner. With respect to the condition-related survey carried out for individual structural components, a poor state is indicated if considerable damages for the fittings, furnishings and equipment are ascertained for a significant share of furnished rooms, measured in proportion of a school's overall usable floor area by means of a weighing factor. Regarding the underlying data sample, a poor state is determined in particular if the general and special furnishings and equipment are found to be in a poor condition (i.e. category D in the questionnaire for the cost groups 611 and 612 according to DIN 276-1:2006-11) for a stated reference quantitiy of 75% of a property's usable floor area (see Appendix B)

In correspondence with previous remarks on other types of municipal repair costs, a trivariate regression model is again described and favoured for predicting the total outlay for repair measures on the fittings, furnishings and equipment. The multivariate regression model supports continuous predictions for school complexes of various sizes (measured in m² UFA) and additionally allows taking different rates of increase in the total repair costs (Y) into account. Fig. 17 illustrates these model assumptions in cases where the fittings, furnishings and equipment are found to be in a good condition with $b_2=0.290$ and at $b_{1,2}=1.925$ where they are found to be in a poor state.

Tab. 77:   Model description for estimating total repair costs of fittings, furnishings and equipment

| Dependent variable | Transf. | R² | R² adj. | SEE | F-value | Sign. | Durbin-Watson-Statistic | | N |
|---|---|---|---|---|---|---|---|---|---|
| Repair costs of fittings, furnishings and equipment (€ p.a.) | - | 0.618 | 0.611 | 3773 | 85.052 | 0.000 | 2.098 | | 108 |

| Factors | Transf. | B | St. Error | Beta | t-value | Sign. | Lower CL | Upper CL | T | VIF |
|---|---|---|---|---|---|---|---|---|---|---|
| Constant | - | 293.79 | 734.40 | | 0.400 | 0.690 | -1162 | 1750 | | |
| Poor condition of fittings, furnishings and equipment*m² UFA | | 1.635 | 0.141 | 0.736 | 11.561 | 0.000 | 1.354 | 1.915 | 0.897 | 1.115 |
| Usable floor area (UFA in m²) | - | 0.290 | 0.144 | 0.128 | 2.009 | 0.047 | 0.004 | 0.576 | 0.897 | 1.115 |

**Dependent variable:** Repair costs of fittings, furnishings and equipment (€ p.a.), costs including VAT, based on 2008 figures

$$\hat{Y} = 293.794 + 1.635X_1^* + 0.290X_2 \qquad \text{(Model 19.A)}$$

Where:     $\hat{Y}$ :   Repair costs of fittings, furnishings and equipment (€ p.a.)

$X_1^*$ :   Poor condition of fittings, furnishings and equipment*m² usable floor area

$X_2$ :   Usable floor area (m²)

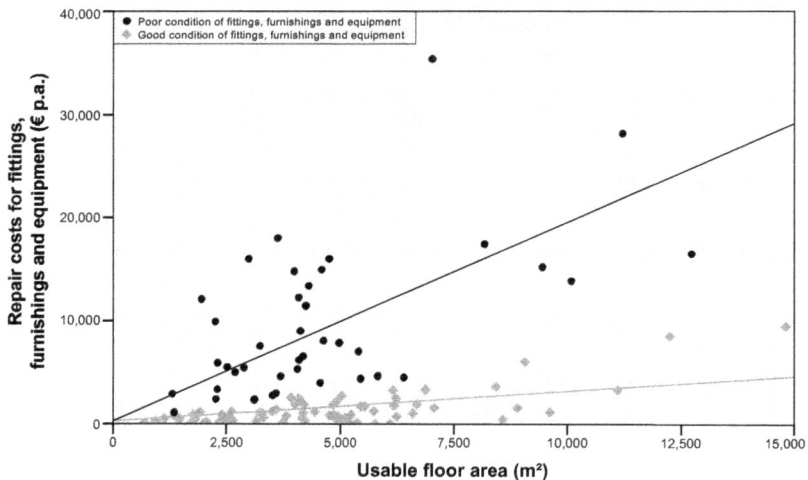

Fig. 17:   Comparison between observed and predicted repair costs of fittings, furnishings and equipment (costs including VAT, based on 2008 figures)

According to Model 19.A, which was evaluated step-by-step, the usable floor area constitutes the appropriate reference area for total cost estimates. Accordingly, this building reference area is used to define Y in €/m² UFA p.a. for the investigation of cost indicators. The initial step of the investigation involves testing whether the whole sample can be used for the approach or whether it is necessary to distinguish between different subsamples for prediction purposes. Based on the causal interrelations revealed in Model 19.A, two significance tests are carried out to examine if the mean values (t-Test) and the sampling distributions (Levene Test) are equal or not for the aspect that the condition of the fittings, furnishings and equipment differs. Both tests are based on an approximately normally distributed cost values for $N_1=68$ (fittings, furnishings and equipment in a good condition) and $N_2=40$ (fittings, furnishings and equipment in a poor condition). The result of both test statistics confirms that the two samples considered in the analysis differ substantially in terms of their mean values and variances, based on a test level of 5%. This is verified statistically for the t-Test at an empirical significance level of 0.00 (empirical t-value is -9.018), and for the Levene Test (F-Test) at an empirical significance level of 0.00 (empirical t-value is set at 60.447).

Based on the aforementioned considerations, the importance of subdivided samples for the following statistical analysis of cost indicators could be confirmed. For the purpose of this study, the indicators were investigated separately for $N_1=68$ (fitting, furnishings and equipment in a good condition) and $N_2=40$ (fittings, furnishings and equipment in a poor condition), but, it was not possible to detect any further causal interrelations between the factors outlined in Section 4.4.1 and the respective outlay for repairs, on the basis of under-lying cost indicators ascertained on property level. Therefore, the analysis failed to confirm any theoretical assumptions made about the influence of different utilization types or propor-tions of UFA 5 per m² UFA, for instance, on the cost indicators examined. On the basis of evaluated condition categories, it is therefore recommended to use the mean value estimate of 0.27 €/m² UFA p.a. in the case that the fittings, furnishings and equipment of a school are found to be in a good state, and an average cost indicator of 2.21 €/m² UFA p.a. for those predictions that refer to a poor condition of these structural components.

*Summary*

In compliance with previous analysis into the repair costs of public schools, it is a trivariate regression model with interaction variable that produces an adequate approximation of the total repair costs for fittings, furnishings and equipment. Total cost predictions are presented by Model 19.A, that allows specifying assumptions in regard to an observed good or poor conditions of the respective structural components. Fig. 17 displays the cost increase rates estimated for 108 schools under investigation. In addition, the usable floor area is evaluated as being the appropriate building reference area for determining cost indicator, at a significance level of 5%.

Based on the analysis into total costs, the requirement for a statistical evaluation of cost indicators is described. Separate cost estimates for different conditions of the fittings, furnishings and equipment are required in order to obtain consistent and unbiased predictions for municipal properties. This requirement is fulfilled in the form of a case distinction for the condition in question when analyzing the cost indicators concerned. It is, however, not possible to confirm any other assumptions regarding possible influential factors based on the underlying sample. Accordingly mean value estimates of 0.27 €/m² UFA p.a. are specified for $N_1$ (fittings, furnishings and equipment in a good condition) and 2.21 €/m² UFA p.a. for $N_2$ (fittings, furnishings and equipment in a poor condition).

In order to forecast the annual outlay required for the repairs concerned, different categories are once again defined for the respective condition by way of distinguishing criterion. If the cost estimates realized in this way are compared with those based on different age categories, it is possible to determine the degree of generalization for age-related estimates (see Fig. 18). Only 45% of the schools in the critical age categories, 35-55 years and 95-115 years respectively, under investigation were found to have their fittings, furnishings and equipment in a poor condition. The empirical examination accordingly shows the quality of cost estimates based on the state of fittings, furnishings and equipment as opposed to more generalized, age-specific predictions for the respective repair costs under analysis in this case.

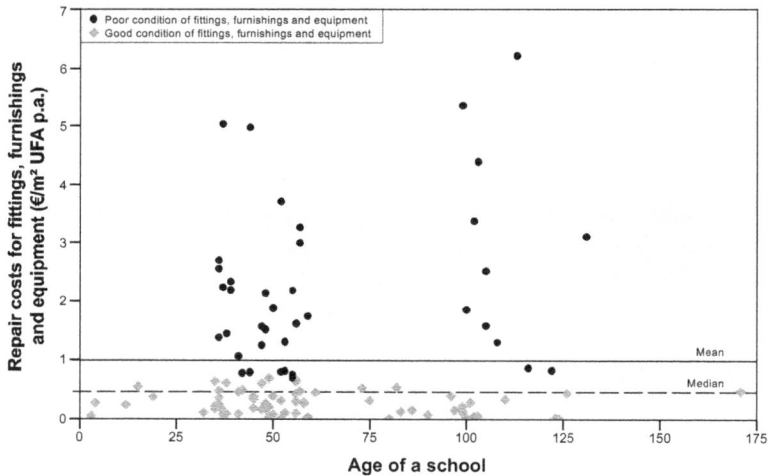

Fig. 18:    Observed repair cost indicators for fittings, furnishings and equipment (costs including VAT, based on 2008 figures)

### 4.4.3    Validation of the model

The validation test described in this section is based on cost data from 108 school complexes and compares empirical cost indicators specified for the repair of fittings, furnishings and equipment. The case distinction formulated above for estimating the repair costs of fittings, furnishings and equipment is used as a basis for the predicted values designated in Tab. 78. The test accordingly takes into account the mean value estimates for $N_1$=68 (fittings, furnishings and equipment in a good condition) and $N_2$=40 (fittings, furnishings and equipment in a poor condition). As regards the five validation cases under consideration, sample Nos. 1 and 2 are found to have their fittings, furnishings and equipment in a poor condition, while those in the other three cases are found to have good state. The prediction accuracy of these cost estimates is compared with the empirical mean and median values of the sample as a whole.

In three out of five validated cases the empirical predictions determined for $N_1$ and $N_2$ provides more accurate estimates and therefore prove to have a good fit. On average, the predictions achieve a MAPE of 61%, that is about 19% more accurate than those estimates using the empirical median, and facilitate a roughly 117% better forecast than the mean value of the overall sample. This practical test, carried out on the basis of 5 schools, consequently reveals that the previously substantiated cost indicators of the repairs of fittings, furnishings and equipment likewise produce good quality estimates for other schools, which had not been included in the modeling process before.

Tab. 78:   Model validation for repair cost indicators of fittings, furnishings and equipment

| No. | Type of school | Observed value | Predicted value | Absolute error % of prediction | Absolute error % of mean | Absolute error % of median | Preference |
|---|---|---|---|---|---|---|---|
| 1 | Elementary school without sports facilities | 0.97 | 2.21 | 128 | 2 | 52 | Mean |
| 2 | Special school with gymnasium | 2.71 | 2.21 | 19 | 64 | 83 | **Prediction** |
| 3 | Secondary school without sports facilities | 0.58 | 0.27 | 53 | 70 | 21 | Median |
| 4 | Secondary school with gymnasium and pool | 0.35 | 0.27 | 22 | 184 | 32 | **Prediction** |
| 5 | Vocational school without sports facilities | 0.15 | 0.27 | 84 | 571 | 212 | Prediction |
| Ø | **Mean Absolute percentage error** | | | 61 | 178 | 80 | **Prediction** |

Observed value: Costs (€/m² usable floor area p.a.), costs including VAT, based on 2008 figures, N=108

## 4.4.4    Cost indicators for the repair of fittings, furnishings and equipment

With regard to the reference area of the usable floor area defined in Section 4.4.2, Tab. 101 describes the measures of the central tendency and dispersion of cost indicators for the repair of fittings, furnishings and equipment for 108 schools. Thus, the average cost indicator is just under 1.00 €/m² UFA p.a. with an empirical interquartile range of around 1.20 €/m² UFA p.a. (costs including VAT, based on 2008 figures). On that basis, the statistical evaluation into municipal schools denominates the condition of fittings, furnishings and equipment as a significant distinguishing criterion for cost estimates and benchmarking purposes, and provides mean value estimates for both a good and a poor state. Tab. 79 compares and contrasts these two empirical estimates for both $N_1$=68 (fittings, furnishings and equipment in a good condition) and $N_2$=40 (fittings, furnishings and equipment in a good condition in a poor condition) and gives additional information on the respective distribution for samples $N_1$ and $N_2$.

As with the repair costs for school grounds and outdoor facilities, a small range of 0.69 €/m² UFA p.a. is indicated for fittings, furnishings and equipment in a good condition, based on the underlying data. By contrast, the reference group (fittings, furnishings and equipment in a poor condition) shows a comparatively wide range of 5.52 €/m² UFA p.a.

This leads to uncertainties in estimates for the latter category which, however, cannot be explained more in detail by using the present sample. The cost indicators given in Tab. 56 for the inspection and maintenance of fittings, furnishings and equipment enable to predict the overall outlay for the maintenance of fittings, furnishings and equipment which, according to DIN 13306:2010-12, comprises both the costs for repairs, and those for the inspection and maintenance.

Tab. 79:   Evaluated cost indicators for the repair of fittings, furnishings and equipment

| Factor level | Minimum | Mean | Median | Maximum | Range |
|---|---|---|---|---|---|
| Fittings, furnishings and equipment in a good condition | 0.01 | 0.27 | 0.25 | 0.69 | 0.69 |
| Fittings, furnishings and equipment in a poor condition | 0.70 | 2.21 | 1.79 | 6.22 | 5.52 |

Dependent variable: Costs (€/m² usable floor area p.a.), costs including VAT, based on 2008 figures, N=108

## 4.5      Aggregate repair costs

### 4.5.1    Empirical and theoretical basis

The analysis of aggregate repair costs (cost group 400, as defined by DIN 18960:2008-2) takes into account the outlay incurred in 2008 for individual repair measures on the building constructions, technical installations, grounds and outdoor facilities as well as on the fittings, furnishings and equipment. At an average rate of 23 €/m² GROFA p.a. (costs including VAT, based on 2008 figures) the aggregate repair costs of 113 school complexes[42] are slightly lower than the mean operating costs (see Tab. 103).

First of all, the investigation takes into consideration all the independent variables that have already been defined as significant factors and distinguishing criteria for individual repair costs earlier on, within the scope of cost types analyzed on the second structural cost level according to DIN 18960:2008-2 (cf. Section 4.1 to 4.4). In particular, these factors comprise specific building floor areas, as defined by DIN 277-1:2005-2, and evaluated condition categories in the form of categorical or interactive variables. Moreover, specific interrelations that exist between individual factors previously assessed over the course of repair analyses are also incorporated in the statistical investigation of aggregate repair costs. Such inter-relations are in the form of ratios between quantified building reference areas, such as the share of the usable floor area per m² GROFA, for example, or arise from a simultaneous existence of different condition categories of structural components, such as a simul-taneously good condition ascertained for both the building constructions and technical installations of a school. Finally, other factors are taken into account, which secondary literature or interviews with experts have determined as relevant predictors for individual repair outlays, such as a school´s type of usage or its standard of technical installations.

---

[42] In accordance with the sample sizes of the cost groups 410 and 420 (according to DIN 18960:2008-2) with the two largest shares of the aggregate repair costs, the underlying sample of this investigation involves 113 schools.

## 4.5.2    Model design and parameters

Estimation models for the total aggregate repair costs (Y) have been developed step-by-step on the basis of sample data from 113 school complexes and compared with one another. The best estimation is realized by Model 20.A, which takes into consideration the gross floor area as well as using descriptions of specific conditions of structural components. The gross floor area was already determined as the relevant building floor area for predicting municipal repair costs for the building constructions in Section 4.1. With regard to specified condition categories, the condition of the building constructions ($X_1$), and the state of the technical installations ($X_3$), are included in the prediction model each as an interaction variable, in relation to their original building reference area (m² GROFA and m² NEFA respectively). From the point of view of content, the two interaction variables $X_1^{*}$ and $X_3^{*}$ incorporated in the multivariate model, indicate that both the condition of the building constructions and that of the technical installations have an influence on the total amount of aggregate repair costs (Y), independently of each other and that these two impacting factors vary with an increased size of school.

By contrast, the influence exerted by the condition of the grounds and outdoor facilities and that of the fittings, furnishings and equipment is taken into account in the form of a qualitative variable. In this case, it is not possible to quantify any individual effects for the two condition categories at a significance level of 5% by means of regression analysis. Due to the specified variable $X_4$ cost planners can, however, estimate the average difference in the outlay of the annual aggregate repair costs assuming that either the grounds and outdoor facilities or the fittings, furnishings and equipment respectively of a school complex are in a poor condition.[43]

Altogether, Model 20.A attributes a separate partial explanation for the differences in the total aggregate outlay for repairs to four independent variables. By taking the total size of a school's gross floor area and the evaluated conditions of specific structural components into consideration, Model 20.A provides continuous estimates for aggregate repair costs and proves with $R^2=0.919$ a convincing goodness-of-fit. Tab. 80 details the reliability of the prediction model and shows the partial regression coefficients bj estimated for individual variable. The interaction variable $X_1^{*}$ (poor condition of building constructions*m² GROFA) describes a big proportion of the overall variation in Y, where $beta_1=0.470$. The slightly lower tolerance values for the two independent variables $X_1^{*}$ and $X_3^{*}$ (poor condition of technical installations*m² NEFA) can be explained from the point of view of content by the often simultaneous presence of poor condition for both building constructions and the technical installations. This is the case in 23 out of the 113 schools investigated in this sample. The investigation does not confirm other influences by any of the other tested variables sufficiently at a significance level of 5%.

---

[43] If cost planner are drawing up their plans on the basis of a sound estimate, taking the eventuality into account that both the grounds and outdoor facilities, and the fittings, furnishings and equipment are in a poor state in the year in question, this assumption can be substantiated even further using the variable $X_4$ in Model 20.A, with x=2, for example.

Tab. 80:   Model description for estimating aggregate repair costs

| Dependent variable | Transf. | R² | R² adj. | SEE | F-value | Sign. | Durbin-Watson-Statistic | | N |
|---|---|---|---|---|---|---|---|---|---|
| Aggregate repair costs (€ p.a.) | - | 0,919 | 0,916 | 53481 | 306,729 | 0,000 | 1,940 | | 113 |

| Factors | Transf. | B | St. Error | Beta | t-value | Sign. | Lower CL | Upper CL | T | VIF |
|---|---|---|---|---|---|---|---|---|---|---|
| Constant | - | -35329 | 10251 | | -3,447 | 0,001 | -55648 | -15011 | | |
| Poor condition of building constructions* m² GROFA | - | 18,122 | 1,310 | 0,470 | 13,834 | 0,000 | 15,525 | 20,718 | 0,650 | 1,538 |
| Gross floor area (GROFA in m²) | - | 14,678 | 0,933 | 0,459 | 15,726 | 0,000 | 12,828 | 16,528 | 0,881 | 1,135 |
| Poor condition of technical installations* m² NEFA | - | 14,002 | 1,642 | 0,298 | 8,528 | 0,000 | 10,748 | 17,256 | 0,613 | 1,632 |
| Grounds and outdoor facilities, or fittings, furnishings and equipment in a poor condition | - | 47281 | 10440 | 0,128 | 4,529 | 0,000 | 26587 | 67976 | 0,932 | 1,072 |

Dependent variable: Aggregate repair costs (€ p.a.), costs including VAT, based on 2008 figures

$$\hat{Y} = -35,329 + 18.122X_1^* + 14.678X_2 + 14.002X_3^* + 47,281X_4 \qquad \text{(Model 20.A)}$$

Where:     $\hat{Y}$ :   Aggregate repair costs (€ p.a.)

$X_1^*$ :   Poor condition of building constructions*m² gross floor area

$X_2$ :   Gross floor area (GROFA in m²)

$X_3^*$ :   Poor condition of technical installations*m² net floor area

$X_4$ :   Grounds and outdoor facilities, or fittings, furnishings and equipment in a poor condition

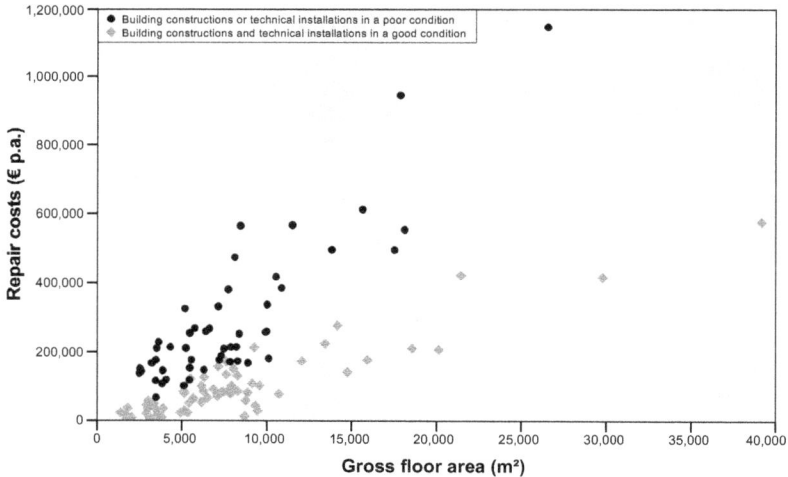

Fig. 19:   Empirical costs for aggregate repair (costs including VAT, based on 2008 figures)

Model 20.A refers to the net floor area by the independent variable $X_3$ to illustrate the causal interrelation between the outlay for the repairs of technical installations and the net floor area described in Section 4.2. Alternatively, it is possible to specify a regression model instead of Model 20.A presented above, using only the gross floor area rather than two building reference areas (gross floor area and net floor area). This simplification would apply to the interaction variable $X_3^*$, which would then be defined as a multiplicative term in relation to the net floor area. The prediction accuracy of a model specified in this way was analyzed in the context of this study and also reveals a good approximation to the observed cost data, when all other model assumptions remained the same.[44] This shows that it is, however, equally possible to imagine a generalization of the variable $X_3$ with regard to the gross floor area.

The subsequent examination of the aggregate repair cost indicators takes the insights gained from the analysis of total costs into account, as defined by Model 20.A above. The gross floor area is used for normalizing the cost data. As in the analyses described above pertaining to the individual repair costs on lower level of hierarchy, the first step is to find out whether the cost indicators can be estimated across the entire sample of 113 schools, or whether it is necessary to create subsamples to estimate and examine the repair cost indicators.

The estimation of the aggregate repair costs (Y) takes the condition of the building construc-tions and those of the technical installations into account in the form of two independent interaction variables verifying influential factors with $beta_1=0.470$ and $beta_3=0.298$ in Model 20.A. Visual inspection of scatter plot reveals that most of the total variation of Y can be ascribed to two positive and linear influences in particular (see Fig. 19). It appears that the overall costs can be broken down into two parts, the lower part being defined by building constructions and technical installations in a good condition, and the upper part of the sample showing either the building constructions in a poor condition or the technical installations found to be in a poor state. To clarify the uncertainty of any subdivided samples with regard to this distinguishing feature, a t-Test is carried out, in order to detect any differences in the mean values, and the Levene Test, by way of an F-Test is applied to examine variance homogeneity. Both significance tests have already been used within previous contemplations relating to individual repair costs on lower structural costs levels.

The empirical sample data for $N_1=63$ (building constructions and technical installations in a good condition) and $N_2=50$ (building constructions or technical installations in a poor condition) form the basis for each investigation. The Kolmogorov-Smirnov test confirms that both empirical cost distributions are approximately normally distributed, with an empirical significance level of 0.617 for $N_1$ and 0.445 for $N_2$, respectively. In addition, the t-Test verifies that, at a significance level of 0.00, the mean values of the two subsamples are not the same, and therefore $H_1(\mu_1 < \mu_2)$ can be accepted. The null hypothesis $H_0(\mu_1 = \mu_2)$ has to be rejected at a test level of 5%, so the discrepancy of 21.10 €/m² GROFA p.a. in the mean values is regarded as significant (costs including VAT, based on 2008 figures). The Levene Test shows that the two samples differ significantly, rather than incidentally, in their variances with an empirical significance level of 0.00, causing the assumption of variance homogeneity to be rejected. The two subsamples that were tested are accordingly found to

---

[44] In the alternative model described, the partial regression coefficients $b_j$ for all independent variables change when $X_3$ (technical installations in a poor condition*m² GROFA) is considered.

differ in terms of their mean values and variances, so the considerations set out below with regard to predicting the aggregate repair cost indicators have to be carried out separately for each of the two samples $N_1$ and $N_2$.

The investigation begins by presenting the cost indicator estimated for $N_1$ in the case of the building constructions are found to be in a good condition, using Model 20.B.1. The single-factor variance analysis makes it possible to substantiate cost estimates based on factor $X_1$ (grounds and outdoor facilities, or fittings, furnishings and equipment in a poor condition). From the point of view of content, the estimation Model 20.B.1 reveals a difference in the average cost indicators for the two manifestations comprising grounds and outdoor facilities, or fittings, furnishings and equipment in a poor condition on the one hand, and both grounds and outdoor facilities and fittings, furnishings and equipment to be in a good condition on the other. This case distinction defined by $X_1$ therefore allows more efficient cost estimates to be realized than using a simple mean value estimate of the overall sample.

Additional information for the estimation Model 20.B.1 is shown in Tab. 81. Where G is the number of factor levels, N is the underlying sample size of 63 schools, and $N_{G1}=37$ and $N_{G2}=26$ are the two subsample sizes for different conditions represented by the mani-festations of the factor $X_1$. Based on a grand mean of 10.142 €/m² GROFA p.a., $b_1=3.386$ indicates the average value of the designated group described by the factor $X_1$ (costs including VAT, based on 2008 figures). Comparing the mean sum of squares (MS), the test result verifies that the factor $X_1$ exerts a significant influence. The variance proportion of $MS_b=175.009$, which is explained by the factor $X_1$, is considerably greater than $MS_w=29.459$, so the model prediction described by Model 20.B.1 is preferable to the overall mean value estimate.[45] In addition, the empirical significance of 0.018 is lower than the stipulated confidence level of 95%, so the null hypothesis can be rejected and the model provides an adequate explanation of the variation measured in Y for $N_1$.

Tab. 81:   Model description for estimating aggregate repair cost indicators
           in case of a good condition of the building constructions and technical installations

| Depentend variable | Transf. | Sum of squares between groups | Sum of squares within groups | F-value | Sign. | MAPE (%) | N |
|---|---|---|---|---|---|---|---|
| Aggregate repair costs (€/m² GROFA p.a.) | - | 175,099 | 1796,974 | 5,944 | 0,018 | 74 | 63 |

| Factors | Transf. | B | Standard Error | T-value | Sign. | Lower CL | Upper CL |
|---|---|---|---|---|---|---|---|
| Constant | - | 10,142 | 0,892 | 11,366 | 0,000 | 8,358 | 11,926 |
| Grounds and outdoor facilities, or fittings, furnishings and equipment in a poor condition | - | 3,386 | 1,389 | 2,438 | 0,018 | 0,609 | 6,164 |

Dependent variable: Aggregate repair costs (€/m² gross floor area p.a.), costs including VAT, based on 2008 figures

---

[45] Where $MS_b$ describes the mean sum of squares between the factor levels g and $MS_w$ describes the mean sum of squares within the factor levels g (see Section 2.6).

| Source | Sum of squares (SS) | Degrees of freedom (df) | Mean sum of squares (MS) |
|---|---|---|---|
| Between | 175,099 | G -1 = 1 | 175,099 |
| Within | 1.796,974 | $(N_{G1} -1) + (N_{G2} -1) = 61$ | 29,459 |
| Total | 1.972,073 | N -1 = 62 | 31,808 |

**Dependent variable:** Aggregate repair costs (€/m² gross floor area p.a.), costs including VAT, based on 2008 figures

$$\hat{Y} = 10.142 + 3.386X_1 \qquad\qquad\qquad\qquad\qquad\text{(Model 20.B.1)}$$

Where:   $\hat{Y}$ :  Aggregate repair cost indicators (€/m² GROFA  p.a.)

$X_1$ :  Grounds and outdoor facilities, or fittings, furnishings and equipment in a poor condition

If the building constructions or technical installations are ascertained to be in a poor condition, however, as is the case with the sample data from $N_2$=50, the best model prediction for aggregate repair costs per m² GROFA and year is achieved by the multivariate regression Model 20.B.2 described in Tab. 82. The specified cost model, in particular, describes a distinguishing required between public schools with their building constructions in a poor condition ($X_1$ with beta$_1$=0.487) and their technical installations found to be in a poor condition ($X_2$ with beta$_2$=0.625). The statistical Model 20.B.2, moreover, takes into account the continuous variables $X_4$ (average storey height) and $X_5$ (share of the usable floor area for teaching, education and culture (UFA 5) per m² GROFA), as well as the qualitative variable $X_5$ (walls, ceilings and roofs in a poor condition) in a similar way to the predictions described for the repair cost of building constructions estimated using Model 16.B.2. In compliance with the aforementioned Model 20.B.1, Model 20.B.2 also takes an assessment of the condition of the grounds and outdoor facilities, as well as of the fittings, furnishings and equipment into account, which are collectively represented by one categorical variable ($X_3$). In this way, six independent variables can be established altogether for estimating the aggregate repair cost indicators. In accordance with the estimation model for the repair costs of technical installations, designated in Section 4.2.2, it is not possible to verify any detailed assumptions with regard to the appearance of different repair costs for technical installations based on the present sample and with an underlying significance level of 5%. It is accordingly the characteristics of the building constructions, in particular, that explain a great proportion of the total variation in the aggregate repair costs for $N_2$ under investigation. Model 20.B.2 displays an excellent prediction quality, with $R^2$=0.735, SEE=7.567 and a calculated MAPE of 15%, and is accordingly given preference over mean value estimates.

Tab. 82:   Model description for estimating aggregate repair cost indicators
           in case of a poor condition of the building constructions or technical installations

| Dependent variable | Transf. | R² | R² adj. | SEE | F-value | Sign. | Durbin-Watson-Statistic | | N |
|---|---|---|---|---|---|---|---|---|---|
| Aggregate repair costs (€/m² GROFA p.a.) | - | 0,735 | 0,699 | 7,567 | 19,928 | 0,000 | 1,939 | | 50 |

| Factors | Transf. | B | St. Error | Beta | t-value | Sign. | Lower CL | Upper CL | T | VIF |
|---|---|---|---|---|---|---|---|---|---|---|
| Constant | - | -36,077 | 9,423 | | -3,828 | 0,000 | -55,081 | -17,073 | | |
| Technical installations in a poor condition | - | 13,454 | 2,373 | 0,487 | 5,669 | 0,000 | 8,668 | 18,240 | 0,835 | 1,198 |
| Building constructions in a poor condition | - | 26,229 | 3,596 | 0,625 | 7,293 | 0,000 | 18,976 | 33,482 | 0,839 | 1,193 |
| Grounds and outdoor facilities, or fittings, furnishings and equipment in a poor condition | - | 9,813 | 2,238 | 0,358 | 4,385 | 0,000 | 5,300 | 14,326 | 0,921 | 1,086 |
| Average storey height (in m) | - | 5,252 | 1,261 | 0,335 | 4,166 | 0,000 | 2,709 | 7,795 | 0,953 | 1,050 |
| Walls, ceilings and roofs in a poor condition | - | 5,891 | 2,329 | 0,210 | 2,529 | 0,015 | 1,193 | 10,589 | 0,896 | 1,116 |
| Share of UFA 5 per m² GROFA | - | 36,109 | 16,891 | 0,172 | 2,138 | 0,038 | 2,044 | 70,173 | 0,945 | 1,058 |

**Dependent variable**: Aggregate repair costs (€/m² gross floor area p.a.), costs including VAT, based on 2008 figures

$$\hat{Y} = -36.077 + 13.454X_1 + 26.229X_2 + 9.813X_3 + 5.252X_4 + 5.891X_5 + 36.109X_6 \qquad \text{(Model 20.B.2)}$$

Where:    $\hat{Y}$ :   Aggregate repair cost indicators (€/m² GROFA p.a.)

$X_1$ :   Technical installations in a poor condition

$X_2$ :   Building constructions in a poor condition

$X_3$ :   Grounds and outdoor facilities, or fittings, furnishings and equipment in a poor condition

$X_4$ :   Average storey height (in m)

$X_5$ :   Walls, ceilings and roofs in a poor condition

$X_6$ :   Share of UFA 5 per m² GROFA

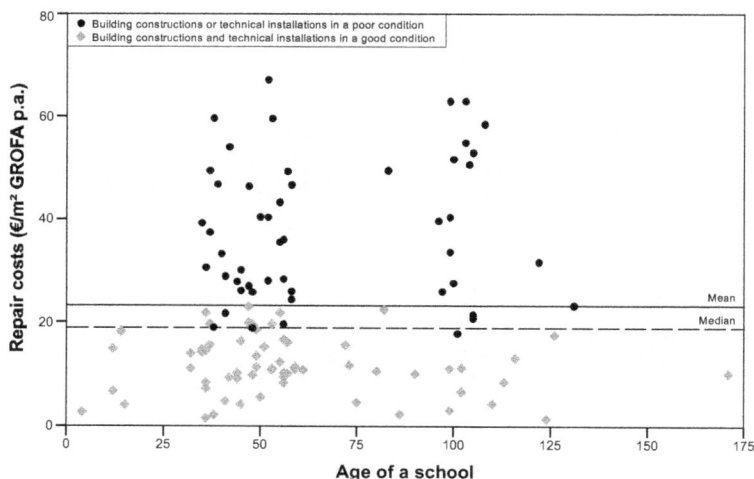

Fig. 20:   Empirical cost indicators for aggregate repair (cost including VAT, based on 2008 figures)

*Summary*

The analysis of aggregate repair costs (cost group 400, as defined by DIN 18960:2008-2) names the gross floor area as the appropriate building reference area for determining the indicators and proceeds to demonstrate the significance of various condition assessments, in particular those for the building constructions, technical installations, grounds and outdoor facilities as well as for fittings, furnishings and equipment, for estimating costs efficiently. As regards the second structural cost level according to DIN 18960:2008-2, the analysis accordingly evaluates the relevant condition categories that need to be distinguished when planning actual repair costs for public schools and describes prediction models for specific indicators for the aggregate outlay

Where the building constructions and technical installations are found to be in a good condition, a single-factor variance analysis is presented for estimating aggregate repair cost indicators based on Model 20.B.1 introduced in this section. This is contrasted with the situation where the building constructions or technical installations of a municipal property are found to be in a poor condition, using the multivariate Model 20.B.2 to substantiate cost prognoses on the basis of sample data from 50 school complexes. Apart from the information pertaining to the state of individual structural components, this regression model also takes 3 independent influences into consideration that were already determined as part of the statistical evaluation of the repair costs for building constructions (Model 16.B.2) for realizing efficient cost estimates. In total, the empirical analysis of aggregate repair costs takes descriptions of the underlying school complexes with regard to technical and functional characteristics into account.

Based on this evaluation, Fig. 20 displays largely constant cost indicators for $N_1$ (building constructions and technical installations in a good condition) regardless of the year in which a school was built, whereas higher mean values and variances are visually apparent in the cost indicators for $N_2$ (building constructions and technical installations in a poor condition). This case distinction yields more accurate prognoses of the annual outlay for repairs, in preference to a frequently favored differentiation and prediction of cost indicators according to the age of a property concerned. In the critical age groups of approximately 50 (40-60) and 100 (90-110) years respectively, only about 54% of the school complexes under investigation featured a poor state of their building constructions and technical installations due to their age. With regard to the cost analyses conducted on lower structural cost level, this figure amounts to about 50% in case of the repair of building constructions, 29% for the repair of technical installations, just 24% for the repair of grounds and outdoor facilities and 45% for the repair of fittings, furnishings and equipment of all schools taken into consideration. This comparison reveals that those cost estimates based on the state of individual components, as presented here for municipal schools, produce a higher level of accuracy for all levels of repair costs.

Based on this evaluation, specific cost indicators for benchmarking purposes can be determined according to various states of repairs and compared with those values provided for different age groups. Comparing the two prediction methods, a classification based on the age of a property yields an average outlay for repairs of 25.83 €/m² GROFA p.a. for those buildings built between 1951-1971 and 1901-1921, for example. This contrasts with the evaluation based on the state of repair, which returns an average cost indicator of 37.82 €/m² GROFA p.a. in the case the building constructions and technical installations are found to be in a poor condition, which displays a better approximation to the observed costs displayed in Fig. 20 (costs including VAT, based on 2008 figures).

### 4.5.3    Validation of the model

The validation test uses the aforementioned Model 20.B.1, where the building constructions and technical installations are simultaneously found to be in a good condition, and takes cost predictions specified by Model 20.B.2, into account, where either the building construc- tions or the technical installations are declared to be in a poor state. The practical test accordingly compares the model predictions specified above, by taking different conditions of structural components into consideration, with empirical mean and median estimates of the overall sample. The underlying cost indicators for aggregate repair costs are measured in €/m² GROFA p.a. include VAT and are based on 2008 figures. In four out of five validated cases, both the building constructions and the technical installations of a school is found to be in a poor condition. In contrast, sample No.4 is described in terms of a poor state of the building constructions or the technical installations.

Comparing the mean absolute percentage errors, those model predictions that are specified by means of ANOVA (Model 20.B.1) or regression analysis (Model 20.B.2) prove to be the most convincing, with the lowest MAPE of just under 26%. The mean value estimates show a higher prediction accuracy in two out of five cases, achieving a MAPE just short of 40%. With regard to the five validated properties cases under comparison, the median shows the highest percentage error with a MAPE of 43% for the aggregated repair costs. The relatively large percentage error in the case of sample No.5 can be partly explained by an existing inaccuracy in the estimated repair costs for the building constructions already discovered in Section 4.1.3. On the whole, both statistical Models 20.B.1 and 20.B.2 show a good predic- tion quality for the aggregate repair costs of five randomly selected school complexes (cost group 400, according to DIN 18960:2008-2).

Tab. 83:   Model validation for aggregate repair cost indicators

| No. | Type of school | Observed value | Predicted value | Absolute error % of prediction | Absolute error % of mean | Absolute error % of median | Preference |
|---|---|---|---|---|---|---|---|
| 1 | Elementary school without sports facilities | 32.45 | 41.66 | **28** | 29 | 42 | **Prediction** |
| 2 | Special school with gymnasium | 33.14 | 48.09 | 45 | **30** | 43 | Mean |
| 3 | Secondary school without sports facilities | 25.05 | 24.49 | **2** | 8 | 25 | **Prediction** |
| 4 | Secondary school with gymnasium and pool | 11.25 | 10.14 | **10** | 106 | 68 | **Prediction** |
| 5 | Vocational school without sports facilities | 30.67 | 10.55 | 66 | **24** | 39 | Mean |
| Ø | **Mean Absolute percentage error** | | | **26** | 39 | 43 | **Prediction** |

**Observed value**: Aggregate repair costs (€/m² gross floor area p.a.), costs including VAT, based on 2008 figures, N=113

### 4.5.4    Cost indicators for aggregate repair

Based on the prediction models introduced and subsequently validated in Sections 4.5.2 and 4.5.3, specific cost indicators for the distinguishing criteria of different conditions will now be presented with regard to individual states of the building constructions, technical installations, grounds and outdoor facilities as well as those of the fittings, furnishings and equipment, see Tab. 84. According to the statistical evaluation of sample data from 113 school complexes, these condition categories explain a great proportion of the overall variation in aggregate repair cost indicators, so their underlying measures of central tendency and dispersion are shown for certain cases of combined conditions and compared with one another. The test results set out in Section 4.5.2 for $N_1$ and $N_2$ are portrayed by means of the values ascertained in the main categories. Based on designated sub-categories, differentiated cost indicators are given for situations where both the grounds and outdoor facilities and the fittings, furnishings and equipment are found to be in a good condition, in contrast to those scenarios where either the grounds and outdoor facilities or the fittings, furnishings and equipment are stated to be in a poor state.

If, for instance, an average cost indicator of 10.14 €/m² GROFA p.a. is stipulated as the reference value in those cases where all the structural components are found to be in a good condition, the corresponding mean in the described worst case scenario (i.e. the building constructions, technical installations, grounds and outdoor facilities as well as the fittings, furnishings and equipment are found to be in a poor condition) amounts to around 41.46 €/m² GROFA p.a. (costs including VAT, based on 2008 figures). In the case that more detailed cost indicators are required, it is possible to carry out continuous cost estimates using the multivariate regression Model 20.B.2, for instance, which particularly substantiate the outlay for the incorporated repairs of building constructions (see Section 4.1.2). Moreover, the outlay for the overall maintenance, as defined by DIN 31051:2003-6, which comprises all costs for the inspection, maintenance and repair measures, can be calculated on the basis of Tab. 60 and Tab. 84.

Tab. 84:   Evaluated cost indicators for aggregate repair

| Factor level | Minimum | Mean | Median | Maximum | Range |
|---|---|---|---|---|---|
| **Building constructions and technical installations in a good condition** | 1,47 | 11,54 | 11,05 | 22,92 | 21,45 |
| Grounds and outdoor facilities and fittings, furnishings and equipment in a good condition | 1,47 | 10,14 | 10,57 | 22,51 | 21,04 |
| Grounds and outdoor facilities, or fittings, furnishings and equipment in a poor condition | 4,77 | 13,53 | 11,84 | 22,92 | 18,15 |
| **Building constructions or technical installations in a poor condition** | 17,86 | 37,82 | 35,72 | 67,00 | 49,14 |
| Grounds and outdoor facilities and fittings, furnishings and equipment in a good condition | 17,86 | 33,55 | 28,87 | 54,89 | 37,03 |
| Grounds and outdoor facilities, or fittings, furnishings and equipment in a poor condition | 19,00 | 41,46 | 40,32 | 67,00 | 47,99 |

**Dependent variable:** Aggregate repair costs (€/m² gross floor area p.a.), costs including VAT, based on 2008 figures, N=113

# 5      Investigation of aggregate operating and repair costs

## 5.1     Empirical and theoretical basis

The empirical investigation of aggregate operating and repair costs for schools is based on contemplations for specific cost categories set out above. The analysis takes into account the total operation and repair costs during the calendar year in question, which can be averaged at 50 €/m² GROFA p.a. and cover a range of 80 €/m² GROFA p.a. according to Tab. 103 (costs including VAT, based on 2008 figures).

First of all, the statistical analysis includes those influential factors that had already been statistically proved to exert substantial effects at a significance level of 5%. Among others, specified categories referring to the condition of single structural components can be mentioned, for example, which were previously defined as relevant criteria impacting on the outlay for individual and aggregate repairs, and from which the current investigation also hopes to draw conclusions as to the overall variation in costs. In addition, the study also takes selected proportions of quantified variables into consideration, such as the ratio between special building reference areas in terms of the share of the usable floor area per m² NEFA, the proportion of the non-built up area per m² GROFA, or the share of the net floor area per m² GROFA, for instance. The latter ratio describes the relationship between the two reference areas whose individual influence in the case of the operating costs (with respect to Model 15.A) and the repair costs (with reference to Model 20.A) was statistically identified, and whose underlying costs within the framework of this investigation are taken into account. Moreover, the present analysis also includes those factors that were substantiated prior to conducting the survey, defined by secondary literature or interviews with experts. The type of usage (such as elementary, secondary or vocational school, for example), may be named which is crucial for cost predictions as well as comparisons of observed values from a theoretical point of view, and therefore of practical relevance for this analysis into aggregate costs. The investigation bears this aspect in mind and takes also secondary utilizations into consideration, which particularly include additional sports facilities, such as gyms and indoor swimming pool for teaching purposes, as well as nursery schools, for instance, in the case of the current data sample. Appendix C shows the aforementioned factors on which the statistical analysis is based in more detail.

## 5.2     Model design and parameters

In accordance with previous investigations into individual operating and repair costs, the analysis begins by defining a suitable building reference area by means of a statistical analysis of the total amount of aggregate costs (Y). The purpose of this preliminary analysis is to determine and provide unbiased cost indicators for the subsequent analysis of normalized costs and, thus, to enable a more precise examination of other influential para-meters. The analysis of total operation and repair costs is based on sample data from 113 school complexes.[46] Using a step-by-step approach, the best cost prediction is achieved by the multivariate regression Model 21.A with regard to the gross floor area. This building floor area was previously already used for estimating and normalizing the aggregate repair costs and describes the total size of the school by definition according to DIN 277-1:2005-2. In addition, Model 21.A incorporates different condition categories in terms of three independent variables describing the state of the building constructions ($X_2$), technical installations ($X_3$) as well as those one of the grounds and outdoor facilities, fittings, furnishings and equipment ($X_4$). All of these condition categories were previously identified as relevant factors by multivariate analysis and used for predictions of costs incurred for aggregate repair costs (cf. Section 4.5.2). The reference areas (GROFA and NEFA respectively) of the interaction variables $X_2^*$ and $X_3^*$ comply with the original reference areas, as defined within the investigation of corresponding cost groups on lower structural cost level (cf. Section 4.1 and Section 4.2).

While these three variables particularly describe variation in the repair costs, as part of the aggregate costs forming the subject of this analysis, the following continuous variables $X_5$ (share of the non-built up plot area per m² GROFA) and $X_6$ (share of the swimming pool utilization area per m² GROFA) express in particular a measured variability in the operating costs (cf. Model 15.A for example). As was already verified in the context of the cost groups investigated for the grounds and outdoor facilities, the size of a school's non-built up plot area does exert an influence, in particular for the cleaning and care, inspection and maintenance, and the repair of grounds and outdoor facilities (cost groups 340, 354 and 430 according to DIN 18960:2008-2).

The swimming pool utilization area describes that specific area of a school complex reserved for the sports as a continuous variable and makes it possible to make a categorical distinction between different types of schools (schools with or without a pool) as well as quantifying the sports facilities concerned. The swimming pool utilization area describes that specific part of a school complex reserved for the respective sports function by means of a continuous variable, measured on room level. Both of the floor areas are depicted in Model 21.A by the variables $X_4$ and $X_5$ in proportion to the gross floor area and, with beta$_4$=0.067 and beta$_5$=0.065 respectively, reveal a positive influence on the total amount of aggregate costs.

Summarizing, the evaluation accordingly includes those factors that were previously identified when analyzing both the operating and the repair costs, and which have therefore already proved to explain a great part of the variation in the individual outlays under consideration. With $R^2$ set at 0.936 and a specified MAPE of 18%, regression Model 21.A yields a good approximation to the observed values and leads to convincing cost estimates. Detailed information on the model design and specifications are displayed in Tab. 85. At a test level of 5%, the constant is not significant which can be disregarded for total costs predictions as previously outlined. The variables $X_2$ and $X_3$ also show lower tolerance and VIF values, with a tolerance of around 0.6 and VIF to be around 1.6 for each predictor. As

---

[46] In compliance with the empirical data sample, on which the evaluation of aggregate repair costs in Section 4.5.2 is based, the random sample in this analysis of aggregate operation and repair costs comprises 113 schools.

described in Section 4.5.2, however, this can also be explained from the point of view of content by the often simultaneous presence of poor condition for both building constructions and technical installations, which can accordingly be disregarded without any signs of having a detrimental effect on the model specification.

Tab. 85:   Model description for estimating total costs for aggregate operation and repair

| Dependent variable | Transf. | R² | R² adj. | SEE | F-value | Sign. | Durbin-Watson-Statistic | | N |
|---|---|---|---|---|---|---|---|---|---|
| Aggregate operating and repair costs (€ p.a.) | - | 0.936 | 0.933 | 73793 | 260.193 | 0.000 | 1.982 | | 113 |

| Factors | Transf. | B | St. Error | Beta | t-value | Sign. | Lower CL | Upper CL | T | VIF |
|---|---|---|---|---|---|---|---|---|---|---|
| Constant | - | -10129 | 14364 | | -0.705 | 0.482 | -38607 | 18349 | | |
| Gross floor area (GROFA in m²) | - | 34.535 | 1.292 | 0.700 | 26.722 | 0.000 | 31.973 | 37.098 | 0.875 | 1.143 |
| Poor condition of building constructions* m² GROFA | - | 18.559 | 1.808 | 0.312 | 10.266 | 0.000 | 14.975 | 22.143 | 0.650 | 1.539 |
| Poor condition of technical installations* m² NEFA | - | 15.945 | 2.268 | 0.220 | 7.031 | 0.000 | 11.449 | 20.441 | 0.611 | 1.636 |
| Grounds and outdoor facilities, or fittings, furnishings and equipment in a poor condition | - | 53140 | 14503 | 0.094 | 3.664 | 0.000 | 24386 | 81894 | 0.920 | 1.087 |
| Share of the non-built up plot area per m² GROFA | LN | 24109 | 8925 | 0.067 | 2.701 | 0.008 | 6414 | 41804 | 0.972 | 1.029 |
| Share of the swimming pool utilization area per m² GROFA | - | 2082539 | 788934 | 0.065 | 2.640 | 0.010 | 518402 | 3646677 | 0.978 | 1.023 |

**Dependent variable**: Aggregate operating and repair costs (€ p.a.), costs including VAT, based on 2008 figures

$$\hat{Y} = -10{,}129 + 34.54\,X_1 + 18.56\,X_2^* + 15.94\,X_3^* + 53{,}140\,X_4 + 24{,}109\,ln\left(X_5\right) + 2{,}082{,}539\,X_6 \quad \text{(Model 21.A)}$$

Where:     $\hat{Y}$ :    Aggregate operating and repair cost indicators (€ p.a.)

$X_1$ :    Gross floor area (GROFA in m²)

$X_2^*$ :    Poor condition of building constructions*m² gross floor area

$X_3^*$ :    Poor condition of technical installations*m² net floor area

$X_4$ :    Grounds and outdoor facilities, or fittings, furnishings and equipment in a poor condition

$X_5$ :    Share of the non-built up plot area per m² GROFA

$X_6$ :    Share of the swimming pool utilization area per m² GROFA

As depicted by Fig. 21, the best way to describe the distribution of the total aggregate operating and repair costs in this instance and bivariate terms is again to apply the method of case distinction with regard to the condition of the building constructions and technical installations. As outlined in Section 4.5.2, this perspective allows to clearly visualizing the different increase rates in the outlay when comparing the situation where both the building constructions and the technical installations are found to be in a good condition with that where at least one of these structural components is stated to be in a poor state of repair.

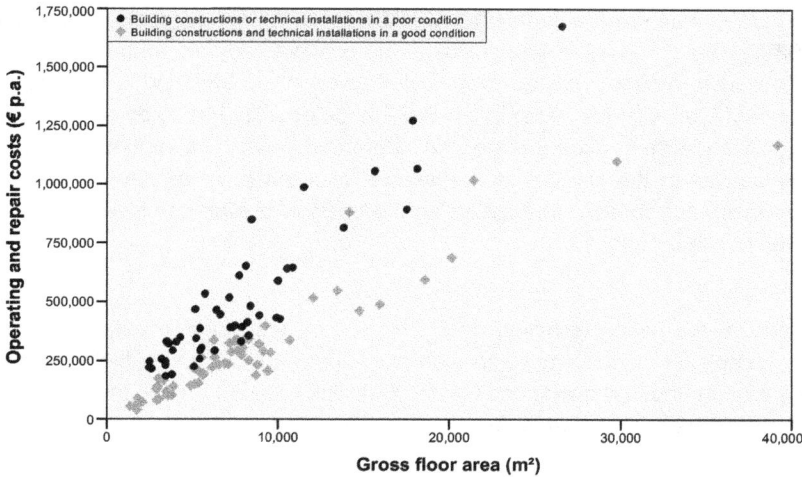

Fig. 21:    Empirical costs for aggregate operation and repair (costs including VAT, based on 2008 figures)

In an bivariate context, Fig. 21 displays the effect that different conditions have on aggregate cost estimates, which particularly can be substantiated by the two variables $X_2$ (with $beta_2=0.312$) and $X_3$ (with $beta_3=0.220$) in Model 21.A. In addition, this survey includes the proportionate repair costs for which significant differences in the empirical cost indicators already could be verified in Section 4 across all the structural cost levels of DIN 18960:2008-2 under analysis. Based on these initial insights from preliminary investigations, the investigation accordingly proceeds to test whether it is possible to formulate cost predictions for the overall sample or a definition of subsamples is required in order to predict and examine the underlying cost indicators.

Against this background, it is examined whether any substantial differences are to be expected between the average cost indicators (€/m² GROFA p.a.), and the variances for $N_1$ (building constructions and technical installations in a good condition) and $N_2$ (building constructions or technical installations in a poor condition) or the deviations between the both subsamples $N_1=63$ and $N_2=50$ occur incidental. As with the earlier contemplations, the analysis therefore differentiates between a case distinction previously discussed in this section, i.e. where both the building constructions and the technical installations are in a good condition compared with that situation where at least one of these two structural components is found to be in a poor state of repair (see Fig. 21). To this end, the t-Test is applied for mean value comparisons (where $H_0(\mu_1 = \mu_2)$ and $H_1(\mu_1 < \mu_2)$) and the Levene Test is carried out for the analysis of variance, where $H_0(\sigma_1 = \sigma_2)$ and $H_1(\sigma_1 \neq \sigma_2)$. Both tests are based on almost normally distributed cost indicators, which is confirmed by the Kolmogorov-Smirnov Test (KS-test) in terms of a statistical test with an empirical significance level of 0.813 for $N_1=63$ and 0.377 for $N_2=50$ respectively based at an underlying significance level of 5%. The t-Test verifies with an empirical significance level of 0.00 (the empirical t-value is -12.148), that the mean cost indicator of $N_2$ is greater than the mean value of $N_1$. At a test level of $\alpha = 5\%$ the null hypothesis accordingly has to be rejected, so the difference in the mean value amounting to 28.93 €/m² GROFA p.a. (costs including VAT, based on 2008 figures) is regarded as significant and consequently not random. In addition, the Levene Test also verifies, with an empirical F-value of 32.555 and a corresponding significance level of 0.00, that the assumption of variance equality has to be rejected. In this way, both significance tests corroborate the aforementioned assumptions concerning possible discrepancies in the sample data available from the point of view of their mean values and variances, which were formulated on the basis of preliminary investigations and visual inspection of scatter plot.

Taking into account the case distinction described above, the study now takes a look at those school complexes whose building constructions and technical installations are simultaneously found to be in a good condition (N=63). The relevant factors that influence on the amount of aggregate cost indicators are described based on Model 21.B.1 below.

Tab. 86:  Model description for estimating cost indicators for aggregate operation and repair
in case of a good condition of the building constructions and technical installations

| Dependent variable | Transf. | R² | R² adj. | SEE | F-value | Sign. | Durbin-Watson-Statistic | | N |
|---|---|---|---|---|---|---|---|---|---|
| Aggregate operating and repair costs (€/m² GROFA p.a.) | - | 0,297 | 0,261 | 7,260 | 8,309 | 0,000 | 1,978 | | 63 |

| Factors | Transf. | B | St. Error | Beta | t-value | Sign. | Lower CL | Upper CL | T | VIF |
|---|---|---|---|---|---|---|---|---|---|---|
| Constant | - | 33,907 | 1,210 | | 28,032 | 0,000 | 31,486 | 36,327 | | |
| Share of the swimming pool utilization area per m² GROFA | - | 426,570 | 126,533 | 0,371 | 3,371 | 0,001 | 173,379 | 679,762 | 0,985 | 1,015 |
| Share of the non-built up plot area per m² GROFA | LN | 2,661 | 1,088 | 0,268 | 2,446 | 0,017 | 0,484 | 4,837 | 0,993 | 1,007 |
| Grounds and outdoor facilities, or fittings, furnishings and equipment in a poor condition | - | 3,810 | 1,872 | 0,224 | 2,035 | 0,046 | 0,064 | 7,556 | 0,985 | 1,015 |

**Dependent variable**: Aggregate operating and repair costs (€/m² gross floor area p.a.), costs including VAT, based on 2008 figures

$$\hat{Y} = 33.907 + 426.570 X_1 + 2.661 \ln(X_2) + 3.810 X_3 \qquad\qquad \text{(Model 21.B.1)}$$

Where:    $\hat{Y}$ :   Aggregate operating and repair cost indicators (€/m² GROFA p.a.)

$X_1$ :   Share of the swimming pool utilization area per m² GROFA

$X_2$ :   Share of the non-built up plot area per m² GROFA

$X_3$ :   Grounds and outdoor facilities, or fittings, furnishings and equipment in a poor condition

The best model prediction is achieved regarding the two continuous variables $X_1$ (share of the swimming pool utilization area per m² GROFA) and $X_2$ (share of the non-built up plot area of per m² GROFA), and distinguishing between the respective condition of the grounds and outdoor facilities, fittings, furnishings and equipment using $X_3$. All three independent variables were already included in Model 21.A to explain differences ascertained in the total aggregate operation and repair costs. These variables, moreover, were already identified as being significant factors for estimating proportionate costs in the context of the statistical analysis of operation cost indicators (Model 15.B)[47], as well as the univariate variance analysis (ANVOA) of comparable repair cost indicators (Model 20.B.1). Details of the individual partial regression coefficients $b_j$ and their statistical measures are provided in Tab. 86. In total, the estimation Model 12.B.1 makes it possible to realize simple cost predictions using descriptions relating to specific areas of a school property and its state of repair. With $R^2=0.297$ and SEE=7.260, however, the estimation model for the cost data concerned only provides a marginally better prediction quality than the mean value estimation for $N_1$.

The following section focuses on those schools that are found to have their building constructions or technical installations in a poor state of repair. The statistical approach shows that the best regression prediction is achieved using the multivariate Model 21.B.2 for estimating operating and repair cost indicators (€/m² GROFA p.a.). In correspondence with Model 20.B.2, defined for predicting the repair cost indicators for schools with an equal state of repair, the estimation model presented here for aggregate operating and repair cost indicators (Y) takes three categorical variables into account for evaluating the conditions of four structural components as defined by DIN 276-1:2008-12. The data evaluation reveals substantial differences in the costs indicators under analysis with regard to the condition categories identified above using sample data of 50 school complexes ($N_2$). The prediction model takes into account the individual influences exerted by different states of the building constructions ($X_1$) and technical installations ($X_2$) and quantifies the independent impacts of these two independent variables on Y separately, in the multivariate context. In the same way as Model 21.B.1, this estimation model also incorporates at the influence delineated by the condition of the grounds and outdoor facilities, fittings, furnishings and equipment in the form of one categorical variable.

Similarly to Model 15.B used for predicting operating cost indicators, the regression analysis also verifies a negative and nonlinear influence exerted by a building reference area; which is the gross floor area in this case and the net floor area in terms of Model 15.B. From the point of view of content, this variable reflects a phenomenon frequently cited in the literature. Among others, BMI (2008), DETR (1998) and JLL (2011) point out that, the larger a building, the lower the anticipated occupancy cost indicator, in general. Based on a significance level of 5%, this statement can also be verified for the underlying sample of schools.

To summarize, the multivariate Model 21.B.2 evaluated for estimating specific aggregate operating and repair cost indicators, not only takes into account previously verified factors influencing on the proportionate amount of repair costs, but also of the operating costs. With $R^2$ of 0.650 and SEE equivalent to 10.091, the regression model displays a convincing goodness-of-fit and prediction accuracy. Further information on the collinearity statistics, coefficient estimates and the empirical significance for each variable are presented in Tab. 87. A comparison between the observed and predicted cost indicators for aggregate operation and repair is visualized in Fig. 22.

---

[47] With regard to the underlying building reference area (NEFA) of Model 15.B, the variable $X_2$ (share of the swimming pool utilization area per m² NEFA) is specified for estimating the operating cost indicators.

Tab. 87:   Model description for estimating cost indicators for aggregate operation and repair
           in case of a poor condition of the building constructions or technical installations

| Dependent variable | Transf. | R² | R² adj. | SEE | F-value | Sign. | Durbin-Watson-Statistic | | N |
|---|---|---|---|---|---|---|---|---|---|
| Aggregate operating and repair costs (€/m² GROFA p.a.) | - | 0,650 | 0,619 | 10,091 | 20,886 | 0,000 | 2,144 | | 50 |

| Factors | Transf. | B | St. Error | Beta | t-value | Sign. | Lower CL | Upper CL | T | VIF |
|---|---|---|---|---|---|---|---|---|---|---|
| Constante | - | 110,54 | 24,735 | | 4,469 | 0,000 | 60,727 | 160,363 | | |
| Technical installations in a poor condition | - | 17,365 | 3,086 | 0,530 | 5,627 | 0,000 | 11,150 | 23,580 | 0,878 | 1,139 |
| Building constructions in a poor condition | - | 28,733 | 4,729 | 0,577 | 6,076 | 0,000 | 19,208 | 38,258 | 0,862 | 1,160 |
| Gross floor area (GROFA in m²) | LN | -9,738 | 2,675 | -0,326 | -3,640 | 0,001 | -15,126 | -4,350 | 0,970 | 1,031 |
| Grounds and outdoor facilities, or furnishings and equipment in a poor condition | - | 10,340 | 2,973 | 0,319 | 3,478 | 0,001 | 4,353 | 16,327 | 0,928 | 1,078 |

**Dependent variable:** Aggregate operating and repair costs (€/m² gross floor area p.a.), costs including VAT, based on 2008 figures

$$\hat{Y} = 110.545 + 17.365\,X_1 + 28.733\,X_2 - 9.738\,ln\left(X_3\right) + 10.340\,X_4 \qquad \text{(Model 21.B.2)}$$

Where:    $\hat{Y}$ :   Aggregate operating and repair cost indicators (€ p.a.)

          $X_1$ :   Technical installations in a poor condition

          $X_2$ :   Building constructions in a poor condition

          $X_3$ :   Gross floor area (GROFA in m²)

          $X_4$ :   Grounds and outdoor facilities, or fittings, furnishings and equipment in a poor condition

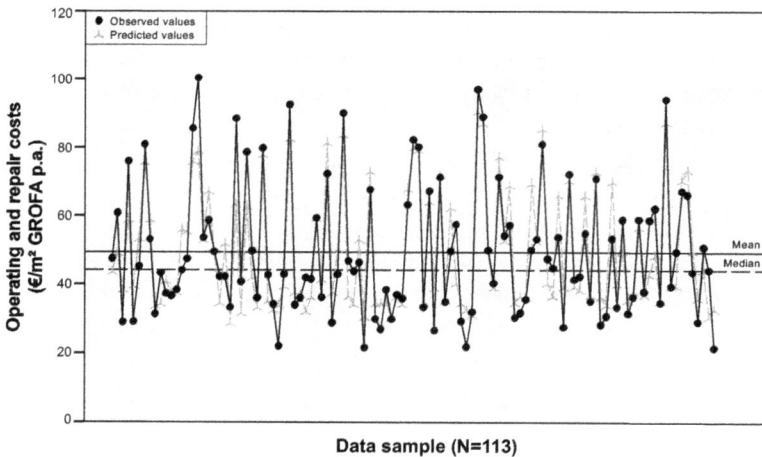

Fig. 22:   Comparison between observed and predicted cost indicators for aggregate operation
           and repair (costs including VAT, based on 2008 figures)

*Summary*

The evaluation of aggregate operating and repair costs presented in this section is based on previously introduced statistical analyses of individual operating costs and repair costs, as defined on the second and third structural cost level by DIN 18960:2008-2. To this end, the investigation looks at detailed sample data describing differences in school utilization as well as functional, technical and local characteristics of 113 school complexes in Germany. Based on this information, the statistical analysis defines the gross floor area as the appropriate building reference area for predictions into total cost and normalizing cost data, and describes specific estimates for cost indicators. In accordance with the case distinction introduced in Section 4 to distinguish between the respective condition categories for repair cost indicators, the operating and repair cost indicators for different states of the building constructions and technical installations are likewise evaluated separately. In compliance with the variables previously determined and quantified by means of a statistical approach for both the annual operating costs and repair expenditures, the study reveals that a distinguishing between four categories is particularly of relevance in order to estimate the relevant cost indicators in an appropriate manner. These categories pertain to different states of the building constructions, technical installations, grounds and outdoor facilities, as well as the fittings, furnishings and equipment in the form of 3 independent variables. Moreover, as with the estimation of operation cost indicators, three continuous variables are incorporated: the gross floor area, the share of the non-built up plot area per m² GROFA and the proportionate swimming pool utilization area per m² GROFA. All variables determined for reliable estimates of aggregate costs were considered by means of individual cost group analysis for the operating cost and repair costs that preceded this analysis. This emphasizes the significance of interrelations ascertained between the driving factors of these two cost groups for investigating the overall outlay. As regards the classification of evaluated pre-dictors, all independent variables used to forecast and compare aggregate costs originate from the type of school usage, functional building characteristics, and, in particular, technical characteristics with the focus on classified conditions.

## 5.3     Validation of the model

The validation test carried out for aggregate cost indicators is based on 5 randomly selected school complexes which had not been part of the model development process outlined above. The model predictions for aggregate operating and repair cost indicators are described in Tab. 88 and compared with empirical mean and median values of the overall sample. On the whole, the validation test reveals that the aggregate cost estimates based on specific regression models are fairly accurate, thus proving a high transferability of assumptions about causal interrelations depicted between influential factors and the aggregate costs for the schools under investigation in this section. However, the observed cost value of 57.29 €/m² GROFA p.a. (costs including VAT, based on 2008 figures) in the case of sample No.5 (vocational school with a technical focus), can only partially be explained by model assumptions specified in Model 21.B.1 and Model 21.B.2, leading to a deterioration in the indicated percentage error of the overall statistics for five validation cases. On average, with a mean absolute percentage error (MAPE) of 15%, the mean value estimate shows a better overall result than the model predictions in terms of all validation cases forming the subject of this practical test. A fairly large percentage error of roughly 43% in evidence here for the prediction value of sample No.5 can largely be explained by an estimation inaccuracy found in the case of the repair costs for building constructions. As described in Section 4.1.3, it may be due to a measuring error, that a good condition of the building constructions is stated for this case, instead of a poor condition. If sample No.5 was excluded from the comparison, the MAPE would be just under 11% for the model predictions, whereas the mean absolute percentage errors for the mean value estimation would remain constant at 15% and the median at 22% for N=4. In comparing the three prediction methods outlined below, the empirical median delivers the worst prediction quality, not only for individual cases but also in the overall average with a MAPE of just under 23%.

Tab. 88:   Model validation for aggregate operation and repair cost indicators

| No. | Type of school | Observed value | Predicted value | Absolute error % of prediction | Absolute error % of mean | Absolute error % of median | Preference |
|---|---|---|---|---|---|---|---|
| 1 | Elementary school without sports facilities | 69.96 | 82.72 | 18 | 29 | 37 | Prediction |
| 2 | Special school with gymnasium | 67.67 | 66.94 | 1 | 27 | 35 | Prediction |
| 3 | Secondary school without sports facilities | 49.11 | 58.65 | 19 | 1 | 10 | Mean |
| 4 | Secondary school with gymnasium and pool | 48.42 | 46.70 | 4 | 2 | 9 | Mean |
| 5 | Vocational school without sports facilities | 57.29 | 32.87 | 43 | 14 | 23 | Mean |
| Ø | Mean Absolute percentage error | | | 17 | 15 | 23 | Mean |

Observed value: Aggregate operating and repair costs (€/m² gross floor area p.a.), costs including VAT, based on 2008 figures, N=125

Tab. 89:   Estimation preferences in validated cost indicators

| No. | Type of school | Cost level 3 | | | Cost level 2 | | | Cost level 1 | | | Aggregate costs | | |
|---|---|---|---|---|---|---|---|---|---|---|---|---|---|
| | | Prediction | Mean | Median | Prediction | Mean | Median | Prediction | Mean | Median | Prediction | Mean | Median |
| 1 | Elementary school without sports facilities | 4 | 1 | 1 | 4 | 5 | - | 2 | - | - | 1 | - | - |
| 2 | Special school with gymnasium | 3 | 3 | 1 | 4 | 4 | 1 | 1 | 1 | - | 1 | - | - |
| 3 | Secondary school without sports facilities | 4 | 1 | 1 | 5 | 2 | 1 | 1 | - | 1 | - | 1 | - |
| 4 | Secondary school with gymnasium and pool | 5 | 1 | - | 8 | - | 1 | 2 | - | - | - | 1 | - |
| 5 | Vocational school without sports facilities | 5 | - | 1 | 6 | 2 | 1 | - | 2 | - | - | 1 | - |
| Ø | Mean Absolute percentage error | 21 | 6 | 4 | 27 | 13 | 4 | 6 | 3 | 1 | 2 | 3 | - |

Note: Estimation preferences in validated cost indicators (cell frequencies per cost level according to DIN 18960:2008-2, cost group 300 to 400)

Within the scope of the study, 19 validation test for individual cost groups as defined by DIN 18960:2008-2 have been carried out and presented in order to assess the model predictions beyond the underlying framework of the statistical approach. By comparing the three prediction methods applied across all the cost groups and five validation properties concerned, the validation tests reveal that the statistical model estimates provide more convincing results than the empirical mean and median values.

Model predictions are given preference as opposed to central value predictions in 56 of the 90 cost estimates (62%) that were carried out (see Tab. 89). More accurate cost estimates are in particular achieved by regression and variance analysis at lower structural cost levels according to DIN 18960:2008-2. In contrast, mean estimates increasingly gain in importance at higher structural cost levels. Those estimates performed by the empirical median reveal, with only 10% of the test decisions, by far the worst compliance with the observed values. This estimation method is therefore not appropriate for the respective schools examined.

## 5.4    Cost indicators for aggregate operation and repair

For the sample of 113 school complexes under investigation, an overall mean of around 50 €/m² GROFA p.a. is obtained with a standard deviation of almost 19.09 €/m² GROFA p.a. (see Tab. 101). The cost indicators described include VAT and are based on 2008 figures. The corresponding indexing table for annual price adjustments is provided by Destatis (2011b). If this empirical distribution of cost data is used as part of an actual cost estimate or benchmarking, considerable prediction uncertainties and deviations should be taken into account. In order to reduce these prediction uncertainties and enable more efficient cost predictions, a statistical evaluation of ascertained cost data is carried out in Section 5.2. This is used to quantify the relevant influential parameters, which make it possible to achieve more precise cost prognoses for the aggregate operating and repair cost indicators con-sidered here. As shown by the evaluation of the proportionate repair costs earlier in this study, the statistical analysis of school complex defines the condition of different structural components as relevant factors for estimating and classifying the outlay for operating and repair. The respective condition categories concerned are specified for the building con-structions, technical installations, grounds and outdoor facilities, and the fittings, furnishings and equipment (cf. DIN 276-1:2008-12).

The analysis into aggregate operating and repair costs evaluates the significance and impact for each condition category separately and uses this information here to provide specific cost indicators within a two-stage classification system. The representative cost indicators are shown in Tab. 90 below. A case distinction for different conditions of the building constructions and technical installations is provided on the first stage and a distin-guishing between evaluated conditions of grounds and outdoor facilities, fittings, furnishings and equipment is simultaneously described on the second stage. Based on this classifi-cation, the aggregate cost values set out in Tab. 90 can easily being compared with the overall repair cost indicators displayed in Tab. 84 (see Section 4.5.4). As regards the aggre-gate costs, the average cost indicator for operation and repair is 36.70 €/m² GROFA p.a. where the cost planner bases his calculations on both the building constructions and technical installations being in a good state of repair. In the case in question, where either the building constructions or the technical installations are found to be in a poor condition, the comparative mean value amounts to 65.63 €/m² GROFA p.a. The given range for the two categories under comparison is somewhere between 40 and 60 €/m² GROFA p.a.

Tab. 90 also shows additional cost values for designated subcategories, taking furhter condition assessments into consideration. By comparing the different condition categories described below, a best scenario can be particularly defined in which all four structural components are taken to be in a good state of repair. By contrast, a worst case scenario is represented by the combination where either the grounds and outdoor facilities, or the fittings, furnishings and equipment are found to be in a poor condition within the category that constitute a poor state of the building constructions or technical installations. In addition, more differentiated cost indicators are described in Section 5.2, which enable continuous cost estimates incorporating other additional criteria.

Tab. 90:   Evaluated cost indicators for aggregate operation and repair

| Factor level | Minimum | Mean | Median | Maximum | Range |
|---|---|---|---|---|---|
| **Building constructions and technical intallations in a good condition** | **21.59** | **36.70** | **36.02** | **62.07** | **40.48** |
| Grounds and outdoor facilities and fittings, furnishings and equipment in a good condition | 21.59 | 34.73 | 34.15 | 53.71 | 32.12 |
| Grounds and outdoor facilities, or fittings, furnishings and equipment in a poor condition | 26.64 | 39.52 | 37.78 | 62.07 | 35.43 |
| **Building constructions or technical intallations in a poor condition** | **42.23** | **65.63** | **61.96** | **100.40** | **58.17** |
| Grounds and outdoor facilities and fittings, furnishings and equipment in a good condition | 42.23 | 61.09 | 58.72 | 88.60 | 46.37 |
| Grounds and outdoor facilities, or fittings, furnishings and equipment in a poor condition | 42.94 | 69.49 | 67.12 | 100.40 | 57.47 |

**Dependent variable**: Costs ($€/m^2$ gross floor area p.a.), costs including VAT, based on 2008 figures, N=113

## 6      Summary of the investigation

The study examines the causes of measured differences in the outlay for operation and repair measures with the objective of evaluating the appropriate building reference areas for the definition of unbiased cost indicators and, subsequently, of making the critical para-meters for cost estimates and comparisons available to municipal real estate authorities. To this end, the causal interrelations assumed between property and usage-related charac-teristics of schools and their underlying occupancy expenditures are examined based on a data sample of 130 properties of the state capital Stuttgart (Germany). The cost data concerned include VAT and have been uniformly compiled for the calendar year 2008 in accordance with the cost structure of DIN 18960:2008-2, cost groups 300 to 400.

The statistical evaluation begins with a descriptive classification of individual operating and repair costs and their respective utility consumption figures pertaining to the building type under investigation. Comparing the cost data reveals that the aggregate operating costs averaging almost at 26 €/m² GROFA p.a., which is about 52% of the overall outlay for operating and repair, only slightly exceeds the average outlay for aggregate repair costs of around 23 €/m² GROFA p.a. which results from a corrective maintenance strategy consistently applied for the complete sample. The variability of these two cost groups indicates distinct differences, however. The operating costs have a standard deviation of around 5 €/m² GROFA p.a., whereas the corresponding value of the repair expenses amounts to approximately 17 €/m² GROFA p.a. The provision of efficient and consistent cost estimates for repair measures is accordingly found to be of particular importance over the course of model analyses to enable the relevant assumptions and parameters to be identified and to enhance occupancy cost prediction and valuation. Still on the subject of repair costs, the outlay for structural repair measures on the building constructions not only constitutes the most substantial share, 68% of the cost group 400, at an average of almost 16 €/m² GROFA p.a. but also the greatest variance with a standard deviation of around 12 €/m² GROFA p.a., followed by the outlay for the repair of technical installations.

With regard to the empirical analysis of localization and dispersion parameters ascertained for individual operating costs, the main emphasis for the schools under analysis is on the outlay for utilities (cost group 310), with an average cost indicator of almost 10 €/m² GROFA p.a., followed by the annual outlay for the cleaning and care of buildings (cost group 330) with an average cost value of around 8.50 €/m² GROFA p.a. and, some way behind that, the average outlay for the operation, inspection and maintenance (cost group 350) at around 3.50 €/m² GROFA p.a. (cf. Tab. 103). Comparing these figures for public schools with the empirical cost distribution for office buildings shows that the expenses for electricity, and often also those for the operation, inspection and maintenance of schools are below the annual outlays for office buildings. By contrast, schools often incur higher costs for the cleaning and care of buildings due to higher service level agreements (SLAs), which amount to a share of around 33% of the operating costs in the case of the underlying data sample.

Based on a descriptive classification of the operating and repair costs examined, the results of the statistical data evaluation are presented. According to DIN 18960:2008-2, differences in occupancy expenditures are best explained by three factor groups, i.e. the type of usage, functional, technical and organizational characteristics of a building, and external influences from the environment which cannot be influenced by local authorities. The data evaluation starts at this point by differentiating the relevant factor groups for the current analysis of school complexes in more detail, and subdividing them into measurable factors for the purpose of a statistical approach. The appropriate building reference area for each cost group is determined to provide a valid basis for the evaluation of consumption and cost indicators. As an example, the net floor area, as defined by DIN 277-1:2005-2, is identified as being the relevant building reference area for cost comparisons pertaining to technical installation measures, regardless of whether costs are taken as a basis for the inspection and maintenance (cost group 353) or the repairs (cost group 420) of the respective structural components. In contrast to this, the heatable gross floor area according to VDI 3807-1:2007-3 is determined for normalizing heating energy consumption and cost values, for instance.

The subsequent investigation of operating costs substantiates the aforementioned assumption of existing cost influences that are associated with specific usage characteristics of the underlying schools. The type of school utilization, such as elementary, secondary or vocational school, therefore represents a substantial factor for explaining annual cost differences. By contrast, variation measured in the repair costs examined cannot specifically be ascribed to usage-related characteristics.

Within the factor group utilization, the sports facilities integrated in a school complex acquire particular importance and are classified and assessed by way of further distinguishing features for the purpose of cost comparison and prediction. This study therefore enables a differentiated analysis of heterogeneous school utilization profiles, whereas often, in theory and practice, only a classification of different school types, such as elementary vs. secondary schools for example, is taken into consideration. The existence of an indoor swimming pool is of particular significance and becomes an essential component of introduced estimation models. The corresponding variable is not only employed for predicting and evaluating aggregate operating expenditure, but also as a basis for the assessment of cost differences measured in individual costs, i.e. in the outlay for utility supply, the cleaning and care of buildings and the costs for the operation, inspection and maintenance. As an example, the empirical cost analysis for these cost groups reveals an average outlay for schools with include an indoor swimming pool that is around 1.3 to 1.5 times higher than that outlay for schools without additional swimming facilities.

In addition, the study allows a detailed examination of the maintenance costs as defined by DIN 31051:2003-6 or DIN EN 13306:2010-12 respectively at an international level. The model parameters, i.e. quantified factors and building reference areas, are evaluated separately for both the individual and aggregate outlay of operation, inspection and maintenance (cost group 350), and for the outlay for repair measures (cost group 400 according to DIN 18960:2008-2). As a result, the empirical analysis in particular verifies usage-related influences on the amount of operating, inspection and maintenance costs and proceeds to assess the causes for the different levels of wear and tear that occur in the various schools examined. The study accordingly determines influences exerted by the type of school, such as elementary or vocational schools, the usage intensity expressed by the number of pupils per m² NEFA for instance, and functional characteristics in the form of the proportionate technical floor area per m² NEFA, or defined as the share of UFA 5 per m² UFA. All of these determinants are identified as being of particular relevance for the prediction and comparison of the annual outlay for the operation, inspection and mainten-ance of schools. By contrast, the analysis of repair costs demonstrates the significance of different condition assessments that have to be taken into consideration when planning and budgeting the repair costs for public schools. Against this backdrop, the analysis of repair costs evaluates the impact of the relevant condition categories for individual structural components as defined by DIN 276-1:2008-12, i.e. the condition of the building construc-tions, technical installations, grounds and outdoor facilities, as well as of the fittings, furni-shings and equipment.

A simplified overview of the model parameters evaluated over the course of this study is given in Fig. 23. The importance of various characteristics of the factor groups utilization, functional and technical characteristics, strategy and operation are depicted for different cost groups according to DIN 18960:2008-2 and levels of contemplation, respectively. The reference areas determined for individual cost types are included in the category functional characteristics. The author recommends to take these building floor areas, in particular, as a basis for refined planning and benchmarking studies of consumption and cost indicators (see Section 7). Further details of the statistical models and the measurement levels of their underlying variables are provided for individual analysis in Sections 3 to 5.

| Factor group | Factor | Cost group according to DIN 18960:2008-2 | Water | Heating | Electricity | Utilities | Waste disposal | Cleaning and care of buildings | Cleaning und care of grounds and outdoor facilities | Inspection and maintenance of building constructions | Inspection and maintenance of technical installations | Inspection and maintenance of grounds and outdoor facilities | Inspection and maintenance of fittings, furnishings and equipment | Operation, inspection and maintenance | Security and surveillance services | Statutory charges and contributions | Operating costs | Repair of building constructions | Repair of technical installations | Repair of grounds and outdoor facilities | Repair of fittings, furnishings and equipment | Repair costs | Cost for operating and repair |
|---|---|---|---|---|---|---|---|---|---|---|---|---|---|---|---|---|---|---|---|---|---|---|---|
| Type of utilization | Elementary School | | | | | | | • | • | | | • | | | | | | | | | | | |
| | Special School | | | | | | | • | • | | | • | | | | | | | | | | | |
| | Vocational school | | | | | | • | | | • | | • | | | | | | | | | | | |
| | Sport hall | | | | | • | • | | | • | | • | | | | | | | | | | | |
| | Indoor swimming pool | | • | • | • | | | • | | • | | • | | | | • | | | | | | • | |
| | Kindergarten | | | | | | | | • | | | | | | | | | | | | | | |
| Intensity of utilization | Number of pupils | | | | | | | | • | | | • | | | | | | | | | | | |
| | Number of school classes | | • | | | | | | | | | | | | | | | | | | | | |
| | Water volume in m³ of complete pool refillings p.a. | | • | | | | • | | | | | | | | | | | | | | | | |
| Functional characteristics | Gross floor area (GROFA) | | | | | | | | • | | | • | | | | • • | • | | • | | | | |
| | Net floor area (NEFA) | | • | | • | | | • | | | • | | • | | | • | | | • | | | | |
| | Usable floor area (UFA) | | • | | | | | | | | • | • | | | | • | | | • | | | | |
| | Usable floor area for education, teaching and culture | | | | | | | | | • | | | | | | | | | | | | | |
| | Technical floor area (TEFA) | | | | | | | | | • | | | | | | | | | | | | | |
| | Average storey height | | | | | | | | | | | | | | | | | | • | | | | |
| | Gross floor area of the ground floor | | | | | | • | | | | | | | | | | | | | | | | |
| | Heatable gross floor area (H-GROFA) | | • | | • | | | | | | | | | | | • | | | | | | | |
| | Sanitary area | | • | | | | | • • | | | | | | | | | | | | | | | |
| Technical characteristics | Heat storage capacity | | • | | | | | | | | | | | | | | | | | | | | |
| | External glass area | | • | | • | | | | | | | | | | | | | | | | | | |
| | Condition of building constructions | | | | | | | | | | | | | | | | • | | | | • | • | |
| | Condition of walls and ceilings | | | | | | | | | | | | | | | | • | | | | • | • | |
| | Condition of roof structures | | | | | | | | | | | | | | | | • | | | | • | | |
| | Condition of technical installations | | | | | | | | | | | | | | | | | • | | | • | | |
| | Condition of heat supply systems | | • | | • | | | | | | | | | | | | | | | | | | |
| | Standard of ground and outdoor facilities | | | | | | | | • | | | | | | | | | | | | | | |
| | Non-built up area of the plot | | | | | | | | • | | | • | • | | | • | | | • | | • | | • |
| | School playground area (hard surfaces) | | | | | | | | • | | | • | | | | | | | | | | | |
| | Outdoor sports area (hard surfaces) | | | | | | | | • | | | • | | | | | | | | | | | |
| | Outdoor cleaning area | | | | | | | | • | | | | | | | | | | | | | | |
| | Water impermeable surface of the plot | | | | | | • | | | | | | | | | | | | | | | | |
| | Condition of grounds and outdoor facilities | | | | | | | | | | | | | | | | | | • | | • • | • | |
| | Condition of fittings, furnishings and equipment | | | | | | | | | | | | | | | | | | | • | • | • | |
| Strategy and operation | Outsourcing rate of services for security and monitoring | | | | | | | | | | | | | • | | | | | | | | |

Legend:   ●   Significant interrelation revealed for occupancy cost planning and benchmarking      No significant interrelation revealed for occupancy cost planning and benchmarking

Fig. 23:     Overview of the relevant factors evaluated in the investigation

# 7        Application examples

The statistical investigation determines the appropriate building reference areas and significant cost influential factors for the operating and repair costs of schools in order to provide an adequate basis for occupancy cost prediction and comparison. The resulting occupancy cost indicators that are presented for various cost groups and evaluated factor levels serve for diverse occupancy cost planning and benchmarking purposes. In this section, several application examples for the research findings of this study are provided for both disciplines and different levels of detail. Each approach is initially described by a rough approximation. More sophisticated procedures are then employed to stepwise elaborate the approximation and to reach a higher evaluation standard. A detailed explanation is given on the individual working stages and the data specifications that are required for the implementation of the concept within building construction planning and operation.

Both the occupancy cost planning and benchmarking approach are exemplified by a concrete school that had not previously been part of any model development or validation process. Some impressions of the underlying school and its floor plans are shown in Fig. 24. The building is a grammar school with gymnasium, located on a hillside and operated by the state capital Stuttgart. The historic building is listed for preservation and was built in 1995. It comprises 7,815 m² GROFA and accommodates around 444 pupils. Further information on the building and its utilization is available in the object documentation No. 4100-090 in BKI NK1 (Stoy & Beusker, 2010, p.110 et seqq.). The cost structure of DIN 18960:2008-2 is taken as a basis and the respective cost types that are taken into account for the application examples are compiled in accordance with the cost structure of this study as shown in Tab. 4. The underlying cost data includes VAT and refers to the calendar year 2008. In addition, detailed descriptions of the empirical data sample that serves as an evaluation basis for both of the application examples are given in Appendix C.

## 7.1     Planning of operating and repair costs

The practical application field of occupancy cost planning is exemplified in the following. The prediction of operating and repair costs is demonstrated in more detail on the basis of the general approach described in Section 1.4. The process of continuous cost approximation is outlined for three different types of cost identification and periods in time respectively in a manner as it could be performed during the construction planning process, for instance. The individual estimation methods are delineated for the concrete grammar school and calendar year stated above.

In a first step, the operating and repair costs are roughly approximated with regard to the gross floor area of the school. Such a single-factor estimation is appropriate as long as no more detailed information is available for the planned construction measure and the building reference areas according to DIN 277-1:2005-2 for instance. At the time of requirements planning, an adequate cost indicator in €/m² GROFA p.a. can be identified within the overall distribution of aggregate operating and repair cost indicators depicted in Tab. 103.

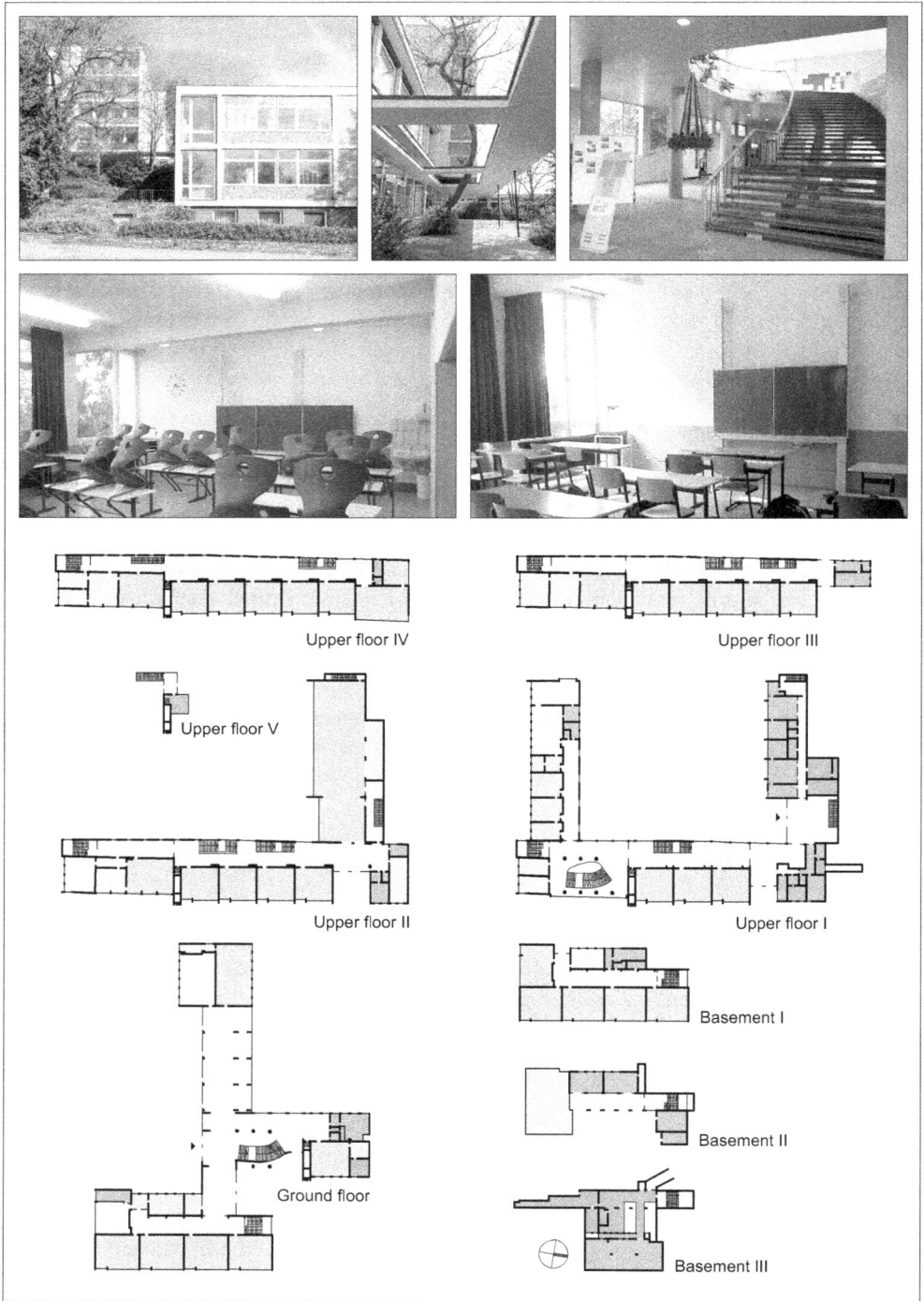

Fig. 24:   Overview of the application example (BKI NK1, No. 4100-090)

Taking the empirical mean as a basis, the first projection of aggregate costs reveals an expected outlay for the property concerned of around 390,000 € p.a. (costs including VAT, based on 2008 figures) that is calculated as follows:

*50.00 €/m² GROFA p.a. * 7,800 m² GROFA = 390,000 € p.a.*

With the progress in construction planning and detail, this estimate can be constantly refined at lower structural cost levels according to DIN 18960:2008-2. The following examples represent such an effort in terms of both a preliminary and approximate cost prediction as they are in particular carried out from the basis of the schematic and final design for the respective grammar school. In accordance with the object information available from the planning documents at a specific planning stage, this study allows the cost planner to specify empirical cost indicators for the operation and repair with regard to determined building reference areas and evaluated factor levels. The preliminary estimation presented in Tab. 91 exemplifies an occupancy cost approximation that is performed at first structural cost level according to DIN 18960:2008-2. The corresponding reference sources are outlined in Appendix C. in the form of empirical cost indicator distributions. In addition, both the gross floor area and the net floor area, specified as 7,815 m² and 6,887 m² respectively, are taken as calculation base for this preliminary estimate.

The statistical analysis revealed that the operating costs of a school (in €/m² NEFA p.a.) are primarily dependent on the proportionate swimming pool utilization area per m² NEFA, and are subsequently influenced by the share of the non-built up plot area per m² NEFA, and the total size of a school's net floor area (measured in m² NEFA), cf. Section 3.8. The individual distributions of operating cost indicators are shown in Tab. 66 for the corresponding factor levels examined. Regarding the current grammar school under consideration, the empirical mean of 27.09 €/m² NEFA p.a. is defined as being the appropriate cost indicator according to the depicted category 'schools without indoor swimming pools and a total NEFA ≥ 6,000 m²'.

This decision is comprehensible if it is assumed that the cubature and the ground floor area of the building in particular have not yet been determined at this preliminary stage of design. Planning documents of alternative building designs are available within this time period which lead to different sizes in the non-built up plot area and therefore restrict further considerations with regard to other classification criteria, such as the share of the non-built up plot area per m² NEFA. Furthermore, it can be noted that an average outlay for the school's operation is expected in this instance. In general, alternative contemplations about the expected outlay for the actual grammar school are also conceivable that would consequently lead to the identification of another cost indicator within a given distribution. As an example, the empirical median value stated at 26.57 €/m² NEFA p.a. in Tab. 66 could also be determined as an adequate reference value for the operating costs (i.e. cost group 300).

As with the identification of an appropriate operating cost indicator for the building, a representative repair cost indicator is subsequently determined at first structural cost level according to DIN 18960:2008-2. A first guideline for the definition of an adequate cost value is described in Section 4 which includes empirical distributions of repair costs by means of scatter plot. As the underlying school falls into a maintenance-intensive period after 52 years of operation, a cost indicator of 32.46 €/m² GROFA p.a. is defined according to the upper quartile of the empirical distribution shown in Tab. 101. Even when it is not possible at an early planning stage to foresee whether the condition of the building constructions or technical installations, among others, will be found to be in a good or poor condition within the respective year, the selection of a representative repair cost indicator that is located above the median value of the empirical distribution can already be justified with regard to the critical age categories described in this study (cf. Section 4). When compared with an overall mean of 23.17 €/m² GROFA p.a., the chosen reference value for the preliminary cost estimate therefore exceeds the average repair cost indicator by 9.29 €/m² GROFA p.a. (costs including VAT, based on 2008 figures).

On the basis of this data base ascertained, the subsequent calculations for estimating the total outlay for operating and repair are illustrated in Tab. 91. With respect to the individual building reference areas determined for the cost groups 300 and 400 according to DIN 189660:2008-2, the total outlay for both of the considered cost groups is determined in a first step and afterwards added to the aggregate costs for operation and repair. As a result, this preliminary estimation reveals a total outlay of around 440,000 €/m² GROFA p.a. In comparison with the first cost projection outlined above, the expected outlay is adjusted by 13% upwards due to more differentiated assumptions regarding the repair costs in particular. In addition, an overall cost indicator of around 56 €/m² GROFA p.a. can be specified for the entirety of expected services and measures for the operation and repair of the concrete school building and respective calendar year.

Tab. 91:   Basic data for a preliminary estimate of operating and repair costs (application example)

| Cost group | Evaluated unit | Building reference area (m²) | Evaluated cost indicator (€/m² reference area p.a.) | Evalutated factor level | Total costs (€ p.a.) | Cost Indicator (€/m² GROFA p.a.) |
|---|---|---|---|---|---|---|
| 300   Operating costs | €/m² NEFA p.a. | 6,887 | 27.09 | School without swimming pool, NEFA ≥ 6,000 m² | 186,577 | 23.87 |
| 400   Repair costs | €/m² GROFA p.a. | 7,815 | 32.46 | Overall distribution | 253,637 | 32.46 |
| Total Aggregate costs | €/m² GROFA p.a. | 7,815 | | | 440,214 | 56.33 |

Note: Operating and repair costs, costs including VAT, based on 2008 figures

In compliance with the procedure outlined above for a preliminary cost estimate, the calculation method for an approximate estimate of operating and repair costs is subsequently described. The planning documents available for the final building design provide more differentiated information, such as details on individual building floor areas according to DIN 277-1:2005-2 for instance. This can now be used for more specific assumptions which enable refined cost approximations to be made at second structural cost level according to DIN 18960:2008-2. The relevant distributions of cost indicators are again provided by the research findings of this study, i.e. with respect to specific building reference areas examined for the normalization of individual cost types, and evaluated determinants for the definition of the relevant cost categories. From this basis, the proceeding can be described as follows. In a first step, cost planners determine an appropriate cost indicator for each of the cost groups taken into account. Subsequently, a calculation is made of the sum of the total outlay that is expected for the period of consideration, i.e. the calendar year 2008 in this example. The result of such an approximate estimate for the operation and repair costs is shown in Tab. 92 for the actual application example.

Tab. 92:   Basic data for an approximate estimate of operating and repair costs (application example)

| Cost group | Evaluated unit | Building reference area (m²) | Evaluated cost indicator (€/m² reference area p.a.) | Evalutated factor level | Total costs (€ p.a.) | Cost Indicator (€/m² GROFA p.a.) | Percentage (%) |
|---|---|---|---|---|---|---|---|
| 310 Utilities | €/m² H-GROFA p.a. | 7,404 | 10.46 | School without swimming pool | 77,478 | 9.91 | 18 |
| 320 Waste disposal | €/m² UFA p.a. | 4,122 | 0.80 | School without swimming pool | 3,316 | 0.42 | 1 |
| 330 Cleaning and care of buildings | €/m² NEFA p.a. | 6,887 | 8.99 | School without swimming pool, Grammer school | 61,919 | 7.92 | 14 |
| 340 Cleaning and care of grounds and outdoor facilities | €/m² non-built up plot area p.a. | 7,265 | 0.86 | Share of the outdoor cleaning area per m² non-built up plot area between 0.5 and 1.0 | 6,264 | 0.80 | 1 |
| 350 Operation, inspection and maintenance | €/m² NEFA p.a. | 6,887 | 3.55 | Grammer school, School without swimming pool | 24,434 | 3.13 | 6 |
| 360 Security and surveillance services | €/m² GROFA p.a. | 7,815 | 0.39 | Overall distribution | 3,064 | 0.39 | 1 |
| 370 Statutory charges and contributions | €/m² GROFA p.a. | 7,815 | 1.56 | Overall distribution | 12,168 | 1.56 | 3 |
| 410 Repair of building constructions | €/m² GROFA p.a. | 7,815 | 21.93 | Overall distribution | 171,389 | 21.93 | 40 |
| 420 Repair of technical installations | €/m² NEFA p.a. | 6,887 | 9.45 | Overall distribution | 65,082 | 8.33 | 15 |
| 430 Repair of grounds and outdoor facilities | €/m² non-built up plot area p.a. | 7,265 | 0.36 | Overall distribution | 2,615 | 0.33 | 1 |
| 440 Repair of fittings, furnishings and equipment | €/m² UFA p.a. | 4,122 | 1.36 | Overall distribution | 5,596 | 0.72 | 1 |
| Total Aggregate costs | €/m² GROFA p.a. | 7,815 | | | 433,325 | 55.45 | 100 |

Note: Operating and repair costs, costs including VAT, based on 2008 figures

Whereas most of the operating cost indicators are specified with respect to the factor 'type of school', i.e. a grammar school without swimming pool in the considered example of Object No. 4100-090, the cost value for the cleaning and care of grounds and out-door facilities is determined from the characteristic 'proportionate outdoor cleaning area per m² non-built-up plot area'. The statistical data analysis previously carried out revealed a positive effect of this factor, i.e. the proportionate outdoor cleaning area of a school property per m² non-built-up plot area (see Section 3.4.2). The corresponding cost indicators are depicted in Tab. 40 for three different factor levels of this characteristic. With a proportionate outdoor cleaning area per m² non-built up plot area of 0.59, the underlying grammar school falls into the category 'share between 0.5 and 1.0' of the respective factor.

In this example of an approximate occupancy cost estimate, reference is made to the average operating cost indicator of designated factor levels in Section 3.8.4, whereas the empirical cost values of the upper quartiles are again seen as being appropriate for specifying the expected outlay of designated repair measures (cf. cost groups 410 to 440 according to DIN 18960:2008-2 in Tab. 101). As outlined above, the probability of higher repair cost indicators is reasonable for a grammar school which has been in operation for 52 years. This consequently leads to the definition of cost indicators which, in this example, lie above the empirical median of each distribution.

In well-founded cases, cost planners in general can also refer to other reference values within a stated distribution, or even can define more specific cost indicators by taking further cost influential factors into account. If the cost planner assumes, because of his experience on the life expectancy of an installed heat supply system, that there is a great possibility that a technical installation will be in a poor condition in the respective year, for example, reference can be made to other cost indicators as described in Tab. 73. A further example can be described for the outlay for the cleaning and care of grounds and outdoor facilities mentioned above. Here, the statistical investigation of 125 school properties indicated higher average cost indicators, for instance, when an elementary, special or nursery school exists on site (see Model 7.B). The multivariate analyses carried out for individual cost types therefore provide supplementary information for cost planners which supports the selection of appropriate cost indicators within the empirical distributions.

Based on the cost indicators evaluated for individual cost groups at second structural cost level according to DIN 18960:2008-2, the aggregate operating and repair costs for the underlying grammar school are estimated to be around 433,000 € p.a. by means of the approximate estimate (costs including VAT, based on 2008 figures). Tab. 93 gives an overview of the different cost predictions presented in this section for three different types of occupancy cost identification. By comparing the approximate estimate with the preliminary estimation described above, the total costs are revised downwards by 2%. Furthermore, the deviation between the last cost prediction carried out (i.e. an approximate estimate) and the real outlay for the operating and repair ascertained for the respective school can be quantified. With respect to the total outlay of around 421,000 € documented in BKI NK1, the cost difference amounts to 3% which can be evaluated as being a good approximation result. The example therefore demonstrates excellent estimates with regard to both the influential factors and building reference evaluated in this study for individual cost types.

In addition, the cost indicators per m² gross floor area (GROFA) and also the proportionate share (%) of each cost group in reference to the aggregate operating and repair costs are depicted in Tab. 93. With respect to the object information and factor levels taken into account at the period of the final design stage, the cost planner gains an overview of the distribution of estimated operating and repair expenditure. The outlay for utility supply (18%) and for the cleaning and care of the school building (14%), together with the repair costs of the building constructions and technical installations that represent around 55% of the aggregate operating and repair costs, therefore constitute the relevant cost items for the actual estimate.

According to the underlying cost structure of the investigation, no predictions of the capital and object management costs (cost group 100 and 200 according to DIN 18960:2008-2) are yet included in the different types of cost identifications outlined above. These expenditures are to a great extent independent of property-related characteristics. They are rather influenced by other determinants, such as the interest rate and the operating lifetime of a building, as well as by the scope of building management services performed. In compliance with the estimation of the outlay for operating and repair, both the capital and object management costs must also be supplemented in each type of cost identification and also be constantly updated in accordance with the level of detail considered. According to DIN 18960:2008-2, such an approximate estimate that includes the aggregate outlay for total occupancy costs, i.e. cost groups 100 to 400, mainly serves, in combination with an approximate estimate of the building construction costs as defined by DIN 276-1:2008-12, as a basis for decisions regarding the financing and the evaluation of alternative building designs during the final design stage, i.e. working stage (LP) 3 according to HOAI 2009-4. The approximate estimate is to be continually updated, in particular according to the planning progress and changes made in planning that particularly affect the expected outlay (cf. DIN 18960:2008-2), until the final occupancy cost estimate is drawn up.

Tab. 93:   Comparison of different types of cost determination (application example)

| Type of cost determination | Period of time | Total operating and repair costs (€ p.a.) | Deviation (%) |
|---|---|---|---|
| First projection | Requirements planning | 390,000 | 7 |
| Preliminary estimate | Building planning (Preliminary design stage) | 440,214 | 5 |
| Approximate estimate | Building planning (Final design stage) | 433,325 | 3 |
| **Final statement** | **Building operation** | **420,937** | |

Note: Operating and repair costs, costs including VAT, based on 2008 figures

Summing up, in this section three different types of occupancy cost estimates are described for a concrete school building in order to exemplify the continuous process of cost identification and concretization over the building construction process. The individual calculation methods are demonstrated for each of the approaches as they are carried out at different periods in time. The prediction results, as compared with one another and also confronted with the observed outlay for the respective school, reveal a convincing accuracy of the estimation based on the research findings presented in this study. The occupancy costs determined in this section for different planning stages therefore serve as a transparent and well-founded basis for decision making and cost control. Delineated proceedings are in general transferable to other building types as far as the respective cost data required is provided for evaluated factor levels by means of a reference building or sample.

When comparing different types of cost identification during cost monitoring, the calculation basis in the form of drawings, building quantities and descriptions that is available at a specific stage of progress has been particularly taken into consideration. For cost planners, a comparison between the final statement of observed expenditure and previous cost estimates becomes especially relevant in practice, because such a consideration gives an excellent opportunity to directly compare the predicted outlay with the actually incurred outlay for a specific property. In this way, cost planners can evaluate the accuracy of cost predictions that were previously carried out and can adjust or expand the underlying data base if appropriate. As an example, from the basis of the observed outlay, further cost indicators can be deduced and determined for future cost estimates of other properties. Such cost indicators can be defined with regard to a final statement on one year, for example, or even more sophisticatedly, be based on descriptive statistics of time-series analyses. The observed costs of an operated building or portfolio can then be used to generate cost indicators for future predictions of other school properties.

According to DIN 18960:2008-2, an accounting period of one year is appropriate for final occupancy cost statements. Regarding the previously mentioned comparison between the final statement and previous occupancy cost estimates, it should be noted that the cost data compiled for the first year of operation does generally not determine a representative occupancy cost standard. Facilities services are often customized at the beginning of buildings operation and the technical installations, such as heating control and building automation systems, for instance, must often also be adjusted to the operating requirements during the first accounting period. A comparatively higher outlay for the first accounting period could therefore be generated in terms of the costs for utility supply or for the cleaning and care of buildings for example. It is therefore advisable to compile the cost data for the first year of operation separately from the cost data of the following years, particularly for those buildings with a comparably high standard of technical installations. How a further comparison of observed cost indicators can be carried out for various levels of detail during buildings operation is exemplified in the following.

## 7.2    Benchmarking of operating and repair costs

In this section, the benchmarking approach for operating and repair costs is demonstrated by means of an example of how it could be performed for the purpose of cost monitoring and assessment during real estate operation. Building up from the empirical cost indicators presented in this study, different evaluation methods of performance indicators are delineated and compared with each other for a concrete building. The benchmarking procedures described for the second structural cost level according to DIN 18960:2008-2 differ particularly in their level of detail and thus the scope of data considered. The different working stages required for each assessment of observed cost indicators are described and supplemented by practical advice as well as by an outlook for potential subsequent considerations. The underlying school building under review is documented in BKI NK1 (Object No. 4100-090) and the cost survey considered corresponds to the cost structure of this study outlined in Tab. 4 (costs including VAT, based on 2008 figures).

The initial benchmarking study is performed as an approximate validation of observed cost indicators. To this end, the plausibility of the actual figures is reviewed with a minimum of effort in data collection and processing. The survey of the actual performance (status quo) therefore comprises the ascertainment of the cost postings for utility supply, operation services and repair measures as documented for the underlying school building and year at second structural cost level according to DIN 18960:2008-2. Regarding the scope of supplementary object descriptions that are considered, this approach only includes the gross floor area (as the overall building size) for the definition of consistent cost indicators. This building floor area amounts to 7,815 m² in the case of the underlying school building. The uniformly prepared cost figures per m² GROFA are outlined in Tab. 94 for both the individual cost groups and their aggregate cost values, which in total amount to almost 54 €/m² GROFA p.a. for the actual building under review. In addition, the percentage of each cost group is outlined in reference to the aggregate cost indicator for operating and repair.

Tab. 94: Basic data for a preliminary benchmarking of operating and repair costs (application example)

| Cost group | | Observed cost indicator | Empirical Mean (Benchmark) | Deviation (%) | Percentage (%) |
|---|---|---|---|---|---|
| 310 | Utilities | 12.39 | 9.61 | 29 | 23 |
| 320 | Waste disposal | 0.28 | 0.51 | 46 | 1 |
| 330 | Cleaning and care of buildings | 8.83 | 8.49 | 4 | 16 |
| 340 | Cleaning and care of grounds and outdoor facilities | 0.95 | 1.02 | 7 | 2 |
| 350 | Operation, inspection and maintenance | 7.27 | 3.44 | 111 | 14 |
| 360 | Security and surveillance services | 2.30 | 0.39 | 487 | 4 |
| 370 | Statutory charges and contributions | 1.94 | 1.56 | 24 | 4 |
| 300 | **Aggregate operating costs** | **33.95** | **25.03** | **36** | **63** |
| 410 | Repair of building constructions | 8.09 | 15.83 | 49 | 15 |
| 420 | Repair of technical installations | 10.64 | 6.54 | 63 | 20 |
| 430 | Repair of grounds and outdoor facilities | 0.06 | 0.44 | 86 | 0 |
| 440 | Repair of fittings, furnishings and equipment | 1.12 | 0.60 | 86 | 2 |
| 400 | **Aggregate repair costs** | **19.91** | **23.41** | **15** | **37** |
| Total | **Aggregate operating and repair costs** | **53.86** | **48.44** | **11** | **100** |

Note: Occupancy cost indicators (€/m² gross floor area p.a.), costs including VAT, based on 2008 figures

Based on the compilation of cost data for the actual building under review, an adequate benchmarking standard has also to be specified. For the purpose of an initial review of observed cost performance, reference is made to the empirical distributions of cost indicators (€/m² GROFA p.a.) provided in Tab. 103. The respective statistics are compiled for the maximum number of school complexes examined in this study. The required reference values are determined according to the mean cost indicator of each cost group at second structural cost level by means of an approximate point estimation. In this way, the evaluation of observed cost indicators takes distortion into account to a certain degree. This arises on the one hand by a generalized definition of the building reference area (i.e. the gross floor area here) across all of the considered cost groups and, on the other hand, because further cost influential factors which could justify the identification of a more appropriate cost indicator within the depicted limits of a given cost indicator distribution in Tab. 103 are neglected. On the basis of this reference data, however, the mean cost figures are compiled for the second structural cost level according to DIN 18960:2008-2 and shown in Tab. 94. As with the calculation of the aggregate cost indicator for the actual school building, the overall reference value is finally determined (i.e. 48 €/m² GROFA p.a.). In addition, the absolute deviations incurred between each of the compared cost indicators are delineated.

On this evaluation basis, the initial assessment of the building's cost performance reveals that the aggregate cost indicator, at almost 54 €/m² GROFA p.a., exceeds the aggregate benchmarking indicator by 11%. In a first instance, this outcome neither indicates a convincing performance for the grammar school under review nor any alerting conspicuousness at this level of inspection. This appraisal can be furthermore substantiated by the overall distribution of aggregate cost indicators provided in Tab. 103. The observed cost indicator therefore lies some distance above the empirical median of 44 €/m² GROFA p.a. but still below the upper quartile stated at around 59 €/m² GROFA p.a. It can therefore be concluded that, when compared with the underlying performance standard determined, the respective building does not indicate a substantiated suspicion of a systematic discrepancy.

On the basis of deviations outlined at lower structural cost level in Tab. 94, it is furthermore possible to delineate the sources for this cost indicator overstepping in more detail. The benchmarking indicator for operating costs is exceeded by 36%, whereas the observed repair cost indicator falls below its reference value by 15%. In addition, a further inspection of the relevant operating costs reveals that this benchmark exceeding is particularly determined by the cost values of utility supply, the cleaning and care of the actual grammar school under review and its underlying operation, inspection and maintenance services. The cost groups 310, 330 and 350 are therefore mainly responsible for this reduced benchmarking result. These cost figures account in total for around 84% of the overall operating cost figure of around 34 €/m² GROFA p.a. and are thus the major causes of a reduced overall cost performance. In contrast to this, the aggregate repair cost indicator can withstand the benchmarking value of around 23 €/m² GROFA p.a. The repair costs of both the building constructions and technical installations, however, constitute a significant proportion (94%) of the cost group 400 and are therefore of particular relevance for the current benchmarking study. As a first result, it can be summarized that the aforementioned cost groups which constitute a substantial share of the overall costs should be continuously reviewed in the following years and evaluated with respect to the underlying operating and repair strategies of the actual building. In how far this benchmarking approach can withstand a more detailed analysis is described in the following.

During the next stage, this preliminary assessment of observed cost indicators is elaborated in more detail by making use of additional details for the definition of more representative cost indicators according to the research findings of this study. These affect the application of specific building floor areas as well as cost influential factors evaluated for both the actual grammar school under review and its respective benchmarking source. The following approach is built on the distributions of specified cost indicators (in €/m² reference area p.a.) and factor levels described in Sections 3 to 5. It therefore implements more sophisticated indicators with respect to individual property and usage-related characteristics.

Tab. 95:   Empirical distribution of relevant cost indicators (application example)

| Cost group | | Evaluated unit | Minimum | Mean | Maximum | Factor level |
|---|---|---|---|---|---|---|
| 310 | Utilities | €/m² H-GROFA p.a. | 7.78 | **11.06** | 15.33 | School without swimming pool |
| | | | | | | Heat supply systems in a poor condition |
| 320 | Waste disposal | €/m² UFA p.a. | 0.37 | **0.80** | 1.43 | School without swimming pool |
| 330 | Cleaning and care of buildings | €/m² NEFA p.a. | 5.47 | **8.99** | 13.48 | School without swimming pool |
| | | | | | | Grammer school |
| 340 | Cleaning and care of grounds and outdoor facilities | €/m² non-built up plot area p.a. | 0.14 | **0.86** | 3.08 | Share of the outdoor cleaning area per m² non-built up plot area is 0.59 |
| 350 | Operation, inspection and maintenance | €/m² NEFA p.a. | 1.68 | **3.55** | 5.41 | Grammer school |
| | | | | | | School without swimming pool |
| 360 | Security and surveillance services | €/m² GROFA p.a. | 0.00 | **0.39** | 8.51 | Overall distribution |
| 370 | Statutory charges and contributions | €/m² GROFA p.a. | 0.10 | **1.56** | 3.52 | Overall distribution |
| 410 | Repair of building constructions | €/m² GROFA p.a. | 0.70 | **7.62** | 15.59 | Building constructions in a good condition |
| 420 | Repair of technical installations | €/m² NEFA p.a. | 9.27 | **17.04** | 33.15 | Technical installations in a poor condition |
| 430 | Repair of grounds and outdoor facilities | €/m² non-built up plot area p.a. | 0.01 | **0.13** | 0.37 | Grounds and outdoor facilities in a good condition |
| 440 | Repair of fittings, furnishings and equipment | €/m² UFA p.a. | 0.01 | **0.27** | 0.69 | Fittings, furnishings and equipment in a good condition |

**Note**: Occupancy cost indicators (€/m² reference area p.a.), costs including VAT, based on 2008 figures

Tab. 96:   Basic data for an elaborated benchmarking of operating and repair costs (application example)

| Cost group | | Evaluated unit | Observed cost indicator | Evaluated cost indicator (Benchmark) | Deviation (%) | Reference area (m²) | Total costs (€ p.a.) |
|---|---|---|---|---|---|---|---|
| 310 | Utilities | €/m² H-GROFA p.a. | 13.08 | 11.06 | 18 | 7,404 | 81,847 |
| 320 | Waste disposal | €/m² UFA p.a. | 0.52 | 0.80 | 35 | 4,122 | 3,316 |
| 330 | Cleaning and care of buildings | €/m² NEFA p.a. | 10.02 | 8.99 | 11 | 6,887 | 61,919 |
| 340 | Cleaning and care of grounds and outdoor facilities | €/m² non-built up plot area p.a. | 1.02 | 0.86 | 18 | 7,265 | 6,264 |
| 350 | Operation, inspection and maintenance | €/m² NEFA p.a. | 8.25 | 3.55 | 133 | 6,887 | 24,434 |
| 360 | Security and surveillance services | €/m² GROFA p.a. | 2.30 | 4.45 | 48 | 7,815 | 34,779 |
| 370 | Statutory charges and contributions | €/m² GROFA p.a. | 1.94 | 2.54 | 24 | 7,815 | 19,843 |
| 410 | Repair of building constructions | €/m² GROFA p.a. | 8.09 | 7.62 | 6 | 7,815 | 59,523 |
| 420 | Repair of technical installations | €/m² NEFA p.a. | 12.07 | 17.04 | 29 | 6,887 | 117,352 |
| 430 | Repair of grounds and outdoor facilities | €/m² non-built up plot area p.a. | 0.07 | 0.13 | 49 | 7,265 | 960 |
| 440 | Repair of fittings, furnishings and equipment | €/m² UFA p.a. | 2.12 | 0.27 | 680 | 4,122 | 1,119 |
| **Total** | **Aggregate costs** | €/m² GROFA p.a. | 53.86 | 52.64 | 2 | 7,815 | 411,357 |

**Note**: Occupancy cost indicators (€/m² reference area p.a.), costs including VAT, based on 2008 figures

Correspondingly to the general proceeding described in Section 1.4, the first step is the determination of the relevant cost determinants that influence the performance to be benchmarked and which shall be taken into consideration within this benchmarking study. The relevant building reference areas that are identified for the definition of unbiased cost indicators are outlined in Tab. 95. In addition, those characteristics are stated for which the statistical investigation revealed significant variation in cost indicators. As opposed to the point estimation outlined above, the current benchmarking employs the empirical distributions of cost indicators which pertain to the parameters depicted in Tab. 95. In this way, an appropriate reference source for the current benchmarking process is compiled that contains the individual distributions of cost indicators in conjunction with specified determinants for the respective factor levels considered. Finally, as with the preparation of the benchmarking values, the performance indicators (€/m² reference area p.a.) are uniformly compiled for the actual school building at second structural cost level according to DIN 18960:2008-2 (see Tab. 96).

On the basis of the two data surveys compiled for the concrete school building under review and the supplementary information available in the form of the object documentation (Object No. 4100-090 in BKI NK1), the subsequent evaluation of observed performance indicators is carried out step-by-step and described in the following with regard to Tab. 95 and Tab. 96 shown above. The underlying school building without swimming pool is characterized by a stated poor condition of the heat supply systems which applies to the heat distribution networks in particular. Taking a given distribution of utility cost indicators determined between 7.80 €/m² H-GROFA p.a. up to 15.30 €/m² GROFA p.a. as a basis, the observed cost indicator stated at 13 €/m² H-GROFA p.a. can be evaluated as being adequate within a first step. Furthermore, the average cost indicator of the depicted factor level, given as 11.06 €/m² H-GROFA p.a., is identified as the appropriate benchmarking indicator and is therefore regarded as basis for evaluating the observed cost indicator for utility supply (cost group 310 according to DIN 18960:2008-2).

By comparing the deviations which occur between the two benchmarking procedures, the revised benchmark that is specified on the basis of two considered factor levels causes a reduction in the initial deviation of 29% to 18%. This indicates only a slight overstepping of the observed cost value to the extent of around 2 €/m² H-GROFA p.a. With regard to the mean benchmarking indicator of the underlying factor group described in Tab. 96, it can be stated that the hillside building, surrounded by dense trees and with windows that were modernized to a great extent in 1990 (i.e. 75% of modernized glass areas of external walls) does not indicate any significant deviation in the utility supply. The evaluation therefore does not reveal any urgent need for action. A possible potential for optimization can, however, already be identified with regard to the current condition of the heat supply systems. It is therefore conceivable that in a long term this technical installation is maintained or replaced in order to improve the heating energy performance and thus the outlay for utility supply that frequently represents a share of 70% of the heating costs in the case of the school building type. The dimension of a possible saving potential for this repair measure can be traced with regard to Tab. 28. The empirical sample data indicates a mean reference value of around 10 €/m² H-GROFA p.a. and a minimum benchmarking indicator of 6 €/m² H-GROFA p.a. for those schools without indoor swimming pools and the heat supply systems found to be in a good state of repair. With regard to the empirical distribution outlined in Tab. 95, it can be stated that a need for more differentiated analyses of individual utility expenditures (i.e. the outlay for water, heating and electricity supplies) is particularly required, should the maximum value of 15.30 €/m² GROFA p.a. be exceeded in the future by otherwise constant basic conditions in building operation.

Carrying on with the evaluation of the observed cost indicators for waste disposal and the cleaning and care of the building, the mean cost indicators of 0.80 €/m² UFA p.a. and 8.99 €/m² NEFA p.a. respectively are selected as reference values of the corresponding factor groups against which the measured performances of the respective grammar school is assessed. Quantified deviations in Tab. 96 indicate that the actual property can withstand both of the indicator comparisons. The observed cost value for waste disposal lies between the minimum and mean benchmarking indicator and therefore verifies a good performance. This cost group, however, contributes only a relatively small proportion of the overall operating costs, i.e. around 1% in this instance, which reduces the significance of this evaluation for any benchmarking of aggregate expenditure.

In contrast to this, deviations that occur in the outlay for the cleaning and care of school buildings are in general more important as this cost group frequently contributes a share of around 33% of the overall operating costs (cf. Tab. 103). In the actual benchmarking approach, the grammar school under review reveals a cost indicator that slightly exceeds the average reference value by 11% within the stated distribution limits. Based on this appraisal, a more detailed analysis is not considered to be necessary. Different options are however conceivable to proceed with in order to specify the benchmark even more precisely and to conduct the evaluation more comprehensively. As a starting point, further cost influential factors determined by this study could be taken into account. The statistical analysis described in Section 3.3.2 revealed a positive influence of both the proportionate sanitary and ground floor area of a school which justifies the selection of a benchmarking cost value above the chosen mean cost indicator when the actual school has an above-average share of one or both of these building areas. Because a more differentiated data survey for the actual grammar school under review is not regarded to be necessary at this point, both of the assumptions can be examined for a rough approximation according to the floor plans shown in Fig. 24. Here, the hillside building with gymnasium can be seen to have a relatively large proportionate area of both wet rooms and entrance cleaning areas that extend over two entry levels. The assumption of a higher service-level and annual outlay for the cleaning and care of the respective school operated by the municipality Stuttgart can therefore already be substantiated by a visual inspection of the floor plans.

Besides a classification of the underlying SLAs, the cost postings documented in BKI NK1 for the calendar year under review also cause a founded exceeding of the empirical mean benchmarking indicator. Several special cleanings and renewals of protective coatings carried out for the floors of both the school and the gymnasium also justify the previously revealed deviation of the cost indicator for the cleaning and care of the building examined. Moreover, the observed outlay includes a charge for regular caretaker services connected with the cleaning and care of buildings which also explains the measured difference of the underlying reference cost indicator of 9 €/m² NEFA p.a. As stated above, such a detailed analysis of further cost determinants and individual cost postings is not necessarily required when a quantified deviation of only 1 €/m² NEFA p.a. is revealed by an analysis carried out at second structural cost level for the cost group 330 according to DIN 18960:2008-2. The remarks exemplify how more differentiated analyses can be performed in order to gain a better notion about the implemented cleaning services, quality standards and their associated cost, however.

The statistical analysis of the cleaning and care of the grounds and outdoor school facilities (cost group 340), revealed a significant influence of the proportionate outdoor cleaning area per m² non-built up plot area. This determinant is accordingly taken as a basis for the comparative investigation of cost figures. With a share of the outdoor cleaning area per m² non-built up plot area at 0.59, the reference value for the actual school is determined within the distribution of cost indicators of those schools which have a proportionate outdoor cleaning area per m² non-built up plot area that is found to be between 0.5 and 1.0. The result is that the observed cost indicator of 1.02 €/m² non-built up plot area p.a. slightly exceeds the empirical mean cost value of the corresponding factor group by 18%. This can be evaluated as being good for this cost group and does not indicate a need for further benchmarking considerations.

The observed cost indicator of 8.25 €/m² NEFA p.a. for the operation, inspection and maintenance is subsequently benchmarked against the mean cost indicator of the empirical reference sample, i.e. grammar schools without indoor swimming pools. The comparison reveals that the cost indicator greatly exceeds the empirical value stated as 3.55 €/m² NEFA p.a. An explanation for this deviation incurred between the two cost indicators compared is provided by BKI NK1 which documents that the respective cost group again contains a charge for regular caretaker services (i.e. about 4 €/m² NEFA p.a. for the aggregate operating, inspection and maintenance costs within the calendar year reviewed). This explains the comparatively decreased performance of the actual school building under review and justifies the appearance of a significant cost difference.

In the case of the outlays for security and surveillance services and for statutory charges and contributions, this study could not reveal any significant influences on cost indicators based on the sample data of 122 school complexes and an underlying significance level of 5%. With regard to the building-related descriptions available for the actual school, a reference value is determined for the historic building with gym which lies in both cases above the mean value of each empirical distribution shown in Tab. 96. The average value between the overall mean and maximum cost indicator of each distribution is therefore taken as a basis which indicates an adequate performance standard for each of the observed cost indicators (i.e. 2.30 €/m² GROFA p.a. for security and surveillance services and 1.94 €/m² GROFA p.a. for statutory charges and contributions).

The evaluation of repair cost indicators is based on a condition assessment of structural components according to DIN 276-1:2006-11 and is carried out with regard to the empirical reference values published in this study for different condition categories. The individual distributions of cost indicators for the relevant factor levels of the actual school building are described in Tab. 95. Whereas the overall state of repair can be evaluated as being good for the building constructions, grounds and outdoor facilities as well as for the fittings, furnishings and equipment, the condition of the technical installations is classified as being in a poor state of repair, particularly because of deficiencies documented for the heat supply system, power installations and telecommunication systems.

Taking the mean cost indicator for each cost group as a basis, only a significant upward deviation is disclosed for the cost group 440, i.e. for an observed repair cost indicators for the fittings, furnishings and equipment stated at 2.12 €/m² UFA p.a. This can be accepted in this instance because of the comparatively small proportion of the overall costs that this outlay represents. In contrast, an adequate appraisal of the repair cost indicators for both the building constructions and the technical installations is more substantial because these have values that total to a share of around 35% of the aggregate operating and repair costs for the actual school building. In this instance, the benchmarking standard of the revised approach which is achieved on the basis of evaluated building reference areas and condition categories can be assessed as being satisfactory.

A comparison of the actual benchmarking results for both of the cost groups 410 and 420 with the initial analysis outlined in Tab. 94, shows a relativization of the initially assumed deviations and, in particular, a change in the direction of incurred deviations for both, i.e. deviations of -49% vs. +6% for the cost group 410 and +63% vs. -29% for the cost group 420. An examination of the underlying cost postings for the actual school building and calendar year leads to the conclusion that the accuracy level achieved by this more detailed benchmarking approach is more appropriate and provides a valid basis for the subsequent evaluation of the aggregate outlay.

The indicator required for benchmarking the aggregate costs is calculated on the basis of the underlying cost groups that are considered on lower structural cost level. Whereas this overall cost value was previously ascertained directly by summation of the individual cost indicators (€/m² GROFA p.a.), an intermediate calculation is required to determine the proportionate outlay per m² GROFA for each cost group considered. The respective working stages are outlined in Tab. 96. The subsequent comparison of the two aggregate cost indicators finally reveals a plausible benchmarking result on the basis of the different factor levels considered. The observed value of 53.86 €/m² GROFA p.a. slightly exceeds the reference benchmark by 2% which confirms a good performance for the actual grammar school reviewed and therefore does not indicate any major requirement for an intervention, i.e. a control measure. As outlined above, this deviation can be in particular explained in the case of the actual grammar school with regard to an overstepping of the specified reference values of the operation, inspection and maintenance as well as with regard to quantified deviations incurred in the outlay for utility supply, the cleaning and care of the school building and for the repair of the building constructions. A key characteristic of the benchmarking study carried out is that it primarily relates to those characteristics, i.e. factor levels, which correspond very well with the actual performance of the underlying school building. In addition, it was also pointed out that the definition of further benchmarks can be carried out with regard to the cost indicator distributions and influential factors determined in this study. With regard to the client's objective, the benchmarking cost indicator can also be determined as the best competitive value of a given distribution with respect to either a current or an aspired factor level, such as an assumed good condition of the heat supply system, as example. In the latter case, moreover the investment measures and associated costs that are required to achieve the desired status should also be taken into account in the evaluation procedure by means of DIN 276-1:2006-11 for example.

Summarizing, the multi-stage evaluation process carried out for an actual school building exemplifies the benchmarking approach by means of different basic information and thus assessment standards. By comparing the two techniques applied, the more detailed evaluation procedure, which utilizes cost determinants that are evaluated over the course of this study, adjusts the initial set reference value, 48 €/m² GROFA p.a., up to a reference benchmark of almost 53 €/m² GROFA p.a. by means of an 8% upward correction. The direction of the first appraisal is hereby particularly revised with regard to five cost groups that are reviewed on second structural cost level of DIN 18960:2008-2, i.e. cost groups 330 and 350 to 420. The two-stage approach performed on the underlying cost data indicates plausible cost indicators for both the individual and aggregate outlay for operating and repair. There is therefore no need to perform a more extensive cost examination of the contracts for operating services or the scope of repair measures, for instance. Taking advantage of the property and usage-related characteristics determined in this study in the form of just five building reference areas and eight cost influential factors in total, the plausibility test that utilizes this information results in an adequate cost assessment for the actual school across all of the cost types reviewed. The results of the statistical analysis, i.e. the empirical distributions of cost indicators for determined building reference areas and significant factors, therefore provide a valid basis for the evaluation of the financially performance of the actual school building. Quantified deviations between the observed and reference values could be satisfactorily explained with respect to the utilization type of the respective school, technical characteristics such as the condition of structural components, and supplementary information available by means of object documentation.

If the client is furthermore interested in a more detailed cost review, the examination should be extended to the third structural cost level according to DIN 18960:2008-2 and, moreover, should include additional levels of cost classification. The basis for such a detailed inspection of individual cost types for utilities (cost group 310, comprising water, heating and electricity supply) as well as for individual inspection and maintenance measures (cost group 350) is comprehensible in the context of this study and described by evaluated cost drivers in Sections 3.1 and 3.5. For the latter cost group 350, the positive cost influential effect of a school's technical floor area (measured in proportion to the overall net floor area) or of the proportionate gymnasium area per m² UFA, for example, could be taken into account for determining an adequate inspection and maintenance benchmark for the respective technical installations and building constructions. As significant distinguishing features that allow for a more detailed benchmarking analysis of individual utilities (cost group 310), the size of an indoor swimming pool (measured by the water volume of complete pool refillings p.a.), or a categorical distinction between vocational schools and other school types, can be additionally regarded, for instance. Such an investigation, however, would also require the compilation of additional cost and property-related information, which, on the basis of the present benchmarking result, is not regarded as being necessary because of the deviation of only 2% found between the observed and benchmarking cost indicator for aggregate costs.

In order to constantly monitor the incurred outlay for utility supply, operating services and repair measures, the process described above should be regularly carried out during the following years with regard to both the comparative values of other reference samples and the observed indicators of previous years. Based on this examination, it is possible to specify the dimension and direction of deviations which occur and to intervene in the applied operating and maintenance strategies at an early stage.

For the client, the assessment that is carried out represents an excellent evaluation basis and starting point for subsequent benchmarking approaches of both the actual building as well as other schools with different characteristics and utilization patterns. On the one hand, the compilation of observed cost indicators for evaluated factor levels constitutes a meaning-ful reference source for future benchmarking studies of the actual building. On the other hand, the indicators assessed for the actual building and year can be used for other control processes, such as for an internal evaluation of occupancy costs for example, both in the present form of a single observation, or in the long term for establishing descriptive statistics on the client's own portfolio. It is furthermore conceivable that cost indicators ascertained at different structural cost levels according to DIN 18960:2008-2 can be used for the purpose of occupancy cost predictions, i.e. first projection up to final estimate (see Section 1.4).

In the case that the client or cost planner, i.e. architect, facilities or property manager, wants to gradually establish his or her own benchmarking data base, it is generally advisable to compile the cost data for the first year of operation separately. As outlined in Section 7.1, this results particularly from customizing facilities services and adapting technical installations such as heating control and building automation systems, for example, for specific operating requirements which might generate a comparatively higher outlay for the first accounting period, in terms of the costs for utility supply or the cleaning and care of buildings, for instance. This could therefore lead to distortion between the outlay incurred within the first year of operation and that incurred in following years.

In this section, the iterative benchmarking process for the definition and evaluation of operating and repair cost indicators is exemplified by means of an operated building which can be in general applied to other school or building types. In the case, the approach is applied for other schools properties, an appropriate benchmarking standard can be determined from the empirical cost data published in this study, such as from the descriptive measures for central tendency and dispersion of aggregate or individual operating and repair cost indicators as described in Sections 3 to 4. The reference data required for any benchmarking of other building types, i.e. cost indicators for evaluated cost determinants and reference quantities, are to be processed and uniformly compiled for the respective level of inspection.

## 8      Conclusion

This empirical investigation is directed against the uncertainties in the prediction and evaluation of operating and repair costs that exist in current real estate management practice and make an economically sustainable provision of real estate as demanded by federal and state governments difficult. In collaboration with the state capital Stuttgart (Germany), the study strives towards the common objective, to reach a greater reliability in cost estimation and thus a higher degree of transparency in cost planning and bench-marking. For this purpose, the calculation bases required for a better assessment of occu-pancy costs are evaluated in order to enhance grading of the cost variation in practice. In addition, the practical application fields of the research findings are demonstrated in detail by means of various examples for early planning stages and benchmarking purposes.

The investigation is carried out for schools, as these often represent a major part of the public building stock and therefore offer a considerable saving potential for property-related expenditure. The annual outlay for operating and repair measures is examined for this type of utilization with regard to both the individual and aggregate costs as defined by DIN 18960:2008-2. Their cost influential factors are empirically determined and quantified by means of sample data obtained from 130 school complexes.

An extensive discussion at the beginning of the study on the appropriate observation unit resulted in the definition of the school property level. This level of observation corresponds with real-built structures of school complexes that include main facilities with outbuildings, adjacent sports facilities and canteens, for example, and therefore allows the corresponding consumption and cost data, as well as further descriptions of the school properties, to be uniformly ascertained for the objective of the data analysis. School visits and on-site interviews enabled data of around 300 school buildings and 140 sports facilities to be consistently compiled. The statistical evaluation of consumption and cost data for the operation and repair of schools is carried out by means of multivariate analyses, in particular regression and variance analysis. On this basis, specific building reference areas are determined for the definition and evaluation of individual consumption and cost indicators, as well as for benchmarking purposes in general. An extensive literature review and dis-cussions with experts, including specialists of the technical, infrastructural and commercial building management, made it furhtermore possible to specifiy and subsequently validate prediction models for individual cost groups and, based on this, provide consumption and cost indicators for the planning practice with respect to decisive parameters.

The investigation reveals fundamental differences between the outlay for the operating and repair costs of the public schools concerned, and proceeds to describe the consequences that arise for valid cost estimates and comparisons. Whereas stable and consistent cost predictions can be formulated for the operating costs of various types of school usage and characteristics without exception, it is not possible to generalize this finding for the repair costs of the schools examined. The properties consistently maintained by a corrective maintenance strategy rather require a differentiated evaluation of their repair costs with regard to different condition categories (cf. Section 6). The study therefore determines the relevant condition categories for the outlay of individual repair measures according to

DIN 18960:2008-2 and additionally describes a required differentiation of basic condition categories for aggregate repair costs, especially with regard to both the condition of the building constructions and technical installations. Based on this, the study draws up cost predictions for budgeting the repair and maintenance costs respectively that are easy to apply in planning practice and allow more accurate forecasts to be made compared with those estimates that refer to age categories.

The approach allows a comprehensive evaluation of various consumption and cost quantities under consideration of numerous basic conditions of the schools examined, in particular, property and usage-related characteristics (see Section 7). The study therefore is to be regarded as part of present efforts towards the provision of specific cost indicators and the definition of benchmarking standards. An empirical investigation always has limitations, however. It is on the one hand important to clarify those for the current study to ensure an appropriate application of the models and presented cost indicator. On the other hand, the limitations associated with this survey constitute challenges for further research work. The restrictions of this examination can be in particular described with regard to the underlying data sample, or rather, and in general, with respect to the diversity of data and the extent to which the empirical sample results are representative.

This investigation comprises public schools of a single proprietor located in the south of Germany. The underlying sample therefore allows in particular a detailed comparison and evaluation of certain characteristics of the school facilities and their utilizations. Influences of other parameters which are regarded to be constant in this survey could not been evaluated, however. With regard to the relatively restricted location of the properties, this comprises in particular characteristics of the provision and operation of the schools examined that are found to be equal in the underlying data sample. The practical application of the statistical models and transferability of the consumption and cost indicators presented here are reduced under different basic conditions, such as different maintenance strategies, operating concepts and outsourcing rates of services, for example. The individual models and cost indicator distributions are discussed in Sections 3 to 5 and the empirical data base of the investigation is additionally shown in Appendix C in order to support a conscientious application of the research findings in planning practice. Cost planners can therefore validate the basic parameters of the empirical sample examined to the frame conditions of other portfolios and thus formulate well founded estimates and benchmarks. When there are systematic deviations in either the outlay for individual costs or the respective school characteristics identified, the predictions then need to be renewed with fundamental changes in model assumptions. Furthermore, the occupancy cost indicators presented in this study serve as an appropriate basis for initial rough cost predictions, i.e. first cost projections up to approximate estimates that are carried out at least to the second structural cost level according to DIN 18960:2008-2 (cf. Section 1.4). In contrast, the present study does not provide more detailed cost values and descriptions which are required for final occupancy cost estimates, for example.

As indicated above, other interesting fields of research are opened up by the limitations stated for this approach. Further qualitative and quantitative analyses are conceivable in the context of occupancy cost planning and benchmarking and a few possibilities are briefly outlined in the following. The empirical data base can be extended with regard to the utilization type examined in order to validate and supplement the findings described in this study to other schools in Germany, or even on an international level. The validation tests carried out are already a first step for such considerations which could furthermore be extended in future to validate the quality of the prediction models described, for example. In addition, it could also be of interest to simultaneously take different method comparisons into account. Further to these, an extension of the scope of cost data and its level of detail is also conceivable, by supplementing the outlay for building-independent services, for instance, or giving consideration to even more detailed types of operating and repair cost as defined on the third structural cost level according to DIN 18960:2008-2, for example.

An inter-municipal extension of the survey could similarly be of interest, with a comparison of various building management services or maintenance strategies, as defined by DIN EN 13306:2010-12 for example, which then should also include a comparison of the respective management costs, i.e. cost group 200 according to DIN 18960:2008-2. Time series analysis of cumulated repair costs, or general maintenance costs, with an important proportionate outlay of the overall occupancy costs opens another interesting field of research. First considerations have already been made on this in the context of Section 4. In the opinion of the author, life-cycle costing (LCC) which also employs the application of reliable occupancy cost indicators that are transferable to other basic conditions will cover a wide area of growing interest. This empirical investigation on the planning and bench-marking of both the operating and repair costs already provides a solid basis for LCC of the building type schools.

## Bibliography

Ages, 2005. Verbrauchskennwerte 2005: Energie- und Wasserverbrauchskennwerte in der Bundesrepublik. Münster: Ages.

APQC, 2010. Benchmarking Code of Conduct. American Productivity & Quality Center (APQC), [internet]. Available at: http://www.apqc.org/benchmarking-methodology [Accessed 14 December 2010].

Argebau, 2010. Bauwerkszuordnungskatalog (BWZ-Katalog). Bauministerkonferenz der für Städtebau, Bau-und Wohnungswesen zuständigen Minister und Senatoren der Länder. Fachkommission Bau- und Kostenplanung.

Ashworth, A., 1996. Estimating the life expectancies of building components in life-cycle costing calculations. Structural Survey, 14(2), pp.4-8. MCB University Press.

Backhaus, K. Erichson, B. Plinke, W. & Weiber, R., 2008. Multivariate Analysemethoden: Eine anwendungsorientierte Einführung. Berlin: Springer.

Balck, H., 2022. Facilities Management und Projektentwicklung im Lebenszyklus der Immobilie. In: K-W. Schulte & S. Bone-Winkel, eds. 2002. Handbuch Immobilien Projektentwicklung. Köln: Rudolf Müller, pp.343-379.

Bahr, C., 2008. Realdatenanalyse zum Instandhaltungsaufwand öffentlicher Hochbauten: Ein Beitrag zur Budgetierung. Universität Karlsruhe. Karlsruhe: Universitätsverlag.

Balaras, C.A. Gaglia, A.G. Georgopoulou, E. Mirasgedis, S. Sarafidis, Y. & Lalas, D.P., 2007. European residential buildings and empirical assessment of the Hellenic building stock, energy consumption, emissions and potential energy savings. Building and Environment, 42, pp.1298-1314.

Barrett, P.S. & Baldry, D., 2003. Facilities Management: Towards Best Practice, 2$^{nd}$ ed. Oxford: Blackwell Science.

Becker, R. Goldberger, I. & Paciuk, M., 2007. Improving energy performance of school buildings while ensuring indoor air quality ventilation. Building and Environment, 41, pp.3261-3276.

BCIS Building Cost Information Service, 2009. Occupancy Cost of Primary Schools. London: RICS Business Services.

BCIS Building Cost Information Service, 1991. Standard Form of Property Occupancy Cost Analysis: Principles, Instructions and Definitions. London: RICS Business Services.

Benninghaus, H., 2007. Deskriptive Statistik: Eine Einführung für Sozialwissenschaftler. Wiesbaden: Springer VS.

BHO, 2010-12. Bundeshaushaltsordnung (BHO). Bundesministerium.

Bleymüller, J. Gehlert, G. & Gülicher, H., 2008. Statistik für Wirtschaftswissenschaftler. München: Vahlen.

BMI Building Maintenance Information, 2000. Occupancy Costs of Offices. BMI Special Report Serial 294. London: RICS Business Services.

BMI Building Maintenance Information, 2003. Review of Occupancy Costs 2003. BMI Special Report Serial 322. London: RICS Business Services.

BMVBS Bundesministerium für Verkehr, Bau und Stadtentwicklung, 2011. Leitfaden Nachhaltiges Bauen. Berlin: BMVBS.

Camp, R.C., 1992 Learning from the Best Leads to Superior Performance. Journal of Business Strategy, 13(3), pp.3-6.

CEEC Code of Measurement for Cost Planning 2008-1. European Committee of Construction Economists (CEEC).

Cheng, C.L. & Hong, Y.T., 2004. Evaluating water utilization in primary schools. Building and Environment, 39, pp.837-845.

Cock, R. & French, N., 2001. Internal Rents and Corporate Property Management: A study into the use of internal rents in UK corporate organizations. Reading: University of Reading.

Corgnati, S.P. Corrado, V. & Filippi, M., 2008. A method for heating consumption assessment in existing buildings: A field survey concerning 120 Italian schools. Energy and Buildings, 40, pp.801-809.

DAC-BW Department of Asset and Construction of Baden-Württemberg, 2005. Betriebskosten und Verbräuche: Kennwerte von Hochbauten. Stuttgart: Finanzministerium Baden-Württemberg, Vermögen und Bau Baden-Württemberg.

DAC-BW Department of Asset and Construction of Baden-Württemberg, 2006. Leistungsdaten und Energiebedarf: Kennwerte Gebäudetechnischer Anlagen. Stuttgart: Finanzministerium Baden-Württemberg, Vermögen und Bau Baden-Württemberg.

Depecker, P. Menezo, C. Virgone, J. & Lepers, S., 2001. Design of buildings shape and energetic consumption. Building and Environment, 36, pp.627-635.

Destatis, Statistisches Bundesamt, 2011a. Finanzen und Steuern: Schulden der öffentlichen Haushalte. Wiesbaden: Statistisches Bundesamt.

Destatis, Statistisches Bundesamt, 2011b. Indizes Deutschland, [internet]. Available at: https://www-genesis.destatis.de/genesis/online/data;jsessionid=6553A50A732B26B1783 43798F7FD2288.tomcat_GO_1_1?operation=abruftabelleAbrufen&selectionname=6111 1-0006&levelindex=1&leveled=1336288822780&index=6 [Assessed 15 December 2011].

DETR, 1997. Cost-effective low energy buildings in further and higher education. Good Practice Guide 207. Department of the Environment, Transport and the Regions.

DETR, 1998. Saving Energy in Schools. Energy Consumption Guide 73. Department of the Environment, Transport and the Regions.

DGNB, 2008: Gebäudebezogene Kosten im Lebenszyklus: Kriteriensteckbrief Büro- und Verwaltungsgebäude. Stuttgart: Deutsche Gesellschaft für Nachhaltiges Bauen.

DIN 18205:1996-4. Bedarfsplanung im Bauwesen. Deutsches Institut für Normung (DIN). Berlin: Beuth Verlag.

DIN 18960:1999-8. Running costs of buildings. English version. Deutsches Institut für Normung (DIN). Berlin: Beuth Verlag.

DIN 18960:2008-2. Nutzungskosten im Hochbau. Deutsches Institut für Normung (DIN). Berlin: Beuth Verlag.

DIN 276-1:2006-11. Building costs - Part 1: Building construction. English version. Deutsches Institut für Normung (DIN). Berlin: Beuth Verlag.

DIN 276-1:2008-12. Kosten im Bauwesen - Teil 1: Hochbau. Deutsches Institut für Normung (DIN). Berlin: Beuth Verlag.

DIN 277-1:2005-2. Grundflächen und Rauminhalte von Bauwerken im Hochbau - Teil 1: Begriffe, Ermittlungsgrundlagen. Deutsches Institut für Normung (DIN). Berlin: Beuth Verlag.

DIN 277-2:2005-2. Grundflächen und Rauminhalte von Bauwerken im Hochbau -Teil 2: Gliederung der Netto-Grundfläche (Nutzflächen, Technische Funktionsflächen und Verkehrsflächen). Deutsches Institut für Normung (DIN). Berlin: Beuth Verlag.

DIN 277-3:2005-4. Grundflächen und Rauminhalte von Bauwerken im Hochbau - Teil 3: Mengen und Bezugseinheiten. Deutsches Institut für Normung (DIN). Berlin: Beuth Verlag.

DIN 31051:2003-6. Grundlagen der Instandhaltung. Deutsches Institut für Normung (DIN). Berlin: Beuth Verlag.

DIN 32736:2000-8. Gebäudemanagement: Begriffe und Leistungen. Deutsches Institut für Normung (DIN). Berlin: Beuth Verlag.

DIN EN 1176-1:2008-8. Spielplatzgeräte und Spielplatzböden - Teil 1: Allgemeine sicherheitstechnische Anforderungen und Prüfverfahren. German version. Deutsches Institut für Normung (DIN). Berlin: Beuth Verlag.

DIN EN 13306:2010-12. Maintenance - Maintenance terminology. Trilingual version. Deutsches Institut für Normung (DIN). Berlin: Beuth Verlag.

El-Haram, M.A. & Horner, M.W., 2002. Factors affecting housing maintenance costs. Journal of Quality in Maintenance Engineering, 8(2), pp.115-123.

EN 15341:2005-9 Draft. Maintenance - Maintenance Key Performance Indicators. English Version. European Committee for Standardization (CEN).

EN ISO 9004:2000-12. Qualitätsmanagementsysteme: Leitfaden zur Leistungsverbesserung. Trilingual version. Deutsches Institut für Normung (DIN). Berlin: Beuth Verlag.

Ernst & Young, 2010. Kommunen in der Finanzkrise: Status Quo und Handlungsoptionen. Ergebnisse einer Befragung von 300 deutschen Kommunen. Stuttgart: Ernst & Young.

Facilities Society, 2011. Strategies for facilities management, [internet]. Available at: http://www.facilities.ac.uk/j/cpd/62-facility-management/118-strategies-for-facility-management [Assessed 14 December 2011].

Filippin, C., 2000. Benchmarking the energy efficiency and greenhouse gases emissions of school buildings in central Argentina. Building and Environment, 35, pp.407-414.

Firth, S. Lomar, K. Wright, A. & Wall, R. 2008. Identifying trends in the use of domestic appliances from household electricity consumption measurements. Energy and Buildings, 40, pp.926-936.

Flores-Colen, I. & Brito, J., 2010. A systematic approach for maintenance budgeting of buildings facades based on predictive and preventive strategies. Construction and Building Materials, 24, pp.1718-1729.

GEFMA 200:2004-7 Draft. Kosten im Facility Management. German Facility Management Association (GEFMA).

GEFMA 300:1996-6 Draft. Benchmarking im Facility Management. German Facility Management Association (GEFMA).

GemHVO, 2009-11. Verordnung des Innenministeriums über die Hauswirtschaft der Gemeinden. Baden-Württemberg: Gemeindehaushaltsverordnung (GemHVO).

Gibson, V., 1994. Strategic Property Management: How Can Local Authorities Develop a Property Strategy? Property Management, 12(3), pp.9-14.

GSD Graduate School of Design, 2003. Public Housing Operating Cost Study: Final Report. Cambridge: Harvard University.

Hasan, A. Vuolle, M. & Sirén K., 2008. Minimisation of life cycle cost of a detached house using combined simulation and optimization. Building and Environment, 43, pp.2022-2034.

Hernandez, P. Burke, K. & Lewis, J.O. 2008. Development of energy performance benchmarks and building energy ratings for non-domestic buildings: An example for Irish primary schools. Energy and Buildings, 40, pp.249-254.

Hinkle, D.E. Wiersma, W. & Jurs, S.G., 1998. Applied Statistics For The Behavioral Sciences. Boston: Houghton Mifflin Company.

HOAI, 2009-4. Honorarordnung für Architekten und Ingenieure.

IFB Institut für Bauforschung, 2006. Bau-Nutzungskosten: Bau-Nutzungskosten-Kennwerte für Wohngebäude. Stuttgart: Frauenhofer IRB Verlag.

IFMA-Switzerland, 2006. ProLeMo, Prozess-/ LeistungsModel im Facility Management. International Facility Management Association Switzerland.

IFMA-Switzerland, 2011. Lebenszykluskosten- Ermittlung von Immobilien. Schweizerische Zentralstelle für Baurationalisierung CRB, International Facility Management Association Switzerland. Zürich: vdf Verlag.

IP Bau, 1995. Grobdiagnose: Zustandserfassung und Kostenschätzung von Gebäuden. 2nd ed. Bern: Bundesamt für Konjunkturfragen.

ISO 15686-5: 2008 Final draft. Buildings and constructed assets - Service-life planning - Part 5: Life-cycle costing. Geneva: International Organization for Standardization.

JLL Jones Lang LaSalle, 2011. OSCAR, Büronebenkostenanalyse 2011. Jones Lang LaSalle.

Kalusche, W., 2002. Projekt-Management in der Bauplanung und Bauausführung. In: K-W. Schulte & S. Bone-Winkel, eds. 2002. Handbuch Immobilien-Projektentwicklung. Köln: Rudolf Müller.

Kalusche, W., 2004. Technische Lebensdauer von Bauteilen und wirtschaftliche Nutzungsdauer eines Gebäudes. Cottbus: Brandenburgische Technische Universität Cottbus (btu).

Kalusche, W., 2008. Lebenszykluskosten von Gebäuden - Grundlage ist die neue DIN 18960:2008-2, Nutzungskosten im Hochbau.  Bauingenieur, 11/2008, pp.495-501. Düsseldorf: Springer VDI, 287-342.

KGSt, 2009. Gebäude kennzahlengestützt steuern. Köln: KGSt.

KMK, 2011. The Education System in the Federal Republic of Germany 2010/2011: A description of the responsibiliites, structures and developments in education policy for the exchange of information in Europe. Bonn: Sekretariat der Ständigen Konferenz der Kultusminister der Länder in der Bundesrepublik Deutschland.

Kouzmin, A. Löffler, E. Klages, H. & Korac-Kakabadse, N. 1999.  Benchmarking and performance measurement in public sectors: Towards learing for agency effectiveness. International Journal of Public Sector Management, 12(2), pp.121-144.

Krengel, U., 2005. Einführung in die Wahrscheinlichkeitstheorie und Statistik. Wiesbaden: Springer Vieweg.

LH Landeshauptstadt Stuttgart, 2007. Neustrukturierung der Innenverwaltung des Schulverwaltungsamts. Stuttgart.

LH Landeshauptstadt Stuttgart, 2009. Schulbericht, Schulverwaltungsamt. Stuttgart: Referat für Kultur, Bildung und Sport.

Loosemore, M. & Hsin, Y.Y., 2001. Customer-focused benchmarking for facilities management. Facilities, 19(13), pp.464-476.

Lucertini, M. Nicolo, F. & Telmon, D., 1995. Integration of Benchmarking and Benchmarking of Integration. International Journal of Production Economics, 38, pp.59-71.

McDougall, G. & Hinks, J. 2000. Identifying priority issues in facilities management benchmarking. Facilities, 18(10), pp. 427-434.

Naber, S., 2002. Planung unter Berücksichtigung der Baunutzungskosten als Aufgabe des Architekten im Feld des Facility Management. Brandenburgische Technische Universität Cottbus (btu). Frankfurt am Main: Lang.

Neil, N.O. & Brümmer, D.G., 2007. Factors influencing water consumption in South African schools. Journal of Engineering, Design and Technology, 5(1), pp.81-94.

NEN 2632:1980-9: Exploitatiekosten van gebouwen, Begripsomschrijvingen en indeling. Rijswijk: Nederlandse Normalisatie Instituut (NEN).

NS 3454:1998. Life cycle costs for building and civil engineering work: Principles and classifications. English version.

OECD, 2002. Use of Benchmark Data to Align or Derive Quarterly/Monthly Estimates, [Paper] 24-25 June. OECD Short-term Economic Statistics Expert Group. Paris: Organisation for Economic Co-operation and Development (OECD)

ÖNOMRM B1801-2:1997-6: Kosten im Hoch- und Tiefbau: Objektdaten - Objektnutzung. Wien: Österreichisches Normungsinstitut (ON).

ÖNOMRM B1801-2:2011-1 Draft. Bauprojekt- und Objektmanagement: Teil 2: Objekt-Folgekosten. Wien: Österreichisches Normungsinstitut (ON).

Pathirage, C. Haigh, R. Amaratunga, D. & Baldry, D., 2008. Knowledge management practices in facilities organisations: a case study, Journal of Facilities Management, 6(1), pp.5-22.

Pom+Consulting, 2008. Der Schweizer Facility Management-Markt unter der Lupe. Zürich: Pom+Consulting.

Pratt, K.T., 2003. Introducing a service level culture. Facilities, 21(11/12), pp.253-359.

REFA, 2004. Handbuch Objektbezogene Leistungskennzahlen für den Reinigungsdienst in Schulen. Meschede: REFA Fachausschuss Gebäudereinigung.

Riegel, G.W., 2004. Ein softwaregestütztes Berechnungsverfahren zur Prognose und Be-urteilung der Nutzungskosten von Bürogebäuden. Technische Universität Darmstadt.

Shetty, Y.K., 1993. Aiming High: Competitive Benchmarking for Superior Performance. Long Range Planning, 26(1),pp.39-44.

SIA 112/1:2004 Recommodation. Nachhaltiges Bauen - Hochbau. Zürich: Schweizerischer Ingenieur- und Architektenverein (SIA).

SIA 380/1:2009. Thermische Energie im Hochbau. Zürich: Schweizerischer Ingenieur- und Architektenverein (SIA).

SIA 380/4:1995. Recomodation. Elektrische Energie im Hochbau. Zürich: Schweizerischer Ingenieur- und Architektenverein (SIA).

SIA 416/1:2007. Kennzahlen für die Gebäudetechnik: Bauteilabmessungen, Bezugsgrössen und Kennzahlen für Bauphysik, Energie- und Gebäudetechnik. Zürich: Schweizerischer Ingenieur- und Architektenverein (SIA).

Stadt Zürich, 2006. Lukretia, Schlussbericht. Zürich: Stadt Zürich.

Statistische Ämter des Bundes und der Länder, 2011. Volkswirtschaftliche Gesamtrechnungen der Länder: Arbeitnehmerentgelt, Bruttolöhne und -gehälter in den Ländern und Ost-West-Großraumregionen Deutschlands 1991 bis 2010. Frankfurt am Main: Statistik und Wahlen.

Stoy, C., 2005. Benchmarks und Einflussfaktoren der Baunutzungskosten. ETH Zürich. Zürich: vdf Hochschulverlag.

Stoy, C. & Beusker, E., 2010. BKI Objektdaten NK1: Nutzungskosten. Stuttgart: Baukosten-informationszentrum (BKI).

Stoy, C. Pollalis, S. & Fiala, D., 2009. Estimating buildings' energy consumption and energy costs in early project phases. Facilities, 27(5/6), pp.187-201.

Then, D.S.S.,1999. An integrated resource management view of facilities management. Facilities, 17(12/13), pp. 462-469.

Urban, D. & Mayerl, J. 2008. Regressionsanalyse: Theorie, Technik und Anwendung. 3$^{rd}$ ed. Wiesbaden: Springer VS.

VDI 3807-1:2007-3. Energie- und Wasserverbrauchskennwerte für Gebäude: Grundlagen. Düsseldorf: Verein Deutscher Ingenieure (VDI).

VDI 3807-2:1998-6. Energieverbrauchskennwerte für Gebäude: Heizenergie- und Stromverbrauchskennwerte. Düsseldorf: Verein Deutscher Ingenieure (VDI).

VDI 3807-3:2000-7. Wasserverbrauchskennwerte für Gebäude und Grundstücke. Düsseldorf: Verein Deutscher Ingenieure (VDI).

Walker, R., 1992. Rank Xeros - Management Revolution. Long Range Planning, 25(1), pp.9-21.

Watson, G.H., 2007. Strategic benchmarking reloaded with Six Sigma: Improve your company's performance using global best practice. Hoboken: John Wiley & Sons.

Williams, B., 1996. Cost-effective facilities management: a practical approach. Facilities, 14(5),pp.26-38.

Zhang, T. Siebers, P-O. & Aickelin, U., 2011. Modeling electricity consumption in office buildings: An agent based approach. Energy and Buildings 43, pp.2882-2892.

## Glossary

*Circulation area (CICA):* The circulation area as defined by DIN 277:2005-2 (Part 1 and 2) is that part of gross floor area that enables access to individual rooms. By definition, this building area is neither part of the usable floor area nor of the technical floor area and comprises areas such as corridors, entrance halls, staircases and lifts.

*Gross floor area (GROFA):* The gross floor area comprises the net floor area and the construction area. According to DIN 277-1:2005-2, this building area corresponds to the sum of all floor areas of a building and their constructional enclosures, excluding unusable building surfaces, such as empty roof spaces or tracks that are solely used for maintenance purposes.

*Heatable gross floor area (H-GROFA):* The heatable gross floor area is calculated as a building's gross floor area minus major non-heatable gross floor areas. According to the German guideline VDI 3807-1:2007-3, this surface constitutes the total of all floor areas that can be heated, whether the corresponding space is used, or not.

*Nett floor area (NEFA):* The net floor area is part of the gross floor area. It breaks down into the usable floor area, technical floor area and the circulation area of a building. According to DIN 277-1:2005-2, this building area includes the respective floor areas of free-standing fittings and furnishings, permanently attached fixtures, lifts or other technical installations.

*Non-built up area of the plot:* The non-built up plot area is defined as a specific part of the property area that includes all open areas with their specifically designated sections, such as hard surfaces of school playground areas and sports areas (sports fields, football pitches, tracks or basketball courts) as well as green areas. According to this definition, those parts of the property area that are overbuilt by buildings are not part of the non-built up area of a plot.

*Outdoor cleaning area:* The external cleaning area consists of the hard surfaces of a school property comprising school playground areas, sports areas, external grounds and roof areas, as well as of public sidewalks adjacent to a school property for which a school has cleaning responsibility in Germany.

*Technical floor area (TEFA):* According to DIN 277-1:2005-2, this building floor area is that specific part of the net floor area which is reserved for technical installations and equipments, such as areas for installed sewage, water and heat supply systems, power installations and technical building automation, for example, which are required to operate a building.

*Usable floor area (UFA):* The usable floor area is part of the net floor area. It includes all floor areas of a building that are designated for specific types of usage as defined by DIN 277-2:2005-2, i.e. living and recreation; office work; production, manual and machine work, experiments; education, teaching and culture; healing and care, as well as rooms being used as wardrobes and storage, showers or restrooms, for instance.

*Usable floor area for living and recreation (UFA 1)*: This building floor area is part of the usable floor area according to DIN 277-2:2005-2 and covers those areas which are dedicated for living space, common and social areas, conference and meeting rooms, waiting rooms, cafeterias and canteens, for instance.

*Usable floor area for office work (UFA 2)*: As defined by DIN 277-2:2005-2, the usable floor area for office work is that part of the usable floor area that provides space for individual offices, open-plan offices, conference and control rooms, for example.

*Usable floor area for education, teaching and culture (UFA 5)*: This building area is part of the usable floor area and incorporates all usable floor areas intended for education, teaching and culture, such as space for school lessons or physical education; seminar, conference and reading rooms; libraries and language labs; assembly rooms; gyms and multipurpose halls, lecture rooms and sacral spaces, for example (cf. DIN 277-2:2005-2).

*Water impermeable surface of the plot:* The water impermeable area of a plot comprises all areas of a plot which are covered by hard surfaces or buildings.

# Appendices

## Appendix A:  Interviewed experts

Tab. 97:   Expert interviews during the development process of the questionnaire

| Company/ Municipality | Position/ Field | Number of interviews |
|---|---|---|
| Municipality Stuttgart | Owner/ Head of Building management department for schools and sport facilities | 1 |
| | Head of Building construction department, Architect | 1 |
| | Facilities Manager (Technical building management) | 5 |
| | Facility Manager (Infrastructural building management) | 2 |
| | Architect, Facilities Manager (Commercial building management) | 1 |
| | Facilities Manager (Floor-space management) | 2 |
| | Architect, ICT manager | 1 |
| Municipality Reutlingen | Architect | 1 |
| | Facilities Manager (Technical building management) | 2 |
| | Facilities Manager (Infrastructural building management) | 2 |
| University of Stuttgart | Head of Building management department for offices and university buildings | 1 |
| | Facilities Manager (Technical building management) | 1 |
| | Facilities Manager (Floor-space management) | 1 |
| BMW Group | Head of Quality and Information management, Floor-space management (REM, FM) | 1 |
| Ages Ltd | Head of Ages, Company for energy planning and system engineering | 1 |
| FairEnergie Ltd | Energy management | 2 |
| KIRU Property management | Information and property management | 2 |

## Appendix B:  Questionnaire (in German)

**Universität Stuttgart** Germany

STUTTGART

**Erhebungsbogen**

Im Rahmen der Erhebung werden Kenngrößen zum Bauwerk und seinen Außenanlagen einheitlich erfasst. Darauf aufbauend werden flächen- und verbrauchsbezogene Kennwerte für verschiedene Merkmalsklassen (z.B. Art der Schule, Nutzungsintensität, Baujahr) für die Nutzungskostenplanung von Immobilien im Hochbau bereitgestellt. Die Erhebung der Bestandsgebäude erfolgt während eines Ortstermins und in Absprache mit dem/der Stammhausmeister/-in. Ich bitte Sie, zuerst das Gebäude beginnend vom Dach an zu begehen und im Anschluss den Fragebogen zu beantworten.

**Inhaltsverzeichnis**

Objekt-ID:
Objektbezeichnung:
Gebäudeart:

Datum der Erhebung:
Bezugsjahr:
Name des Nutzers:
Name des Hausmeisters/ der Hausmeisterin:
Name des/der Bearbeiter/-in:

---

**Erhebungsbogen**

**1. Allgemeine Angaben zum Objekt**

Baujahr des Gebäudes:

Standort:   o Innerstädtisch   o Städtisch   o Ländlich

Bauraum:   o Beengt   o Freier Bauraum   o Baulücke

Gelände:   o Ebenes   o Geneigtes Gelände   o Hanglage

Größe der Sportstätte gemessen an der Anzahl der Hallenfelder:
o Einfachhalle   o Dreifachhalle
o Zweifachhalle   o Nicht vorhanden

Anzahl der Nebenräume (Umkleide-, Sanitärräume):
o Zweifach   o Sechsfach
o Vierfach   o Nicht vorhanden

Ist-Anzahl der Zuschauersitzplätze:

**2. Nutzerinterview**

**Angaben zum Schulbetrieb**

Schulkindbetreuung:
o Regelschule   o Ganztagsschule
o Regelschule mit Übermittagsbetreuung   o Sonstige ...

Art der Verpflegung (bei Übermittagsbetreuung, Ganztagsbetreuung):
o Überwiegend Catering: Anlieferung von Speisen, Essensausgabe in Kantine.
o Überwiegend Küchenbetrieb: Speisezubereitung, Essensausgabe in Kantine.
o Kiosk: keine Küche, keine Kantine.
o Keine Verpflegung (Küche, Kantine, Kiosk) im Gebäude
o Sonstiges ...

- 1 -

## Erhebungsbogen

### Eigen- und Fremdnutzung des Gebäudes

Bitte tragen Sie die durchschnittliche Betriebszeit des Gebäudes während der Schulzeit ein und geben Sie die Anzahl Schüler für die drei aufgeführten Betreuungssequenzen an.

| | Montag | Dienstag | Mittwoch | Donnerstag | Freitag | Samstag | Anzahl Schüler |
|---|---|---|---|---|---|---|---|
| Vormittags: | - Uhr - | - Uhr - | - Uhr - | - Uhr - | - Uhr - | - Uhr - | |
| Mittagszeit: | - Uhr - | - Uhr - | - Uhr - | - Uhr - | - Uhr - | - Uhr - | |
| Nachmittags: | - Uhr - | - Uhr - | - Uhr - | - Uhr - | - Uhr - | - Uhr - | |

### Angaben zur Nutzerzufriedenheit

Äußere Belastungen aus der Umgebung (Lärm, Luft/Klima und Licht):

- ○ Gering / Keine äußeren Belastungen.
- ○ Eher gering / Geringe äußere Belastungen, vereinzelt
- ○ Eher hoch / Geringe äußere Belastungen, beständig.
- ○ Hoch / Hohe äußere Belastungen (z.B. Verkehrslärm).

Anmerkung:

Nutzerzufriedenheit in Bezug auf Luft/Klima im Gebäude:

- ○ Gut / Gebäudeautomation gut eingestellt, Regulationsmöglichkeiten in Außenhaltbereichen vorhanden.
- ○ Eher gut / Gebäudeautomation gut eingestellt, wenige Regulationsmöglichkeiten in Außenhaltsbereichen vorhanden.
- ○ Eher schlecht / Gebäudeautomation unzureichend eingestellt, keine Regulationsmöglichkeiten in Außenhaltsräumen, vereinzelt Zugerscheinungen.
- ○ Schlecht / Gebäudeautomation nicht vorhanden oder unzureichend eingestellt, keine Regulationsmöglichkeiten in Außenhaltsräumen, häufig Zugerscheinungen.

Anmerkung:

### Flächenangebot im Gebäude (Unterrichts-, Gemeinschafts-, Speiseräume, etc.):

- ○ Gut (oberer Standard) / Flächenangebot entspricht den Nutzungsanforderungen.
- ○ Eher gut / Flächenangebot entspricht weitestgehend den Nutzungsanforderungen.
- ○ Eher schlecht / Flächenangebot entspricht weitestgehend nicht den Nutzungsanforderungen.
- ○ Schlecht (unterer Standard) / Flächenangebot zu gering, entspricht nicht den Nutzungsanforderungen.

Anmerkung:

### Standard der Technischen Anlagen:

- ○ Gut (oberer Standard) / Ausbaustandard der Technischen Anlagen entspricht den Nutzungsanforderungen.
- ○ Eher hoch / Ausbaustandard der Technischen Anlagen entspricht weitestgehend den Nutzungsanforderungen.
- ○ Eher niedrig / Technischen Anlagen teils veraltet, Ausbaustandard entspricht weitestgehend nicht den Nutzungsanforderungen.
- ○ Niedrig (unterer Standard) / Technischen Anlagen veraltet, Ausbaustandard entspricht nicht den Nutzungsanforderungen.

Anmerkung:

---

## Erhebungsbogen

Ist-Anzahl der EDV-Arbeitsplätze im Gebäude:

Ergänzungen zum Nutzerinterview:

### 3. Hausmeisterinterview

### Standard der Technischen Anlagen:

Standard der Gebäudeautomation:

- ○ Hoch (Raumregelung) / Raumweise Regelung von Wärme, Luft/ Klima, Licht zentral möglich.
- ○ Eher hoch (Gruppenregelung) / Tlw., Geschossweise Regelung von Wärme, Luft/ Klima, Licht zentral möglich.
- ○ Eher niedrig / Gebäudeweise Regelung von Wärme, Luft/ Klima, Licht zentral möglich.
- ○ Niedrig / Keine zentrale Regelung möglich.

Anmerkung:

Standard der Heizungssteuerung:

- ○ Hoch (Tagesprogramm)
- ○ Eher hoch (Wochenprogramm)
- ○ Erfüllt.
- ○ Niedrig (Jahresprogramm)

Lufttechnische Anlagen:

- ○ Abluftanlagen
- ○ Zuluftanlagen
- ○ Zu- und Abluftanlagen
- ○ Teilklimaanlage mit Wärmerückgewinnung
- ○ Teilklimaanlage ohne Wärmerückgewinnung
- ○ Vollklimaanlage mit Wärmerückgewinnung
- ○ Vollklimaanlage ohne Wärmerückgewinnung
- ○ Sonstige ...
- ○ Keine Klimaanlage vorhanden.

Mit welcher Auslastung wurde die Klimaanlage im Betrachtungszeitraum betrieben?

- ○ Hoch / Die Klimaanlage ist voll ausgelastet (> 90%)
- ○ Eher hoch (> 70%)
- ○ Eher niedrig (> 40%)
- ○ Niedrig / Die Klimaanlage ist überdimensioniert (< 40%)

### Entsorgung:

Entsorgungskonzept hinsichtlich Zentralität und Abtransport:

- ○ Gut / Zentrale Sammelstellen für optimale Arbeitenbergung, Abtransport optimal gelöst
- ○ Eher gut
- ○ Eher schlecht
- ○ Schlecht / Sammelstelle nicht zentral, Abtransport aufwendig

Ergänzungen zum Bewirtschafterinterview:

Erhebungsbogen

## 3. Zustandserfassung

Im Folgenden bitten wir Sie, den Zustand aufgeführter Teile des Bauwerks, der Außenanlagen und der Ausstattung auf einer Skala von A (guter Zustand) bis D (schlechter Zustand) zu bewerten. Sind verschiedene Typen einer Kostengruppe aufgeführt (z.B. Typ 1 Stahlbeton, Typ 2 Mauerwerk), wählen Sie bitte die passenden Typen zum Gebäude aus und bestimmen deren Zustand und Prozentanteil. Sollte ein bestimmter Typ einer Kostengruppe nicht aufgeführt sein, können Sie diesen handschriftlich ergänzen.

### 3.1 Zustandserfassung Baukonstruktionen

### 320 Gründung

324 Unterböden und Bodenplatten:

- ☐ A  Gebäude in statisch gutem Zustand. Keine Risse und Abplatzungen an Unterböden und aufgehenden Bauteilen sichtbar. Keine kostenwirksamen Maßnahmen.
- ☐ B  Spuren von Hisarrissen und Abplatzungen an Unterböden und aufgehenden Bauteilen. Dilatationen teilweise defekt. Beschädigte Flächen (< 5%). Beton sanieren, inkl. Dilatationen. Isolierung gegen aufsteigende Feuchtigkeit.
- ☐ C  Spuren von Hisarrissen und Abplatzungen an Unterböden und aufgehenden Bauteilen. Dilatationen teilweise defekt. Beschädigte Flächen (< 20%). Beton sanieren, inkl. Dilatationen. Isolierung gegen aufsteigende Feuchtigkeit.
- ☐ D  Erhebliche Risse und Abplatzungen. Wasseneintritt ins Gebäude durch Feuchtigkeits- und Schimmelschäden erkennbar. Ausbildungen bei erdberührenden Bauteilen. Dilatationen großenteils beschädigt. Beton sanieren, inkl. Dilatationen, Bauwerksabdichtung und Isolierung gegen aufsteigende Feuchtigkeit, sachgemäßer Einbau von Fugenblechen, Fugenbändern oder Verpressschläuchen.
- ☐ E  Nicht vorhanden.

Anmerkung:

Bodenplatte Wärmedämmung:

- ☐ A  Wärmedämmung fachgerecht verlegt und geschützt. Keine kostenwirksamen Maßnahmen.
- ☐ B  Wärmedämmung mit örtlichen Beschädigungen (<10%). Ausbesserung der beständenden Wärmedämmung (<10%), Energiebilanz und Prüfung auf Wärmebrücken durchführen.
- ☐ C  Erhebliche Risse und Abplatzungen. Wasseneintritt ins Gebäude durch Feuchtigkeits- und Schimmelschäden erkennbar. Ausbildungen bei erdberührenden Bauteilen. Dilatationen großenteils beschädigt. Beschädigte Flächen (< 40 %).
- ☐ D  Beton sanieren, inkl. Dilatationen, Bauwerksabdichtung und Isolierung gegen aufsteigende Feuchtigkeit, sachgemäßer Einbau von Fugenblechen, Fugenbändern oder Verpressschläuchen. Erhebliche Risse und Abplatzungen. Wasseneintritt ins Gebäude durch Feuchtigkeits- und Schimmelschäden erkennbar. Ausbildungen bei erdberührenden Bauteilen. Dilatationen großenteils beschädigt. Beton sanieren, inkl. Dilatationen, Bauwerksabdichtung und Isolierung gegen aufsteigende Feuchtigkeit, sachgemäßer Einbau von Fugenblechen, Fugenbändern oder Verpressschläuchen.
- ☐ E  Nicht vorhanden.

Anmerkung:

Erhebungsbogen

### 330 Außenwände

331 Tragende Außenwände, 332 Nichttragende Außenwände

Außenwände – Typ 1 Stahlbeton:

Prozentanteil der Außenwandfläche: _____ 100 %

- ☐ A  Gebäude im statisch guten Zustand. Keine Risse und Abplatzungen sichtbar.
- ☐ B  Spuren von Haarrissen und Abplatzungen an Außenwänden. Dilatationen teilweise beschädigt. Beschädigte Fläche (<10 %). Keine weiteren Bewegungen zu erwarten. Beton äußerlich sanieren, inkl. Dilatationen (< 10%). Schützen der Außenhaut, Oberflächenbehandlung.
- ☐ C  Spuren von Haarrissen und Abplatzungen an Außenwänden. Dilatationen teilweise beschädigt. Beschädigte Fläche (< 40%). Keine weiteren Bewegungen zu erwarten. Beton äußerlich sanieren, inkl. Dilatationen (< 40%). Schützen der Außenhaut durch Oberflächenbehandlung.
- ☐ D  Erhebliche Risse und Abplatzungen. Dilatationen großenteils beschädigt. Beschädigte Flächen. Weitere Bewegungen zu erwarten. Beton äußerlich sanieren, inkl. Dilatationen. Schutzanstrich für sämtliche Oberflächen.
- ☐ E  Nicht vorhanden.

Anmerkung:

Außenwände – Typ 2 Mauerwerk:

Prozentanteil der Außenwandfläche: _____ %

- ☐ A  Gebäude im statisch guten Zustand. Keine Anzeichen von Setzungsrissen. Keine kostenwirksamen Maßnahmen.
- ☐ B  Risse vorhanden. Gebäude hat Anzeichen von Setzungen (< 10%). Rissesanierung (< 10%), Konstruktionsteile erneuern und statisch verstärken.
- ☐ C  Risse vorhanden. Gebäude hat Anzeichen von Setzungen (< 40%). Rissesanierung (<40%), Konstruktionsteile erneuern und statisch verstärken.
- ☐ D  Durchgehende Risse an den Wänden. Anzeichen von Setzungen. Weitere Bewegungen zu erwarten. Rissesanierung, Konstruktionsteile erneuern oder statisch verstärken. Weiteren Bewegungen vorbeugen.
- ☐ E  Nicht vorhanden.

Anmerkung:

Außenwände – Typ 3 Holzkonstruktion:

Prozentanteil der Außenwandfläche: _____ %

- ☐ A  Gebäude im statisch guten Zustand. Keine Anzeichen von Setzungsrissen, Durchbiegungen, Durchbiegungen etc. Keine kostenwirksamen Maßnahmen.
- ☐ B  Risse vorhanden. Örtliche Durchbiegungen. Anzeichen von Verwitterung (< 10%). Rissesanierung (< 10%), Konstruktionsteile erneuern und statisch verstärken.
- ☐ C  Risse vorhanden. Örtliche Setzungen, Durchbiegungen. Anzeichen von Verwitterung (< 40%). Rissesanierung (<40%), Konstruktionsteile erneuern und statisch verstärken.
- ☐ D  Verwendet Auftreten von Holzfäuchte, Anzeichen von Pilz-, Insektenbefall oder Verrottung. Korrosion an metallischen Verbindungsmitteln. Durchgehende Risse, Durchbiegungen und Setzungen im Gebäude. Weitere Bewegungen zu erwarten. Rissesanierung, Maßnahmen des konstruktiven oder chemischen Holzschutzes, Verbindungsmittel und Konstruktionsteile in beanspruchten Bereichen erneuern oder statisch verstärken. Weiteren Bewegungen vorbeugen.
- ☐ E  Nicht vorhanden.

Anmerkung:

**Erhebungsbogen**

## Außenwände – Typ 4 Pfosten-Riegel Konstruktion:

Prozentanteil der Außenwandfläche: _____ %

| | | |
|---|---|---|
| ○ | A | Gebäude ist statisch guter Zustand. Keine Anzeichen von Durchbiegungen, Korrosion. Keine kostenwirksamen Maßnahmen. |
| ○ | B | Erfüllt. |
| ○ | C | Gebäude hat Anzeichen von Durchbiegungen und Korrosion (< 10%). Keine weiteren Bewegungen zu erwarten. Konstruktionsteile erneuern und statisch verstärken (< 10%). Korrosionsschutz. |
| ○ | D | Gebäude hat Anzeichen von Durchbiegungen und Korrosion (< 40%). Keine weiteren Bewegungen zu erwarten. Konstruktionsteile erneuern und statisch verstärken (< 40%). Korrosionsschutz. |
| ○ | | Gebäude hat Anzeichen von Durchbiegungen und Korrosion. Weitere Bewegungen zu erwarten. Konstruktionsteile erneuern oder statisch verstärken. Korrosionsschutz. Maßnahmen gegen weitere Bewegung. |
| ○ | E | Nicht vorhanden. |

Anmerkung:

## 333 Außenstützen

### Außenstützen – Typ 1 Stahlbeton:

| | | |
|---|---|---|
| ○ | A | Gebäude ist statisch guter Zustand. Keine Risse und Abplatzungen sichtbar. Keine kostenwirksamen Maßnahmen. |
| ○ | B | Erfüllt. |
| ○ | C | Spuren von Haarrissen und Abplatzungen. Distaltionen teilweise beschädigt. Beschädigte Fläche (<10 %). Keine weiteren Bewegungen zu erwarten. Beton äußerlich sanieren, inkl. Distaltionen (< 10%). Schutzen der Außenhaut durch Oberflächenbehandlung. |
| ○ | D | Erhebliche Risse und Abplatzungen. Distaltionen größtenteils beschädigt. Weitere Bewegungen zu erwarten. Beton äußerlich sanieren, inkl. Distaltionen. Schutzanstrich für sämtliche Oberflächen. |
| ○ | E | Nicht vorhanden. |

Anmerkung:

### Außenstützen – Typ 2 Holzkonstruktion:

| | | |
|---|---|---|
| ○ | A | Gebäude ist statisch guter Zustand. Keine Anzeichen von Setzungsrissen, Durchfeuchtungen, Durchbiegungen etc. |
| ○ | B | Erfüllt. |
| ○ | C | Risse vorhanden. Örtliche Setzungen oder Durchbiegungen (< 10%). Konstruktionsteile erneuern und statisch verstärken. |
| ○ | D | Vereinzelt Auftreten von Holzfeuchte, Anzeichen von Pilz-, Insektenbefall oder Vermorschung, Korrosion an metallischen Verbindungsmitteln, Durchgehende Risse, Durchbiegungen und Setzungen im Gebäude. Weitere Bewegungen zu erwarten. Ressanierung. Maßnahmen des konstruktiven oder chemischen Holzschutzes. Verbindungsmittel und Konstruktionsteile in beanspruchten Bereichen erneuern oder statisch verstärken. Weitere Bewegungen vorbeugen. |
| ○ | E | Nicht vorhanden. |

Anmerkung:

---

**Erhebungsbogen**

## Außenstützen – Typ 3 Stahlkonstruktion:

| | | |
|---|---|---|
| ○ | A | Gebäude ist statisch guter Zustand. Keine Anzeichen von Durchbiegungen, Korrosion. Keine kostenwirksamen Maßnahmen. |
| ○ | B | Erfüllt. |
| ○ | C | Gebäude hat Anzeichen von Durchbiegungen und Korrosion (< 10%). Keine weiteren Bewegungen zu erwarten. Konstruktionsteile erneuern und statisch verstärken (< 10%). Korrosionsschutz. |
| ○ | D | Fortgeschrittene Korrosionserscheinungen. Setzungen im Gebäude. Weitere Bewegungen zu erwarten. Verbindungsmittel und Konstruktionsteile in beanspruchten Bereichen erneuern oder statisch verstärken. Weiteren Bewegungen vorbeugen. |
| ○ | E | Nicht vorhanden. |

Anmerkung:

## 334 Außentüren und -fenster      100 %

### Außentüren und -fenster – Typ 1 Kunststoff:

Prozentanteil der Außentüren-, fensterfläche: _____ %

Jahr der Modernisierung: _____

Prozentanteil modernisierter Türen- und Fenster: _____ %

| | | |
|---|---|---|
| ○ | A | Sämtliche Außentüren und -fenster in gutem Zustand. Dämmung genügend. Schließzeug funktioniert. Keine kostenwirksamen Maßnahmen. |
| ○ | B | Oberflächen außen verschmutzt, teils beschädigt (< 10%). Schließzeug funktioniert. Äussere Oberflächenbehandlung mit Versiegelung gegen Außenwand (< 10%). |
| ○ | C | Oberflächen innen und außen verschmutzt, beschädigt (<40%). Schließzeug funktioniert, vereinzelt undichte Stellen. Beschläge teilweise lose. Komplette Oberflächenbehandlung und Versiegelung gegen Außenwand (< 40%). Neue Kittfugen oder Glasleisten. Beschläge richten Energienachweis. |
| ○ | D | Sämtliche Außentüre und -fenster beschädigt. Schließzeug und Bedienung größtenteils nicht funktionstüftig. Ungenügende Wärmedämmung. Kompletter Ersatz und Versiegelung gegen Mauerwerk. Energiebereiter hinzuziehen. |
| ○ | E | Nicht vorhanden. |

Anmerkung:

### Außentüren und -fenster – Typ 2 Holz:

Prozentanteil der Außentüren-, fensterfläche: _____ %

Jahr der Modernisierung: _____

Prozentanteil modernisierter Türen- und Fenster: _____ %

| | | |
|---|---|---|
| ○ | A | Sämtliche Außentüren und -fenster in gutem Zustand. Dämmung genügend. Schließzeug funktioniert. Keine kostenwirksamen Maßnahmen. |
| ○ | B | Oberflächen außen verschmutzt, teils beschädigt (< 10%). Schließzeug funktioniert. Äussere Oberflächenbehandlung mit Versiegelung gegen Außenwand (< 10%). |
| ○ | C | Oberflächen innen und außen verschmutzt, beschädigt (<40%). Schließzeug funktioniert, vereinzelt undichte Stellen. Beschläge teilweise lose. Komplette Oberflächenbehandlung und Versiegelung gegen Außenwand (< 40%). Neue Kittfugen oder Glasleisten. Beschläge richten Energienachweis. |
| ○ | D | Sämtliche Außentüre und -fenster beschädigt. Schließzeug und Bedienung größtenteils nicht funktionstüftig. Ungenügende Wärmedämmung. Kompletter Ersatz und Versiegelung gegen Mauerwerk. Energiebereiter hinzuziehen. |
| ○ | E | Nicht vorhanden. |

Anmerkung:

Erhebungsbogen

## Außentüren und -fenster – Typ 3 Aluminium:

Prozentanteil der Außentüren-, fensterfläche: _____ %

Jahr der Modernisierung: _____

Prozentanteil modernisierter Türen- und Fenster: _____ %

- O  A  Sämtliche Außentüren und -fenster in gutem Zustand. Dämmung genügend. Schliessung funktioniert. Keine kostenwirksamen Maßnahmen.
- O  B  Oberflächen außen verschmutzt, teils beschädigt (< 10%). Schliessung funktioniert. Aussere Oberflächenbehandlung mit Versiegelung gegen Außenwand (< 10%).
- O  C  Oberflächen innen und außen verschmutzt, beschädigt (<40%). Schliessung funktioniert, vereinzelt undichte Stellen. Beschläge teilweise lose. Komplette Oberflächenbehandlung und Versiegelung gegen Außenwand (< 40%). Neue Kittfugen oder Glasleisten. Beschläge richten Energienachweis.
- O  D  Sämtliche Außentüre und -fenster beschädigt. Schliessung und Bedienung größtenteils nicht funktionsfähig. Ungenügende Wärmedämmung. Kompletter Ersatz und Versiegelung gegen Mauerwerk. Energieberater hinzuziehen.
- O  E  Nicht vorhanden.

Anmerkung:

## Außentüren und -fenster – Typ 4 Stahl:

Prozentanteil der Außentüren-, fensterfläche: _____ %

Jahr der Modernisierung: _____

Prozentanteil modernisierter Türen- und Fenster: _____ %

- O  A  Sämtliche Außentüren und -fenster in gutem Zustand. Dämmung genügend. Schliessung funktioniert. Keine kostenwirksamen Maßnahmen.
- O  B  Oberflächen außen verschmutzt, teils beschädigt (< 10%). Schliessung funktioniert. Aussere Oberflächenbehandlung mit Versiegelung gegen Außenwand (< 10%).
- O  C  Oberflächen innen und außen verschmutzt, beschädigt (<40%). Schliessung funktioniert, vereinzelt undichte Stellen. Beschläge teilweise lose. Komplette Oberflächenbehandlung und Versiegelung gegen Außenwand (< 40%). Neue Kittfugen oder Glasleisten. Beschläge richten Energienachweis.
- O  D  Sämtliche Außentüre und -fenster beschädigt. Schliessung und Bedienung größtenteils nicht funktionsfähig. Ungenügende Wärmedämmung. Kompletter Ersatz und Versiegelung gegen Mauerwerk. Energieberater hinzuziehen.
- O  E  Nicht vorhanden.

Anmerkung:

## 335 Außenwandbekleidungen, außen

## Außenwandbekleidungen, außen – Typ 1 Putz:                                    100 %

Prozentanteil der Außenbekleidungsfläche der Außenwand: _____ %

- O  A  Keine sichtbaren Schäden. Anstrich sauber. Keine kostenwirksamen Maßnahmen.
- O  B  Anstrich verwittert. Putzschäden der Fassadenoberfläche (< 20%). Neuer Grund- und Deckputz bei schadhaften Stellen (< 20%). Reinigung und Anstrich der Fassade.
- O  C  Anstrich verwittert. Putzschäden (<50%) der Fassadenfläche. Neuer Grund- und Deckputz bei schadhaften Stellen (< 50%) Reinigung und Anstrich der Fassade.
- O  D  Anstrich verwittert. Putzschäden der Fassadenfläche. Entfernen des bestehenden Putzes. Reinigen des Mauerwerks, Aufbau des Putzes, Anstrich Fassade.
- O  E  Nicht vorhanden.

Anmerkung:

- 8 -

---

Erhebungsbogen

## Außenwandbekleidungen, außen – Typ 2 Sichtmauerwerk:

Prozentanteil der Außenbekleidungsfläche der Außenwand: _____ %

- O  A  Keine Anzeichen von Verschmutzung, Abblätterungen oder Rissen. Keine kostenwirksamen Maßnahmen.
- O  B  Verunreinigungen und punktuelle Beschädigungen (< 20 %). Fassade reinigen und imprägnieren.
- O  C  Verunreinigung mit Ausblühungen, Beschädigungen und Abplatzungen (< 50%) der Fassadenfläche. Schäden an Fugen. Sanieren, Reinigen und Imprägnieren des Mauerwerks. Nacharbeiten der Fugen.
- O  D  Verunreinigung mit Ausblühungen, Beschädigungen und Abplatzungen der Fassadenfläche. Schäden an Fugen. Sanieren, Reinigen und Imprägnieren des Mauerwerks. Nacharbeiten der Fugen.
- O  E  Nicht vorhanden.

Anmerkung:

## Außenwandbekleidungen, außen – Typ 3 Vorgehängte Verkleidung (Metall):

Prozentanteil der Außenbekleidungsfläche der Außenwand: _____ %

- O  A  Oberflächen sauber. An- und Abschlüsse intakt, keine Anzeichen von Schäden an Befestigung. Keine kostenwirksamen Maßnahmen.
- O  B  Fassaden verwittert, einzelne Elemente beschädigt (< 20%). An- und Abschlüsse undicht. Keine Anzeichen von Schäden an Befestigung. Auswechseln beschädigter Fassadenelemente auf bestehender Unterkonstruktion (< 20%). Ausbilden aller An- und Abschlüsse. Oberflächenbehandlung der Fassade.
- O  C  Fassaden verwittert, einzelne Elemente beschädigt (< 50%). An- und Abschlüsse undicht. Keine Anzeichen von Schäden an Befestigung. Auswechseln beschädigter Fassadenelemente auf bestehender Unterkonstruktion (< 50%). Ausbilden aller An- und Abschlüsse. Oberflächenbehandlung der Fassade.
- O  D  Großteil der Fassadenelemente beschädigt, verwittert, korrodiert. Schäden an der Befestigung. An- und Abschlüsse undicht. Teilersatz nicht möglich, kein Ersatzmaterial erhältlich. Entfernen und Entsorgen der bestehenden Konstruktion. Neuaufbau ab bestehendem Mauerwerk inkl. Wärmedämmung.
- O  E  Nicht vorhanden.

Anmerkung:

## Außenwandbekleidungen, außen – Typ 4 Vorgehängte Steinplatten:

Prozentanteil der Außenbekleidungsfläche der Außenwand: _____ %

- O  A  Oberflächen intakt und sauber. Keine Anzeichen von Schäden an Befestigungen und Aufhängungen. Keine kostenwirksamen Maßnahmen.
- O  B  Oberflächen verschmutzt. Fugen punktuell beschädigt (< 20%). Keine Anzeichen von Schäden der Platten, Befestigung und Aufhängung. Instandsetzen und Imprägnieren der Oberflächen. Erneuern der Fugen (< 20%).
- O  C  Oberflächen stark angegriffen mit Abplatzungen. Fugen beschädigt (< 50%). Keine Anzeichen von Schäden an Befestigung und Aufhängung. Beschädigte Platten auswechseln (< 50%). Erneuern der Fugen. Komplette Oberflächenbehandlung.
- O  D  Beschädigte Platten angegriffen mit Abplatzungen. Anzeichen von korrodierten Befestigungen und Aufhängungen. Die Sicherheit ist gefährdet. Erhebliche Schäden durch mangelhafte Wärmedämmung. Neuer Aufbau der Konstruktion.

Anmerkung:

- 9 -

**Erhebungsbogen**

## Außenwände Wärmedämmung:

- A   Wärmedämmung flächengerecht verlegt und geschützt. Keine kostenwirksamen Maßnahmen.
- B   Wärmedämmung mit örtliche Beschädigungen (< 10%). Ausbesserung der bestehenden Wärmedämmung (< 10%). Energiebilanz und Prüfung auf Wärmebrücken durchführen.
- C   Wärmedämmung unvollständig oder mit örtlichen Beschädigungen (< 40%). Erneuerung und Erneuerung der bestehenden Wärmedämmung. Energiebilanz und Prüfung auf Wärmebrücken durchführen.
- D   Wärmedämmung unvollständig oder mit örtlichen Beschädigungen. Erneuerung und Erneuerung der bestehenden Wärmedämmung. Energiebilanz und Prüfung auf Wärmebrücken durchführen.
- E   Nicht vorhanden.

Anmerkung:

## 338 Sonnenschutz    100 %

### Sonnenschutz – Typ 1 Markise, elektrisch gesteuert:

Prozentanteil des Sonnenschutzes: _____ %

- A   Markisen funktionsfähig, Stoffteile in Ordnung. Keine kostenwirksamen Maßnahmen.
- B   Markisen funktionsfähig, Stoffteile stark verwittert oder beschädigt (< 10%). Bedienungselemente teilweise abgenutzt, defekt.
- C   Markisen funktionsunfähig, Stoffteile stark verwittert oder beschädigt (< 40%). Bedienungselemente funktionsunfähig. Ersatz der Stoffteile und Bedienungselemente (< 40%). Prüfung auf Wärmebrücken durchführen.
- D   Großteil der Markisen nicht funktionsfähig. Stoffteile stark verwittert oder beschädigt. Bedienungselemente defekt. Totalersatz der Markisen. Energienachweis und Prüfung auf Wärmebrücken durchführen.
- E   Nicht vorhanden.

Anmerkung:

### Sonnenschutz – Typ 2 Rollläden, manuell gesteuert:

Prozentanteil des Sonnenschutzes: _____ %

- A   Rollläden in gutem Zustand. Oberflächen sauber. Keine kostenwirksamen Maßnahmen.
- B   Rollläden in Ordnung. Bedienungselemente teilweise abgenutzt (< 10%). Ersetzen von Bedienungselementen. Kleinere Instandsetzungsarbeiten (< 10%).
- C   Panzer stark verwittert und teilweise defekt. Bedienungselemente größtenteils abgenutzt, defekt (< 40%). Ersetzen der Panzer durch Bedienungselemente (< 40%). Prüfung auf Wärmebrücken durchführen.
- D   Rollläden nicht mehr funktionstüchtig. Kompletter Ersatz durch neue Rollläden. Energienachweis und Prüfung auf Wärmebrücken durchführen.
- E   Nicht vorhanden.

Anmerkung:

---

**Erhebungsbogen**

### Sonnenschutz – Typ 3 Lamellenstoren (außenliegend), elektrisch gesteuert:

Prozentanteil des Sonnenschutzes: _____ %

- A   Lamellenstoren in gutem Zustand. Oberflächen sauber. Keine kostenwirksamen Maßnahmen.
- B   Lamellenstoren in Ordnung. Bedienungselemente teilweise abgenutzt (< 10%). Ersetzen von Bedienungselementen. Kleinere Instandsetzungsarbeiten (< 10%).
- C   Lamellenstoren stark verwittert, teilweise defekt. Bedienungselemente abgenutzt, defekt (< 40%). Ersetzen der Lamellengeräte durch Bedienungselemente (< 40%). Prüfung auf Wärmebrücken durchführen.
- D   Lamellenstoren nicht mehr funktionsfähig. Kompletter Ersatz durch neue Lamellenstoren. Energienachweis und Prüfung auf Wärmebrücken durchführen.
- E   Nicht vorhanden.

Anmerkung:

### Sonnenschutz – Typ 4 Stoffbahnen (außenliegend), elektrisch gesteuert:

Prozentanteil des Sonnenschutzes: _____ %

- A   Stoffbahnen in gutem Zustand. Oberflächen sauber. Keine kostenwirksamen Maßnahmen.
- B   Stoffbahnen in Ordnung. Bedienungselemente teilweise abgenutzt (< 10 %). Ersetzen von Bedienungselementen. Kleinere Instandsetzungsarbeiten (< 10%).
- C   Stoffbahnen stark verwittert, teilweise defekt. Bedienungselemente abgenutzt, defekt (< 40%). Ersetzen der Lamellengeräte durch Bedienungselemente (< 40%). Prüfung auf Wärmebrücken durchführen.
- D   Stoffbahnen nicht mehr funktionsfähig. Kompletter Ersatz durch neue Stoffbahnen. Energienachweis und Prüfung auf Wärmebrücken durchführen.
- E   Nicht vorhanden.

Anmerkung:

## 340 Innenwände

## 341 Tragende Innenwände, 342 Nichttragende Innenwände    100 %

### Innenwände – Typ 1 Stahlbeton:

Prozentanteil der Innenwandfläche: _____ %

- A   Gebäude im statisch guten Zustand. Keine Risse und Abplatzungen sichtbar. Keine kostenwirksamen Maßnahmen.
- B   Spuren von Haarrissen und Abplatzungen. Dilatationen teilweise defekt. Beschädigte Fläche (< 10%). Keine weiteren Bewegungen zu erwarten. Schadhaft Stellen ausbessern, inkl. Dilatationen (< 10%). Oberflächenbehandlung.
- C   Spuren von Haarrissen und Abplatzungen. Dilatationen teilweise defekt. Beschädigte Fläche (< 40%). Keine weiteren Bewegungen zu erwarten. Schadhaft Stellen ausbessern, inkl. Dilatationen (< 40%). Oberflächenbehandlung.
- D   Erhebliche Risse und Abplatzungen. Dilatationen größtenteils beschädigt. Weitere Bewegungen zu erwarten. Betonsanierung, inkl. Dilatationen. Oberflächenbehandlung. Maßnahmen gegen weitere Bewegung.
- E   Nicht vorhanden.

Anmerkung:

Erhebungsbogen

## Innenwände – Typ 2 Mauerwerk:

Prozentanteil der Innenwandfläche: _____ %

| | | |
|---|---|---|
| O | A | Gebäude im statisch guten Zustand. Keine Anzeichen von Setzungsrissen. Keine kostenwirksamen Maßnahmen. |
| O | B | Risse vorhanden. Gebäude hat Anzeichen von Setzungen (< 10%). Keine weiteren Bewegungen zu erwarten. |
| O | C | Rissesanierung. Konstruktionsteile erneuern und statisch verstärken (< 10%). Risse vorhanden. Gebäude hat Anzeichen von Setzungen (< 40%). Keine weiteren Bewegungen zu erwarten. |
| O | D | Rissesanierung. Konstruktionsteile erneuern und statisch verstärken (< 40%). Durchgehende Risse an den Wänden. Anzeichen von Setzungen feststellbar. Weitere Bewegungen zu erwarten. Rissesanierung. Konstruktionsteile erneuern oder statisch verstärken. Maßnahmen gegen weitere Bewegung. |
| O | E | Nicht vorhanden. |

Anmerkung:

## Innenwände – Typ 3 Holzkonstruktion:

Prozentanteil der Innenwandfläche: _____ %

| | | |
|---|---|---|
| O | A | Gebäude im statisch guten Zustand. Keine Anzeichen von Setzungsrissen. Keine kostenwirksamen Maßnahmen. |
| O | B | Risse vorhanden. Örtliche Setzungen oder Durchbiegungen (< 10%). Keine weiteren Bewegungen zu erwarten. Rissesanierung (< 10%). Konstruktionsteile erneuern und statisch verstärken. |
| O | C | Risse vorhanden. Örtliche Setzungen oder Durchbiegungen (< 40%). Keine weiteren Bewegungen zu erwarten. Rissesanierung (< 40%). Konstruktionsteile erneuern und statisch verstärken. |
| O | D | Durchgehende Risse, Durchbiegungen und Setzungen. Weitere Bewegungen zu erwarten. Rissesanierung. Maßnahmen des konstruktiven Holzschutzes. Verbindungsmittel und Konstruktionsteile in beanspruchten Bereichen erneuern oder statisch verstärken. Weitere Bewegungen vorbeugen. |
| O | E | Nicht vorhanden. |

Anmerkung:

## Innenwände – Typ 4 Metall-, Holzständerwand:

Prozentanteil der Innenwandfläche: _____ %

| | | |
|---|---|---|
| O | A | Keine sichtbaren Schäden. Keine Anzeichen von Stauchungen, Durchbiegungen. Keine kostenwirksamen Maßnahmen. |
| O | B | Örtliche Durchbiegungen. Vereinzelt lockere An- und Abschlüsse (< 10%). Austausch schadhafter Konstruktionsteile, beschädigte An-, Abschlüsse erneuern (< 10%). |
| O | C | Örtliche Durchbiegungen. Vereinzelt lockere An- und Abschlüsse (< 40%). Austausch schadhafter Konstruktionsteile, beschädigte An-, Abschlüsse erneuern (< 40%). |
| O | D | Metall-, Holzständer weisen großflächig Durchbiegungen auf. Lockere An-, Abschlüsse. Beanspruchte Konstruktionsteile und Verbindungsmittel erneuern. |
| O | E | Nicht vorhanden. |

Anmerkung:

---

Erhebungsbogen

## Innenwände – Typ 5 Verglasung:

Prozentanteil der Innenwandfläche: _____ %

| | | |
|---|---|---|
| O | A | Keine Verschmutzungen oder schadhafte Stellen. Keine kostenwirksamen Maßnahmen. |
| O | B | Vereinzelt lockere An- und Abschlüsse. Glasschäden (< 10%). Oberflächen verschmutzt. Beschädigte Glasscheiben, An- und Abschlüsse erneuern (< 10%). Glasreinigung. |
| O | C | Vereinzelt lockere An- und Abschlüsse. Glasschäden (< 40%). Oberflächen verschmutzt. Beschädigte Glasscheiben, An- und Abschlüsse erneuern (< 40%). Glasreinigung. |
| O | D | Lockere An- und Abschlüsse. Beschädigungen am Glas. Beschädigte Glasscheiben, An- und Abschlüsse erneuern. Glasreinigung. |
| O | E | Nicht vorhanden. |

Anmerkung:

## 343 Innenstützen

## Innenstützen – Typ 1 Stahlbeton:

| | | |
|---|---|---|
| O | A | Gebäude im statisch guten Zustand. Keine Risse und Abplatzungen sichtbar. Keine kostenwirksamen Maßnahmen. |
| O | B | Entfällt. |
| O | C | Spuren von Haarrissen und Abplatzungen. Dilatationen teilweise beschädigt. Beschädigte Fläche (< 10%). Beton äußerlich sanieren, inkl. Dilatationen (< 10%). Oberflächenbehandlung. |
| O | D | Erhebliche Risse und Abplatzungen. Dilatationen großflächig beschädigt. Beschädigte Flächen. Beton äußerlich sanieren, inkl. Dilatationen. Oberflächenbehandlung. |
| O | E | Nicht vorhanden. |

Anmerkung:

## Innenstützen – Typ 2 Holzkonstruktion:

| | | |
|---|---|---|
| O | A | Gebäude im statisch guten Zustand. Keine Anzeichen von Setzungsrissen, Durchbiegungen etc. Keine kostenwirksamen Maßnahmen. |
| O | B | Entfällt. |
| O | C | Risse vorhanden. Örtliche Setzungen oder Durchbiegungen (< 10%). Rissesanierung (< 10%). Konstruktionsteile erneuern und statisch verstärken. |
| O | D | Durchgehende Risse, Durchbiegungen und Setzungen. Weitere Bewegungen zu erwarten. Rissesanierung. Maßnahmen des konstruktiven Holzschutzes. Verbindungsmittel und Konstruktionsteile in beanspruchten Bereichen erneuern oder statisch verstärken. Weitere Bewegungen vorbeugen. |
| O | E | Nicht vorhanden. |

Anmerkung:

## Innenstützen – Typ 3 Stahlkonstruktion:

| | | |
|---|---|---|
| O | A | Gebäude im statisch guten Zustand. Keine Anzeichen von Setzungsrissen, Durchbiegungen etc. Keine kostenwirksamen Maßnahmen. |
| O | B | Entfällt. |
| O | C | Gebäude hat Anzeichen von Durchbiegungen, Korrosion (< 10%). Konstruktionsteile erneuern und statisch verstärken (< 10%). Korrosionsschutz. |
| O | D | Fortgeschrittene Korrosionserscheinungen. Setzungen im Gebäude. Weitere Bewegungen zu erwarten. Konstruktionsteile in beanspruchten Bereichen erneuern, verstärken. Weitere Bewegungen vorbeugen. |
| O | E | Nicht vorhanden. |

Anmerkung:

Erhebungsbogen

**344 Innentüren und -fenster**

**Innentüren und -fenster – Typ 1 Kunststoff:**    100 %

Prozentanteil der Innentüren-, Innenfensterfläche: _____ %

| | | |
|---|---|---|
| ○ | A | Innentüren in Ordnung. Keine Beanstandungen. Keine Kostenwirksamen Maßnahmen. |
| ○ | B | Oberflächen teils verschmutzt. Garnituren teils gelöst (< 20%). Oberflächen säubern. Richten der Garnituren (< 20 %). |
| ○ | C | Oberflächen verschmutzt. Unsaubere Türläuffen. Teile der Verglasung beschädigt. Garnituren lose oder fehlend (<50 %). |
| ○ | D | Oberflächen säubern. Beschädigte Schwelleneisen und Sockelbleche austauschen. Verglasung austauschen. Garnituren ersetzen (<50 %). Innentüren genügen den Anforderungen nicht mehr. Flügel, Rahmen und Garnituren stark beschädigt. Erneuerung schadhafter Innentüren, inkl. Beschläge und Garnituren. |
| ○ | E | Nicht vorhanden. |

Anmerkung:

**Innentüren und -fenster – Typ 2 Holz:**    _____ %

Prozentanteil der Innentüren-, Innenfensterfläche: _____ %

| | | |
|---|---|---|
| ○ | A | Holzteile in gutem Zustand. Oberflächen sauber und gepflegt. Beschläge in Ordnung. Keine Kostenwirksamen Maßnahmen. |
| ○ | B | Holzteile in gutem Zustand. Beschläge vereinzelt beschädigt. Oberflächen punktuell schadhaft (< 20%). Beschläge teilweise ersetzen und richten. Anstriche ausbessern (< 20%). |
| ○ | C | Holzteile und Beschläge nicht mehr funktionstüchtig (< 50%). Oberflächen schadhaft. Ersatz der Holzteile und Beschläge (< 50%). Komplette Oberflächenbehandlung. |
| ○ | D | Sämtliche Holzteile in schlechtem Zustand. Oberflächen sind stark verschmutzt. Totalersatz aller Holzteile, komplette Oberflächenbehandlung. |
| ○ | E | Nicht vorhanden. |

Anmerkung:

**Innentüren und -fenster – Typ 3 Aluminium:**    _____ %

Prozentanteil der Innentüren-, Innenfensterfläche: _____ %

| | | |
|---|---|---|
| ○ | A | Innentüren in Ordnung. Keine Beanstandungen. Keine Kostenwirksamen Maßnahmen. |
| ○ | B | Oberflächen teils verschmutzt. Garnituren teils gelöst (< 20%). Oberflächen säubern. Richten der Garnituren (< 20%). |
| ○ | C | Oberflächen verschmutzt. Unsaubere Türläuffen. Teile der Verglasung beschädigt. Garnituren lose oder fehlend (< 50%). Oberflächen säubern. Beschädigte Schwelleneisen und Sockelbleche austauschen. Verglasung ausbessern. Garnituren ersetzen (< 50%). |
| ○ | D | Innentüren genügen den Anforderungen nicht mehr. Flügel, Rahmen und Garnituren stark beschädigt. Erneuerung schadhafter Außentüren, inkl. Beschläge und Garnituren. |
| ○ | E | Nicht vorhanden. |

Anmerkung:

- 14 -

---

Erhebungsbogen

**Innentüren und -fenster – Typ 4 Stahl:**    _____ %

Prozentanteil der Innentüren-, Innenfensterfläche: _____ %

| | | |
|---|---|---|
| ○ | A | Schliessung und Schaltdämmung in Ordnung. Keine Beanstandungen. Keine Kostenwirksamen Maßnahmen. |
| ○ | B | Oberflächen teils verschmutzt. Schliessung ungenügend (< 20%). Schlechte Schaltdämmung. Anstrich. Garnituren teils gelöst. Oberflächen säubern, streichen. Richten der Garnituren (< 20%). Schloss erneuern, zusätzliche Filzdichtungen. |
| ○ | C | Oberflächen verschmutzt. Schlechte Schaltdämmung und Schliessung (< 50%). Garnituren lose oder fehlend. Oberflächen säubern. Beschädigte Schwelleneisen und Sockelbleche austauschen. Garnituren ersetzen (< 50%). |
| ○ | D | Innentüren genügen den Anforderungen nicht mehr. Flügel, Rahmen und Garnituren stark beschädigt. Schlechte Schaltdämmung. Totalersatz Flügel und Rahmen, inkl. Schliessung und Spion. Oberflächenbehandlung innen und aussen. |
| ○ | E | Nicht vorhanden. |

Anmerkung:

**Innenliegende Wandbekleidungen**
**(345 Innenwandbekleidungen, 336 Außenwandbekleidungen, innen)**    100 %

**Innenliegende Wandbekleidungen – Typ 1 Anstriche:**    _____ %

Prozentanteil der innenliegenden Wandbekleidungsfläche: _____ %

| | | |
|---|---|---|
| ○ | A | Anstriche in gutem Zustand. Keine oder nur leichte Verschmutzung. Keine kostenwirksamen Maßnahmen. |
| ○ | B | Untergrund in Ordnung. Oberflächen schmutzig oder abgenutzt. Örtliche Risse und Abblätterungen (<20 %). Untergrund neu streichen (< 20%). |
| ○ | C | Oberflächen schmutzig oder abgenutzt. Untergrund teilweise gerissen oder beschädigt. Risse und Abblätterungen (< 50%). Untergrund instand setzen (< 50%). Komplett neuer Anstrich. |
| ○ | D | Oberflächen und Untergrund in schlechtem Zustand. Zahlreiche Beschädigungen, Risse und Abblösungen. Bestehende Anstriche vollständig entfernen. Untergrund ausbessern. Komplett neuer Anstrich. |
| ○ | E | Nicht vorhanden. |

Anmerkung:

**Innenliegende Wandbekleidungen – Typ 2 Tapeten:**    _____ %

Prozentanteil der innenliegenden Wandbekleidungsfläche: _____ %

| | | |
|---|---|---|
| ○ | A | Tapeten in gutem Zustand. Es sind keine losen Stellen sichtbar. Keine kostenwirksamen Maßnahmen. |
| ○ | B | Tapeten lose, verschmutzt oder beschädigt (< 20%). Untergrund in Ordnung. Bestehende Tapeten entfernen. Wände neu tapezieren. |
| ○ | C | Tapeten lose, verschmutzt oder beschädigt (< 50%). Untergrund in Ordnung. Bestehende Tapeten entfernen (< 50%). Wände neu tapezieren. |
| ○ | D | Tapeten total verschmutzt oder beschädigt. Untergrund mit Rissen, Unebenheiten oder losen Stellen. Bestehende Tapeten entfernen (< 50%). Untergrund ausbessern und neu tapezieren. |
| ○ | E | Nicht vorhanden. |

Anmerkung:

- 15 -

**Erhebungsbogen**

## Innenliegende Wandbekleidungen – Typ 3 Holzverkleidung:

Prozentanteil der innenliegenden Wandbekleidungsfläche _____ %

- O  A  Holzverkleidung in gutem Zustand. Oberflächen sauber. Keine kostenwirksamen Maßnahmen.
- O  B  Holzverkleidung in gutem Zustand. Oberflächen verschmutzt oder abgenutzt (< 20%). Komplette Oberflächenbehandlung.
- O  C  Örtliche Schwindrisse und Beschädigungen. Oberflächen verschmutzt (<50%). Komplette Oberflächenbehandlung.
- O  D  Holzverkleidung in schlechtem Zustand. Fugen offen, Schwindrisse und Beschädigungen sichtbar. Oberflächen verschmutzt. Holzverkleidung ersetzen, inkl. Unterkonstruktion. Komplette Oberflächenbehandlung.
- O  E  Nicht vorhanden.

Anmerkung:

## Innenliegende Wandbekleidungen – Typ 4 Prallschutz (Nadelvlies):

Prozentanteil der innenliegenden Wandbekleidungsfläche _____ %

- O  A  Prallschutz in gutem Zustand. Oberflächen sauber. Keine kostenwirksamen Maßnahmen.
- O  B  Prallschutz in gutem Zustand. Oberflächen verschmutzt oder abgenutzt (< 20%). Komplette Oberflächenbehandlung.
- O  C  Oberflächen verschmutzt mit örtlichen Beschädigungen (<50%). Teilersatz des Prallschutzes (< 50%). Komplette Oberflächenbehandlung.
- O  D  Prallschutz in schlechtem Zustand. Oberflächen großflächig verschmutzt und beschädigt. Neuer Prallschutz.

Anmerkung:

## Innenliegende Wandbekleidungen – Typ 5 Ballwurfsichere Kassetten:

Prozentanteil der innenliegenden Wandbekleidungsfläche _____ %

- O  A  Metallpaneelen in gutem Zustand. Oberflächen sauber. Keine kostenwirksamen Maßnahmen.
- O  B  Metallpaneelen in gutem Zustand. Oberflächen verschmutzt oder abgenutzt (< 20%). Komplette Oberflächenbehandlung.
- O  C  Oberflächen verschmutzt mit örtlichen Beschädigungen (< 50 %). Austausch beschädigter Metallpaneelen (< 50 %). Komplette Oberflächenbehandlung.
- O  D  Metallpaneelen in schlechtem Zustand. Oberflächen großflächig verschmutzt, beschädigt. Ersatz ballwurfsicherer Kassetten.

Anmerkung:

## Innenliegende Wandbekleidungen – Typ 6 Keramik (Bad/WC):

Prozentanteil der innenliegenden Wandbekleidungsfläche _____ %

- O  A  Plattenbeläge einwandfrei und sauber. Keine kostenwirksamen Maßnahmen.
- O  B  Plattenbeläge einwandfrei. Fugen teilweise ausgebrochen oder verschmutzt (< 20%). Fugen reinigen oder erneuern (< 20%).
- O  C  Plattenbeläge einwandfrei. Fugen teilweise ausgebrochen oder verschmutzt (< 50%). Fugen reinigen oder erneuern (< 50%).
- O  D  Plattenbeläge schadhaft und gelöst. Fugen stark verschmutzt, teils ausgebrochen. Plattenbeläge komplette erneuern.
- O  E  Nicht vorhanden.

Anmerkung:

---

**Erhebungsbogen**

## Innenwände Dämmung:

- O  A  Schalldämmung in ausreichender Stärke vorhanden, fachgerecht verlegt und geschützt. Keine kostenwirksamen Maßnahmen.
- O  B  Schalldämmung in ausreichender Stärke vorhanden. Örtliche Beschädigungen (< 20%). Ausbesserung der bestehenden Schalldämmung (< 20%).
- O  C  Schalldämmung größtenteils nicht in ausreichender Stärke vorhanden. Örtliche Beschädigungen (< 50 %). Ausbesserung der bestehenden Schalldämmung (< 50%).
- O  D  Schalldämmung unvollständig, Stärke der Dämmschicht ist ungenügend. Erneuerung der bestehenden Schalldämmung in ausreichender Stärke.
- O  E  Nicht vorhanden.

Anmerkung:

## 350  Decken

### 351  Deckenkonstruktionen     100 %

### Deckenkonstruktionen – Typ 1 Stahlbeton:

Prozentanteil der Deckenkonstruktionsfläche _____ %

- O  A  Gebäude in statisch gutem Zustand. Keine Anzeichen von Rissen, Abplatzungen und Durchbiegungen. Keine kostenwirksamen Maßnahmen.
- O  B  Entfällt.
- O  C  Spuren von Haarrissen und Abplatzungen erkennbar. Dilatationen teilweise defekt. Beschädigte Fläche (< 10%). Beton sanieren, inkl. Dilatationen (< 10%).
- O  D  Erhebliche Risse und Abplatzungen. Durchbiegungen sichtbar. Dilatationen großflächig beschädigt. Beschädigte Flächen. Beanspruchte Deckenkonstruktionen ersetzen oder verstärken.
- O  E  Nicht vorhanden.

Anmerkung:

### Deckenkonstruktionen – Typ 2 Holzbalkendecke:

Prozentanteil der Deckenkonstruktionsfläche: _____ %

- O  A  Gebäude in statisch gutem Zustand. Holzwerk gesund. Keine Anzeichen von Setzungsrissen, Verformung und Durchbiegungen. Keine kostenwirksamen Maßnahmen.
- O  B  Entfällt.
- O  C  Risse vorhanden. Örtliche Setzungen oder Durchbiegungen (< 10%). Keine weiteren Bewegungen zu erwarten. Rissesanierung (< 10%). Beanspruchte Konstruktionsteile auswechseln oder statisch verstärken.
- O  D  Wichtige Teile des Tragwerks zeigen durchgehende Risse. Durchbiegungen und Setzungen im Gebäude. Weitere Setzungsrisse. Verbindungsmittel und Konstruktionsteile in beanspruchten Bereichen erneuern oder statisch verstärken. Weitere Bewegungen vorbeugen.
- O  E  Nicht vorhanden.

Anmerkung:

Erhebungsbogen

## Treppen, Rampen – Typ 1 Betontreppe:

Prozentanteil der Betontreppen im Gebäude: _____ %

| | | |
|---|---|---|
| ○ | A | Treppenwangen, Stufen und Geländer in gutem Zustand. Keine Risse oder Verschleissspuren. Oberflächen sauber. Keine kostenwirksamen Massnahmen. |
| ○ | B | Treppenwangen und Geländer in gutem Zustand. Punktuelle Schäden an Stufen und Treppenwangen, freiliegende Haarrisse und Fugen (< 10%). Oberflächen schmutzig. Örtliche Betonsanierung (< 10%). Materialausgänge ausfugen. Tritte reinigen und imprägnieren. Streichen der Geländer. |
| ○ | C | Treppenwangen, Stufen und Beläge beschädigt oder abgelöst (< 40%). Sanieren aller Oberflächen. Materialausgänge ausfugen. Wiederherstellung der Bodenbeläge. Geländer richten und streichen. Verankerung überprüfen. |
| ○ | D | Erhebliche Schäden, Risse und Abplatzungen an Stufen und Treppenwangen. Verankerung des Geländers teils locker. Sicherheit beeinträchtigt. Totalersatz der Treppe inkl. Geländer. |
| ○ | E | Nicht vorhanden. |

Anmerkung:

## Treppen, Rampen – Typ 2 Holz-, Stahltreppe:

Prozentanteil der Holz- oder Stahltreppen im Gebäude: _____ %

| | | |
|---|---|---|
| ○ | A | Treppenwangen, Stufen und Geländer in gutem Zustand. Keine Risse oder Verschleissspuren. Keine kostenwirksamen Massnahmen. |
| ○ | B | Treppenwangen und Geländer in gutem Zustand. Punktuelle Schäden an Stufen und Treppenwangen, freiliegende Haarrisse (< 10%). Oberflächen schmutzig. Örtliche Ausbesserungen (< 10%). Tritte reinigen und imprägnieren. Streichen der Geländer. |
| ○ | C | Treppenwangen, Stufen und Beläge beschädigt oder abgelöst (< 40%). Richten der Stufen und Wangen. Neue Bodenbeläge. Rechen der Geländer. Verankerung überprüfen. Streichen aller Teile. |
| ○ | D | Erhebliche Schäden an Stufen und Treppenwangen. Verformungen der Treppenanlage sichtbar. Geländer an vielen Stellen gelöst. Sicherheit beeinträchtigt. Totalersatz der Treppe inkl. Geländer. |
| ○ | E | Nicht vorhanden. |

Anmerkung:

## Balkone, Loggien:

| | | |
|---|---|---|
| ○ | A | Keine sichtbaren Schäden am Balkonplatten, Belägen, Brüstungen und Anschlüssen. Entwässerung einwandfrei. Keine Kondensatschäden an Decke oder Boden in Balkonnähe sichtbar. Keine kostenwirksamen Massnahmen. |
| ○ | B | Unterwerk und Brüstungen verschmutzt. Örtliche Haarrisse vorhanden. Kleinere Schäden am Belag. Metallteile mit Oberflächenkorrosion und teilweise mangelhafter Verankerung. Schadhafte Stellen (< 10%). Entwässerung funktionsfähig. Punktuelle Betonrandbehandlung (< 10%). Belag erneuern. Metallteile teilweise neu verankern und Korrosionsschutz auffragen. Reinigung und Oberflächenbehandlung der Unterseiten und Brüstung. Prüfung auf Wärmebrücken durchführen. |
| ○ | C | Zahlreiche Risse und Abplatzungen (< 40%). Grössere Ablösungen am Bodenbelag. Entwässerung teils nicht funktionstüchtig. Metallteile korrodiert mit mangelhafter Verankerung. Fortgeschrittene Korrosionsschäden. Instandsetzen von Beton und Mauerwerk (< 40%). Erneuern von Belag und Entwässerung. Metallteile neu verankern und Korrosionsschutz aller Oberflächen. Prüfung auf Wärmebrücken durchführen. |
| ○ | D | Beträchtliche Risse und Abplatzungen. Vollständige Ablösung des Bodenbelags. Entwässerung nicht funktionstüchtig. Metallteile durchgerostet mit mangelhafter Verankerung. Beeinträchtigung der Sicherheit. Ausbessern (< 40%). Ganze Fläche schleifen und imprägnieren. Korrosionsschutz an Decke oder Boden in Balkonnähe. Erneuerung der Balkonplatte. Ersetzen von Brüstung und Metallteilen. Neuer Bodenbelag. Behandlung aller Oberflächen. Neue Entwässerung. Prüfung auf Wärmebrücken durchführen. |
| ○ | E | Nicht vorhanden. |

Anmerkung:

---

Erhebungsbogen

## 352 Deckenbeläge und 325 Bodenbeläge:                                     100 %

### Boden- und Deckenbeläge – Typ 1 Estrich:

| | | |
|---|---|---|
| ○ | A | Keine Risse und Abplatzungen erkennbar. Keine kostenwirksamen Massnahmen. |
| ○ | B | Spuren von Haarrissen und Abplatzungen. Dilatationen teilweise defekt. Beschädigte Fläche (< 10%). Estrich sanieren, inkl. Dilatationen. Isolierung gegen aufsteigende Feuchtigkeit. |
| ○ | C | Spuren von Haarrissen und Abplatzungen. Dilatationen teilweise defekt. Beschädigte Fläche (< 40%). Estrich sanieren, inkl. Dilatationen. Isolierung gegen aufsteigende Feuchtigkeit. |
| ○ | D | Flächige Risse, Abplatzungen. Erkennbarer Höhenversatz an Rissrändern. Beschädigte Flächen. Estrich sanieren, inkl. Dilatationen. Sachgemässer Einbau von Schwellfugen und Isolierung gegen aufsteigende Feuchtigkeit. Prüfung der Materialfestigkeit. |
| ○ | E | Nicht vorhanden. |

Anmerkung:

### Boden- und Deckenbeläge – Typ 2 Beton- und Naturwerkstein:

| | | |
|---|---|---|
| ○ | A | Belag in Ordnung. Fugen ausgefüllt. Sockelplatten vorhanden. Keine kostenwirksamen Massnahmen. |
| ○ | B | Stellenweise gelöste oder beschädigte Platten (<10%). Fugen teilweise ausgebrochen. Ersetzen von einzelnen Boden- und Sockelplatten (< 10%). Fugen nachbehalten. |
| ○ | C | Stellenweise gelöste oder beschädigte Platten (< 40%). Fugen teilweise ausgebrochen. Ersetzen von einzelnen Boden- und Sockelplatten (< 40%). Fugen nachbehalten. |
| ○ | D | Belag gelöst. Kein Reservematerial vorhanden. Neuer Plattenbelag. |
| ○ | E | Nicht vorhanden. |

Anmerkung:

### Boden- und Deckenbeläge – Typ 3 Kunststoff und textile Beläge:

| | | |
|---|---|---|
| ○ | A | Beläge in Ordnung. Keine Flecken oder Verschleissstellen. Sockelleisten in Ordnung. Keine kostenwirksamen Massnahmen. |
| ○ | B | Beläge teilweise erneuern (< 10%). Befestigung der gelösten Stellen. Sockelleisten ersetzen. |
| ○ | C | Teilweise Ablösungen und Verschleissstellen (< 40%). Sockelleisten beschädigt oder Nicht vorhanden. Beläge teilweise erneuern (< 40%). Befestigung der gelösten Stellen. Sockelleisten ersetzen. |
| ○ | D | Belag vollständig gelöst. Grössere Flecken und Verschleissstellen. Verbreitet Schäden an Unterlagsboden. Unterlagsboden teilweise neu erstellen. Komplett neuer Bodenbelag inkl. Sockelleisten. |
| ○ | E | Nicht vorhanden. |

Anmerkung:

### Boden- und Deckenbeläge – Typ 4 Parkett:

| | | |
|---|---|---|
| ○ | A | Parkett und Sockelleisten in Ordnung. Keine Flecken und Beschädigungen. Keine kostenwirksamen Massnahmen. |
| ○ | B | Parkett eben und in Ordnung. Örtliche Flecken und Verschleissstellen (< 10%). Sockelleisten beschädigt oder Nicht vorhanden. Schleifen und versiegeln. Sockelleisten ersetzen (< 10%) |
| ○ | C | Zahlreiche Flecken und Beschädigungen. Einheitsmässige Abnützung des Bodenbelags. Einheitsmässig teils (< 40%). Flecken und Verschleissstellen verbreitet. Sockelleisten beschädigt oder Nicht vorhanden. Schleifen und versiegeln. Sockelleisten ersetzen. |
| ○ | D | Lose Parkettlamellen und verbreitet Beschädigungen. Komplett neuer Parkettbelag inkl. Sockelleisten. Vorbehandlung des Unterlagsbodens. |
| ○ | E | Nicht vorhanden. |

Anmerkung:

**Erhebungsbogen**

Bodenbeläge – Typ 5 Hallenboden (Parkett, Linoleum):

Prozentanteil der Bekleidungsfläche: _____ %

| | | |
|---|---|---|
| ○ | A | Belag sauber und in gutem Zustand. Keine Flecken oder Verschleissstellen. Spielfeldmarkierungen einwandfrei. Keine kostenwirksamen Maßnahmen. |
| ○ | B | Örtliche Verschußstellen, Schutzbelag und Spielfeldmarkierungen vereinzelt beschädigt (< 10%). Spielfeldmarkierungen erneuern (< 10%). Oberflächenbehandlung. |
| ○ | C | Örtliche Verschußstellen, Schutzbelag und Spielfeldmarkierungen vereinzelt beschädigt (< 40%). Spielfeldmarkierungen erneuern (< 40%). Oberflächenbehandlung. |
| ○ | D | Belag vom Unterlagsboden teils gelöst. Grössere Flecken und Verschleissstellen. Schutzbelag und Spielfeldmarkierungen großflächig beschädigt. Unterlagsboden teilweise neu erstellen. Komplett neuer Bodenbelag inkl. Oberflächenbehandlung. |
| ○ | E | Nicht vorhanden. |

Anmerkung: _____

Boden- und Deckenbeläge – Typ 6 Keramik:

| | | |
|---|---|---|
| ○ | A | Belag in Ordnung, Fugen ausgefüllt. Sockelplatten vorhanden. Keine kostenwirksamen Maßnahmen. |
| ○ | B | Stellenweise gelöste oder beschädigte Platten. Fugen teilweise ausgebrochen (< 10%). |
| ○ | C | Stellenweise gelöste oder beschädigte Platten. Fugen teilweise ausgebrochen (< 40%). Fugen nacharbeiten. Ersetzen von einzelnen Boden- und Sockelplatten (<10%). Fugen nacharbeiten. |
| ○ | D | Belag gelöst. Kein Reservematerial vorhanden. Neuer Plattenbelag. Ersetzen von einzelnen Boden- und Sockelplatten (< 40%). |
| ○ | E | Nicht vorhanden. |

Anmerkung: _____

Decke Trittschalldämmung:

| | | |
|---|---|---|
| ○ | A | Trittschalldämmung in ausreichender Stärke vorhanden, flächengerecht verlegt und geschützt. Keine kostenwirksamen Maßnahmen. |
| ○ | B | Trittschalldämmung in ausreichender Stärke vorhanden. Örtliche Beschädigungen (< 10 %). Ausbesserung der bestehenden Trittschalldämmung (< 10%). |
| ○ | C | Trittschalldämmung unvollständig (< 40%). Stärke der Dämmschicht ist ungenügend. Erneuerung der bestehenden Trittschalldämmung, neuer Bodenaufbau in ausreichender Stärke. |
| ○ | D | Trittschalldämmung unvollständig, Stärke der Dämmschicht ist ungenügend. Beheglichkeit ungenügend. Erneuerung der bestehenden Trittschalldämmung, neuer Bodenaufbau in ausreichender Stärke. |
| ○ | E | Nicht vorhanden. |

Anmerkung: _____

**353  Deckenbekleidungen und 364 Dachbekleidungen**          100 %

Decken- und Dachbekleidungen – Typ 1 Gipskartondecke:

Prozentanteil der Bekleidungsfläche: _____ %

| | | |
|---|---|---|
| ○ | A | Deckenbekleidung in gutem Zustand. Oberflächen sauber. Keine kostenwirksamen Maßnahmen. |
| ○ | B | Oberfläche verschmutzt, örtliche Haarrisse (< 10%). Untergrund in gutem Zustand. Risse ausbessern (< 10%). Oberflächen neu streichen. |
| ○ | C | Ablösungen und Risse (< 40%). Oberfläche verschmutzt. Untergrund ausbessern. Einzelne Platten ersetzen (< 40%). Oberflächen streichen. |
| ○ | D | Oberfläche und Untergrund stark verschmutzt, beschädigt. Unabenheiten, Ablösungen, Platzeffekt, Risse. Untergrund neu erstellen und Deckenbekleidung erneuern (evtl. herabhängende Decke, Akustikdecke). |
| ○ | E | Nicht vorhanden. |

Anmerkung: _____

- 20 -

---

**Erhebungsbogen**

Decken- und Dachbekleidungen – Typ 2 Metallkassettendecke:

Prozentanteil der Bekleidungsfläche: _____ %

| | | |
|---|---|---|
| ○ | A | Deckenbekleidung in gutem Zustand. Oberflächen sauber. Keine kostenwirksamen Maßnahmen. |
| ○ | B | Oberfläche verschmutzt, vereinzelt Ablösungen (< 10%). Untergrund in gutem Zustand. Schadhafte Stellen ausbessern (< 10%). Oberflächen reinigen. |
| ○ | C | Ablösungen und Durchbiegungen (< 40%). Oberfläche verschmutzt. Untergrund ausbessern. Einzelne Platten ersetzen (< 40%). Oberflächen reinigen. |
| ○ | D | Die Oberfläche ist stark verschmutzt und beschädigt. Untergrund in schlechtem Zustand, Ablösungen und Durchbiegungen. Untergrund neu erstellen und Deckenbekleidung erneuern (evtl. herabhängende Decke, Akustikdecke). |
| ○ | E | Nicht vorhanden. |

Anmerkung: _____

Decken- und Dachbekleidungen – Typ 3 Holzverkleidung:

Prozentanteil der Bekleidungsfläche: _____ %

| | | |
|---|---|---|
| ○ | A | Holzverkleidung und Oberflächen in gutem Zustand. Keine kostenwirksamen Maßnahmen. |
| ○ | B | Holzverkleidung in gutem Zustand, Oberflächen verschmutzt, vereinzelte Risse (< 10 %). Komplette Oberflächenbehandlung. |
| ○ | C | Holzverkleidung teilweise beschädigt (< 40%). Oberflächen verschmutzt. Teilersatz der Holzverkleidung (< 40%). Komplette Oberflächenbehandlung. |
| ○ | D | Holzverkleidung in schlechtem Zustand, Fugen offen, Oberflächen verschmutzt. Holzverkleidung ersetzen inkl. Unterkonstruktion. Komplette Oberflächenbehandlung (evtl. herabhängende Decke, Akustikdecke). |
| ○ | E | Nicht vorhanden. |

Anmerkung: _____

Decken- und Dachbekleidungen – Typ 4 Ballwurfsichere Kassetten:

Prozentanteil der innenliegenden Wandbekleidungsfläche: _____ %

| | | |
|---|---|---|
| ○ | A | Metallpaneelen in gutem Zustand, genügt den behördlichen Vorschriften nach DIN 18032. Keine kostenwirksamen Maßnahmen. |
| ○ | B | Metallpaneelen in gutem Zustand, Oberflächen verschmutzt oder abgenutzt (< 10%). Komplette Oberflächenbehandlung. |
| ○ | C | Oberflächen verschmutzt mit örtlichen Beschädigungen (< 40%). Austausch beschädigter Metallpaneelen (< 40%). Komplette Oberflächenbehandlung. |
| ○ | D | Metallpaneelen in schlechtem Zustand. Oberfläche großflächig verschmutzt und beschädigt. Ersatz ballwurfsicherer Kassetten. |

Anmerkung: _____

- 21 -

Erhebungsbogen

# 360 Dächer

## 361 Dachkonstruktionen                                           100 %

**Dachkonstruktionen – Typ 1 Geneigte Dächer (Holzkonstruktion):**

Prozentanteil der Gründungsfläche (projizierte Dachfläche): _____ %

- O  A  Tragwerk in gutem Zustand. Keine Schäden oder Verformungen. Verbindungen intakt. Holzwerk gesund. Dachneigung und Dachüberstand ausreichend. Keine kostenwirksamen Maßnahmen.
- O  B  Tragwerk in Ordnung. Holzwerk gesund. Anzeichen von vereinzeltem Schädigungsbefall (< 10%). Holzschutzbehandlung für gesamtes Tragwerk.
- O  C  Teile des Tragwerks sind verformt. Schädigungsbefall (< 40%). Tragfähigkeit von Verbindungen vereinzelt beeinträchtigt. Beanspruchte Teile des Tragwerkes auswechseln oder verstärken (< 40%). Neue Verbindungen. Holzschutzbehandlung für gesamtes Tragwerk. Belüftung verbessern.
- O  D  Wichtige Teile des Tragwerks sind zerstört durch Insektenbefall (Hausbock). Durchgehende Risse und Verformungen sichtbar. Tragfähigkeit von Verbindungen beeinträchtigt. Vollständiger Ersatz des Tragwerkes. Dachneigung und Dachüberstand besichten.
- O  E  Nicht vorhanden.

Anmerkung:

**Dachkonstruktionen – Typ 2 Geneigte Dächer (Stahlkonstruktion):**

Prozentanteil der Gründungsfläche (projizierte Dachfläche): _____ %

- O  A  Tragwerk in gutem Zustand. Keine Schäden oder Verformungen sichtbar. Dachneigung und Dachüberstand ausreichend. Keine kostenwirksamen Maßnahmen.
- O  B  Tragwerk in Ordnung. Vereinzelt Anzeichen von Verformungen (< 10%). Beanspruchte Teile des Tragwerkes auswechseln oder verstärken.
- O  C  Teile des Tragwerkes sind verformt (< 40%). Tragfähigkeit von Verbindungen vereinzelt beeinträchtigt. Beanspruchte Teile des Tragwerkes auswechseln oder verstärken (< 40%).
- O  D  Wichtige Teile des Tragwerks sind zerstört Verformungen sichtbar. Tragfähigkeit von Verbindungen beeinträchtigt. Vollständiger Ersatz des Tragwerkes. Dachneigung und Dachüberstand besichten.
- O  E  Nicht vorhanden.

Anmerkung:

**Dachkonstruktionen – Typ 3 Flachdach:**

Prozentanteil der Gründungsfläche (projizierte Dachfläche): _____ %

- O  A  Tragwerk in gutem Zustand. Keine Durchbiegungen, Abplatzungen, Anschlüsse, Entwässerung intakt. Keine kostenwirksamen Maßnahmen.
- O  B  Tragwerk in Ordnung, keine Durchbiegungen. Örtliche Haarrisse (< 10%). Punktuelle Betonsanierung (< 10%).
- O  C  Zahlreiche Risse und Abplatzungen ohne Beeinträchtigung der Sicherheit. Dilatationen teilweise defekt. Teile des Tragwerks stark verformt. Örtliches Eindringen von Feuchtigkeit (< 40%). Beanspruchte Teile des Tragwerkes auswechseln oder verstärken. Verbindungen und Dilatationen erneuern (< 40%). Prüfung auf Wärmebrücken durchführen.
- O  D  Wichtige Teile des Tragwerks sind zerstört. Tragfähigkeit von Verbindungen beeinträchtigt. Zahlreiche Risse und Abplatzungen mit Beeinträchtigung der Sicherheit. Entwässerung nicht funktionsfähig. Vollständiger Ersatz des Tragwerks, inkl. Entwässerung. Prüfung auf Wärmebrücken.
- O  E  Nicht vorhanden.

Anmerkung:

---

Erhebungsbogen

**Dachkonstruktionen – Typ 4 Flachdach, begrünt:**

Prozentanteil der Gründungsfläche (projizierte Dachfläche): _____ %                     100 %

- O  A  Tragwerk in gutem Zustand. Keine Durchbiegungen und Abplatzungen. Anschlüsse und Entwässerung intakt. Keine kostenwirksamen Maßnahmen.
- O  B  Tragwerk in Ordnung, keine Durchbiegungen. Örtliche Haarrisse (< 10%). Punktuelle Betonsanierung (< 10%).
- O  C  Zahlreiche Risse und Abplatzungen ohne Beeinträchtigung der Sicherheit. Dilatationen teilweise defekt. Teile des Tragwerks stark verformt. Örtliches Eindringen von Feuchtigkeit (< 40%). Beanspruchte Teile des Tragwerkes auswechseln oder verstärken. Verbindungen und Dilatationen erneuern (< 40%). Prüfung auf Wärmebrücken durchführen.
- O  D  Wichtige Teile des Tragwerks sind zerstört. Tragfähigkeit von Verbindungen beeinträchtigt. Zahlreiche Risse und Abplatzungen mit Beeinträchtigung der Sicherheit. Entwässerung nicht funktionsfähig. Vollständiger Ersatz des Tragwerks, inkl. Entwässerung. Prüfung auf Wärmebrücken.
- O  E  Nicht vorhanden.

Anmerkung:

## 362 Dachfenster, Dachöffnungen                                 100 %

**Dachfenster – Typ 1 Kunststoff:**

Prozentanteil der Dachfläche: _____ %

- O  A  Sämtliche Fenster in gutem Zustand. Dämmung geeignet. Schliessung funktioniert. Keine kostenwirksamen Maßnahmen.
- O  B  Oberflächen außen verschmutzt, beschädigt (< 10%). Schliessung funktioniert. Aussere Oberflächenbehandlung mit Versiegelung gegen Außenwand (< 10%).
- O  C  Oberflächen innen und außen verschmutzt oder beschädigt (< 40%). Schliessung funktioniert, vereinzelt undichte Stellen. Beschläge teilweise lose. Komplette Oberflächenbehandlung und Versiegelung gegen Außenwand. Neue Kittfugen oder Glasleisten (< 40%). Beschläge richten. Energienachweis.
- O  D  Sämtliche Fenster beschädigt. Schliessung und Bedienung nicht funktionsfähig. Ungenügende Wärmedämmung. Kompletter Ersatz der Fenster und Versiegelung gegen Mauerwerk. Energieberater hinzuziehen.
- O  E  Nicht vorhanden.

Anmerkung:

**Dachfenster – Typ 2 Holz:**

Prozentanteil der Dachfläche: _____ %

- O  A  Sämtliche Fenster in gutem Zustand. Dämmung geeignet. Schliessung funktioniert. Keine kostenwirksamen Maßnahmen.
- O  B  Oberflächen außen beschädigt (< 10%). Schliessung funktioniert. Aussere Oberflächenbehandlung mit Versiegelung gegen Außenwand (< 10%).
- O  C  Oberflächen innen und außen beschädigt (< 40%). Schliessung funktioniert, vereinzelt undichte Stellen. Beschläge teilweise lose. Komplette Oberflächenbehandlung und Versiegelung gegen Außenwand. Neue Kittfugen oder Glasleisten (< 40%). Beschläge richten. Energienachweis.
- O  D  Sämtliche Fenster beschädigt. Flügel und Rahmen verwittert. Schliessung und Bedienung nicht funktionsfähig. Ungenügende Wärmedämmung. Kompletter Ersatz der Fenster. Oberflächenbehandlung und Versiegelung gegen Mauerwerk. Energieberater hinzuziehen.
- O  E  Nicht vorhanden.

Anmerkung:

**Erhebungsbogen**

## Dachfenster – Typ 3 Aluminium:

Prozentanteil der Dachfläche: _____ %

| | | |
|---|---|---|
| ○ | A | Sämtliche Fenster in gutem Zustand. Dämmung genügend. Schliessung funktioniert. Keine kostenwirksamen Massnahmen. |
| ○ | B | Oberflächen aussen verschmutzt, beschädigt (< 10%). Schliessung funktioniert. Aussere Oberflächenbehandlung mit Versiegelung gegen Aussenwand (<10%). |
| ○ | C | Oberflächen innen und aussen verschmutzt, beschädigt (< 40%). Schliessung funktioniert, vereinzelt undichte Stellen. Beschläge teilweise lose. Komplette Oberflächenbehandlung und Versiegelung gegen Aussenwand. Neue Kittfugen oder Glasleisten (< 40 %). Beschläge richten. Energienachweis. |
| ○ | D | Sämtliche Fenster beschädigt. Schliessung und Bedienung nicht funktionsfähig. Ungenügende Wärmedämmung. Kompletter Ersatz der Fenster und Versiegelung gegen Mauerwerk. Energieberater hinzuziehen. |
| ○ | E | Nicht vorhanden. |

Anmerkung:

## Dachöffnungen – Typ 1 Dachgaube, Putz:

Prozentanteil der Dachfläche: _____ %

| | | |
|---|---|---|
| ○ | A | Aufbauten in gutem Zustand und sauber. Keine Risse vorhanden. Blechteile in gutem Zustand. Keine kostenwirksamen Massnahmen. |
| ○ | B | Putzschäden, Anstrich schmutzig und verwittert. Blechteile teilweise gelöst (<10%). Ausbessern des Putzes, neue Oberflächenbehandlung. Befestigen der Blechteile (< 10%). |
| ○ | C | Umfangreiche Putzschäden und Risse. Anstrich schmutzig und verwittert. Blechteile gelöst und beschädigt (< 40%). Putzsanierung der Oberfläche, Blechteile ersetzen (< 40%). Neue Oberflächenbehandlung |
| ○ | D | Putzschäden über ganze Fläche. Blechteile grösstenteils gelöst und beschädigt. Neu verputzen der gesamten Oberfläche inkl. Streichen. Alte Blechteile ersetzen. |
| ○ | E | Nicht vorhanden. |

Anmerkung:

## Dachöffnungen – Typ 2 Dachgaube, Verkleidung:

Prozentanteil der Dachfläche: _____ %

| | | |
|---|---|---|
| ○ | A | Abdeckung und Verkleidung in gutem Zustand. Dämmung ausreichend. An- und Abschlüsse an die Dachhaut intakt. Keine kostenwirksamen Massnahmen. |
| ○ | B | Abdeckung in gutem Zustand, Verkleidung, An- und Abschlüsse gelöst oder beschädigt (< 10%). Dichtigkeit nicht mehr sichergestellt. Auswechseln von Abdeckung und Verkleidung (<10 %). Neue An- und Abschlüsse. |
| ○ | C | Abdeckung in gutem Zustand, Verkleidung, An- und Abschlüsse gelöst oder beschädigt (< 40%). Dichtigkeit nicht mehr sichergestellt. Auswechseln von Abdeckung und Verkleidung (< 40%). Neue An- und Abschlüsse. |
| ○ | D | Erhebliche Schäden an Abdeckung und Verkleidung. Wärmedämmung mangelhaft. An- und Abschlüsse an Dachhaut in schlechtem Zustand. Undichte Stellen. Neuaufbau ab bestehender Dachkonstruktion. Wärmedämmung, hinterlüftete Blechverkleidung. Neue An- und Abschlüsse an die Dachhaut. |
| ○ | E | Nicht vorhanden. |

Anmerkung:

- 24 -

---

**Erhebungsbogen**

### 363 Dachbeläge

## Dachbeläge – Typ 1 Geneigte Dächer: Ziegeldach

Prozentanteil der Dachfläche: _____ %

| | | |
|---|---|---|
| ○ | A | Deckung in sauberem und gutem Zustand. Wasserdichtheit gewährleistet. Abschlüsse in Ordnung. Keine kostenwirksamen Massnahmen. |
| ○ | B | Deckung in gutem Zustand. Diverse Ziegel verschmutzt und verschoben. Teile der Firstziegel gelöst. Wasserdichtheit gewährleistet. Abschlüsse aus Holz teilweise lose und verschmutzt (< 10%). Auswechseln von Ziegeln (< 10%). Abschlüsse in Holz richten, streichen. |
| ○ | C | Ziegel grösstenteils von verschmutzten und defekt. Firstziegel gelöst und verschoben. Örtliche Wassereintritte. Abschlüsse aus Holz beschädigt. Metallteile rostig (< 40%). Auswechseln von Ziegeln (< 40%). Abschlüsse in Holz teilweise ersetzen und streichen. Metallteile auswechseln. |
| ○ | D | Deckung erheblich beschädigt. Verbreitet Wassereintritte. Lüftung teilweise verlauft. Dachdeckung vollständig ersetzen inkl. Konterlattung, Holzabschlüsse, Metallteile ersetzen. |
| ○ | E | Nicht vorhanden. |

Anmerkung:

## Dachbeläge – Typ 2 Geneigte Dächer: Schieferdach:

Prozentanteil der Dachfläche: _____ %

| | | |
|---|---|---|
| ○ | A | Deckung in sauberem und gutem Zustand. Wasserdichtheit gewährleistet. Abschlüsse in Ordnung. Keine kostenwirksamen Massnahmen. |
| ○ | B | Deckung in gutem Zustand. Diverse Platten verschmutzt und verschoben. Teile der Firstziegel gelöst. Wasserdichtheit gewährleistet. Abschlüsse aus Holz teilweise lose und verschmutzt (< 10%). Auswechseln von Platten (< 10%). Abschlüsse in Holz richten, streichen. |
| ○ | C | Platten grösstenteils von verschmutzten und defekt. Firstziegel gelöst und verschoben. Örtliche Wassereintritte. Abschlüsse aus Holz beschädigt. Metallteile rostig (< 40%). Auswechseln von Platten (< 40%). Abschlüsse in Holz teilweise ersetzen und streichen. Metallteile auswechseln. |
| ○ | D | Deckung erheblich beschädigt. Verbreitet Wassereintritte. Lüftung teilweise verlauft. Dachdeckung vollständig ersetzen inkl. Konterlattung, Holzabschlüsse, Metallteile ersetzen. |
| ○ | E | Nicht vorhanden. |

Anmerkung:

## Dachbeläge – Typ 3 Geneigte Dächer: Metalldach (Trapezblech, Stehfalzdach)

Prozentanteil der Dachfläche: _____ %

| | | |
|---|---|---|
| ○ | A | Dach ist dicht. An- und Abschlüsse intakt. Metallbleche sind sauber, vollfarbig vorhanden. Keine kostenwirksamen Massnahmen. |
| ○ | B | Dach ist dicht. Örtlicher Abblätterungen von An- und Abschlüssen (< 10%). An- und Abschlüsse örtlich neu ausführen (< 10%). |
| ○ | C | Dach ist dicht. Örtlicher Abblätterungen von An- und Abschlüssen (< 40%). An- und Abschlüsse örtlich neu ausführen (< 40%). |
| ○ | D | Dach ist undicht. An- und Abschlüsse an mehreren Stellen abgelöst oder beschädigt. Neuer Dachaufbau mit allen An- und Abschlüssen. |

Anmerkung:

- 25 -

Erhebungsbogen

## Dachbeläge – Typ 4 Geneigte Dächer: Wellzementplatten

Prozentanteil der Dachfläche: _____ %

| | | |
|---|---|---|
| O | A | Dach ist dicht. An- und Abschlüsse intakt. Zementplatten sind sauber, vollflächig vorhanden. Keine kostenwirksamen Maßnahmen. |
| O | B | Dach ist dicht. Örtlicher Ablösungen von An- und Abschlüssen (< 10%). |
| O | C | Dach ist dicht. Örtlicher Ablösungen von An- und Abschlüssen (< 40%). An- und Abschlüsse örtlich neu ausführen. |
| O | D | Dach ist undicht. An- und Abschlüsse an mehreren Stellen abgelöst oder beschädigt. Neuer Dachaufbau mit allen An- und Abschlüssen. |

Anmerkung:

## Dachbeläge – Typ 5 Flachdach begehbar:

Prozentanteil der Dachfläche: _____ %

| | | |
|---|---|---|
| O | A | Flachdach ist dicht. An- und Abschlüsse intakt. Brüstungen und Geländer in Ordnung. Gehbelag ist eben und sauber. Keine kostenwirksamen Maßnahmen. |
| O | B | Flachdach ist dicht trotz örtlicher Ablösungen von An- und Abschlüssen. Schäden an Brüstungen und Geländer. Gehbelag uneben, Fugen vermoost (< 10%). Brüstung und Geländer reparieren. Gehbelag richten und defekte Platten ersetzen (< 10%). |
| O | C | Flachdach ist dicht trotz örtlicher Ablösungen von An- und Abschlüssen. Schäden an Brüstungen und Geländer. Gehbelag uneben, Fugen vermoost (< 40%). An- und Abschlüsse örtlich neu ausführen. Brüstung und Geländer reparieren. Gehbelag richten und defekte Platten ersetzen (< 40%). |
| O | D | Flachdach undicht. An- und Abschlüsse an mehreren Stellen abgelöst oder beschädigt. Gehbelag uneben und Fugen vermoost. Brüstungen und Geländer beschädigt. Sicherheit nicht gewährleistet. Neuer Aufbau des Flachdaches mit allen An- und Abschlüssen. Neuer Gehbelag, Brüstung und Geländer erneuern. |
| O | E | Nicht vorhanden. |

Anmerkung:

## Dachbeläge – Typ 6 Flachdach nicht begehbar:

Prozentanteil der Dachfläche: _____ %

| | | |
|---|---|---|
| O | A | Flachdach ist dicht. Schutzschicht ist sauber und vollflächig vorhanden. Keine kostenwirksamen Maßnahmen. |
| O | B | Flachdach ist dicht trotz örtlicher Ablösungen von An- und Abschlüssen. Schutzschicht ist ungleichmäßig und vermoost (< 10%). |
| O | C | Flachdach ist dicht trotz örtlicher Ablösungen von An- und Abschlüssen. Schutzschicht ist ungleichmäßig und vermoost (< 40%). Schutzschicht erneuern. |
| O | D | Flachdach undicht. An- und Abschlüsse an mehreren Stellen abgelöst oder beschädigt. Schutzschicht ungleichmäßig und vermoost. Neuer Aufbau des Flachdaches mit allen An- und Abschlüssen. Neue Schutzschicht. |
| O | E | Nicht vorhanden. |

Anmerkung:

Erhebungsbogen

## Dachbeläge – Dachabschlüsse, Dachentwässerung:

| | | |
|---|---|---|
| O | A | Alle Blechteile intakt. Keine Korrosion. An- und Abschlüsse fachgerecht ausgeführt. Keine kostenwirksamen Maßnahmen. |
| O | B | Blechteile beschädigt oder mit Korrosionsstellen (< 10%). Funktion nicht beeinträchtigt. |
| O | C | Blechteile reparieren (< 10%) und mit einem Schutzanstrich versehen. |
| O | D | Blechteile beschädigt oder mit Korrosionsstellen (< 40%). Funktion nicht beeinträchtigt. Blechteile reparieren (< 40%) und mit neuem Schutzanstrich versehen. |
| O | D | Blechteile vielfalt, erhebliche Korrosionsschäden. Rinnen und Ablaufrohre mit Leckstellen. Alle Blechteile ersetzen unter Verwendung von korrosionsfreien Materialien. |
| O | E | Nicht vorhanden. |

Anmerkung:

## Dach Wärmedämmung:

| | | |
|---|---|---|
| O | A | Wärmedämmung fachgerecht verlegt und geschützt. Keine kostenwirksamen Maßnahmen. |
| O | B | Wärmedämmung mit örtliche Beschädigungen (<10%). |
| O | C | Ausbesserung der bestehenden Wärmedämmung (< 10%). Energiebilanz und Prüfung auf Wärmebrücken durchführen. |
| O | C | Wärmedämmung mit örtliche Beschädigungen (<40%). Ausbesserung der bestehenden Wärmedämmung (< 40%). Prüfung auf Wärmebrücken durchführen. |
| O | D | Wärmedämmung unvollständig oder Stärke der Dämmschicht ist ungenügend. Örtliche Durchnässung oder Beschädigung. Neue Wärmedämmung ab bestehender Dampfbremse. Nicht zugängliche Hohlräume mit umweltfreundlichen Dämmmaterial füllen. Energiebilanz und Prüfung auf Wärmebrücken durchführen. |
| O | E | Nicht vorhanden. |

Anmerkung:

## 370 Baukonstruktive Einbauten
## 371 Allgemeine Einbauten – Einbauten wie Gestühle, Garderoben, Einbauküchen:

| | | |
|---|---|---|
| O | A | Oberflächen, Beschläge, An- und Abschlüsse in gutem Zustand. Keine kostenwirksamen Maßnahmen. |
| O | B | Oberflächen, Beschläge, An- und Abschlüsse verschmutzt und leicht beschädigt (< 20%). Komplette Oberflächenbehandlung. |
| O | C | Oberflächen, Beschläge, An- und Abschlüsse verschmutzt und beschädigt (< 50%). Teilersatz der Beschläge, Verkleidungen (< 50 %), komplette Oberflächenbehandlung. |
| O | D | Oberflächen, Beschläge, An- und Abschlüsse in schlechtem Zustand, offene Fugen, Komplette Erneuerung der Einbauten. |
| O | E | Nicht vorhanden. |

Anmerkung:

## 372 Besondere Einbauten (wie Tafeln in Unterrichtsräumen, Einbauten in naturwissen-schaftlichen Räumen, Werkbänke in Werkhalle und dgl.):

| | | |
|---|---|---|
| O | A | Besondere Einbauten neu oder in gut gepflegtem Zustand. Keine kostenwirksamen Maßnahmen. |
| O | B | Großteil der Einbauten neu oder in gutem Zustand. Vereinzelt Beschädigungen (< 20 %). Beschädigte Elemente austauschen. Fugen auslösen. Oberflächenbehandlung. |
| O | C | Großteil der Einbauten neu oder in gutem Zustand. Vereinzelt Beschädigungen, offene Kanten und Fugen (< 50%). Beschädigte Elemente austauschen. Fugen auslösen. Oberflächenbehandlung. |
| O | D | Großteil der Einbauten veraltet und in schlechtem Zustand. Offene Kanten und Fugen. Neue Einbauten. Erforderliche Nutzungsflexibilität beachten. |
| O | E | Nicht vorhanden. |

Anmerkung:

Erhebungsbogen

## 3.2 Zustandserfassung Technische Anlagen

### 410 Abwasser-, Wasser-, Gasanlagen

### 411 Abwasseranlagen:

- [ ] A   Abläufe und Abwasserleitungen intakt. Keine Beanstandungen. Keine kostenwirksamen Maßnahmen.
- [ ] B   Abläufe und Abwasserleitungen intakt. Durchfluss örtlich nicht gewährleistet (< 10%). Geräuschemissionen.
- [ ] C   Ausbohren und Spülen der Leitungen (< 10%). Dämmungen an zugänglichen Stellen. Abläufe und Abwasserleitungen funktionsfähig. Durchfluss örtlich nicht gewährleistet (< 40%). Punktuelle Korrosionsstellen. Aufhängungen beschädigt. Teilersatz des Leitungsnetzes (< 40 %). Spülen der Leitungen.
- [ ] D   Fortgeschrittene Korrosionsanscheinungen am ganzen Leitungsnetz. Ungenügendes Gefälle wie z.B. geschweisste Stahlrohre. Schlechter Abfluss Durchfluss nicht gewährleistet. Totalersatz des Leitungsnetzes.
- [ ] E   Nicht vorhanden.

Anmerkung:

### 412 Wasseranlagen – Rohleitungen:

- [ ] A   Leitungen in Ordnung, keine Beschädigungen sichtbar. Guter Durchfluss, Leitungsarmaturen sind dicht und regulierbar. Dämmung vollständig (bei dezentraler Wassererwärmung). Keine kostenwirksamen Maßnahmen.
- [ ] B   Leitungen in Ordnung. Guter Durchfluss. Leitungsarmaturen vereinzelt undicht oder schlecht regulierbar (< 10%). Dämmung teilweise mangelhaft (bei dezentraler Wassererwärmung).
- [ ] C   Leitungen in Ordnung. Guter Durchfluss. Leitungsarmaturen vereinzelt undicht oder schlecht regulierbar (< 40%). Dämmung teilweise mangelhaft (bei dezentraler Wassererwärmung). Auswechseln beschädigter Armaturen und Teilstücken (< 10%). Ausbessern der Dämmung soweit zugänglich (bei dezentraler Wassererwärmung).
- [ ] D   Ganzes Leitungsnetz beschädigt oder korrodiert. Schlechter Durchfluss infolge Verkalkung. Leitungsarmaturen undicht oder schlecht regulierbar. Totalersatz des Leitungsnetzes inkl. Dämmung und Einbau von Durchflussbegrenzern.
- [ ] E   Nicht vorhanden.

### Wasseranlagen – Dezentrale Wassererwärmer:

Anzahl dezentraler Wassererwärmer im Gebäude: _____ Stück

- [ ] A   Dezentrale Wassererwärmer in Ordnung. Warmwassermenge genügend bei einer Temperatur von 60°C. Keine kostenwirksamen Maßnahmen.
- [ ] B   Dezentrale Wassererwärmer beschädigt oder korrodiert. Leitungsarmaturen teilweise undicht (< 10%). Auswechseln von Wassererwärmer, beschädigter Dichtungen und Leitungsarmaturen (< 10%). Bei Wunsch nach zentraler Wassererwärmung: Energieberater hinzuziehen.
- [ ] C   Dezentrale Wassererwärmer beschädigt oder korrodiert. Leitungsarmaturen teilweise undicht (< 40%). Auswechseln von Wassererwärmer, beschädigter Dichtungen und Leitungsarmaturen (< 40%). Bei Wunsch nach zentraler Wassererwärmung: Energieberater hinzuziehen.
- [ ] D   Fortgeschrittene Korrosionserscheinungen an Wassererwärmer und Leitungen. Defekte Leitungsarmaturen, schlechte Dämmung. Wassermenge ungenügend. Ersetzen der Wassererwärmer und Warmwasserleitungen. Bei Wunsch nach zentraler Wassererwärmung: Energieberater hinzuziehen.
- [ ] E   Nicht vorhanden.

Anmerkung:

- 28 -

---

Erhebungsbogen

### Wasseranlagen – Sanitärobjekte Typ 1 mit wassergespülten Urinalen:

Anzahl wassergespülter Urinale (grob): _____ %

- [ ] A   Sanitäre Apparate (Armaturen, Waschbecken, WCs, Urinale) intakt, elektrische Installationen genügend. Keine kostenwirksamen Maßnahmen.
- [ ] B   Sanitäre Apparate mit leichten Abnutzungen. Elastische Fugen teilweise ausgebrochen oder verschmutzt (<10%). Elektrische Installationen genügend und intakt. Auswechseln beschädigter sanitären Apparaten (<10%). Schadhafte Armaturen erneuern.
- [ ] C   Einzelne sanitäre Apparate beschädigt (<40%). Bedienungsarmaturen veraltet und undicht. Fugen verschmutzt, teils ausgebrochen. Elektrische Installationen intakt. Auswechseln beschädigter sanitären Apparaten (<40%). Schadhafte Armaturen erneuern.
- [ ] D   Sanitäre Apparate in Bad/WCs, größtenteils beschädigt. Bedienungsarmaturen veraltet und undicht. Fugen verschmutzt, größtenteils ausgebrochen. Elektrische Installationen teils nicht funktionsfähig. Neue Sanitäreinrichtungen mit Warmwasser-Durchflussbegrenzer. Neue elektrische Installationen.
- [ ] E   Nicht vorhanden.

Anmerkung:

### Wasseranlagen – Sanitärobjekte Typ 2 mit wasserlosen Urinalen:

Anzahl wasserloser Urinale (grob): _____ %

- [ ] A   Sanitäre Apparate (Armaturen, Waschbecken, WCs, Urinale) intakt, elektrische Installationen genügend. Keine kostenwirksamen Maßnahmen.
- [ ] B   Sanitäre Apparate mit leichten Abnutzungen. Elastische Fugen teilweise ausgebrochen oder verschmutzt (< 10%). Elektrische Installationen genügend und intakt. Auswechseln beschädigter sanitären Apparaten (<10%). Schadhafte Armaturen erneuern.
- [ ] C   Einzelne sanitäre Apparate beschädigt (< 40%). Bedienungsarmaturen veraltet und undicht. Fugen verschmutzt, teils ausgebrochen. Elektrische Installationen intakt. Auswechseln beschädigter sanitären Apparaten (< 40%). Schadhafte Armaturen erneuern.
- [ ] D   Sanitäre Apparate in Bad/WCs, größtenteils beschädigt. Bedienungsarmaturen veraltet und undicht. Fugen verschmutzt, größtenteils ausgebrochen. Elektrische Installationen teils nicht funktionsfähig. Neue Sanitäreinrichtungen mit Warmwasser-Durchflussbegrenzer. Neue elektrische Installationen.
- [ ] E   Nicht vorhanden.

Anmerkung:

### 420 Wärmeversorgungsanlagen

### 421 Wärmeerzeugungsanlagen

### Wärmeerzeugungsanlagen – Typ 1: mit zentraler Warmwassererwärmung: _____ 100 %

Prozentanteil der Wärmeerzeugungsanlagen im Gebäude: _____ %

- [ ] A   Wärmeerzeugung in gutem Zustand. Anlage genügt den Vorschriften. Keine kostenwirksamen Maßnahmen.
- [ ] B   Pumpen und Verteiler revisionsbedürftig. Dämmung teilweise beschädigt. Gelegentliche Klagen über zu hohe oder zu tiefe Raumtemperaturen (< 10%). Revision der Pumpen und des Verteilers (< 10%). Dämmung ausbessern. Energieberater hinzuziehen.
- [ ] C   Pumpen und Verteiler revisionsbedürftig. Dämmung teilweise beschädigt. Gelegentliche Klagen über zu hohe oder zu tiefe Raumtemperaturen (< 40%). Revision der Pumpen und des Verteilers (< 40%).
- [ ] D   Pumpen und Verteiler revisionsbedürftig. Korrosionsschäden an diversen Stellen. Dämmung mangelhaft. Vereinzelt Klagen über zu hohe oder zu tiefe Raumtemperaturen. Vollständiger Ersatz der Anlage. Energieberater hinzuziehen. Rechtliche Rahmenbedingungen und Auflagen abklären. Einbau Wärmezähler.
- [ ] E   Nicht vorhanden.

Anmerkung:

- 29 -

**Erhebungsbogen**

Wärmeerzeugungsanlagen – Typ 2: ohne zentrale Warmwassererwärmung:

Prozentanteil der Wärmeversorgungsanlagen im Gebäude: _____ %

| | | |
|---|---|---|
| ○ | A | Wärmeerzeugung in gutem Zustand. Anlage genügt den Vorschriften. Keine kostenwirksamen Maßnahmen. |
| ○ | B | Pumpen und Verteiler revisionsbedürftig, Dämmung teilweise beschädigt. Gelegentliche Klagen über zu hohe oder zu tiefe Raumtemperaturen (< 10%). Revision der Pumpen und des Verteilers (< 10%). Dämmung ausbessern. Energieberater hinzuziehen. |
| ○ | C | Pumpen und Verteiler revisionsbedürftig, Dämmung teilweise beschädigt. Gelegentliche Klagen über zu hohe oder zu tiefe Raumtemperaturen (< 40%). Revision der Pumpen und des Verteilers (< 40%). Dämmung ausbessern. Energieberater hinzuziehen. |
| ○ | D | Pumpen und Verteiler revisionsbedürftig. Korrosionsschäden an diversen Stellen. Dämmung mangelhaft. Verstärkt Klagen über zu hohe oder zu tiefe Raumtemperaturen. Vollständiger Ersatz der Anlage. Energieberater hinzuziehen. Rechtliche Rahmenbedingungen und Auflagen abklären. Einbau Wärmezähler. |
| ○ | E | Nicht vorhanden. |

Anmerkung.

422  Wärmeverteilnetze (mit/ ohne zentraler Warmwassererwärmung):

| | | |
|---|---|---|
| ○ | A | Keine sichtbaren Roststellen. Armaturen funktionstüchtig. Verteilung tadellos gedämmt. Keine kalten Heizkörper oder Störungsgeräusche. Keine kostenwirksamen Maßnahmen. |
| ○ | B | Punktuelle Roststellen und teilweise undichte Stellen an den Armaturen. Dämmung teilweise mangelhaft (< 10%). Geräusche. Anlage schlecht entlüftbar. Einige Heizkörper werden nicht richtig warm. Strömungsgeräusche hörbar. Reparaturen am Netz. Ausbesserung der Dämmung (< 10%). Hydraulischer Abgleich. |
| ○ | C | Verteilung hat Lecks und Roststellen (< 40%). Dämmung nicht vorhanden oder ungenügend. Teilersatz der Kellerverteilung und Armaturen. Verteilung neu dämmen (< 40%). Einbau Wärmezähler im Rahmen der Erneuerung der Heizungsanlage. |
| ○ | D | Verteilung hat Lecks und Roststellen. Dämmung nicht vorhanden oder ungenügend. Vollersatz der horizontalen Leitungen. Ersatz von Steigsträngen. Einbau Wärmezähler im Rahmen der Erneuerung der Heizungsanlage. |
| ○ | E | Nicht vorhanden. |

Anmerkung.

423  Raumheizflächen                    100 %

Raumheizflächen – Typ 1 Heizkörper:

Prozentanteil der beheizbaren Fläche: _____ %

| | | |
|---|---|---|
| ○ | A | Heizkörper in gutem Zustand, sauber und ohne Roststellen. Regulierung und Entlüftung funktionieren. Vorlauftemperatur liegt im Normalfall unter 60 °C. Keine sichtbaren Roststellen. Armaturen funktionstüchtig. Keine kostenwirksamen Maßnahmen. |
| ○ | B | Einzelne Heizkörper verschmutzt, schlechter Durchfluss. Anlage verschlammt (< 10%). Vorlauftemperatur liegt im Normalfall über 60 °C. Dämmung der Rohrleitungen. Heizkörper entsprechen nicht mehr den Vorschriften. Alte Aufputzanlagen. Aus- und Einbau, Entschlammen und Streichen der Heizkörper (< 10%). Fühler, Entlüften der Anlage. |
| ○ | C | Heizkörper verschmutzt Korrosionsschäden. Schlechter Durchfluss. Anlage verschlammt. Ventile schlecht regulierbar. Anschlüsse undicht (< 40%). Vorlauftemperatur liegt im Normalfall unter 60 °C. Dämmung der Rohrleitungen und Heizkörper teils ungenügend. Ersatz aller Ventile durch Thermostatventile. Teilersatz durch neue Heizkörper (< 40%). Ausbau der übrigen Heizkörper, Entschlammen und Streichen. |
| ○ | D | Sanitäre Heizkörper veraltet, beschädigt und schlecht regulierbar. Standorte ungünstig. Mangelhafte Dämmung der Rohrleitungen und Heizkörper. Ersatz durch neue Heizkörper mit Thermostatventilen. Dämmung der Rohrleitungen und Heizkörper. Energieberater hinzuziehen. |
| ○ | E | Nicht vorhanden. |

Anmerkung.

---

**Erhebungsbogen**

Raumheizflächen – Typ 2 Boden- oder Deckenheizung:

Prozentanteil der beheizbaren Fläche: _____ %

| | | |
|---|---|---|
| ○ | A | Anlage funktioniert und ist gut regulierbar. Keine kostenwirksamen Maßnahmen. |
| ○ | B | Anlage funktioniert und ist schlecht regulierbar. Vereinzelt Beschwerden über zu hohe oder zu niedrige Raumtemperaturen (< 10%). Anlage bleibt bestehen. Ventile und Armaturen auswechseln (< 10%). Durchspülen der Anlage. |
| ○ | C | Anlage funktioniert und ist schlecht regulierbar. Vereinzelt Beschwerden über zu hohe oder zu niedrige Raumtemperaturen (< 40%). Anlage bleibt bestehen. Ventile und Armaturen auswechseln (< 40%). Durchspülen der Anlage. |
| ○ | D | Anlage mangelhaft und beschädigt. Teilbereiche der Anlage fallen aus, nicht mehr regulierbar. Anlage stilllegen, Systemwechsel auf Heizkörper. Energieberater hinzuziehen. |
| ○ | E | Nicht vorhanden. |

Anmerkung.

430  Lufttechnische Anlagen

Lüftungsanlagen – Teilklimaanlagen, Klimaanlagen:

| | | |
|---|---|---|
| ○ | A | Luftaustausch ausreichend. Keine Geruchs wahrnehmbar. Anlage funktionstüchtig und gut regulierbar. Keine kostenwirksamen Maßnahmen. |
| ○ | B | Luftaustausch ausreichend. Vereinzelt Klagen über Luftmenge/ -qualität, Zugerscheinungen einzelner Räume (< 10%). Überprüfung der Ventilatoren. Kanäle einzelner Räume. Teilersatz der bestehenden Anlage (< 10%). |
| ○ | C | Luftaustausch ausreichend. Vereinzelt Klagen über Luftmenge/ -qualität, Zugerscheinungen einzelner Räume (< 40%). Überprüfung der Ventilatoren. Kanäle einzelner Räume. Teilersatz der bestehenden Anlage (< 40%). |
| ○ | D | Be- und Entlüftung/ Klimatisierung der Räume ungenügend. Gerüche und Feuchtigkeit. Modernisierung der Anlage in bestehenden oder neuen Kanälen. Elektrische Installationen. Wärmerückgewinnung integrieren. |
| ○ | E | Nicht vorhanden. |

Anmerkung.

440  Starkstromanlagen

441  Hoch- und Mittelspannungsanlagen, 445 Beleuchtungsanlagen:

| | | |
|---|---|---|
| ○ | A | Keine offensichtlichen Mängel und Widersprüche gegenüber den Vorschriften. Keine kostenwirksamen Maßnahmen. |
| ○ | B | Elektrische Installationen teilweise mangelhaft, zu schwache Absicherung (< 10%). Neuinstallation von Unterzuteilungen (< 10%). Neue Unterverteilung mit Fehlerstromschutzschalter. |
| ○ | C | Elektrische Installationen teilweise mangelhaft, zu schwache Absicherung (< 40%). Neuinstallation von Unterzuteilungen (< 40%). Neue Unterverteilung mit Fehlerstromschutzschalter. |
| ○ | D | Installationen veraltet, entsprechen nicht mehr den Vorschriften. Alte Aufputzanlagen. Absicherung zu schwach. Totalersatz der Elektroinstallationen. Neue Unterverteilung abgesichert Fehlerstromschutzschalter. |
| ○ | E | Nicht vorhanden. |

Anmerkung.

Erhebungsbogen

## 442 Eigenstromversorgungsanlagen – Photovoltaik (Eigenbedarf):

- ○ A | Ausreichende Modulfläche für Leistungsbezug. Anlage funktioniert. Guter Wirkungsgrad. Keine kostenwirksamen Maßnahmen.
- ○ B | Entfällt.
- ○ C | Anlage funktioniert. Modulfläche für Leistungsbezug zu gering ausgelegt. Strombezug vernachlässigbar. Erweiterung der Anlage für besseren Wirkungsgrad.
- ○ D | Anlage funktioniert nicht störungsfrei. Schlechter Wirkungsgrad. Modernisierung der Anlage entsprechend Leistungsbedarf.
- ○ E | Nicht vorhanden.

Anmerkung:

## 450 Fernmelde- und Informationstechnische Anlagen:

### 451 Telekommunikationsanlagen, 457 Übertragungsnetze:

- ○ A | Telekommunikationsanlagen und Übertragungsnetze funktionieren und sind in gutem Zustand. Keine Kostenwirksamen Maßnahmen.
- ○ B | Einzelne Teile der Anlagen und Übertragungsnetze veraltet und mangelhaft (< 10%). Austausch veralteter Anlagenteile und Übertragungsnetzteile (<10%).
- ○ C | Teile der Anlagen und Übertragungsnetze veraltet und mangelhaft (< 40%). Austausch veralteter Anlagenteile und Übertragungsnetze (< 40%).
- ○ D | Gesamte Anlage veraltet und mangelhaft. Totalersatz der gesamten Anlage und Übertragungsnetze.
- ○ E | Nicht vorhanden.

Anmerkung:

### 452 Such- und Signalanlagen, 456 Gefahrenmelde- und Alarmanlagen:

- ○ A | Such- und Signalanlagen (Personenrufanlagen, Klingelanlagen, etc.) sowie Gefahrenmelde- und Alarmanlagen (Brand, Überfall, Einbruchmeldeanlage, etc.) funktionieren und sind in gutem Zustand. Keine kostenwirksamen Maßnahmen.
- ○ B | Einzelne Teile der Anlagen und Übertragungsnetze veraltet und mangelhaft (< 10%). Austausch veralteter Anlagenteile und Übertragungsnetze (< 10%).
- ○ C | Teile der Anlagen und Übertragungsnetze veraltet und mangelhaft (< 40%). Austausch veralteter Anlagenteile und Übertragungsnetze (< 40%).
- ○ D | Gesamte Anlage veraltet und mangelhaft. Totalersatz der gesamten Anlage und Übertragungsnetze.
- ○ E | Nicht vorhanden.

Anmerkung:

---

Erhebungsbogen

## 460 Förderanlagen

### 461 Aufzugsanlagen:

Anzahl der Anlagen: _____ Stück

Durchschnittliche Anzahl der Aufzugshaltepunkte eines Aufzugs: _____ Stück

- ○ A | Personen- und Lastenaufzüge funktionieren und werden regelmäßig gewartet. Keine Beanstandungen. Keine kostenwirksamen Maßnahmen.
- ○ B | Anlagen funktionieren. Türschliessungen und Steuerung ungenügend (< 10%). Erhöhter Wartungsaufwand. Innere Oberflächen verschmutzt. Vereinzelt fehlende Beschriftung. Austausch einzelner Anlagenteile (< 10%). Reinigung der Kabine. Neue Beschriftung.
- ○ C | Anlagen funktionieren. Türschliessungen und Steuerung ungenügend (< 40%). Hohe Störanfälligkeit, hoher Wartungsaufwand. Innere Oberflächen verschmutzt. Fehlende Beschriftung. Nachrüsten der Anlage (Steuerung, Türen, Tragseile mit. Generalrevision) (< 40%). Reinigung der Kabine. Neue Beschriftung.
- ○ D | Zustand der Anlagen ist unbefriedigend, häufige Störungen. Anlagen genügen nicht mehr den behördlichen Vorschriften. Nachrüstung der Anlage nicht möglich. Neue elektromagnetische Aufzugsanlagen. Nachrüsten der Maschinenräume. Oberflächenbehandlung der Schächte und Maschinenräume.
- ○ E | Nicht vorhanden.

Anmerkung:

## 470 Nutzungsspezifische Anlagen

### 471 Küchentechnische Anlagen:

Anzahl der Kochzeilen: _____ Stück

- ○ A | Küchentechnische Anlagen funktionieren und sind in gutem Zustand. Keine Beanstandungen, Mängel und Widersprüche gegenüber den Vorschriften, Oberflächen, Beschläge, An- und Abschlüsse in gutem Zustand. Keine kostenwirksamen Maßnahmen.
- ○ B | Küchentechnische Anlagen wenig funktional. Oberflächen, Beschläge, An- und Abschlüsse teils verschmutzt und leicht beschädigt (< 10%). Erneuerung schadhafter Oberflächen, Beläge (< 10%).
- ○ C | Küchentechnische Anlagen wenig funktional. Oberflächen, Beschläge, An- und Abschlüsse teils verschmutzt und leicht beschädigt (< 40%). Erneuerung schadhafter Oberflächen, Beläge (< 40%).
- ○ D | Anlagen veraltet, entsprechen nicht mehr den Vorschriften oder Nutzeranforderungen. Beschläge, An- und Abschlüsse in schlechtem Zustand, offene Fugen, Oberflächen verschmutzt. Neue Einbauküchen entsprechend Nutzeranforderungen.
- ○ E | Nicht vorhanden.

Anmerkung:

### 472 Wäscherei- und Reinigungsanlagen:

Anzahl der Anlagen: _____ Stück

- ○ A | Wäscherei- und Reinigungsanlagen funktionieren und sind in gutem Zustand. Keine Beanstandungen, Mängel und Widersprüche gegenüber den Vorschriften. Keine kostenwirksamen Maßnahmen.
- ○ B | Wäscherei- und Reinigungsanlagen veraltet oder wenig funktional (< 10%). Austausch veralteter Anlagen (< 10%).
- ○ C | Wäscherei- und Reinigungsanlagen veraltet oder wenig funktional (< 40%). Austausch veralteter Anlagen (< 40%).
- ○ D | Anlagen veraltet, entsprechen nicht mehr den behördlichen Vorschriften. Ersatz der Anlagen und elektrischen Installationen.
- ○ E | Nicht vorhanden.

Anmerkung:

Erhebungsbogen

## 476 Badtechnische Anlagen – Aufbereitungsanlagen für Schwimmbeckenwasser:

Breite des Schwimmbeckens: _____ m

Länge des Schwimmbeckens: _____ m

Durchschnittliche Tiefe des Schwimmbeckens: _____ m

- A. Badtechnische Anlagen in gutem Zustand. Keine Beanstandungen, Mängel und Widersprüche gegenüber den Vorschriften. Keine kostenwirksamen Maßnahmen.
- B. Badtechnische Anlagen veraltet und defekt (< 10%). Austausch beschädigter Anlagenteile und elektrischen Installationen (< 10%).
- C. Badtechnische Anlagen veraltet und defekt (< 40%). Austausch beschädigter Anlagenteile und elektrischen Installationen (< 40%).
- D. Badtechnische Anlagen größtenteils veraltet, entsprechen nicht mehr den behördlichen Vorschriften. Ersatz der Anlage und elektrischen Installationen.
- E. Nicht vorhanden.

Anmerkung:

## 478 Entsorgungsanlagen – Presscontainer:

Anzahl der Presscontainer: _____ Stück

- A. Presscontainer funktionsfähig, ausreichend vorhanden. Abfallsammelstellen in Ordnung. Keine kostenwirksamen Maßnahmen.
- B. Erfüllt.
- C. Erfüllt.
- D. Presscontainer schlecht zugänglich oder in zu geringer Anzahl vorhanden. Anlieferung und Abtransport von Sammelstelle nicht funktional. Neuorganisation der Abfallsammelstelle. Anschaffung weiterer Presscontainer entsprechend Abfallaufkommen.
- E. Nicht vorhanden.

Anmerkung:

## 480 Gebäudeautomation

## 481 Automationssysteme: Gebäudeautomationssysteme (Überwachungs- und Steuereinrichtungen auf Gebäudeebene):

- A. Gebäudeautomationssysteme mit Bedien- und Beobachtungseinrichtungen funktionstüchtig und in gutem Zustand. Keine kostenwirksamen Maßnahmen.
- B. Anlagen teils veraltet. Funktionalität ungenügend (<10%). Ersatz beschädigter Anlagenteile und elektrischen Installationen (< 10%).
- C. Anlagen teils veraltet. Funktionalität ungenügend (< 40%). Ersatz beschädigter Anlagenteile und elektrischen Installationen (< 40%).
- D. Anlagen veraltet, nicht funktional. Hohe Störanfälligkeit. Totalersatz der Anlage und elektrischen Installationen, ggf. Aufrüstung.
- E. Nicht vorhanden.

Anmerkung:

---

Erhebungsbogen

## 484 Raumautomationssysteme (Sonnenschutzsteuerung, Raumklimaregelung auf Raumebene):

Prozentanteil der Netto-Grundfläche mit Raumautomationssystemen: _____ %

- A. Raumautomationssysteme mit Bedien- und Anzeigeeinrichtungen funktionstüchtig und in gutem Zustand. Keine kostenwirksamen Maßnahmen.
- B. Anlagen teils veraltet. Zustand ungenügend (< 10%). Ersatz beschädigter Anlagenteile und elektrischen Installationen (< 10%).
- C. Anlagen teils veraltet. Zustand ungenügend (< 40%). Ersatz beschädigter Anlagenteile und elektrischen Installationen (< 40%).
- D. Anlagen veraltet. Hohe Störanfälligkeit. Totalersatz der Anlage und elektrischen Installationen.
- E. Nicht vorhanden.

Anmerkung:

## 3.3 Zustandserfassung Außenanlagen

## 500 Außenanlagen

## 520 Befestigte Flächen (Wege, Plätze, Stellplätze, Sportplatz-, Spielplatzflächen):

- A. Befestigte Flächen in gutem Zustand. Unterhaltsarbeiten regelmäßig ausgeführt. Keine kostenwirksamen Maßnahmen.
- B. Befestigte Flächen in gutem Zustand, vereinzelt leichte Beschädigungen und Unebenheiten (< 20%). Ausbesserungen an beschädigten Hartflächen (< 20%).
- C. Befestigte Flächen weisen Beschädigungen und Unebenheiten auf (< 50%). Wiederherrichten beschädigter Hartflächen (<50%).
- D. Befestigte Flächen sind stark beschädigt, großflächige Unebenheiten. Oberflächenentwässerung nicht mehr gewährleistet. Instandsetzung befestigter Flächen, inkl. Schächte und Entwässerung.
- E. Nicht vorhanden.

Anmerkung:

## 530 Baukonstruktionen in Außenanlagen (Mauern, Treppen, Überdachungen):

- A. Baukonstruktionen in Außenanlagen in gutem Zustand. Keine kostenwirksamen Maßnahmen erforderlich.
- B. Leichte Beschädigungen an Holz-, Beton-, Stein und Stahlkonstruktionen (< 20%). Teilweise beschädigter Baukonstruktionen (< 20%).
- C. Beschädigungen an Holz-, Beton-, Stein und Stahlkonstruktionen (< 50%). Teilweise beschädigter Baukonstruktionen (< 50%).
- D. Großteil der Baukonstruktionen in Außenanlagen beschädigt. Verkehrsgefahr. Totalersatz der Baukonstruktionen entsprechend den behördlichen Vorschriften.
- E. Nicht vorhanden.

Anmerkung:

Erhebungsbogen

**540 Technische Anlagen in Außenanlagen**

**542 Wasseranlagen – Beregnungsanlagen:**

Bewässerte Außenanlagenfläche: _____ m²

- A  Bewässerungsanlage einwandfrei und ausreichend dimensioniert. Keine kostenwirksamen Maßnahmen.
- B  Bewässerungsanlage zu gering ausgelegt (<20%). Teilersatz oder Aufstockung der bestehenden Beregnungsanlage (<20%).
- C  Bewässerungsanlage zu gering ausgelegt (<50%). Teilersatz oder Aufstockung der bestehenden Beregnungsanlage (<50%).
- D  Bewässerungsanlage zu gering ausgelegt, nicht funktional. Teilersatz oder Aufstockung der bestehenden Beregnungsanlage.
- E  Nicht vorhanden.

Anmerkung:

**546 Starkstromanlagen – Außenbeleuchtung:**

- A  Außenleuchten in gutem Zustand, Stromversorgung intakt. Keine kostenwirksamen Maßnahmen erforderlich.
- B  Teil der Außenleuchten stark verschmutzt und nicht funktionsfähig (< 20%). Austausch beschädigter Außenleuchten, Instandsetzung der Elektroinstallationen (< 20%).
- C  Teil der Außenleuchten stark verschmutzt und nicht funktionsfähig (< 50%). Austausch beschädigter Außenleuchten, Instandsetzung der Elektroinstallationen (< 50%).
- D  Großteil der Außenleuchten ist stark verschmutzt, beschädigt und nicht funktionsfähig. Erneuerung sämtlicher Außenleuchten und Elektroinstallationen.
- E  Nicht vorhanden.

Anmerkung:

**550 Einbauten in Außenanlagen**

Einbauten in Außenanlagen (wie Fahrradständer, Sport- und Spielanlagen und dgl.):

- A  Einbauten in gutem Zustand. Unterhaltbarkeiten regelmässig ausgeführt. Keine kostenwirksamen Maßnahmen erforderlich.
- B  Leichte Beschädigungen an Holz, Beton-, Stein und Stahlkonstruktionen (< 20%). Teilersatz beschädigter Einbauten (< 20%). Vollständige Oberflächenbehandlung.
- C  Leichte Beschädigungen an Holz, Beton-, Stein und Stahlkonstruktionen (< 50%). Teilersatz beschädigter Einbauten (< 50%). Vollständige Oberflächenbehandlung.
- D  Großteil der Einbauten beschädigt, Verletzungsgefahr. Ersatz beschädigter Einbauten an geeigneten Standorten.
- E  Nicht vorhanden.

Anmerkung:

Erhebungsbogen

**570 Pflanz- und Saatflächen – Pflanzen, Rasen und Ansaaten:**

- A  Pflanz- und Saatflächen gepflegt, Gärtnerarbeiten regelmässig ausgeführt. Keine kostenwirksamen Maßnahmen erforderlich.
- B  Pflanz- und Saatflächen zum Teil verwildert (< 20%). Wiederherrichten der Pflanz- und Saatflächen (< 20%).
- C  Pflanz- und Saatflächen zum Teil verwildert (< 50%). Wiederherrichten der Pflanz- und Saatflächen (< 50%).
- D  Großteil der Pflanz- und Saatflächen verwildert. Wiederherrichten sämtlicher Pflanz- und Saatflächen. Neuplanung.
- E  Nicht vorhanden.

Anmerkung:

**3.4 Zustandserfassung Ausstattung**

**600 Ausstattung und Kunstwerke**

**611 Allgemeine Ausstattung**

Allgemeine Möbel, Schränke, Regale, Tische, Textilien:

- A  Ausstattung neu oder gut gepflegt. Keine kostenwirksamen Maßnahmen erforderlich.
- B  Gebrauchsspuren, leichte Beschädigungen vereinzelt sichtbar (< 20%). Austausch beschädigter Teile, Oberflächenbehandlung (< 20%).
- C  Gebrauchsspuren, erhebliche Beschädigungen sichtbar (< 50%). Austausch beschädigter Teile, Oberflächenbehandlung (< 50%).
- D  Ausstattung größtenteils beschädigt und veraltet, Verletzungsgefahr. Wertvechende Maßnahmen, Totalersatz.
- E  Nicht vorhanden.

Anmerkung:

**612 Besondere Ausstattung**

Besondere Ausstattung – technische Geräte mit besonderer Zweckbestimmung:

- A  Ausstattung neu oder gut gepflegt. Keine kostenwirksamen Maßnahmen erforderlich.
- B  Gebrauchsspuren, leichte Beschädigungen vereinzelt sichtbar (< 20%). Austausch beschädigter Teile, Oberflächenbehandlung (< 20%).
- C  Gebrauchsspuren, erhebliche Beschädigungen sichtbar (< 50%). Austausch beschädigter Teile, Oberflächenbehandlung (< 50%).
- D  Ausstattung größtenteils beschädigt und veraltet, Verletzungsgefahr. Wertvechende Maßnahmen, Totalersatz.
- E  Nicht vorhanden.

Anmerkung:

Erhebungsbogen

**619   Besondere Ausstattung**

Ausstattung, sonstiges – Schilder, Orientierungstafeln:

| | |
|---|---|
| A | Ausstattung neu oder gut gepflegt. Keine kostenwirksamen Maßnahmen erforderlich. |
| B | Gebrauchsspuren, leichte Beschädigungen vereinzelt sichtbar (< 20%). Austausch beschädigter Teile (< 20%). |
| C | Gebrauchsspuren, erhebliche Beschädigungen sichtbar (< 50%). Austausch beschädigter Teile (< 50%). |
| D | Ausstattung größtenteils beschädigt und veraltet. Totalersatz. |
| E | Nicht vorhanden. |

Anmerkung:

**Kostengruppe ... – Typ ... Ergänzung:**

| | |
|---|---|
| A | Bauteil in Ordnung. Keine kostenwirksamen Maßnahmen. |
| B | Bauteil vereinzelt beschädigt (< 20%). Austausch beschädigter Teile (< 20%). |
| C | Bauteil erheblich beschädigt (< 50%). Austausch beschädigter Teile (< 50%). |
| D | Bauteil größtenteils beschädigt und veraltet. Totalersatz. |
| E | Nicht vorhanden. |

Anmerkung:

**4.   Angaben zu den Planunterlagen**

Eckdaten zum Gebäude:

Kernnutzung (Unterricht) im untersten Geschoss (ja/nein):

Oberste Geschoss bei Steildach (Dachgeschoss) ausgebaut (ja/nein):

Entlüftete Fläche (m² NGF):

Be- und entlüftete Fläche (m² NGF):

Teilklimatisierte Fläche (m² NGF):

Klimatisierte Fläche (m² NGF):

Leerstandsflächenanteil im Gebäude (m² NGF):

Leerstand: Durchschnittliche Dauer ungenutzter Flächen im Gebäude (Monate im Jahr):

Bauweise:

| | | |
|---|---|---|
| Einzelhaus | | Doppel-/Reihenanbauhaus |
| Hausgruppe | | Geschlossene Bauweise |

Tragsystem:

| | | |
|---|---|---|
| Skelettbau | | Längswandtyp |
| Querwandtyp | | Kreuzwandtyp |

- 38 -

Erhebungsbogen

Konstruktion:

| | |
|---|---|
| Schwere, einschalige Außenwand (%) | Pfosten-Riegel-Konstruktion (%) |
| Schwere, mehrschalige Außenwand (%) | Sonstige ... (%) |

Ausrichtung des Gebäudes:

| | |
|---|---|
| | Längsseite in Nord-, Südrichtung |
| | Längsseite in Ost-, Westrichtung |
| | Keine Ausrichtung (z.B. sternförmiger Grundriss) |

**Wärmedämmung**

Wärmedämmung des Daches (in Prozent der Dachfläche):

Jahr der Modernisierung (falls vorhanden):

| | |
|---|---|
| % | Nach gesetzlichem Standard, zum Zeitpunkt der Erstellung. |
| % | Nach gesetzlichem Standard, zum Zeitpunkt der Modernisierung des Daches. |
| % | Über dem gesetzlichem Standard im Betrachtungsjahr. |
| % | Nicht vorhanden. |

Wärmedämmung der Außenwände (in Prozent Außenbekleidungsfläche der Außenwand):

Jahr der Modernisierung (falls vorhanden):

| | |
|---|---|
| % | Nach gesetzlichem Standard, zum Zeitpunkt der Erstellung. |
| % | Nach gesetzlichem Standard, zum Zeitpunkt der Modernisierung der Außenwände. |
| % | Über dem gesetzlichem Standard im Betrachtungsjahr. |
| % | Nicht vorhanden. |

Wärmedämmung der Bodenplatte (in Prozent der Gründungsfläche):

Jahr der Modernisierung (falls vorhanden):

| | |
|---|---|
| % | Nach gesetzlichem Standard, zum Zeitpunkt der Erstellung. |
| % | Nach gesetzlichem Standard, zum Zeitpunkt der Modernisierung der Bodenplatte. |
| % | Über dem gesetzlichem Standard im Betrachtungsjahr. |
| % | Nicht vorhanden. |

Standard der Außentüren, -fenster (in Prozent der Außentüren-, Außenfensterfläche):

Jahr der Modernisierung (falls vorhanden):

| | |
|---|---|
| % | Einscheibenverglasung |
| % | Zweischeibenverglasung |
| % | Dreischeibenverglasung |
| % | Sonstige ... |

- 39 -

**Erhebungsbogen**

## Erschließung

**Art und Anzahl der äußeren Erschließung:**

| | |
|---|---|
| Windfang | Zugang über Flur |
| Zugang über Eingangshalle | Zugang über Gruppenraum |
| Zugang über Treppenhaus | Zugang über separatem Vorraum |
| Sonstige ... | |

**Vertikalerschließung (Hauptterschließung) im Gebäude:**

| | | |
|---|---|---|
| ○ offene Treppe, verdeckt | ○ Punktterschließung, Treppenhaus | |
| ○ Punktterschließung, offene Treppe | ○ Sonstige ... | |
| ○ nicht vorhanden | | |

**Horizontale Erschließung im Gebäude:**

| | |
|---|---|
| ○ Gangerschließung | ○ Spännererschließung |
| ○ Großraumerschließung | ○ Sonstige ... |

**Nordfassade:**

**Art der Konstruktion (in Prozent der Außenwandfläche):**

| | |
|---|---|
| ____ % | Schwere, einschalige Außenwand |
| ____ % | Schwere, mehrschalige Außenwand |
| ____ % | Pfosten-Riegel-Konstruktion |
| ____ % | Sonstige ... |
| ____ % | Fassade nicht vorhanden |

**Glasflächenanteil der Nordfassade (gesamte Außenwandfläche inkl. Untergeschosse):**

| ○ 0 % | ○ < 5 % ____ % | ○ < 20 % ____ % |
|---|---|---|
| ○ < 30 % ____ % | ○ < 50 % ____ % | ○ > 49 % ____ % |

**Außenliegender Sonnenschutz (in Prozent der Außentüren, -fensterfläche):**

| | |
|---|---|
| ____ % | Markisen |
| ____ % | Rollläden |
| ____ % | Lamellentüren, außenliegend |
| ____ % | Stoffbahnen, außenliegend |
| ____ % | Sonstige ... |
| ____ % | Nicht vorhanden |

**Indirekte Verschattung der Nordfassade (durch Bäume, Gebäude):**

| ○ Ja. | ○ Nein. |
|---|---|

- 40 -

---

**Erhebungsbogen**

**Ostfassade:**

**Art der Konstruktion (in Prozent der Außenwandfläche):**

| | |
|---|---|
| ____ % | Schwere, einschalige Außenwand |
| ____ % | Schwere, mehrschalige Außenwand |
| ____ % | Pfosten-Riegel-Konstruktion |
| ____ % | Sonstige ... |
| ____ % | Fassade nicht vorhanden |

**Glasflächenanteil der Ostfassade (gesamte Außenwandfläche inkl. Untergeschosse):**

| ○ 0 % | ○ < 5 % ____ % | ○ < 20 % ____ % |
|---|---|---|
| ○ < 30 % ____ % | ○ < 50 % ____ % | ○ > 49 % ____ % |

**Außenliegender Sonnenschutz (in Prozent der Außentüren, -fensterfläche):**

| | |
|---|---|
| ____ % | Markisen |
| ____ % | Rollläden |
| ____ % | Lamellentüren, außenliegend |
| ____ % | Stoffbahnen, außenliegend |
| ____ % | Sonstige ... |
| ____ % | Nicht vorhanden |

**Indirekte Verschattung der Nordfassade (durch Bäume, Gebäude):**

| ○ Ja. | ○ Nein. |
|---|---|

**Südfassade:**

**Art der Konstruktion (in Prozent der Außenwandfläche):**

| | |
|---|---|
| ____ % | Schwere, einschalige Außenwand |
| ____ % | Schwere, mehrschalige Außenwand |
| ____ % | Pfosten-Riegel-Konstruktion |
| ____ % | Sonstige ... |
| ____ % | Fassade nicht vorhanden |

**Glasflächenanteil der Südfassade (gesamte Außenwandfläche inkl. Untergeschosse):**

| ○ 0 % | ○ < 5 % ____ % | ○ < 20 % ____ % |
|---|---|---|
| ○ < 30 % ____ % | ○ < 50 % ____ % | ○ > 49 % ____ % |

- 41 -

**Erhebungsbogen**

Außenliegender Sonnenschutz (in Prozent der Außentüren, -fensterfläche):

| % | Markisen |
| % | Rollläden |
| % | Lamellenstoren, außenliegend |
| % | Stoffbahnen, außenliegend |
| % | Sonstige .... |
| % | Nicht vorhanden |

Indirekte Verschattung der Nordfassade (durch Bäume, Gebäude):

o Ja.    o Nein.

**Westfassade:**

Art der Konstruktion (in Prozent der Außenwandfläche):

| % | Schwere, einschalige Außenwand |
| % | Schwere, mehrschalige Außenwand |
| % | Pfosten-Riegel-Konstruktion |
| % | Sonstige ... |
| % | Fassade nicht vorhanden |

Glasflächenanteil der Westfassade (gesamte Außenwandfläche inkl. Untergeschosse):

| o 0 % ...... % | o < 5 % ...... % | o < 20 % ...... % |
| o < 30 % ...... % | o < 50 % ...... % | o > 49 % ...... % |

Außenliegender Sonnenschutz (in Prozent der Außentüren, -fensterfläche):

| % | Markisen |
| % | Rollläden |
| % | Lamellenstoren, außenliegend |
| % | Stoffbahnen, außenliegend |
| % | Sonstige ... |
| % | nicht vorhanden |

Indirekte Verschattung der Nordfassade (durch Bäume, Gebäude):

o Ja.    o Nein.

---

**Erhebungsbogen**

**Kubaturtypologie:**

| o Turm (Längsseite : Höhe > 1 : 4) | o liegende Scheibe (Längsseite : Höhe < 1 : 2) | o gestaffelte Form, gegliederter Baukörper |
| o stehende Scheibe (Längsseite : Höhe > 1 : 2) | o Atrium | o stark gegliederter Baukörper |
| | | o sonstige... |

**Grundrisstypologie:**

Bitte geben Sie die Grundrisstypologie des Gebäudes an und weisen Sie schematisch die Heizungsgruppen (Wärmeverteilnetze) aus:

Beispiel:

☒ U-Form (Seitenverhältnisse irrelevant)

Nordflügel     Südflügel

| o Quadrat (Breite : Tiefe < 1 : 2) | o Ring (Seitenverhältnisse irrelevant) |
| o Rechteck (Breite : Tiefe > 1 : 2) | o L-förmiger Grundriss: |
| o Stern (Seitenverhältnisse irrelevant) | o U-förmiger Grundriss: |
| o sonstige... (z. B. zusammengesetzt) | |

Anmerkungen vom Bearbeiter/in: _____

## Appendix C: Database of the investigation

## Dependent variables: Occupancy consumptions and costs

### Total utility consumption p.a.

Tab. 98: Database of the investigation: Total utility consumption

| Cost group | Designation | Unit | Lower quartile | Mean | Median | Upper quartile | Standard deviation | N | Model |
|---|---|---|---|---|---|---|---|---|---|
| 311 | Water | m³ p.a. | 667 | 1,215 | 947 | 1,522 | 875 | 125 | 1.A.1 |
| 312 - 315 | Heating | kWh p.a. | 395,816 | 651,208 | 548,753 | 866,457 | 413,510 | 125 | 2.A.1 |
| 316 | Electricity | kWh p.a. | 57,120 | 127,778 | 84,987 | 142,210 | 131,967 | 125 | 3.A.1 |

Note: Utility consumption (m² or kWh p.a.), 2008

### Total operating and repair costs p.a.

Tab. 99: Database of the investigation: Total operating and repair costs

| Cost group | Designation | Unit | Lower quartile | Mean | Median | Upper quartile | Standard deviation | N | Model |
|---|---|---|---|---|---|---|---|---|---|
| 300 | Aggregate operating costs | € p.a. | 120,877 | 196,184 | 174,650 | 240,533 | 119,470 | 125 | 15.A |
| 310 | Utilities | € p.a. | 46,111 | 78,279 | 65,672 | 98,983 | 52,627 | 125 | 4.A |
| 311 | Water | € p.a. | 2,487 | 4,431 | 3,467 | 5,607 | 3,131 | 125 | 1.A.2 |
| 312 - 315 | Heating | € p.a. | 33,055 | 53,296 | 46,534 | 71,656 | 32,452 | 125 | 2.A.2 |
| 316 | Electricity | € p.a. | 9,035 | 19,817 | 14,407 | 22,542 | 19,147 | 125 | 3.A.2 |
| 320 | Waste disposal | € p.a. | 2,310 | 3,988 | 3,322 | 4,510 | 2,767 | 125 | 5.A |
| 330 | Cleaning and care of buildings | € p.a. | 37,563 | 68,035 | 58,263 | 80,031 | 43,325 | 122 | 6.A |
| 340 | Cleaning und care of grounds and outdoor facilities | € p.a. | 3,342 | 7,090 | 5,404 | 9,355 | 5,831 | 125 | 7.A |
| 350 | Operation, inspection and maintenance | € p.a. | 15,203 | 30,286 | 22,403 | 34,372 | 25,406 | 105 | 12.A |
| 352 | Inspection and maintenance of building constructions | € p.a. | 5,211 | 10,520 | 8,273 | 13,312 | 7,932 | 125 | 8.A |
| 353 | Inspection and maintenance of technical installations | € p.a. | 7,026 | 16,522 | 11,291 | 18,189 | 18,675 | 125 | 9.A |
| 354 | Inspection and maintenance of grounds and outdoor facilities | € p.a. | 377 | 2,025 | 1,074 | 2,050 | 2,886 | 114 | 10.A |
| 355 | Inspection and maintenance of fittings, furnishings and equipment | € p.a. | 240 | 1,145 | 658 | 1,346 | 1,562 | 100 | 11.A |
| 360 | Security and surveillance services | € p.a. | 175 | 1,422 | 287 | 699 | 4,017 | 122 | 13.A |
| 370 | Statutory charges and contributions | € p.a. | 6,078 | 10,923 | 8,875 | 14,864 | 6,700 | 122 | 14.A |
| 400 | Aggreage repair costs | € p.a. | 66,045 | 184,280 | 140,064 | 219,241 | 184,636 | 113 | 20.A |
| 410 | Repair of building constructions | € p.a. | 38,260 | 124,799 | 86,540 | 160,566 | 121,214 | 113 | 16.A |
| 420 | Repair of technical installations | € p.a. | 14,321 | 52,297 | 32,101 | 65,303 | 67,532 | 113 | 17.A |
| 430 | Repair of grounds and outdoor faciities | € p.a. | 535 | 2,765 | 1,532 | 3,626 | 3,319 | 71 | 18.A |
| 440 | Repair of fittings, furnishings and equipment | € p.a. | 679 | 4,430 | 1,879 | 5,776 | 6,051 | 108 | 19.A |
| ∑ (300;400) | Aggregate operating and repair costs | € p.a. | 216,436 | 385,143 | 304,172 | 462,997 | 284,706 | 113 | 21.A |

Note: Operating and repair costs (€ p.a.), costs including VAT, based on 2008 figures

## Utility consumption indicators in consumption/m² reference area p.a.

Tab. 100: Database of the investigation: Utility consumption indicators per m² reference area

| Cost group | Designation | Unit | Lower quartile | Mean | Median | Upper quartile | Standard deviation | N | Model |
|---|---|---|---|---|---|---|---|---|---|
| 311 | Water | m³/m² UFA p.a. | 0.17 | 0.24 | 0.21 | 0.27 | 0.12 | 125 | 1.B.1 |
| 312 - 315 | Heating | kWh/m² H-GROFA p.a. | 74.25 | 92.08 | 88.78 | 105.65 | 27.62 | 125 | 2.B.1 |
| 316 | Electricity | kWh/m² NEFA p.a. | 11.21 | 16.00 | 15.66 | 19.70 | 5.55 | 125 | 3.B.1 |

Note: Utility consumption (consumption/ m² reference area p.a.), 2008

## Operating and repair cost indicators in €/m² reference area p.a.

Tab. 101: Database of the investigation: Operating and repair cost indicators per m² reference area

| Cost group | Designation | Unit | Lower quartile | Mean | Median | Upper quartile | Standard deviation | N | Model |
|---|---|---|---|---|---|---|---|---|---|
| 300 | Aggregate operating costs | €/m² NEFA p.a. | 25.27 | 29.43 | 28.63 | 31.79 | 5.91 | 125 | 15.B |
| 310 | Utilitties | €/m² H-GROFA p.a. | 9.02 | 10.82 | 10.71 | 12.05 | 2.55 | 125 | 4.B |
| 311 | Water | €/m² UFA p.a. | 0.62 | 0.87 | 0.78 | 1.00 | 0.41 | 125 | 1.B.2 |
| 312 - 315 | Heating | €/m² H-GROFA p.a. | 6.17 | 7.56 | 7.43 | 8.60 | 2.05 | 125 | 2.B.2 |
| 316 | Electricity | €/m² NEFA p.a. | 1.87 | 2.55 | 2.50 | 3.15 | 0.86 | 125 | 3.B.2 |
| 320 | Waste disposal | €/m² UFA p.a. | 0.62 | 0.82 | 0.82 | 0.95 | 0.26 | 125 | 5.B |
| 330 | Cleaning and care of buildings | €/m² NEFA p.a. | 8.36 | 9.70 | 9.49 | 10.67 | 1.95 | 122 | 6.B |
| 340 | Cleaning und care of grounds and outdoor facilities | €/m² non built up plot area p.a. | 0.40 | 0.76 | 0.65 | 0.96 | 0.52 | 125 | 7.B |
| 350 | Operation, inspection and maintenance | €/m² NEFA p.a. | 3.03 | 3.91 | 3.65 | 4.57 | 1.32 | 105 | 12.B |
| 352 | Inspection and maintenance of building constructions | €/m² GROFA p.a. | 0.81 | 1.38 | 1.26 | 1.74 | 0.70 | 125 | 8.B |
| 353 | Inspection and maintenance of technical installations | €/m² NEFA p.a. | 1.47 | 2.07 | 1.91 | 2.37 | 1.02 | 125 | 9.B |
| 354 | Inspection and maintenance of grounds and outdoor facilities | €/m² non built up plot area p.a. | 0.07 | 0.19 | 0.12 | 0.21 | 0.22 | 114 | 10.B |
| 355 | Inspection and maintenance of fittings, furnishings and equipment | €/m² UFA p.a. | 0.06 | 0.23 | 0.15 | 0.32 | 0.28 | 100 | 11.B |
| 360 | Security and surveillance services | €/m² GROFA p.a. | 0.03 | 0.39 | 0.05 | 0.10 | 1.43 | 122 | - |
| 370 | Statutory charges and contributions | €/m² GROFA p.a. | 1.06 | 1.56 | 1.53 | 1.99 | 0.71 | 122 | - |
| 400 | Aggreage repair costs | €/m² GROFA p.a. | 10.73 | 23.17 | 18.85 | 32.46 | 16.51 | 113 | 20.B.1 20.B.2 |
| 410 | Repair of building constructions | €/m² GROFA p.a. | 6.38 | 15.83 | 12.84 | 21.93 | 12.42 | 113 | 16.B.2 |
| 420 | Repair of technical installations | €/m² NEFA p.a. | 2.37 | 7.41 | 4.91 | 9.45 | 6.82 | 113 | - |
| 430 | Repair of grounds and outdoor facilities | €/m² non built up plot area p.a. | 0.07 | 0.35 | 0.15 | 0.36 | 0.50 | 71 | - |
| 440 | Repair of fittings, furnishings and equipment | €/m² UFA p.a. | 0.18 | 0.99 | 0.46 | 1.36 | 1.27 | 108 | - |
| Σ (300;400) | Aggregate operating and repair costs | €/m² GROFA p.a. | 34.93 | 49.50 | 44.11 | 59.19 | 19.09 | 113 | 21.B.1 21.B.2 |

Note: Operating and repair costs (€/m² reference area p.a.), costs including VAT, based on 2008 figures

## Utility consumption indicators in consumption/m² gross floor area p.a.

Tab. 102: Database of the investigation: Utility consumption indicators per m² gross floor area

| Cost group | Designation | Lower quartile | Mean | Median | Upper quartile | Standard deviation | N |
|---|---|---|---|---|---|---|---|
| 311 | Water | 0.10 | 0.16 | 0.13 | 0.17 | 0.18 | 125 |
| 312 - 315 | Heating | 64.11 | 81.75 | 78.62 | 94.80 | 26.07 | 125 |
| 316 | Electricity | 9.94 | 14.05 | 13.78 | 17.19 | 5.11 | 125 |

Note: Consumption indicators (utility consumption/ m² gross floor area p.a.), 2008

## Operating and repair cost indicators in €/m² gross floor area p.a.

Tab. 103: Database of the investigation: Operating and repair cost indicators per m² gross floor area

| Cost group | Designation | Lower quartile | Mean | Median | Upper quartile | Standard deviation | N |
|---|---|---|---|---|---|---|---|
| 300 | Aggregate operating costs | 22.31 | 25.93 | 25.09 | 28.28 | 5.29 | 125 |
| 310 | Utilitties | 7.87 | 9.61 | 9.40 | 10.94 | 2.44 | 125 |
| 311 | Water | 0.39 | 0.53 | 0.49 | 0.63 | 0.25 | 125 |
| 312 - 315 | Heating | 5.32 | 6.72 | 6.71 | 7.89 | 1.96 | 125 |
| 316 | Electricity | 1.63 | 2.23 | 2.19 | 2.76 | 0.79 | 125 |
| 320 | Waste disposal | 0.40 | 0.51 | 0.50 | 0.60 | 0.16 | 125 |
| 330 | Cleaning and care of buildings | 7.32 | 8.49 | 8.38 | 9.52 | 1.90 | 122 |
| 340 | Cleaning und care of grounds and outdoor facilities | 0.45 | 1.02 | 0.76 | 1.37 | 0.80 | 125 |
| 350 | Operation, inspection and maintenance | 2.63 | 3.44 | 3.21 | 4.07 | 1.24 | 105 |
| 352 | Inspection and maintenance of building constructions | 0.81 | 1.38 | 1.26 | 1.74 | 0.70 | 125 |
| 353 | Inspection and maintenance of technical installations | 1.29 | 1.83 | 1.66 | 2.11 | 0.92 | 125 |
| 354 | Inspection and maintenance of grounds and outdoor facilities | 0.06 | 0.29 | 0.16 | 0.35 | 0.37 | 114 |
| 355 | Inspection and maintenance of fittings, furnishings and equipment | 0.04 | 0.14 | 0.09 | 0.19 | 0.17 | 100 |
| 360 | Security and surveillance services | 0.03 | 0.39 | 0.05 | 0.10 | 1.43 | 122 |
| 370 | Statutory charges and contributions | 1.06 | 1.56 | 1.53 | 1.99 | 0.71 | 122 |
| 400 | Aggreage repair costs | 10.73 | 23.17 | 18.85 | 32.46 | 16.51 | 113 |
| 410 | Repair of building constructions | 6.38 | 15.83 | 12.84 | 21.93 | 12.42 | 113 |
| 420 | Repair of technical installations | 2.10 | 6.54 | 4.39 | 8.45 | 6.05 | 113 |
| 430 | Repair of grounds and outdoor facilities | 0.07 | 0.44 | 0.22 | 0.59 | 0.60 | 71 |
| 440 | Repair of fittings, furnishings and equipment | 0.10 | 0.60 | 0.28 | 0.78 | 0.77 | 108 |
| Σ (300;400) | Aggregate operating and repair costs | 34.93 | 49.50 | 44.11 | 59.19 | 19.09 | 113 |

Note: Operating and repair costs (€/m² gross floor area p.a.), costs including VAT, based on 2008 figures

Operating and repair cost indicators in €/m² gross floor area p.a.:
Empirical distribution and median

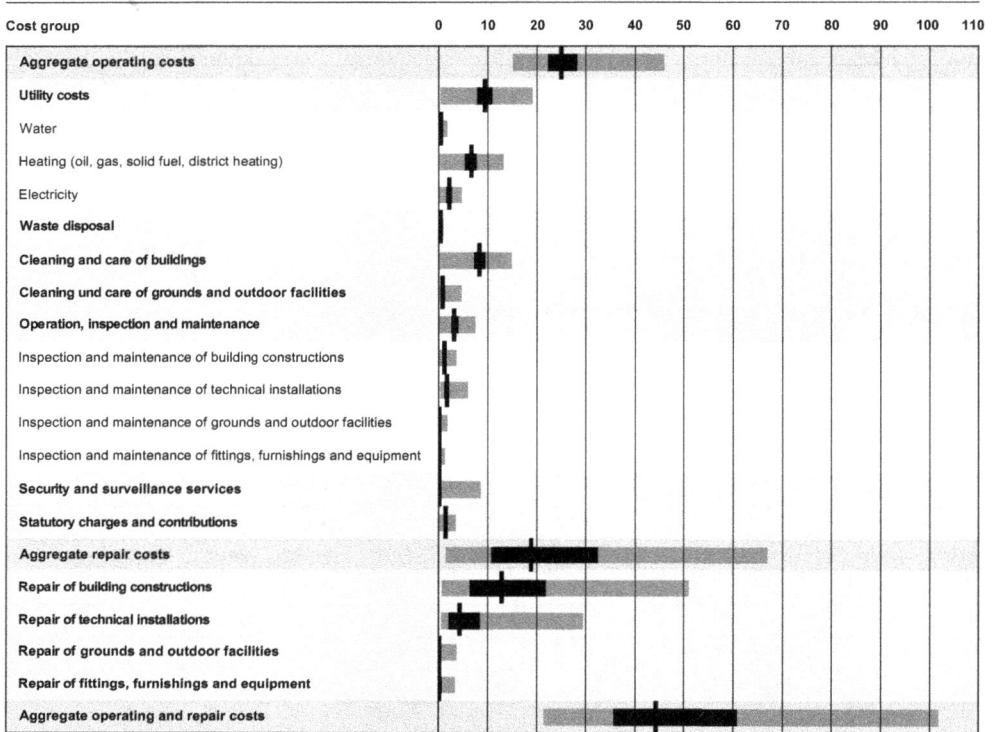

| Cost group | 0 | 10 | 20 | 30 | 40 | 50 | 60 | 70 | 80 | 90 | 100 | 110 |
|---|---|---|---|---|---|---|---|---|---|---|---|---|
| Aggregate operating costs | | | | | | | | | | | | |
| Utility costs | | | | | | | | | | | | |
| Water | | | | | | | | | | | | |
| Heating (oil, gas, solid fuel, district heating) | | | | | | | | | | | | |
| Electricity | | | | | | | | | | | | |
| Waste disposal | | | | | | | | | | | | |
| Cleaning and care of buildings | | | | | | | | | | | | |
| Cleaning und care of grounds and outdoor facilities | | | | | | | | | | | | |
| Operation, inspection and maintenance | | | | | | | | | | | | |
| Inspection and maintenance of building constructions | | | | | | | | | | | | |
| Inspection and maintenance of technical installations | | | | | | | | | | | | |
| Inspection and maintenance of grounds and outdoor facilities | | | | | | | | | | | | |
| Inspection and maintenance of fittings, furnishings and equipment | | | | | | | | | | | | |
| Security and surveillance services | | | | | | | | | | | | |
| Statutory charges and contributions | | | | | | | | | | | | |
| Aggregate repair costs | | | | | | | | | | | | |
| Repair of building constructions | | | | | | | | | | | | |
| Repair of technical installations | | | | | | | | | | | | |
| Repair of grounds and outdoor facilities | | | | | | | | | | | | |
| Repair of fittings, furnishings and equipment | | | | | | | | | | | | |
| Aggregate operating and repair costs | | | | | | | | | | | | |

Note: Operating and repair costs (€/m² gross floor area p.a.), costs including VAT, based on 2008 figures

Fig. 25:    Empirical distribution: Operating and repair cost indicators per m² gross floor area

## Independent variables

### Independent variables: Factor group utilization

## Type of utilization

Tab. 104: Database of the investigation: Type of utilization (quantitative variables, N =130)

| Factors | Minimum | Lower Quartile | Median | Upper Quartile | Maximum | Data processing |
|---|---|---|---|---|---|---|
| Area of school utilization (NEFA of builiding sections in m²) | 779 | 3.002 | 5.072 | 7.072 | 31.363 | Aggregated from builidng sections |
| Area of sports utilization (NEFA of builiding sections in m²) | 0 | 400 | 828 | 1.460 | 5.110 | Aggregated from builidng sections |
| Area of gymnasium utilization (NEFA of builiding sections in m²) | 0 | 378 | 815 | 1.305 | 4.827 | Aggregated from builidng sections |

*(continued)*

| Factors | Minimum | Lower Quartile | Median | Upper Quartile | Maximum | Data processing |
|---|---|---|---|---|---|---|
| Area of swimming pool utilization (NEFA of builiding sections in m²) | 0 | 0 | 0 | 0 | 1.186 | Aggregated from builidng sections |
| Area of sports utilization (UFA 5 on room level in m²) | 0 | 171 | 340 | 561 | 2.135 | Aggregated from room level |
| Area of sports hall utilization (UFA 5 on room level in m²) | 0 | 171 | 340 | 501 | 1.932 | Aggregated from room level |
| Area of swimming pool utilization (UFA 5 on room level in m²) | 0 | 0 | 0 | 0 | 395 | Aggregated from room level |
| Area of swimming pools base (m²) | 0 | 0 | 0 | 0 | 150 | Property level |
| Water volume of swimming pools (m³) | 0 | 0 | 0 | 0 | 230 | Property level |
| Net floor area of underground parking (m²) | 0 | 0 | 0 | 0 | 4.735 | Aggregated from room level |

Tab. 105: Database of the investigation: Type of utilization (qualitative variables, N =130)

| Factors | Levels | N | Data processing |
|---|---|---|---|
| Primary utilization (Type of school) | Elementary school | 31 | Property level |
| | Special school | 15 | Property level |
| | Secondary school | 66 | Property level |
| | Secondary general school | 29 | Property level |
| | Intermediate secondary school | 10 | Property level |
| | Multiple school center | 8 | Property level |
| | Grammar school | 19 | Property level |
| | Vocational school | 18 | Property level |
| | Vocational school with technical focus | 11 | Property level |
| | Vocational school with business focus | 7 | Property level |
| Secondary utilization | School with sports facilities | 107 | Property level |
| | School without sports facilities | 23 | Property level |
| | School with sports halls | 106 | Property level |
| | School without sports halls | 24 | Property level |
| | School with indoor swimming pools | 8 | Property level |
| | School without indoor swimming pools | 122 | Property level |
| | School with nursery schools | 20 | Property level |
| | School without nursery schools | 110 | Property level |
| | School with underground parking garage | 7 | Property level |
| | School with underground parking garage | 123 | Property level |

## Standard of utilization

Tab. 106: Database of the investigation: Standard of utilization (quantitative variables, N =130)

| Factors | Minimum | Lower Quartile | Median | Upper Quartile | Maximum | Data processing |
|---|---|---|---|---|---|---|
| Number of computer workstations | 0 | 10 | 30 | 60 | 800 | Aggregated from building level |

Tab. 107: Database of the investigation: Standard of utilization (qualitative variables, N =130)

| Factors | Levels | N | Data processing |
|---|---|---|---|
| Educational program | Regular school | 30 | Property level |
| | Extended regular school | 57 | Property level |
| | Full-day school | 43 | Property level |
| Canteen service | School based canteen | 28 | Property level |
| | External catering | 49 | Property level |
| | No canteen service | 53 | Property level |

## Intensity of utilization

Tab. 108: Database of the investigation: Intensity of utilization (quantitative variables, N =130)

| Factors | Minimum | Lower Quartile | Median | Upper Quartile | Maximum | Data processing |
|---|---|---|---|---|---|---|
| Average operating time (hours per school week in 2008) | 36 | 68 | 70 | 74 | 94 | Property level |
| Average operating time for schools (hours per school week in 2008) | 27 | 45 | 51 | 60 | 94 | Property level |
| Average operating time for sports facilities (hours per school week in 2008) | 0 | 65 | 70 | 74 | 93 | Property level |
| Average number of schooldays per school week in 2008 | 5 | 5 | 5 | 5 | 6 | Property level |
| Number of pupils | 48 | 245 | 377 | 593 | 1,290 | Weighted value from school level |
| Number of school classes | 4 | 12 | 19 | 26 | 116 | Weighted value from school level |
| Water volume of swimming pools in m³ of complete refillings per year in 2008 | 0 | 0 | 0 | 0 | 691 | Property level |

Tab. 109: Database of the investigation: Intensity of utilization (qualitative variables, N =130)

| Factors | Levels | N | Data processing |
|---|---|---|---|
| Spatial standard | Higher standard | 68 | Weighted value from building level |
| | Lower standard | 62 | Weighted value from building level |

## Independent variables: Factor group building characteristics

## Functional characteristics

Tab. 110: Database of the investigation: Functional characteristics (quantitative variables, N =130)

| Factors | Minimum | Lower Quartile | Median | Upper Quartile | Maximum | Data processing |
|---|---|---|---|---|---|---|
| Gross floor area (GROFA in m²) | 1,396 | 4,461 | 7,192 | 9,742 | 39,160 | Aggregated from room level |
| Net floor area (NEFA in m²) | 1,242 | 3,884 | 6,282 | 8,591 | 33,870 | Aggregated from room level |
| Usable floor area (UFA in m²) | 687 | 2,655 | 4,171 | 6,032 | 18,761 | Aggregated from room level |
| Usable floor area: Living and recreation (UFA 1 in m²) | 39 | 135 | 273 | 455 | 1,372 | Aggregated from room level |
| Usable floor area: Office work (UFA 2 in m²) | 0 | 87 | 139 | 233 | 781 | Aggregated from room level |
| Usable floor area: Prodution, manual and machine work, experiments (UFA 3 in m²) | 0 | 22 | 44 | 97 | 3,893 | Aggregated from room level |
| Usable floor area: Storage, distribution and sale (UFA 4 in m²) | 0 | 158 | 277 | 467 | 1,852 | Aggregated from room level |
| Usable floor area: Eduaction, teaching and culture (UFA 5 in m²) | 226 | 1,725 | 2,443 | 3,433 | 9,209 | Aggregated from room level |
| Usable floor area: Convalescence and care (UFA 6 in m²) | 0 | 0 | 3 | 21 | 90 | Aggregated from room level |
| Usable floor area: Other functions (UFA 7 in m²) | 92 | 397 | 781 | 1,293 | 6,507 | Aggregated from room level |
| Technical floor area (TEFA in m²) | 4 | 127 | 250 | 470 | 2,238 | Aggregated from room level |
| Circulation area (CICA in m²) | 87 | 880 | 1,454 | 2,306 | 16,891 | Aggregated from room level |
| Gross building volume (m³) | 3,193 | 17,420 | 27,455 | 40,137 | 140,615 | Aggregated from building level |
| Gross floor area of the ground floor (m²) | 504 | 1,812 | 2,446 | 3,420 | 12,213 | Aggregated from building level |
| Heatable gross floor area (H-GROFA in m²) | 900 | 3,846 | 6,252 | 8,367 | 36,653 | Aggregated from room level |
| Sanitary area (m²) | 40 | 158 | 235 | 301 | 825 | Aggregated from room level |
| Cleaning floor area (m²) | 768 | 3,699 | 6,222 | 8,482 | 27,123 | Aggregated from room level |
| Share of wood floorings per m² flooring area (%) | 0 | 0 | 7 | 17 | 57 | Aggregated from room level |
| Share of stone floorings per m² flooring area (%) | 1 | 28 | 35 | 40 | 68 | Aggregated from room level |
| Share of carpet floorings per m² flooring area (%) | 0 | 0 | 0 | 2 | 54 | Aggregated from room level |
| Share of synthetic floorings per m² flooring area (%) | 4 | 35 | 48 | 59 | 99 | Aggregated from room level |
| Share of wood linings per m² internal wall lining area (%) | 0 | 0 | 7 | 15 | 73 | Weighted value from building level |
| Share of ceramic linings per m² internal wall lining area (%) | 0 | 5 | 10 | 14 | 50 | Weighted value from building level |
| Share of panel linings per m² internal wall lining area (%) | 0 | 0 | 0 | 0 | 68 | Weighted value from building level |
| Share of painted and wallpapered linings per m² internal wall lining area (%) | 0 | 1 | 1 | 1 | 1 | Weighted value from building level |
| Share of wood linings of ceilings and roof per m² ceiling and roof lining area (%) | 0 | 0 | 2 | 20 | 100 | Weighted value from building level |
| Share of panel linings of ceilings and roof per m² ceiling and roof lining area (%) | 0 | 52 | 86 | 100 | 100 | Weighted value from building level |
| Share of painted and plastered linings of ceilings and roof per m² ceiling and roof lining area (%) | 0 | 0 | 0 | 3 | 70 | Weighted value from building level |
| Share of wallpapered linings of ceilings and roof per m² ceiling and roof lining area (%) | 0 | 0 | 0 | 0 | 10 | Weighted value from building level |

## Technical characteristics

Tab. 111: Database of the investigation: Technical characteristics (quantitative variables, N =130)

| Factors | Minimum | Lower Quartile | Median | Upper Quartile | Maximum | Data processing |
|---|---|---|---|---|---|---|
| Age of a school property (N=115) | 3 | 41 | 53 | 87 | 171 | Property level |
| Share of external wood claddings per m² external wall cladding area (%) | 0 | 0 | 0 | 0 | 100 | Weighted value from building level |
| Share of external stone claddings per m² external wall cladding area (%) | 0 | 0 | 3 | 35 | 100 | Weighted value from building level |
| Share of external concrete claddings per m² external wall cladding area (%) | 0 | 0 | 0 | 12 | 100 | Weighted value from building level |
| Share of external plaster claddings per m² external wall cladding area (%) | 0 | 0 | 50 | 86 | 100 | Weighted value from building level |
| Share of external panel claddings per m² external wall cladding area (%) | 0 | 0 | 0 | 0 | 100 | Weighted value from building level |
| Glass area of external walls and roofs (m²) | 105 | 932 | 1,532 | 2,538 | 8,884 | Aggregated from building level |
| Share of single glazing per m² glass area of external walls (%) | 0 | 0 | 0 | 0 | 90 | Aggregated from building level |
| Share of double glazing per m² glass area of external walls (%) | 0 | 99 | 100 | 100 | 100 | Aggregated from building level |
| Share of triple glazing per m² glass area of external walls (%) | 0 | 0 | 0 | 0 | 81 | Aggregated from building level |
| Share of modernized insulation per m² external wall and roof cladding area (%) | 0 | 75 | 100 | 100 | 100 | Weighted value from building level |
| Share of sloped roofs per m² roof structure area (%) | 0 | 0 | 50 | 100 | 100 | Weighted value from building level |
| Share of flat roofs per m² roof structure area (%) | 0 | 0 | 50 | 100 | 100 | Weighted value from building level |
| Share of defective glass area of external walls per m² glass area of external walls (%) | 0 | 0 | 8 | 32 | 100 | Aggregated from building level |
| Number of decentralized water heaters | 0 | 0 | 2 | 7 | 33 | Aggregated from building level |
| Share of heat supply systems in a poor condition (%) | 0 | 0 | 10 | 20 | 80 | Weighted value from building level |
| Number of lifts | 0 | 0 | 0 | 1 | 3 | Aggregated from building level |
| Average number of lift-stops | 0 | 0 | 0 | 1 | 7 | Mean from property level |
| Number of press containers (waste disposal facilities) | 0 | 0 | 0 | 0 | 3 | Property level |
| Property area (m²) | 906 | 6,335 | 10,783 | 18,074 | 84,511 | Property level |
| Non-built up plot area (part of property area that isn´t built on in m²) | 235 | 4,370 | 7,658 | 14,730 | 72,298 | Property level |
| School playground area (hard surfaces in m²) | 0 | 2,205 | 3,536 | 5,544 | 19,952 | Property level |
| Sports area (hard surfaces in m²) | 0 | 0 | 0 | 145 | 3,152 | Property level |
| Green area (m²) | 0 | 1,455 | 4,015 | 8,875 | 56,921 | Property level |
| Irrigated grounds (m²) | 0 | 0 | 0 | 0 | 1,000 | Property level |
| Water impermeable surface of the plot (m²) | 643 | 4,373 | 6,180 | 9,898 | 30,599 | Property level |
| Outdoor cleaning area in m² (including public sidewalks adjacent to the plot of land) | 0 | 2,876 | 4,484 | 6,395 | 24,452 | Property level |
| Area of public sidewalks in m² (adjacent to plot of land) | 0 | 380 | 510 | 820 | 2,358 | Property level |

Tab. 112: Database of the investigation: Technical characteristics (qualitative variables, N =130)

| Factors | Levels | N | Data processing |
|---|---|---|---|
| Historical building conservation | Historical building conservation exists | 43 | Aggregated from building level |
| | Historical building conservation does not exist | 87 | Aggregated from building level |
| Heat storage capacity | Light thermal mass | 21 | Weighted value from building level |
| | Heavy thermal mass | 109 | Weighted value from building level |
| Condition of building constructions | Good condition | 54 | Weighted value from building level |
| | Poor condition | 76 | Weighted value from building level |
| Condition of walls and ceilings | Good condition | 116 | Weighted value from building level |
| | Poor condition | 14 | Weighted value from building level |
| Condition of glass areas of external walls | Good condition | 78 | Weighted value from building level |
| | Poor condition | 52 | Weighted value from building level |
| Condition of roofs | Good condition | 93 | Weighted value from building level |
| | Poor condition | 37 | Weighted value from building level |
| Condition of permanent fixtures | Good condition | 95 | Weighted value from building level |
| | Poor condition | 35 | Weighted value from building level |
| Type of energy source | Gas | 85 | Property level |
| | District heating | 45 | Property level |
| Standard of technical installations | Higher standard | 91 | Weighted value from building level |
| | Lower standard | 39 | Weighted value from building level |
| Standard of heat generators | With central water heaters | 92 | Weighted value from building level |
| | Without central water heaters | 38 | Weighted value from building level |
| Standard of heating control systems | Higher standard | 73 | Weighted value from building level |
| | Lower standard | 57 | Weighted value from building level |
| Condition of techinical installations | Good condition | 93 | Weighted value from building level |
| | Poor condition | 37 | Weighted value from building level |
| Condition of seweage systems | Good condition | 103 | Weighted value from building level |
| | Poor condition | 27 | Weighted value from building level |
| Condition of water supply systems | Good condition | 107 | Weighted value from building level |
| | Poor condition | 23 | Weighted value from building level |
| Condition of heat supply systems | Good condition | 112 | Weighted value from building level |
| | Poor condition | 18 | Weighted value from building level |
| Condition of power installations | Good condition | 104 | Weighted value from building level |
| | Poor condition | 26 | Weighted value from building level |
| Standard of grounds and outdoor facilities | Higher standard | 93 | Property level |
| | Lower standard | 37 | Property level |

(continued)

| Factors | Levels | N | Data processing |
|---|---|---|---|
| Condition of grounds and outdoor facilities | Good condition | 104 | Property level |
| | Poor condition | 26 | Property level |
| Condition of hard surfaces | Good condition | 98 | Property level |
| | Poor condition | 32 | Property level |
| Condition of outdoor constructions | Good condition | 124 | Property level |
| | Poor condition | 6 | Property level |
| Condition of permanent outdoor fixtures | Good condition | 126 | Property level |
| | Poor condition | 4 | Property level |
| Condition of green areas | Good condition | 124 | Property level |
| | Poor condition | 6 | Property level |
| Standard of furnishings and equipment | Higher standard | 95 | Weighted value from building level |
| | Lower standard | 35 | Weighted value from building level |
| Condition of fittings, furnishings and equipment | Good condition | 80 | Weighted value from building level |
| | Poor condition | 50 | Weighted value from building level |

## Independent variables: Factor group strategy and operation

Tab. 113: Database of the investigation: Strategy and operation (qualitative variables, N =130)

| Factors | Levels | N | Data processing |
|---|---|---|---|
| Disposal concept | Efficient | 121 | Property level |
| | Inefficient | 9 | Property level |
| Outsourcing rate of caretaker services for security and surveillance services | Services completely internal | 115 | Property level |
| | Services completely outsourced | 15 | Property level |

## Independent variables: Factor group location

Tab. 114: Database of the investigation: Location (qualitative variables, N =130)

| Factors | Levels | N | Data processing |
|---|---|---|---|
| Region | Urban | 27 | Property level |
| | Suburban | 84 | Property level |
| | Rural | 19 | Property level |
| Topography | Flat | 76 | Property level |
| | Sloped | 54 | Property level |
| External environmental pollution | Pollution exists | 27 | Property level |
| | Pollution does not exist | 103 | Property level |

www.ingramcontent.com/pod-product-compliance
Lightning Source LLC
Chambersburg PA
CBHW081532190326
41458CB00015B/5533